SPEECHES AND OTHER WRITINGS

By ABRAHAM LINCOLN

Speeches and Other Writings
By Abraham Lincoln

Print ISBN 13: 978-1-4209-7346-4
eBook ISBN 13: 978-1-4209-7408-9

Cover Image: a detail of a portrait of Abraham Lincoln, by George Peter Alexander Healy, c. 1887 / National Portrait Gallery, Smithsonian Institution; transfer from the National Gallery of Art; gift of the A.W. Mellon Educational and Charitable Trust, 1942.

Please visit *www.digireads.com*

CONTENTS

TO THE PEOPLE OF SANGAMON COUNTY, NEW
SALEM, ILLINOIS, MARCH 9, 1832.

FELLOW-CITIZENS:—Having become a candidate for the honorable
office of one of your Representatives in the next General Assembly of
this State, in according with an established custom and the principles of
true Republicanism it becomes my duty to make known to you, the
people whom I propose to represent, my sentiments with regard to local
affairs.

Time and experience have verified to a demonstration the public
utility of internal improvements. That the poorest and most thinly
populated countries would be greatly benefited by the opening of good
roads, and in the clearing of navigable streams within their limits, is
what no person will deny. Yet it is folly to undertake works of this or
any other without first knowing that we are able to finish them—as
half-finished work generally proves to be labor lost. There cannot justly
be any objection to having railroads and canals, any more than to other
good things, provided they cost nothing. The only objection is to
paying for them; and the objection arises from the want of ability to
pay.

With respect to the County of Sangamon, some more easy means
of communication than it now possesses, for the purpose of facilitating
the task of exporting the surplus products of its fertile soil, and
importing necessary articles from abroad, are indispensably necessary.
A meeting has been held of the citizens of Jacksonville and the adjacent
country, for the purpose of deliberating and inquiring into the
expediency of constructing a railroad from some eligible point on the
Illinois River, through the town of Jacksonville, in Morgan County, to
the town of Springfield, in Sangamon County. This is, indeed, a very
desirable object. No other improvement that reason will justify us in
hoping for can equal in utility the railroad. It is a never-failing source
of communication between places of business remotely situated from
each other. Upon the railroad the regular progress of commercial
intercourse is not interrupted by either high or low water, or freezing
weather, which are the principal difficulties that render our future hopes
of water communication precarious and uncertain.

Yet, however desirable an object the construction of a railroad
through our country may be, however high our imaginations may be
heated at thoughts of it,—there is always a heart-appalling shock
accompanying the amount of its cost, which forces us to shrink from
our pleasing anticipations. The probable cost of this contemplated
railroad is estimated at $290,000; the bare statement of which, in my
opinion, is sufficient to justify the belief that the improvement of the
Sangamon River is an object much better suited to our infant resources.

Respecting this view, I think I may say, without the fear of being contradicted, that its navigation may be rendered completely practicable as high as the mouth of the South Fork, or probably higher, to vessels of from twenty-five to thirty tons burden, for at least one half of all common years, and to vessels of much greater burden a part of the time. From my peculiar circumstances, it is probable that for the last twelve months I have given as particular attention to the stage of the water in this river as any other person in the country. In the month of March, 1831, in company with others, I commenced the building of a flatboat on the Sangamon, and finished and took her out in the course of the spring. Since that time I have been concerned in the mill at New Salem. These circumstances are sufficient evidence that I have not been very inattentive to the stages of the water. The time at which we crossed the mill-dam being in the last days of April, the water was lower than it had been since the breaking of winter in February, or than it was for several weeks after. The principal difficulties we encountered in descending the river were from the drifted timber, which obstructions all know are not difficult to be removed. Knowing almost precisely the height of water at that time, I believe I am safe in saying that it has as often been higher as lower since.

From this view of the subject it appears that my calculations with regard to the navigation of the Sangamon cannot but be founded in reason; but, whatever may be its natural advantages, certain it is that it never can be practically useful to any great extent without being greatly improved by art. The drifted timber, as I have before mentioned, is the most formidable barrier to this object. Of all parts of this river, none will require so much labor in proportion to make it navigable as the last thirty or thirty-five miles; and going with the meanderings of the channel, when we are this distance above its mouth we are only between twelve and eighteen miles above Beardstown in something near a straight direction; and this route is upon such low ground as to retain water in many places during the season, and in all parts such as to draw two thirds or three fourths of the river water at all high stages.

This route is on prairie-land the whole distance, so that it appears to me, by removing the turf a sufficient width, and damming up the old channel, the whole river in a short time would wash its way through, thereby curtailing the distance and increasing the velocity of the current very considerably, while there would be no timber on the banks to obstruct its navigation in future; and being nearly straight, the timber which might float in at the head would be apt to go clear through. There are also many places above this where the river, in its zigzag course, forms such complete peninsulas as to be easier to cut at the necks than to remove the obstructions from the bends, which, if done, would also lessen the distance.

What the cost of this work would be, I am unable to say. It is probable, however, that it would not be greater than is common to streams of the same length. Finally, I believe the improvement of the Sangamon River to be vastly important and highly desirable to the people of the county; and, if elected, any measure in the Legislature having this for its object, which may appear judicious, will meet my approbation and receive my support.

It appears that the practice of loaning money at exorbitant rates of interest has already been opened as a field for discussion; so I suppose I may enter upon it without claiming the honor or risking the danger which may await its first explorer. It seems as though we are never to have an end to this baneful and corroding system, acting almost as prejudicially to the general interests of the community as a direct tax of several thousand dollars annually laid on each county for the benefit of a few individuals only, unless there be a law made fixing the limits of usury. A law for this purpose, I am of opinion, may be made without materially injuring any class of people. In cases of extreme necessity, there could always be means found to cheat the law; while in all other cases it would have its intended effect. I would favor the passage of a law on this subject which might not be very easily evaded. Let it be such that the labor and difficulty of evading it could only be justified in cases of greatest necessity.

Upon the subject of education, not presuming to dictate any plan or system respecting it, I can only say that I view it as the most important subject which we as a people can be engaged in. That every man may receive at least a moderate education, and thereby be enabled to read the histories of his own and other countries, by which he may duly appreciate the value of our free institutions, appears to be an object of vital importance, even on this account alone, to say nothing of the advantages and satisfaction to be derived from all being able to read the Scriptures, and other works both of a religious and moral nature, for themselves.

For my part, I desire to see the time when education—and by its means, morality, sobriety, enterprise, and industry—shall become much more general than at present, and should be gratified to have it in my power to contribute something to the advancement of any measure which might have a tendency to accelerate that happy period.

With regard to existing laws, some alterations are thought to be necessary. Many respectable men have suggested that our estray laws, the law respecting the issuing of executions, the road law, and some others, are deficient in their present form, and require alterations. But, considering the great probability that the framers of those laws were wiser than myself, I should prefer not meddling with them, unless they were first attacked by others; in which case I should feel it both a privilege and a duty to take that stand which, in my view, might tend most to the advancement of justice.

But, fellow-citizens, I shall conclude. Considering the great degree of modesty which should always attend youth, it is probable I have already been more presuming than becomes me. However, upon the subjects of which I have treated, I have spoken as I have thought. I may be wrong in regard to any or all of them; but, holding it a sound maxim that it is better only sometimes to be right than at all times to be wrong, so soon as I discover my opinions to be erroneous, I shall be ready to renounce them.

Every man is said to have his peculiar ambition. Whether it be true or not, I can say, for one, that I have no other so great as that of being truly esteemed of my fellow-men, by rendering myself worthy of their esteem. How far I shall succeed in gratifying this ambition is yet to be developed. I am young, and unknown to many of you. I was born, and have ever remained, in the most humble walks of life. I have no wealthy or popular relations or friends to recommend me. My case is thrown exclusively upon the independent voters of the county; and, if elected, they will have conferred a favor upon me for which I shall be unremitting in my labors to compensate. But, if the good people in their wisdom shall see fit to keep me in the background, I have been too familiar with disappointments to be very much chagrined.

Your friend and fellow-citizen,

A. LINCOLN.

New Salem, March 9, 1832.

PROTEST ENTERED IN THE ILLINOIS LEGISLATURE,
VANDALIA, ILLINOIS, MARCH 3, 1837.

The following protest was presented to the House, which was read and ordered to be spread in the journals, to wit:

"Resolutions upon the subject of domestic slavery having passed both branches of the General Assembly at its present session, the undersigned hereby protest against the passage of the same.

"They believe that the institution of slavery is founded on both injustice and bad policy, but that the promulgation of abolition doctrines tends rather to increase than abate its evils.

"They believe that the Congress of the United States has no power under the Constitution to interfere with the institution of slavery in the different States.

"They believe that the Congress of the United States has the power, under the Constitution, to abolish slavery in the District of Columbia, but that the power ought not to be exercised, unless at the request of the people of the District.

"The difference between these opinions and those contained in the said resolutions is their reason for entering this protest.

"DAN STONE,
"A. LINCOLN,

"Representatives from the County of Sangamon."

THE PERPETUATION OF OUR POLITICAL INSTITUTIONS,
SPEECH BEFORE THE YOUNG MEN'S LYCEUM OF
SPRINGFIELD, ILLINOIS, JANUARY 27, 1838.

As a subject for the remarks of the evening, "The Perpetuation of our Political Institutions" is selected.

In the great journal of things happening under the sun, we, the American people, find our account running under date of the nineteenth century of the Christian era. We find ourselves in the peaceful possession of the fairest portion of the earth as regards extent of territory, fertility of soil, and salubrity of climate. We find ourselves under the government of a system of political institutions conducing more essentially to the ends of civil and religious liberty than any of which the history of former times tells us. We, when mounting the stage of existence, found ourselves the legal inheritors of these fundamental blessings. We toiled not in the acquirement or establishment of them; they are a legacy bequeathed us by a once hardy, brave, and patriotic, but now lamented and departed, race of ancestors. Theirs was the task (and nobly they performed it) to possess themselves, and through themselves us, of this goodly land, and to uprear upon its hills and its valleys a political edifice of liberty and equal rights; it is ours only to transmit these—the former unprofaned by the foot of an invader, the latter undecayed by the lapse of time and untorn by usurpation—to the latest generation that fate shall permit the world to know. This task gratitude to our fathers, justice to ourselves, duty to posterity, and love for our species in general, all imperatively require us faithfully to perform.

How then shall we perform it? At what point shall we expect the approach of danger? By what means shall we fortify against it? Shall we expect some transatlantic military giant to step the ocean and crush us at a blow? Never! All the armies of Europe, Asia, and Africa combined, with all the treasure of the earth (our own excepted) in their military chest, with a Bonaparte for a commander, could not by force take a drink from the Ohio or make a track on the Blue Ridge in a trial of a thousand years.

At what point then is the approach of danger to be expected? I answer: If it ever reach us it must spring up amongst us; it cannot come from abroad. If destruction be our lot we must ourselves be its author and finisher. As a nation of freemen we must live through all time, or die by suicide.

I hope I am over-wary; but if I am not, there is even now something of ill omen amongst us. I mean the increasing disregard for law which pervades the country—the growing disposition to substitute the wild and furious passions in lieu of the sober judgment of courts, and the worse than savage mobs for the executive ministers of justice. This disposition is awfully fearful in any community; and that it now exists in ours, though grating to our feelings to admit, it would be a violation of truth and an insult to our intelligence to deny. Accounts of outrages committed by mobs form the everyday news of the times. They have pervaded the country from New England to Louisiana; they are neither peculiar to the eternal snows of the former nor the burning suns of the latter; they are not the creature of climate, neither are they confined to the slave holding or the non-slave holding States. Alike they spring up among the pleasure-hunting masters of Southern slaves, and the order-loving citizens of the land of steady habits. Whatever then their cause may be, it is common to the whole country.

It would be tedious as well as useless to recount the horrors of all of them. Those happening in the State of Mississippi and at St. Louis are perhaps the most dangerous in example and revolting to humanity. In the Mississippi case they first commenced by hanging the regular gamblers—a set of men certainly not following for a livelihood a very useful or very honest occupation, but one which, so far from being forbidden by the laws, was actually licensed by an act of the Legislature passed but a single year before. Next, negroes suspected of conspiring to raise an insurrection were caught up and hanged in all parts of the State; then, white men supposed to be leagued with the negroes; and finally, strangers from neighboring States, going thither on business, were in many instances subjected to the same fate. Thus went on this process of hanging, from gamblers to negroes, from negroes to white citizens, and from these to strangers, till dead men were seen literally dangling from the boughs of trees upon every roadside, and in numbers almost sufficient to rival the native Spanish moss of the country as a drapery of the forest.

Turn then to that horror-striking scene at St. Louis. A single victim only was sacrificed there. This story is very short, and is perhaps the most highly tragic of anything of its length that has ever been witnessed in real life. A mulatto man by the name of McIntosh was seized in the street, dragged to the suburbs of the city, chained to a tree, and actually burned to death; and all within a single hour from the time he had been a freeman attending to his own business and at peace with the world.

Such are the effects of mob law, and such are the scenes becoming more and more frequent in this land so lately famed for love of law and order, and the stories of which have even now grown too familiar to attract anything more than an idle remark.

But you are perhaps ready to ask, "What has this to do with the perpetuation of our political institutions?" I answer, It has much to do with it. Its direct consequences are, comparatively speaking, but a small evil, and much of its danger consists in the proneness of our minds to regard its direct as its only consequences. Abstractly considered, the hanging of the gamblers at Vicksburg was of but little consequence. They constitute a portion of population that is worse than useless in any community; and their death, if no pernicious example be set by it, is never matter of reasonable regret with any one. If they were annually swept from the stage of existence by the plague or smallpox, honest men would perhaps be much profited by the operation. Similar too is the correct reasoning in regard to the burning of the negro at St. Louis. He had forfeited his life by the perpetration of an outrageous murder upon one of the most worthy and respectable citizens of the city, and had he not died as he did, he must have died by the sentence of the law in a very short time afterwards. As to him alone, it was as well the way it was as it could otherwise have been. But the example in either case was fearful. When men take it in their heads to-day to hang gamblers or burn murderers, they should recollect that in the confusion usually attending such transactions they will be as likely to hang or burn some one who is neither a gambler nor a murderer as one who is, and that, acting upon the example they set, the mob of to-morrow may, and probably will, hang or burn some of them by the very same mistake. And not only so: the innocent, those who have ever set their faces against violations of law in every shape, alike with the guilty fall victims to the ravages of mob law; and thus it goes on, step by step, till all the walls erected for the defense of the persons and property of individuals are trodden down and disregarded. But all this, even, is not the full extent of the evil. By such examples, by instances of the perpetrators of such acts going unpunished, the lawless in spirit are encouraged to become lawless in practice; and having been used to no restraint but dread of punishment, they thus become absolutely unrestrained. Having ever regarded government as their deadliest bane, they make a jubilee of the suspension of its operations, and pray for nothing so much as its total annihilation. While, on the other hand, good men, men who love tranquility, who desire to abide by the laws and enjoy their benefits, who would gladly spill their blood in the defense of their country, seeing their property destroyed, their families insulted, and their lives endangered, their persons injured, and seeing nothing in prospect that forebodes a change for the better, become tired of and disgusted with a government that offers them no protection, and are not much averse to a change in which they imagine they have nothing to lose. Thus, then, by the operation of this mobocratic spirit which all must admit is now abroad in the land, the strongest bulwark of any government, and particularly of those constituted like ours, may effectually be broken down and destroyed—I mean the attachment of the people. Whenever this effect shall be produced among us; whenever the vicious portion of population shall be permitted to gather in bands of hundreds and thousands, and burn churches, ravage and rob provision-stores, throw printing presses into rivers, shoot editors, and hang and burn obnoxious persons at pleasure and with impunity, depend on it, this government cannot last. By such things the feelings of the best citizens will become more or less alienated from it, and thus it will be left without friends, or with too few, and those few too weak to make their friendship effectual. At such a time, and under such circumstances, men of sufficient talent and ambition will not be wanting to seize the opportunity, strike the blow, and overturn that fair fabric which for the last half century has been the fondest hope of the lovers of freedom throughout the world.

I know the American people are much attached to their government; I know they would suffer much for its sake; I know they would endure evils long and patiently before they would ever think of exchanging it for another,—yet, notwithstanding all this, if the laws be continually despised and disregarded, if their rights to be secure in their persons and property are held by no better tenure than the caprice of a mob, the alienation of their affections from the government is the natural consequence; and to that, sooner or later, it must come.

Here, then, is one point at which danger may be expected.

The question recurs, How shall we fortify against it? The answer is simple. Let every American, every lover of liberty, every well-wisher to his posterity swear by the blood of the Revolution never to violate in the least particular the laws of the country, and never to tolerate their violation by others. As the patriots of seventy-six did to the support of the Declaration of Independence, so to the support of the Constitution and laws let every American pledge his life, his property, and his sacred honor. Let every man remember that to violate the law is to trample on the blood of his father, and to tear the charter of his own and his children's liberty. Let reverence for the laws be breathed by every American mother to the lisping babe that prattles on her lap; let it be taught in schools, in seminaries, and in colleges; let it be written in primers, spelling books, and in almanacs; let it be preached from the pulpit, proclaimed in legislative halls, and enforced in courts of justice. And, in short, let it become the political religion of the nation; and let the old and the young, the rich and the poor, the grave and the gay of all sexes and tongues and colors and conditions, sacrifice unceasingly upon its altars.

While ever a state of feeling such as this shall universally or even very generally prevail throughout the nation, vain will be every effort, and fruitless every attempt, to subvert our national freedom.

When, I so pressingly urge a strict observance of all the laws, let me not be understood as saying there are no bad laws, or that grievances may not arise for the redress of which no legal provisions have been made. I mean to say no such thing. But I do mean to say that although bad laws, if they exist, should be repealed as soon as possible, still, while they continue in force, for the sake of example they should be religiously observed. So also in unprovided cases. If such arise, let proper legal provisions be made for them with the least possible delay, but till then let them, if not too intolerable, be borne with.

There is no grievance that is a fit object of redress by mob law. In any case that may arise, as, for instance, the promulgation of abolitionism, one of two positions is necessarily true—that is, the thing is right within itself, and therefore deserves the protection of all law and all good citizens, or it is wrong, and therefore proper to be prohibited by legal enactments; and in neither case is the interposition of mob law either necessary, justifiable, or excusable.

But it may be asked, Why suppose danger to our political institutions? Have we not preserved them for more than fifty years? And why may we not for fifty times as long?

We hope there is no sufficient reason. We hope all danger may be overcome; but to conclude that no danger may ever arise would itself be extremely dangerous. There are now, and will hereafter be, many causes, dangerous in their tendency, which have not existed heretofore, and which are not too insignificant to merit attention. That our government should have been maintained in its original form, from its establishment until now, is not much to be wondered at. It had many props to support it through that period, which now are decayed and crumbled away. Through that period it was felt by all to be an undecided experiment; now it is understood to be a successful one. Then, all that sought celebrity and fame and distinction expected to find them in the success of that experiment. Their all was staked upon it; their destiny was inseparably linked with it. Their ambition aspired to display before an admiring world a practical demonstration of the truth of a proposition which had hitherto been considered at best no better than problematical—namely, the capability of a people to govern themselves. If they succeeded they were to be immortalized; their names were to be transferred to counties, and cities, and rivers, and mountains; and to be revered and sung, toasted through all time. If they failed, they were to be called knaves and fools, and fanatics for a fleeting hour; then to sink and be forgotten. They succeeded. The experiment is successful, and thousands have won their deathless names in making it so. But the game is caught; and I believe it is true that with the catching end the pleasures of the chase. This field of glory is harvested, and the crop is already appropriated. But new reapers will arise, and they too will seek a field. It is to deny what the history of the world tells us is true, to suppose that men of ambition and talents will not continue to spring up amongst us. And when they do, they will as naturally seek the gratification of their ruling passion as others have done before them. The question then is, Can that gratification be found in supporting and in maintaining an edifice that has been erected by others? Most certainly it cannot. Many great and good men, sufficiently qualified for any task they should undertake, may ever be found whose ambition would aspire to nothing beyond a seat in Congress, a Gubernatorial or a Presidential chair; but such belong not to the family of the lion, or the tribe of the eagle. What! think you these places would satisfy an Alexander, a Caesar, or a Napoleon? Never! Towering genius disdains a beaten path. It seeks regions hitherto unexplored. It sees no distinction in adding story to story upon the monuments of fame erected to the memory of others. It denies that it is glory enough to serve under any chief. It scorns to tread in the footsteps of any predecessor, however illustrious. It thirsts and burns for distinction; and if possible, it will have it, whether at the expense of emancipating slaves or enslaving freemen. Is it unreasonable, then, to expect that some man possessed of the loftiest genius, coupled with ambition sufficient to push it to its utmost stretch, will at some time spring up among us? And when such an one does it will require the people to be united with each other, attached to the government and laws, and generally intelligent, to successfully frustrate his designs.

Distinction will be his paramount object, and although he would as willingly, perhaps more so, acquire it by doing good as harm, yet, that opportunity being past, and nothing left to be done in the way of building up, he would set boldly to the task of pulling down.

Here then is a probable case, highly dangerous, and such an one as could not have well existed heretofore.

Another reason which once was, but which, to the same extent, is now no more, has done much in maintaining our institutions thus far. I mean the powerful influence which the interesting scenes of the Revolution had upon the passions of the people as distinguished from their judgment. By this influence, the jealousy, envy, and avarice incident to our nature, and so common to a state of peace, prosperity, and conscious strength, were for the time in a great measure smothered and rendered inactive, while the deep-rooted principles of hate, and the powerful motive of revenge, instead of being turned against each other, were directed exclusively against the British nation. And thus, from the force of circumstances, the basest principles of our nature were either made to lie dormant, or to become the active agents in the advancement of the noblest of causes—that of establishing and maintaining civil and religious liberty.

But this state of feeling must fade, is fading, has faded, with the circumstances that produced it.

I do not mean to say that the scenes of the Revolution are now or ever will be entirely forgotten, but that, like everything else, they must fade upon the memory of the world, and grow more and more dim by the lapse of time. In history, we hope, they will be read of, and recounted, so long as the Bible shall be read; but even granting that they will, their influence cannot be what it heretofore has been. Even then they cannot be so universally known nor so vividly felt as they were by the generation just gone to rest. At the close of that struggle, nearly every adult male had been a participator in some of its scenes. The consequence was that of those scenes, in the form of a husband, a father, a son, or a brother, a living history was to be found in every family—a history bearing the indubitable testimonies of its own authenticity, in the limbs mangled, in the scars of wounds received, in the midst of the very scenes related—a history, too, that could be read and understood alike by all, the wise and the ignorant, the learned and the unlearned. But those histories are gone. They can be read no more forever. They were a fortress of strength; but what invading foeman could never do the silent artillery of time has done—the leveling of its walls. They are gone. They were a forest of giant oaks; but the all-restless hurricane has swept over them, and left only here and there a lonely trunk, despoiled of its verdure, shorn of its foliage, unshading and unshaded, to murmur in a few more gentle breezes, and to combat with its mutilated limbs a few more ruder storms, then to sink and be no more.

They were pillars of the temple of liberty; and now that they have crumbled away that temple must fall unless we, their descendants, supply their places with other pillars, hewn from the solid quarry of sober reason. Passion has helped us, but can do so no more. It will in future be our enemy. Reason cold, calculating, unimpassioned reason—must furnish all the materials for our future support and defense. Let those materials be molded into general intelligence, sound morality, and in particular, a reverence for the Constitution and laws; and that we improved to the last, that we remained free to the last, that we revered his name to the last, that during his long sleep we permitted no hostile foot to pass over or desecrate his resting place, shall be that which to learn the last trump shall awaken our Washington.

Upon these let the proud fabric of freedom rest, as the rock of its basis; and as truly as has been said of the only greater institution, "the gates of hell shall not prevail against it."

SPEECH ON THE SUB-TREASURY, SPRINGFIELD,
ILLINOIS, DECEMBER 26, 1839.

FELLOW-CITIZENS:—It is peculiarly embarrassing to me to attempt
a continuance of the discussion, on this evening, which has been
conducted in this hall on several preceding ones. It is so because on
each of those evenings there was a much fuller attendance than now,
without any reason for its being so, except the greater interest the
community feel in the speakers who addressed them then than they do
in him who is to do so now. I am, indeed, apprehensive that the few
who have attended have done so more to spare me mortification than in
the hope of being interested in anything I may be able to say. This
circumstance casts a damp upon my spirits, which I am sure I shall be
unable to overcome during the evening. But enough of preface.

The subject heretofore and now to be discussed is the subtreasury
scheme of the present administration, as a means of collecting, safe-
keeping, transferring, and disbursing, the revenues of the nation, as
contrasted with a national bank for the same purposes. Mr. Douglas has
said that we (the Whigs) have not dared to meet them (the Locos) in
argument on this question. I protest against this assertion. I assert that
we have again and again, during this discussion, urged facts and
arguments against the subtreasury which they have neither dared to
deny nor attempted to answer. But lest some may be led to believe that
we really wish to avoid the question, I now propose, in my humble
way, to urge those arguments again; at the same time begging the
audience to mark well the positions I shall take and the proof I shall
offer to sustain them, and that they will not again permit Mr. Douglas
or his friends to escape the force of them by a round and groundless
assertion that we "dare not meet them in argument."

Of the subtreasury, then, as contrasted with a national bank for the
before-enumerated purposes, I lay down the following propositions, to
wit: (1) It will injuriously affect the community by its operation on the
circulating medium. (2) It will be a more expensive fiscal agent. (3) It
will be a less secure depository of the public money. To show the truth
of the first proposition, let us take a short review of our condition under
the operation of a national bank. It was the depository of the public
revenues. Between the collection of those revenues and the
disbursement of them by the government, the bank was permitted to
and did actually loan them out to individuals, and hence the large
amount of money actually collected for revenue purposes, which by
any other plan would have been idle a great portion of the time, was
kept almost constantly in circulation. Any person who will reflect that
money is only valuable while in circulation will readily perceive that
any device which will keep the government revenues in constant

circulation, instead of being locked up in idleness, is no inconsiderable advantage. By the subtreasury the revenue is to be collected and kept in iron boxes until the government wants it for disbursement; thus robbing the people of the use of it, while the government does not itself need it, and while the money is performing no nobler office than that of rusting in iron boxes. The natural effect of this change of policy, every one will see, is to reduce the quantity of money in circulation. But, again, by the subtreasury scheme the revenue is to be collected in specie. I anticipate that this will be disputed. I expect to hear it said that it is not the policy of the administration to collect the revenue in specie. If it shall, I reply that Mr. Van Buren, in his message recommending the subtreasury, expended nearly a column of that document in an attempt to persuade Congress to provide for the collection of the revenue in specie exclusively; and he concludes with these words: "It may be safely assumed that no motive of convenience to the citizens requires the reception of bank paper." In addition to this, Mr. Silas Wright, Senator from New York, and the political, personal and confidential friend of Mr. Van Buren, drafted and introduced into the Senate the first subtreasury bill, and that bill provided for ultimately collecting the revenue in specie. It is true, I know, that that clause was stricken from the bill, but it was done by the votes of the Whigs, aided by a portion only of the Van Buren senators. No subtreasury bill has yet become a law, though two or three have been considered by Congress, some with and some without the specie clause; so that I admit there is room for quibbling upon the question of whether the administration favor the exclusive specie doctrine or not; but I take it that the fact that the President at first urged the specie doctrine, and that under his recommendation the first bill introduced embraced it, warrants us in charging it as the policy of the party until their head as publicly recants it as he at first espoused it. I repeat, then, that by the subtreasury the revenue is to be collected in specie. Now mark what the effect of this must be. By all estimates ever made there are but between sixty and eighty millions of specie in the United States. The expenditures of the Government for the year 1838—the last for which we have had the report—were forty millions. Thus it is seen that if the whole revenue be collected in specie, it will take more than half of all the specie in the nation to do it. By this means more than half of all the specie belonging to the fifteen millions of souls who compose the whole population of the country is thrown into the hands of the public office-holders, and other public creditors comprising in number perhaps not more than one quarter of a million, leaving the other fourteen millions and three quarters to get along as they best can, with less than one half of the specie of the country, and whatever rags and shinplasters they may be able to put, and keep, in circulation. By this means, every office-holder and other public creditor may, and most likely will, set up shaver; and a most glorious harvest will the specie-men have of it,—each specie-man, upon a fair division, having to his share the fleecing of about fifty-nine rag-men. In all candor let me ask, was such a system for benefiting the few at the expense of the many ever before devised? And was the sacred name of Democracy ever before made to indorse such an enormity against the rights of the people?

I have already said that the subtreasury will reduce the quantity of money in circulation. This position is strengthened by the recollection that the revenue is to be collected in Specie, so that the mere amount of revenue is not all that is withdrawn, but the amount of paper circulation that the forty millions would serve as a basis to is withdrawn, which would be in a sound state at least one hundred millions. When one hundred millions, or more, of the circulation we now have shall be withdrawn, who can contemplate without terror the distress, ruin, bankruptcy, and beggary that must follow? The man who has purchased any article—say a horse—on credit, at one hundred dollars, when there are two hundred millions circulating in the country, if the quantity be reduced to one hundred millions by the arrival of pay-day, will find the horse but sufficient to pay half the debt; and the other half must either be paid out of his other means, and thereby become a clear loss to him, or go unpaid, and thereby become a clear loss to his creditor. What I have here said of a single case of the purchase of a horse will hold good in every case of a debt existing at the time a reduction in the quantity of money occurs, by whomsoever, and for whatsoever, it may have been contracted. It may be said that what the debtor loses the creditor gains by this operation; but on examination this will be found true only to a very limited extent. It is more generally true that all lose by it—the creditor by losing more of his debts than he gains by the increased value of those he collects; the debtor by either parting with more of his property to pay his debts than he received in contracting them, or by entirely breaking up his business, and thereby being thrown upon the world in idleness.

The general distress thus created will, to be sure, be temporary, because, whatever change may occur in the quantity of money in any community, time will adjust the derangement produced; but while that adjustment is progressing, all suffer more or less, and very many lose everything that renders life desirable. Why, then, shall we suffer a severe difficulty, even though it be but temporary, unless we receive some equivalent for it?

What I have been saying as to the effect produced by a reduction of the quantity of money relates to the whole country. I now propose to show that it would produce a peculiar and permanent hardship upon the citizens of those States and Territories in which the public lands lie. The land-offices in those States and Territories, as all know, form the great gulf by which all, or nearly all, the money in them is swallowed up. When the quantity of money shall be reduced, and consequently everything under individual control brought down in proportion, the price of those lands, being fixed by law, will remain as now. Of necessity it will follow that the produce or labor that now raises money sufficient to purchase eighty acres will then raise but sufficient to purchase forty, or perhaps not that much; and this difficulty and hardship will last as long, in some degree, as any portion of these lands shall remain undisposed of. Knowing, as I well do, the difficulty that poor people now encounter in procuring homes, I hesitate not to say that when the price of the public lands shall be doubled or trebled, or, which is the same thing, produce and labor cut down to one half or one third of their present prices, it will be little less than impossible for them to procure those homes at all.

In answer to what I have said as to the effect the subtreasury would have upon the currency, it is often urged that the money collected for revenue purposes will not lie idle in the vaults of the treasury; and, farther, that a national bank produces greater derangement in the currency, by a system of contractions and expansions, than the subtreasury would produce in any way. In reply, I need only show that experience proves the contrary of both these propositions. It is an undisputed fact that the late Bank of the United States paid the government $75,000 annually for the privilege of using the public money between the times of its collection and disbursement. Can any man suppose that the bank would have paid this sum annually for twenty years, and then offered to renew its obligations to do so, if in reality there was no time intervening between the collection and disbursement of the revenue, and consequently no privilege of using the money extended to it? Again, as to the contractions and expansions of a national bank, I need only point to the period intervening between the time that the late bank got into successful operation and that at which the government commenced war upon it, to show that during that period no such contractions or expansions took place. If, before or after that period, derangement occurred in the currency, it proves nothing. The bank could not be expected to regulate the currency, either before it got into successful operation, or after it was crippled and thrown into death convulsions, by the removal of the deposits from it, and other hostile measures of the government against it. We do not pretend that a national bank can establish and maintain a sound and uniform state of currency in the country, in spite of the National Government; but we do say that it has established and maintained such a currency, and can do so again, by the aid of that government; and we further say that no duty is more imperative on that government than the duty it owes the people of furnishing them a sound and uniform currency.

I now leave the proposition as to the effect of the subtreasury upon the currency of the country, and pass to that relative to the additional expense which must be incurred by it over that incurred by a national bank as a fiscal agent of the government. By the late national bank we had the public revenue received, safely kept, transferred, and disbursed, not only without expense, but we actually received of the bank $75,000 annually for its privileges while rendering us those services. By the subtreasury, according to the estimate of the Secretary of the Treasury, who is the warm advocate of the system (and which estimate is the lowest made by any one), the same services are to cost $60,000. Mr. Rives, who, to say the least, is equally talented and honest, estimates that these services, under the subtreasury system, cannot cost less than $600,000. For the sake of liberality, let us suppose that the estimates of the secretary and Mr. Rives are the two extremes, and that their mean is about the true estimate, and we shall then find that when to that sum is added the $75,000 which the bank paid us, the difference between the two systems, in favor of the bank and against the subtreasury, is $105,000 a year. This sum, though small when compared to the many millions annually expended by the General Government, is, when viewed by itself, very large; and much too large, when viewed in any light, to be thrown away once a year for nothing. It is sufficient to pay the pensions of more than four thousand Revolutionary soldiers, or to purchase a forty-acre tract of government land for each one of more than eight thousand poor families.

To the argument against the subtreasury, on the score of additional expense, its friends, so far as I know, attempt no answer. They choose, so far as I can learn, to treat the throwing away of $405,000 once a year as a matter entirely too small to merit their Democratic notice.

I now come to the proposition that it would be less secure than a national bank as a depository of the public money. The experience of the past, I think, proves the truth of this. And here, inasmuch as I rely chiefly upon experience to establish it, let me ask how is it that we know anything—that any event will occur, that any combination of circumstances will produce a certain result—except by the analogies of past experience? What has once happened will invariably happen again when the same circumstances which combined to produce it shall again combine in the same way. We all feel that we know that a blast of wind would extinguish the flame of the candle that stands by me. How do we know it? We have never seen this flame thus extinguished. We know it because we have seen through all our lives that a blast of wind extinguishes the flame of a candle whenever it is thrown fully upon it. Again, we all feel to know that we have to die. How? We have never died yet. We know it because we know, or at least think we know, that of all the beings, just like ourselves, who have been coming into the world for six thousand years, not one is now living who was here two hundred years ago. I repeat, then, that we know nothing of what will happen in future, but by the analogy of experience, and that the fair analogy of past experience fully proves that the subtreasury would be a less safe depository of the public money than a national bank. Examine it. By the subtreasury scheme the public money is to be kept, between the times of its collection and disbursement, by treasurers of the mint, custom-house officers, land officers, and some new officers to be appointed in the same way that those first enumerated are. Has a year passed, since the organization of the government, that numerous defalcations have not occurred among this class of officers! Look at Swartwout with his $1,200,000, Price with his $75,000, Harris with his $109,000, Hawkins with his $100,000, Linn with his $55,000, together with some twenty-five hundred lesser lights. Place the public money again in these same hands, and will it not again go the same way? Most assuredly it will. But turn to the history of the national banks in this country, and we shall there see that those banks performed the fiscal operations of the government through a period of forty years, received, safely kept, transferred, disbursed an aggregate of nearly five hundred millions of dollars; and that, in all this time, and with all that money, not one dollar, nor one cent, did the government lose by them. Place the public money again in a similar depository, and will it not again be safe. But, conclusive as the experience of fifty years is that individuals are unsafe depositories of the public money, and of forty years that national banks are safe depositories, we are not left to rely solely upon that experience for the truth of those propositions. If experience were silent upon the subject, conclusive reasons could be shown for the truth of them.

It is often urged that to say the public money will be more secure in a national bank than in the hands of individuals, as proposed in the subtreasury, is to say that bank directors and bank officers are more honest than sworn officers of the government. Not so. We insist on no such thing. We say that public officers, selected with reference to their capacity and honesty (which, by the way, we deny is the practice in these days), stand an equal chance, precisely, of being capable and honest with bank officers selected by the same rule. We further say that with however much care selections may be made, there will be some unfaithful and dishonest in both classes. The experience of the whole world, in all bygone times, proves this true. The Savior of the world chose twelve disciples, and even one of that small number, selected by superhuman wisdom, turned out a traitor and a devil. And it may not be improper here to add that Judas carried the bag—was the subtreasurer of the Savior and his disciples. We, then, do not say—nor need we say to maintain our proposition—that bank officers are more honest than government officers selected by the same rule. What we do say is that the interest of the subtreasurer is against his duty, while the interest of the bank is on the side of its duty. Take instances: A subtreasurer has in his hands one hundred thousand dollars of public money; his duty says,

"You ought to pay this money over," but his interest says, "You ought to run away with this sum, and be a nabob the balance of your life." And who that knows anything of human nature doubts that in many instances interest will prevail over duty, and that the subtreasurer will prefer opulent knavery in a foreign land to honest poverty at home? But how different is it with a bank. Besides the government money deposited with it, it is doing business upon a large capital of its own. If it proves faithful to the government, it continues its business; if unfaithful, it forfeits its charter, breaks up its business, and thereby loses more than all it can make by seizing upon the government funds in its possession. Its interest, therefore, is on the side of its duty—is to be faithful to the government, and consequently even the dishonest amongst its managers have no temptation to be faithless to it. Even if robberies happen in the bank, the losses are borne by the bank, and the government loses nothing. It is for this reason, then, that we say a bank is the more secure. It is because of that admirable feature in the bank system which places the interest and the duty of the depository both on one side; whereas that feature can never enter into the subtreasury system. By the latter the interest of the individuals keeping the public money will wage an eternal war with their duty, and in very many instances must be victorious. In answer to the argument drawn from the fact that individual depositories of public money have always proved unsafe, it is urged that, even if we had a national bank, the money has to pass through the same individual hands that it will under the subtreasury. This is only partially true in fact, and wholly fallacious in argument. It is only partially true in fact, because by the subtreasury bill four receivers-general are to be appointed by the President and Senate. These are new officers, and consequently it cannot be true that the money, or any portion of it, has heretofore passed through their hands. These four new officers are to be located at New York, Boston, Charleston, and St. Louis, and consequently are to be depositories of all the money collected at or near those points; so that more than three fourths of the public money will fall into the keeping of these four new officers, who did not exist as officers under the national-bank system. It is only partially true, then, that the money passes through the same hands, under a national bank, as it would do under the subtreasury. It is true that under either system individuals must be employed as collectors of the customs, receivers at the land-offices, etc., but the difference is that under the bank system the receivers of all sorts receive the money and pay it over to the bank once a week when the collections are large, and once a month when they are small; whereas by the subtreasury system individuals are not only to collect the money, but they are to keep it also, or pay it over to other individuals equally unsafe as themselves, to be by them kept until it is wanted for disbursement. It is during the time that it is thus lying idle in their hands that opportunity is afforded and temptation held out to them to embezzle and escape with it. By the bank system each collector or receiver is to deposit in bank all the money in his hands at the end of each month at most, and to send the bank certificates of deposit to the Secretary of the Treasury. Whenever that certificate of deposit fails to arrive at the proper time, the secretary knows that the officer thus failing is acting the knave; and, if he is himself disposed to do his duty, he has him immediately removed from office, and thereby cuts him off from the possibility of embezzling but little more than the receipts of a single month. But by the subtreasury system the money is to lie month after month in the hands of individuals; larger amounts are to accumulate in the hands of the receivers-general and some others, by perhaps ten to one, than ever accumulated in the hands of individuals before; yet during all this time, in relation to this great stake, the Secretary of the Treasury can comparatively know nothing. Reports, to be sure, he will have; but reports are often false, and always false when made by a knave to cloak his knavery. Long experience has shown that nothing short of an actual demand of the money will expose an adroit peculator. Ask him for reports, and he will give them to your heart's content; send agents to examine and count the money in his hands, and he will borrow of a friend, merely to be counted and then returned, a sufficient sum to make the sum square. Try what you will, it will all fail till you demand the money; then, and not till then, the truth will come.

The sum of the whole matter I take to be this: Under the bank system, while sums of money, by the law, were permitted to lie in the hands of individuals for very short periods only, many and very large defalcations occurred by those individuals. Under the subtreasury system much larger sums are to lie in the hands of individuals for much longer periods, thereby multiplying temptation in proportion as the sums are larger, and multiplying opportunity in proportion as the periods are longer to and for those individuals to embezzle and escape with the public treasure; and therefore, just in the proportion that the temptation and the opportunity are greater under the subtreasury than the bank system, will the peculations and defalcations be greater under the former than they have been under the latter. The truth of this, independent of actual experience, is but little less than self-evident. I therefore leave it.

But it is said, and truly too, that there is to be a penitentiary department to the subtreasury. This, the advocates of the system will have it, will be a "king cure-all." Before I go farther, may I not ask if the penitentiary department is not itself an admission that they expect the public money to be stolen! Why build the cage if they expect to catch no birds? But as to the question how effectual the penitentiary will be in preventing defalcations. How effectual have penitentiaries heretofore been in preventing the crimes they were established to suppress? Has not confinement in them long been the legal penalty of larceny, forgery, robbery, and many other crimes, in almost all the States? And yet are not those crimes committed weekly, daily,—nay, and even hourly,—in every one of those States? Again, the gallows has long been the penalty of murder, and yet we scarcely open a newspaper that does not relate a new case of that crime. If, then, the penitentiary has ever heretofore failed to prevent larceny, forgery, and robbery, and the gallows and halter have likewise failed to prevent murder, by what process of reasoning, I ask, is it that we are to conclude the penitentiary will hereafter prevent the stealing of the public money? But our opponents seem to think they answer the charge that the money will be stolen fully if they can show that they will bring the offenders to punishment. Not so. Will the punishment of the thief bring back the stolen money? No more so than the hanging of a murderer restores his victim to life. What is the object desired? Certainly not the greatest number of thieves we can catch, but that the money may not be stolen. If, then, any plan can be devised for depositing the public treasure where it will never be stolen, never embezzled, is not that the plan to be adopted? Turn, then, to a national bank, and you have that plan, fully and completely successful, as tested by the experience of forty years.

I have now done with the three propositions that the subtreasury would injuriously affect the currency, and would be more expensive and less secure as a depository of the public money than a national bank. How far I have succeeded in establishing their truth, is for others to judge. Omitting, for want of time, what I had intended to say as to the effect of the subtreasury to bring the public money under the more immediate control of the President than it has ever heretofore been, I now ask the audience, when Mr. Calhoun shall answer me, to hold him to the questions. Permit him not to escape them. Require him either to show that the subtreasury would not injuriously affect the currency, or that we should in some way receive an equivalent for that injurious effect. Require him either to show that the subtreasury would not be more expensive as a fiscal agent than a bank, or that we should in some way be compensated for that additional expense. And particularly require him to show that the public money would be as secure in the subtreasury as in a national bank, or that the additional insecurity would be overbalanced by some good result of the proposed change.

No one of them, in my humble judgment, will he be able to do; and I venture the prediction, and ask that it may be especially noted, that he will not attempt to answer the proposition that the subtreasury would be more expensive than a national bank as a fiscal agent of the government.

As a sweeping objection to a national bank, and consequently an argument in favor of the subtreasury as a substitute for it, it often has been urged, and doubtless will be again, that such a bank is unconstitutional. We have often heretofore shown, and therefore need not in detail do so again, that a majority of the Revolutionary patriarchs, who ever acted officially upon the question, commencing with General Washington, and embracing General Jackson, the larger number of the signers of the Declaration, and of the framers of the Constitution, who were in the Congress of 1791, have decided upon their oaths that such a bank is constitutional. We have also shown that the votes of Congress have more often been in favor of than against its constitutionality. In addition to all this, we have shown that the Supreme Court—that tribunal which the Constitution has itself established to decide constitutional questions—has solemnly decided that such a bank is constitutional. Protesting that these authorities ought to settle the question which ought to be conclusive,—I will not urge them further now. I now propose to take a view of the question which I have not known to be taken by any one before. It is that whatever objection ever has or ever can be made to the constitutionality of a bank, will apply with equal force, in its whole length, breadth, and proportions, to the subtreasury. Our opponents say there is no express authority in the Constitution to establish a bank, and therefore, a bank is unconstitutional; but we with equal truth may say there is no express authority in the Constitution to establish a subtreasury, and therefore a subtreasury is unconstitutional. Who, then, has the advantage of this "express authority" argument? Does it not cut equally both ways! Does it not wound them as deeply and as deadly as it does us? Our position is that both are constitutional. The Constitution enumerates expressly several powers which Congress may exercise, superadded to which is a general authority "to make all laws necessary and proper" for carrying into effect all the powers vested by the Constitution in the Government of the United States. One of the express powers given Congress is "to lay and collect taxes, duties, imports, and excises; to pay the debts and provide for the common defense and general welfare of the United States." Now, Congress is expressly authorized to make all laws necessary and proper for carrying this power into execution. To carry it into execution, it is indispensably necessary to collect, safely keep, transfer, and disburse a revenue. To do this, a bank is "necessary and proper." But, say our opponents, to authorize the making of a bank, the necessity must be so great that the power just recited would be nugatory without it; and that that necessity is expressly negatived by the fact that they have got along ten whole years without such a bank. Immediately we turn on them, and say that that sort of necessity for a subtreasury does not exist, because we have got along forty whole years without one. And this time, it may be observed that we are not merely equal with them in the argument, but we beat them forty to ten, or, which is the same thing, four to one. On examination, it will be found that the absurd rule which prescribes that before we can constitutionally adopt a national bank as a fiscal agent, we must show an indispensable necessity for it, will exclude every sort of fiscal agent that the mind of man can conceive. A bank is not indispensable, because we can take the subtreasury; the subtreasury is not indispensable, because we can take the bank. The rule is too absurd to need further comment. Upon the phrase "necessary and proper" in the Constitution, it seems to me more reasonable to say that some fiscal agent is indispensably necessary; but inasmuch as no particular sort of agent is thus indispensable, because some other sort might be adopted, we are left to choose that sort of agent which may be most "proper" on grounds of expediency. But it is said the Constitution gives no power to Congress to pass acts of incorporation. Indeed! What is the passing an act of incorporation but the making of a law? Is any one wise enough to tell! The Constitution expressly gives Congress power "to pass all laws necessary and proper," etc. If, then, the passing of a bank charter be the "making a law necessary and proper," is it not clearly within the constitutional power of Congress to do so?

I now leave the bank and the subtreasury to try to answer, in a brief way, some of the arguments which on previous evenings here have been urged by Messrs. Lamborn and Douglas. Mr. Lamborn admits that "errors," as he charitably calls them, have occurred under the present and late administrations; but he insists that as great "errors" have occurred under all administrations. This we respectfully deny. We admit that errors may have occurred under all administrations; but we insist that there is no parallel between them and those of the two last. If they can show that their errors are no greater in number and magnitude than those of former times, we call off the dogs. But they can do no such thing. To be brief, I will now attempt a contrast of the "errors" of the two latter with those of former administrations, in relation to the public expenditures only. What I am now about to say as to the expenditures will be, in all cases, exclusive of payments on the national debt. By an examination of authentic public documents, consisting of the regular series of annual reports made by all the secretaries of the treasury from the establishment of the government down to the close of the year 1838, the following contrasts will be presented:

(1) The last ten years under General Jackson and Mr. Van Buren cost more money than the first twenty-seven did (including the heavy expenses of the late British war) under Washington, Adams, Jefferson, and Madison.

(2) The last year of J. Q. Adams's administration cost, in round numbers, thirteen millions, being about one dollar to each soul in the nation; the last (1838) of Mr. Van Buren's cost forty millions, being about two dollars and fifty cents to each soul, and being larger than the expenditure of Mr. Adams in the proportion of five to two.

(3) The highest annual expenditure during the late British war—being in 1814, and while we had in actual service rising 188,000 militia, together with the whole regular army, swelling the number to greatly over 200,000, and they to be clad, fed, and transported from point to point, with great rapidity and corresponding expense, and to be furnished with arms and ammunition, and they to be transported in like manner, and at like expense was no more in round numbers than thirty millions; whereas the annual expenditure of 1838, under Mr. Van Buren, and while we were at peace with every government in the world, was forty millions; being over the highest year of the late and very expensive war in the proportion of four to three.

(4) General Washington administered the government eight years for sixteen millions; Mr. Van Buren administered it one year (1838) for forty millions; so that Mr. Van Buren expended twice and a half as much in one year as General Washington did in eight, and being in the proportion of twenty to one; or in other words, had General Washington administered the government twenty years at the same average expense that he did for eight, he would have carried us through the whole twenty for no more money than Mr. Van Buren has expended in getting us through the single one of 1838. Other facts equally astounding might be presented from the same authentic document; but I deem the foregoing abundantly sufficient to establish the proposition that there is no parallel between the "errors" of the present and late administrations and those of former times, and that Mr. Van Buren is wholly out of the line of all precedents.

But Mr. Douglas, seeing that the enormous expenditure of 1838 has no parallel in the olden times, comes in with a long list of excuses for it. This list of excuses I will rapidly examine, and show, as I think, that the few of them which are true prove nothing, and that the majority of them are wholly untrue in fact. He first says that the expenditures of that one year were made under the appropriations of Congress—one branch of which was a Whig body. It is true that those expenditures were made under the appropriations of Congress; but it is untrue that either branch of Congress was a Whig body. The Senate had fallen into the hands of the administration more than a year before, as proven by the passage of the Expunging Resolution; and at the time those appropriations were made there were too few Whigs in that body to make a respectable struggle, in point of numbers, upon any question. This is notorious to all. The House of Representatives that voted those appropriations was the same that first assembled at the called session of September, 1838. Although it refused to pass the Subtreasury Bill, a majority of its members were elected as friends of the administration, and proved their adherence to it by the election of a Van Buren speaker, and two Van Buren clerks. It is clear, then, that both branches of the Congress that passed those appropriations were in the hands of Mr. Van

Buren's friends, so that the Whigs had no power to arrest them, as Mr. Douglas would insist. And is not the charge of extravagant expenditures equally well sustained, if shown to have been made by a Van Buren Congress, as if shown to have been made in any other way? A Van Buren Congress passed the bills, and Mr. Van Buren himself approved them, and consequently the party are wholly responsible for them.

Mr. Douglas next says that a portion of the expenditures of that year was made for the purchase of public lands from the Indians. Now it happens that no such purchase was made during that year. It is true that some money was paid that year in pursuance of Indian treaties; but no more, or rather not as much as had been paid on the same account in each of several preceding years.

Next he says that the Florida war created many millions of this year's expenditure. This is true, and it is also true that during that and every other year that that war has existed, it has cost three or four times as much as it would have done under an honest and judicious administration of the government. The large sums foolishly, not to say corruptly, thrown away in that war constitute one of the just causes of complaint against the administration. Take a single instance. The agents of the government in connection with that war needed a certain steamboat; the owner proposed to sell it for ten thousand dollars; the agents refused to give that sum, but hired the boat at one hundred dollars per day, and kept it at that hire till it amounted to ninety-two thousand dollars. This fact is not found in the public reports, but depends with me, on the verbal statement of an officer of the navy, who says he knows it to be true. That the administration ought to be credited for the reasonable expenses of the Florida war, we have never denied. Those reasonable charges, we say, could not exceed one or two millions a year. Deduct such a sum from the forty-million expenditure of 1838, and the remainder will still be without a parallel as an annual expenditure.

Again, Mr. Douglas says that the removal of the Indians to the country west of the Mississippi created much of the expenditure of 1838. I have examined the public documents in relation to this matter, and find that less was paid for the removal of Indians in that than in some former years. The whole sum expended on that account in that year did not much exceed one quarter of a million. For this small sum, although we do not think the administration entitled to credit, because large sums have been expended in the same way in former years, we consent it may take one and make the most of it.

Next, Mr. Douglas says that five millions of the expenditures of 1838 consisted of the payment of the French indemnity money to its individual claimants. I have carefully examined the public documents, and thereby find this statement to be wholly untrue. Of the forty millions of dollars expended in 1838, I am enabled to say positively that not one dollar consisted of payments on the French indemnities. So much for that excuse.

Next comes the Post-office. He says that five millions were expended during that year to sustain that department. By a like examination of public documents, I find this also wholly untrue. Of the so often mentioned forty millions, not one dollar went to the Post-office. I am glad, however, that the Post-office has been referred to, because it warrants me in digressing a little to inquire how it is that that department of the government has become a charge upon the treasury, whereas under Mr. Adams and the presidents before him it not only, to use a homely phrase, cut its own fodder, but actually threw a surplus into the treasury. Although nothing of the forty millions was paid on that account in 1838, it is true that five millions are appropriated to be so expended in 1839; showing clearly that the department has become a charge upon the treasury. How has this happened? I account for it in this way. The chief expense of the Post-office Department consists of the payments of contractors for carrying the mail. Contracts for carrying the mails are by law let to the lowest bidders, after advertisement. This plan introduces competition, and insures the transportation of the mails at fair prices, so long as it is faithfully adhered to. It has ever been adhered to until Mr. Barry was made postmaster-general. When he came into office, he formed the purpose of throwing the mail contracts into the hands of his friends, to the exclusion of his opponents. To affect this, the plan of letting to the lowest bidder must be evaded, and it must be done in this way: the favorite bid less by perhaps three or four hundred percent than the contract could be performed for, and consequently shutting out all honest competition, became the contractor. The Postmaster-General would immediately add some slight additional duty to the contract, and under the pretense of extra allowance for extra services run the contract to double, triple, and often quadruple what honest and fair bidders had proposed to take it at. In 1834 the finances of the department had become so deranged that total concealment was no longer possible, and consequently a committee of the Senate were directed to make a thorough investigation of its affairs. Their report is found in the Senate Documents of 1833-4, Vol. V, Doc. 422; which documents may be seen at the secretary's office, and I presume elsewhere in the State. The report shows numerous cases of similar import, of one of which I give the substance. The contract for carrying the mail upon a certain route had expired, and of course was to be let again. The old contractor offered to take it for $300 a year, the mail to be transported thereon three times a week, or for $600 transported daily. One James Reeside bid $40 for three times a week, or $99 daily, and of course received the contract. On the examination of the committee, it was discovered that

Reeside had received for the service on this route, which he had contracted to render for less than $100, the enormous sum of $1999! This is but a single case. Many similar ones, covering some ten or twenty pages of a large volume, are given in that report. The department was found to be insolvent to the amount of half a million, and to have been so grossly mismanaged, or rather so corruptly managed, in almost every particular, that the best friends of the Postmaster-General made no defense of his administration of it. They admitted that he was wholly unqualified for that office; but still he was retained in it by the President until he resigned it voluntarily about a year afterward. And when he resigned it, what do you think became of him? Why, he sunk into obscurity and disgrace, to be sure, you will say. No such thing. Well, then, what did become of him? (Postmaster General Barry) Why, the President immediately expressed his high disapprobation of his almost unequaled incapacity and corruption by appointing him to a foreign mission, with a salary and outfit of $18,000 a year! The party now attempt to throw Barry off, and to avoid the responsibility of his sins. Did not the President indorse those sins when, on the very heel of their commission, he appointed their author to the very highest and most honorable office in his gift, and which is but a single step behind the very goal of American political ambition?

I return to another of Mr. Douglas's excuses for the expenditures of 1838, at the same time announcing the pleasing intelligence that this is the last one. He says that ten millions of that year's expenditure was a contingent appropriation, to prosecute an anticipated war with Great Britain on the Maine boundary question. Few words will settle this. First, that the ten millions appropriated was not made till 1839, and consequently could not have been expended in 1838; second, although it was appropriated, it has never been expended at all. Those who heard Mr. Douglas recollect that he indulged himself in a contemptuous expression of pity for me. "Now he's got me," thought I. But when he went on to say that five millions of the expenditure of 1838 were payments of the French indemnities, which I knew to be untrue; that five millions had been for the post-office, which I knew to be untrue; that ten millions had been for the Maine boundary war, which I not only knew to be untrue, but supremely ridiculous also; and when I saw that he was stupid enough to hope that I would permit such groundless and audacious assertions to go unexposed,—I readily consented that, on the score both of veracity and sagacity, the audience should judge whether he or I were the more deserving of the world's contempt.

Mr. Lamborn insists that the difference between the Van Buren party and the Whigs is that, although the former sometimes err in practice, they are always correct in principle, whereas the latter are wrong in principle; and, better to impress this proposition, he uses a figurative expression in these words: "The Democrats are vulnerable in the heel, but they are sound in the head and the heart." The first branch of the figure—that is, that the Democrats are vulnerable in the heel—I admit is not merely figuratively, but literally true. Who that looks but for a moment at their Swartwouts, their Prices, their Harringtons, and their hundreds of others, scampering away with the public money to Texas, to Europe, and to every spot of the earth where a villain may hope to find refuge from justice, can at all doubt that they are most distressingly affected in their heels with a species of "running itch"? It seems that this malady of their heels operates on these sound-headed and honest-hearted creatures very much like the cork leg in the comic song did on its owner: which, when he had once got started on it, the more he tried to stop it, the more it would run away. At the hazard of wearing this point threadbare, I will relate an anecdote which seems too strikingly in point to be omitted. A witty Irish soldier, who was always boasting of his bravery when no danger was near, but who invariably retreated without orders at the first charge of an engagement, being asked by his captain why he did so, replied: "Captain, I have as brave a heart as Julius Caesar ever had; but, somehow or other, whenever danger approaches, my cowardly legs will run away with it." So with Mr. Lamborn's party. They take the public money into their hand for the most laudable purpose that wise heads and honest hearts can dictate; but before they can possibly get it out again, their rascally "vulnerable heels" will run away with them.

Seriously this proposition of Mr. Lamborn is nothing more or less than a request that his party may be tried by their professions instead of their practices. Perhaps no position that the party assumes is more liable to or more deserving of exposure than this very modest request; and nothing but the unwarrantable length to which I have already extended these remarks forbids me now attempting to expose it. For the reason given, I pass it by.

I shall advert to but one more point. Mr. Lamborn refers to the late elections in the States, and from their results confidently predicts that every State in the Union will vote for Mr. Van Buren at the next Presidential election. Address that argument to cowards and to knaves; with the free and the brave it will affect nothing. It may be true; if it must, let it. Many free countries have lost their liberty, and ours may lose hers; but if she shall, be it my proudest plume, not that I was the last to desert, but that I never deserted her. I know that the great volcano at Washington, aroused and directed by the evil spirit that reigns there, is belching forth the lava of political corruption in a current broad and deep, which is sweeping with frightful velocity over the whole length and breadth of the land, bidding fair to leave unscathed no green spot or living thing; while on its bosom are riding, like demons on the waves of hell, the imps of that evil spirit, and fiendishly taunting all those who dare resist its destroying course with the hopelessness of their effort; and, knowing this, I cannot deny that all may be swept away. Broken by it I, too, may be; bow to it I never will. The probability that we may fall in the struggle ought not to deter us from the support of a cause we believe to be just; it shall not deter me. If ever I feel the soul within me elevate and expand to those dimensions not wholly unworthy of its almighty Architect, it is when I contemplate the cause of my country deserted by all the world beside, and I standing up boldly and alone, and hurling defiance at her victorious oppressors. Here, without contemplating consequences, before high heaven and in the face of the world, I swear eternal fidelity to the just cause, as I deem it, of the land of my life, my liberty, and my love. And who that thinks with me will not fearlessly adopt the oath that I take? Let none falter who thinks he is right, and we may succeed. But if, after all, we shall fail, be it so. We still shall have the proud consolation of saying to our consciences, and to the departed shade of our country's freedom, that the cause approved of our judgment, and adored of our hearts, in disaster, in chains, in torture, in death, we never faltered in defending.

ADDRESS TO THE WASHINGTON TEMPERANCE SOCIETY,
SPRINGFIELD, ILLINOIS, FEBRUARY 22, 1842.

Although the temperance cause has been in progress for near twenty years, it is apparent to all that it is just now being crowned with a degree of success hitherto unparalleled.

The list of its friends is daily swelled by the additions of fifties, of hundreds, and of thousands. The cause itself seems suddenly transformed from a cold abstract theory to a living, breathing, active, and powerful chieftain, going forth "conquering and to conquer." The citadels of his great adversary are daily being stormed and dismantled; his temple and his altars, where the rites of his idolatrous worship have long been performed, and where human sacrifices have long been wont to be made, are daily desecrated and deserted. The triumph of the conqueror's fame is sounding from hill to hill, from sea to sea, and from land to land, and calling millions to his standard at a blast.

For this new and splendid success we heartily rejoice. That that success is so much greater now than heretofore is doubtless owing to rational causes; and if we would have it continue, we shall do well to inquire what those causes are.

The warfare heretofore waged against the demon intemperance has somehow or other been erroneous. Either the champions engaged or the tactics they adopted have not been the most proper. These champions for the most part have been preachers, lawyers, and hired agents. Between these and the mass of mankind there is a want of approachability, if the term be admissible, partially, at least, fatal to their success. They are supposed to have no sympathy of feeling or interest with those very persons whom it is their object to convince and persuade.

And again, it is so common and so easy to ascribe motives to men of these classes other than those they profess to act upon. The preacher, it is said, advocates temperance because he is a fanatic, and desires a union of the Church and State; the lawyer from his pride and vanity of hearing himself speak; and the hired agent for his salary. But when one who has long been known as a victim of intemperance bursts the fetters that have bound him, and appears before his neighbors "clothed and in his right mind," a redeemed specimen of long-lost humanity, and stands up, with tears of joy trembling in his eyes, to tell of the miseries once endured, now to be endured no more forever; of his once naked and starving children, now clad and fed comfortably; of a wife long weighed down with woe, weeping, and a broken heart, now restored to health, happiness, and a renewed affection; and how easily it is all done, once it is resolved to be done; how simple his language! there is a logic and an eloquence in it that few with human feelings can resist. They cannot say that he desires a union of Church and State, for he is not a church member; they cannot say he is vain of hearing himself speak, for his whole demeanor shows he would gladly avoid speaking at all; they cannot say he speaks for pay, for he receives none, and asks for none. Nor can his sincerity in any way be doubted, or his sympathy for those he would persuade to imitate his example be denied.

In my judgment, it is to the battles of this new class of champions that our late success is greatly, perhaps chiefly, owing. But, had the old-school champions themselves been of the most wise selecting, was their system of tactics the most judicious? It seems to me it was not. Too much denunciation against dram-sellers and dram-drinkers was indulged in. This I think was both impolitic and unjust. It was impolitic, because it is not much in the nature of man to be driven to anything; still less to be driven about that which is exclusively his own business; and least of all where such driving is to be submitted to at the expense of pecuniary interest or burning appetite. When the dram-seller and drinker were incessantly told not in accents of entreaty and persuasion, diffidently addressed by erring man to an erring brother, but in the thundering tones of anathema and denunciation with which the lordly judge often groups together all the crimes of the felon's life, and thrusts them in his face just ere he passes sentence of death upon him that they were the authors of all the vice and misery and crime in the land; that they were the manufacturers and material of all the thieves and robbers and murderers that infest the earth; that their houses were the workshops of the devil; and that their persons should be shunned by all the good and virtuous, as moral pestilences—I say, when they were told all this, and in this way, it is not wonderful that they were slow to acknowledge the truth of such denunciations, and to join the ranks of their denouncers in a hue and cry against themselves.

To have expected them to do otherwise than they did to have expected them not to meet denunciation with denunciation, crimination with crimination, and anathema with anathema—was to expect a reversal of human nature, which is God's decree and can never be reversed.

When the conduct of men is designed to be influenced, persuasion, kind, unassuming persuasion, should ever be adopted. It is an old and a true maxim that "a drop of honey catches more flies than a gallon of gall." So with men. If you would win a man to your cause, first convince him that you are his sincere friend. Therein is a drop of honey that catches his heart, which, say what he will, is the great highroad to his reason; and which, when once gained, you will find but little trouble in convincing his judgment of the justice of your cause, if indeed that cause really be a just one. On the contrary, assume to dictate to his judgment, or to command his action, or to mark him as one to be shunned and despised, and he will retreat within himself, close all the avenues to his head and his heart; and though your cause be naked truth itself, transformed to the heaviest lance, harder than steel, and sharper than steel can be made, and though you throw it with more than herculean force and precision, you shall be no more able to pierce him than to penetrate the hard shell of a tortoise with a rye straw. Such is man, and so must he be understood by those who would lead him, even to his own best interests.

On this point the Washingtonians greatly excel the temperance advocates of former times. Those whom they desire to convince and persuade are their old friends and companions. They know they are not demons, nor even the worst of men; they know that generally they are kind, generous, and charitable even beyond the example of their more staid and sober neighbors. They are practical philanthropists; and they glow with a generous and brotherly zeal that mere theorizers are incapable of feeling. Benevolence and charity possess their hearts entirely; and out of the abundance of their hearts their tongues give utterance; "love through all their actions runs, and all their words are mild." In this spirit they speak and act, and in the same they are heard and regarded. And when such is the temper of the advocate, and such of the audience, no good cause can be unsuccessful. But I have said that denunciations against dram-sellers and dram-drinkers are unjust, as well as impolitic. Let us see. I have not inquired at what period of time the use of intoxicating liquors commenced; nor is it important to know. It is sufficient that, to all of us who now inhabit the world, the practice of drinking them is just as old as the world itself that is, we have seen the one just as long as we have seen the other. When all such of us as have now reached the years of maturity first opened our eyes upon the stage of existence, we found intoxicating liquor recognized by everybody, used by everybody, repudiated by nobody. It commonly entered into the first draught of the infant and the last draught of the dying man. From the sideboard of the parson down to the ragged pocket of the houseless loafer, it was constantly found. Physicians proscribed it in this, that, and the other disease; government provided it for soldiers and sailors; and to have a rolling or raising, a husking or "hoedown," anywhere about without it was positively insufferable. So, too, it was everywhere a respectable article of manufacture and merchandise. The making of it was regarded as an honorable livelihood, and he who could make most was the most enterprising and respectable. Large and small manufactories of it were everywhere erected, in which all the earthly goods of their owners were invested. Wagons drew it from town to town; boats bore it from clime to clime, and the winds wafted it from nation to nation; and merchants bought and sold it, by wholesale and retail, with precisely the same feelings on the part of the seller, buyer, and bystander as are felt at the selling and buying of ploughs, beef, bacon, or any other of the real necessaries of life. Universal public opinion not only tolerated but recognized and adopted its use.

It is true that even then it was known and acknowledged that many were greatly injured by it; but none seemed to think the injury arose from the use of a bad thing, but from the abuse of a very good thing. The victims of it were to be pitied and compassionated, just as are the heirs of consumption and other hereditary diseases. Their failing was treated as a misfortune, and not as a crime, or even as a disgrace. If, then, what I have been saying is true, is it wonderful that some should think and act now as all thought and acted twenty years ago? and is it just to assail, condemn, or despise them for doing so? The universal sense of mankind on any subject is an argument, or at least an influence, not easily overcome. The success of the argument in favor of the existence of an overruling Providence mainly depends upon that sense; and men ought not in justice to be denounced for yielding to it in any case, or giving it up slowly, especially when they are backed by interest, fixed habits, or burning appetites.

Another error, as it seems to me, into which the old reformers fell, was the position that all habitual drunkards were utterly incorrigible, and therefore must be turned adrift and damned without remedy in order that the grace of temperance might abound, to the temperate then, and to all mankind some hundreds of years thereafter. There is in this some thing so repugnant to humanity, so uncharitable, so cold-blooded and feelingless, that it, never did nor ever can enlist the enthusiasm of a popular cause. We could not love the man who taught it we could not hear him with patience. The heart could not throw open its portals to it, the generous man could not adopt it—it could not mix with his blood. It looked so fiendishly selfish, so like throwing fathers and brothers overboard to lighten the boat for our security, that the noble-minded shrank from the manifest meanness of the thing. And besides this, the benefits of a reformation to be effected by such a system were too remote in point of time to warmly engage many in its behalf. Few can be induced to labor exclusively for posterity, and none will do it enthusiastically. —Posterity has done nothing for us; and, theorize on it as we may, practically we shall do very little for it, unless we are made to think we are at the same time doing something for ourselves.

What an ignorance of human nature does it exhibit to ask or to expect a whole community to rise up and labor for the temporal happiness of others, after themselves shall be consigned to the dust, a majority of which community take no pains whatever to secure their own eternal welfare at no more distant day! Great distance in either time or space has wonderful power to lull and render quiescent the human mind. Pleasures to be enjoyed, or pains to be endured, after we shall be dead and gone are but little regarded even in our own cases, and much less in the cases of others. Still, in addition to this there is something so ludicrous in promises of good or threats of evil a great way off as to render the whole subject with which they are connected easily turned into ridicule. "Better lay down that spade you are stealing, Paddy; if you don't you'll pay for it at the day of judgment." "Be the powers, if ye'll credit me so long I'll take another jist."

By the Washingtonians this system of consigning the habitual drunkard to hopeless ruin is repudiated. They adopt a more enlarged philanthropy; they go for present as well as future good. They labor for all now living, as well as hereafter to live. They teach hope to all-despair to none. As applying to their cause, they deny the doctrine of unpardonable sin; as in Christianity it is taught, so in this they teach— "While—While the lamp holds out to burn, The vilest sinner may return." And, what is a matter of more profound congratulation, they, by experiment upon experiment and example upon example, prove the maxim to be no less true in the one case than in the other. On every hand we behold those who but yesterday were the chief of sinners, now the chief apostles of the cause. Drunken devils are cast out by ones, by sevens, by legions; and their unfortunate victims, like the poor possessed who were redeemed from their long and lonely wanderings in the tombs, are publishing to the ends of the earth how great things have been done for them.

To these new champions and this new system of tactics our late success is mainly owing, and to them we must mainly look for the final consummation. The ball is now rolling gloriously on, and none are so able as they to increase its speed and its bulk, to add to its momentum and its magnitude—even though unlearned in letters, for this task none are so well educated. To fit them for this work they have been taught in the true school. They have been in that gulf from which they would teach others the means of escape. They have passed that prison wall which others have long declared impassable; and who that has not shall dare to weigh opinions with them as to the mode of passing?

But if it be true, as I have insisted, that those who have suffered by intemperance personally, and have reformed, are the most powerful and efficient instruments to push the reformation to ultimate success, it does not follow that those who have not suffered have no part left them to perform. Whether or not the world would be vastly benefited by a total and final banishment from it of all intoxicating drinks seems to me not now an open question. Three fourths of mankind confess the affirmative with their tongues, and, I believe, all the rest acknowledge it in their hearts.

Ought any, then, to refuse their aid in doing what good the good of the whole demands? Shall he who cannot do much be for that reason excused if he do nothing? "But," says one, "what good can I do by signing the pledge? I never drank, even without signing." This question has already been asked and answered more than a million of times. Let it be answered once more. For the man suddenly or in any other way to break off from the use of drams, who has indulged in them for a long course of years and until his appetite for them has grown ten or a hundredfold stronger and more craving than any natural appetite can be, requires a most powerful moral effort. In such an undertaking he needs every moral support and influence that can possibly be brought to his aid and thrown around him. And not only so, but every moral prop should be taken from whatever argument might rise in his mind to lure him to his backsliding. When he casts his eyes around him, he should be able to see all that he respects, all that he admires, all that he loves, kindly and anxiously pointing him onward, and none beckoning him back to his former miserable "wallowing in the mire."

But it is said by some that men will think and act for themselves; that none will disuse spirits or anything else because his neighbors do; and that moral influence is not that powerful engine contended for. Let us examine this. Let me ask the man who could maintain this position most stiffly, what compensation he will accept to go to church some Sunday and sit during the sermon with his wife's bonnet upon his head? Not a trifle, I'll venture. And why not? There would be nothing irreligious in it, nothing immoral, nothing uncomfortable—then why not? Is it not because there would be something egregiously unfashionable in it? Then it is the influence of fashion; and what is the influence of fashion but the influence that other people's actions have on our actions—the strong inclination each of us feels to do as we see all our neighbors do? Nor is the influence of fashion confined to any particular thing or class of things; it is just as strong on one subject as another. Let us make it as unfashionable to withhold our names from the temperance cause as for husbands to wear their wives' bonnets to church, and instances will be just as rare in the one case as the other.

"But," say some, "we are no drunkards, and we shall not acknowledge ourselves such by joining a reformed drunkard's society, whatever our influence might be." Surely no Christian will adhere to this objection. If they believe as they profess, that Omnipotence condescended to take on himself the form of sinful man, and as such to die an ignominious death for their sakes, surely they will not refuse submission to the infinitely lesser condescension, for the temporal, and perhaps eternal, salvation of a large, erring, and unfortunate class of their fellow-creatures. Nor is the condescension very great. In my judgment such of us as have never fallen victims have been spared more by the absence of appetite than from any mental or moral superiority over those who have. Indeed, I believe if we take habitual drunkards as a class, their heads and their hearts will bear an advantageous comparison with those of any other class. There seems ever to have been a proneness in the brilliant and warm-blooded to fall into this vice—the demon of intemperance ever seems to have delighted in sucking the blood of genius and of generosity. What one of us but can call to mind some relative, more promising in youth than all his fellows, who has fallen a sacrifice to his rapacity? He ever seems to have gone forth like the Egyptian angel of death, commissioned to slay, if not the first, the fairest born of every family. Shall he now be arrested in his desolating career? In that arrest all can give aid that will; and who shall be excused that can and will not? Far around as human breath has ever blown he keeps our fathers, our brothers, our sons, and our friends prostrate in the chains of moral death. To all the living everywhere we cry, "Come sound the moral trump, that these may rise and stand up an exceeding great army." "Come from the four winds, O breath! and breathe upon these slain that they may live." If the relative grandeur of revolutions shall be estimated by the great amount of human misery they alleviate, and the small amount they inflict, then indeed will this be the grandest the world shall ever have seen.

Of our political revolution of '76 we are all justly proud. It has given us a degree of political freedom far exceeding that of any other nation of the earth. In it the world has found a solution of the long-mooted problem as to the capability of man to govern himself. In it was the germ which has vegetated, and still is to grow and expand into the universal liberty of mankind. But, with all these glorious results, past, present, and to come, it had its evils too. It breathed forth famine, swam in blood, and rode in fire; and long, long after, the orphan's cry and the widow's wail continued to break the sad silence that ensued. These were the price, the inevitable price, paid for the blessings it bought.

Turn now to the temperance revolution. In it we shall find a stronger bondage broken, a viler slavery manumitted, a greater tyrant deposed; in it, more of want supplied, more disease healed, more sorrow assuaged. By it no Orphans starving, no widows weeping. By it none wounded in feeling, none injured in interest; even the dram-maker and dram-seller will have glided into other occupations so gradually as never to have felt the change, and will stand ready to join all others in the universal song of gladness. And what a noble ally this to the cause of political freedom, with such an aid its march cannot fail to be on and on, till every son of earth shall drink in rich fruition the sorrow-quenching draughts of perfect liberty. Happy day when-all appetites controlled, all poisons subdued, all matter subjected-mind, all-conquering mind, shall live and move, the monarch of the world. Glorious consummation! Hail, fall of fury! Reign of reason, all hail!

And when the victory shall be complete, when there shall be neither a slave nor a drunkard on the earth, how proud the title of that land which may truly claim to be the birthplace and the cradle of both those revolutions that shall have ended in that victory. How nobly distinguished that people who shall have planted and nurtured to maturity both the political and moral freedom of their species.

This is the one hundred and tenth anniversary of the birthday of Washington; we are met to celebrate this day. Washington is the mightiest name of earth long since mightiest in the cause of civil liberty, still mightiest in moral reformation. On that name no eulogy is expected. It cannot be. To add brightness to the sun or glory to the name of Washington is alike impossible. Let none attempt it. In solemn awe pronounce the name, and in its naked deathless splendor leave it shining on.

SPEECH ON THE WAR WITH MEXICO,
WASHINGTON, DC, JANUARY 12, 1848.

MR. CHAIRMAN:—Some if not all the gentlemen on the other side of the House who have addressed the committee within the last two days have spoken rather complainingly, if I have rightly understood them, of the vote given a week or ten days ago declaring that the war with Mexico was unnecessarily and unconstitutionally commenced by the President. I admit that such a vote should not be given in mere party wantonness, and that the one given is justly censurable if it have no other or better foundation. I am one of those who joined in that vote; and I did so under my best impression of the truth of the case. How I got this impression, and how it may possibly be remedied, I will now try to show. When the war began, it was my opinion that all those who because of knowing too little, or because of knowing too much, could not conscientiously approve the conduct of the President in the beginning of it should nevertheless, as good citizens and patriots, remain silent on that point, at least till the war should be ended. Some leading Democrats, including ex-President Van Buren, have taken this same view, as I understand them; and I adhered to it and acted upon it, until since I took my seat here; and I think I should still adhere to it were it not that the President and his friends will not allow it to be so. Besides the continual effort of the President to argue every silent vote given for supplies into an endorsement of the justice and wisdom of his conduct; besides that singularly candid paragraph in his late message in which he tells us that Congress with great unanimity had declared that "by the act of the Republic of Mexico, a state of war exists between that government and the United States," when the same journals that informed him of this also informed him that when that declaration stood disconnected from the question of supplies sixty-seven in the House, and not fourteen merely, voted against it; besides this open attempt to prove by telling the truth what he could not prove by telling the whole truth-demanding of all who will not submit to be misrepresented, in justice to themselves, to speak out, besides all this, one of my colleagues [Mr. Richardson] at a very early day in the session brought in a set of resolutions expressly indorsing the original justice of the war on the part of the President. Upon these resolutions when they shall be put on their passage I shall be compelled to vote; so that I cannot be silent if I would. Seeing this, I went about preparing myself to give the vote understandingly when it should come. I carefully examined the President's message, to ascertain what he himself had said and proved upon the point. The result of this examination was to make the impression that, taking for true all the President states as facts, he falls far short of proving his justification; and that the President would have gone further with his proof if it had not been for the small matter that the truth would not permit him. Under the impression thus made I gave the vote before mentioned. I propose now to give concisely the process of the examination I made, and how I reached the conclusion I did. The President, in his first war message of May, 1846, declares that the soil was ours on which hostilities were commenced by Mexico, and he repeats that declaration almost in the same language in each successive annual message, thus showing that he deems that point a highly essential one. In the importance of that point I entirely agree with the President. To my judgment it is the very point upon which he should be justified, or condemned. In his message of December, 1846, it seems to have occurred to him, as is certainly true, that title-ownership-to soil or anything else is not a simple fact, but is a conclusion following on one or more simple facts; and that it was incumbent upon him to present the facts from which he concluded the soil was ours on which the first blood of the war was shed.

Accordingly, a little below the middle of page twelve in the message last referred to, he enters upon that task; forming an issue and introducing testimony, extending the whole to a little below the middle of page fourteen. Now, I propose to try to show that the whole of this— issue and evidence—is from beginning to end the sheerest deception. The issue, as he presents it, is in these words: "But there are those who, conceding all this to be true, assume the ground that the true western boundary of Texas is the Nueces, instead of the Rio Grande; and that, therefore, in marching our army to the east bank of the latter river, we passed the Texas line and invaded the territory of Mexico." Now this issue is made up of two affirmatives and no negative. The main deception of it is that it assumes as true that one river or the other is necessarily the boundary; and cheats the superficial thinker entirely out of the idea that possibly the boundary is somewhere between the two, and not actually at either. A further deception is that it will let in evidence which a true issue would exclude. A true issue made by the President would be about as follows: "I say the soil was ours, on which the first blood was shed; there are those who say it was not."

I now proceed to examine the President's evidence as applicable to such an issue. When that evidence is analyzed, it is all included in the following propositions:

(1) That the Rio Grande was the western boundary of Louisiana as we purchased it of France in 1803.

(2) That the Republic of Texas always claimed the Rio Grande as her eastern boundary.

(3) That by various acts she had claimed it on paper.

(4) That Santa Anna in his treaty with Texas recognized the Rio Grande as her boundary.

(5) That Texas before, and the United States after, annexation had exercised jurisdiction beyond the Nueces—between the two rivers.

(6) That our Congress understood the boundary of Texas to extend beyond the Nueces.

Now for each of these in its turn. His first item is that the Rio Grande was the western boundary of Louisiana, as we purchased it of France in 1803; and seeming to expect this to be disputed, he argues over the amount of nearly a page to prove it true, at the end of which he lets us know that by the treaty of 1803 we sold to Spain the whole country from the Rio Grande eastward to the Sabine. Now, admitting for the present that the Rio Grande was the boundary of Louisiana, what under heaven had that to do with the present boundary between us and Mexico? How, Mr. Chairman, the line that once divided your land from mine can still be the boundary between us after I have sold my land to you is to me beyond all comprehension. And how any man, with an honest purpose only of proving the truth, could ever have thought of introducing such a fact to prove such an issue is equally incomprehensible. His next piece of evidence is that "the Republic of Texas always claimed this river [Rio Grande] as her western boundary." That is not true, in fact. Texas has claimed it, but she has not always claimed it. There is at least one distinguished exception. Her State constitution the republic's most solemn and well-considered act, that which may, without impropriety, be called her last will and testament, revoking all others-makes no such claim. But suppose she had always claimed it. Has not Mexico always claimed the contrary? So that there is but claim against claim, leaving nothing proved until we get back of the claims and find which has the better foundation. Though not in the order in which the President presents his evidence, I now consider that class of his statements which are in substance nothing more than that Texas has, by various acts of her Convention and Congress, claimed the Rio Grande as her boundary, on paper. I mean here what he says about the fixing of the Rio Grande as her boundary in her old constitution (not her State constitution), about forming Congressional districts, counties, etc. Now all of this is but naked claim; and what I have already said about claims is strictly applicable to this. If I should claim your land by word of mouth, that certainly would not make it mine; and if I were to claim it by a deed which I had made myself, and with which you had had nothing to do, the claim would be quite the same in substance—or rather, in utter nothingness. I next consider the President's statement that Santa Anna in his treaty with Texas recognized the Rio Grande as the western boundary of Texas. Besides the position so often taken, that Santa Anna while a prisoner of war, a captive, could not bind Mexico by a treaty, which I deem conclusive—besides this, I wish to say something in relation to this treaty, so called by the President, with Santa Anna. If any man would like to be amused by a sight of that little thing which the President calls by that big name, he can have it by turning to Niles's Register, vol. 1, p. 336. And if any one should suppose that Niles's Register is a curious repository of so mighty a document as a solemn treaty between nations, I can only say that I learned to a tolerable degree of certainty, by inquiry at the State Department, that the President himself never saw it anywhere else. By the way, I believe I should not err if I were to declare that during the first ten years of the existence of that document it was never by anybody called a treaty— that it was never so called till the President, in his extremity, attempted by so calling it to wring something from it in justification of himself in connection with the Mexican War. It has none of the distinguishing features of a treaty. It does not call itself a treaty. Santa Anna does not therein assume to bind Mexico; he assumes only to act as the President—Commander-in-Chief of the Mexican army and navy; stipulates that the then present hostilities should cease, and that he would not himself take up arms, nor influence the Mexican people to take up arms, against Texas during the existence of the war of independence. He did not recognize the independence of Texas; he did not assume to put an end to the war, but clearly indicated his expectation of its continuance; he did not say one word about boundary, and, most probably, never thought of it. It is stipulated therein that the Mexican forces should evacuate the territory of Texas, passing to the other side of the Rio Grande; and in another article it is stipulated that, to prevent collisions between the armies, the Texas army should not approach nearer than within five leagues—of what is not said, but clearly, from the object stated, it is of the Rio Grande. Now, if this is a treaty recognizing the Rio Grande as the boundary of Texas, it contains the singular feature of stipulating that Texas shall not go within five leagues of her own boundary.

Next comes the evidence of Texas before annexation, and the United States afterwards, exercising jurisdiction beyond the Nueces and between the two rivers. This actual exercise of jurisdiction is the very class or quality of evidence we want. It is excellent so far as it goes; but does it go far enough? He tells us it went beyond the Nueces, but he does not tell us it went to the Rio Grande. He tells us jurisdiction was exercised between the two rivers, but he does not tell us it was exercised over all the territory between them. Some simple-minded people think it is possible to cross one river and go beyond it without going all the way to the next, that jurisdiction may be exercised between two rivers without covering all the country between them. I know a man, not very unlike myself, who exercises jurisdiction over a piece of land between the Wabash and the Mississippi; and yet so far is this from being all there is between those rivers that it is just one hundred and fifty-two feet long by fifty feet wide, and no part of it much within a hundred miles of either. He has a neighbor between him and the Mississippi—that is, just across the street, in that direction—whom I am sure he could neither persuade nor force to give up his habitation; but which nevertheless he could certainly annex, if it were to be done by merely standing on his own side of the street and claiming it, or even sitting down and writing a deed for it.

But next the President tells us the Congress of the United States understood the State of Texas they admitted into the Union to extend beyond the Nueces. Well, I suppose they did. I certainly so understood it. But how far beyond? That Congress did not understand it to extend clear to the Rio Grande is quite certain, by the fact of their joint resolutions for admission expressly leaving all questions of boundary to future adjustment. And it may be added that Texas herself is proven to have had the same understanding of it that our Congress had, by the fact of the exact conformity of her new constitution to those resolutions.

I am now through the whole of the President's evidence; and it is a singular fact that if any one should declare the President sent the army into the midst of a settlement of Mexican people who had never submitted, by consent or by force, to the authority of Texas or of the United States, and that there and thereby the first blood of the war was shed, there is not one word in all the which would either admit or deny the declaration. This strange omission it does seem to me could not have occurred but by design. My way of living leads me to be about the courts of justice; and there I have sometimes seen a good lawyer, struggling for his client's neck in a desperate case, employing every artifice to work round, befog, and cover up with many words some point arising in the case which he dared not admit and yet could not deny. Party bias may help to make it appear so, but with all the allowance I can make for such bias, it still does appear to me that just such, and from just such necessity, is the President's struggle in this case.

Sometime after my colleague [Mr. Richardson] introduced the resolutions I have mentioned, I introduced a preamble, resolution, and interrogations, intended to draw the President out, if possible, on this hitherto untrodden ground. To show their relevancy, I propose to state my understanding of the true rule for ascertaining the boundary between Texas and Mexico. It is that wherever Texas was exercising jurisdiction was hers; and wherever Mexico was exercising jurisdiction was hers; and that whatever separated the actual exercise of jurisdiction of the one from that of the other was the true boundary between them. If, as is probably true, Texas was exercising jurisdiction along the western bank of the Nueces, and Mexico was exercising it along the eastern bank of the Rio Grande, then neither river was the boundary: but the uninhabited country between the two was. The extent of our territory in that region depended not on any treaty-fixed boundary (for no treaty had attempted it), but on revolution. Any people anywhere being inclined and having the power have the right to rise up and shake off the existing government, and form a new one that suits them better. This is a most valuable, a most sacred right—a right which we hope and believe is to liberate the world. Nor is this right confined to cases in which the whole people of an existing government may choose to exercise it. Any portion of such people that can may revolutionize and make their own of so much of the territory as they inhabit. More than this, a majority of any portion of such people may revolutionize, putting down a minority, intermingled with or near about them, who may oppose this movement. Such minority was precisely the case of the Tories of our own revolution. It is a quality of revolutions not to go by old lines or old laws, but to break up both, and make new ones.

As to the country now in question, we bought it of France in 1803, and sold it to Spain in 1819, according to the President's statements. After this, all Mexico, including Texas, revolutionized against Spain; and still later Texas revolutionized against Mexico. In my view, just so far as she carried her resolution by obtaining the actual, willing or unwilling, submission of the people, so far the country was hers, and no farther. Now, sir, for the purpose of obtaining the very best evidence as to whether Texas had actually carried her revolution to the place where the hostilities of the present war commenced, let the President answer the interrogatories I proposed, as before mentioned, or some other similar ones. Let him answer fully, fairly, and candidly. Let him answer with facts and not with arguments. Let him remember he sits where Washington sat, and so remembering, let him answer as Washington would answer. As a nation should not, and the Almighty will not, be evaded, so let him attempt no evasion—no equivocation. And if, so answering, he can show that the soil was ours where the first blood of the war was shed,—that it was not within an inhabited country, or, if within such, that the inhabitants had submitted themselves to the civil authority of Texas or of the United States, and that the same is true of the site of Fort Brown, then I am with him for his justification. In that case I shall be most happy to reverse the vote I gave the other day. I have a selfish motive for desiring that the President may do this—I expect to gain some votes, in connection with the war, which, without his so doing, will be of doubtful propriety in my own judgment, but which will be free from the doubt if he does so. But if he can not or will not do this,—if on any pretence or no pretence he shall refuse or omit it then I shall be fully convinced of what I more than suspect already that he is deeply conscious of being in the wrong; that he feels the blood of this war, like the blood of Abel, is crying to heaven against him; that originally having some strong motive—what, I will not stop now to give my opinion concerning to involve the two countries in a war, and trusting to escape scrutiny by fixing the public gaze upon the exceeding brightness of military glory,—that attractive rainbow that rises in showers of blood, that serpent's eye that charms to destroy,—he plunged into it, and was swept on and on till, disappointed in his calculation of the ease with which Mexico might be subdued, he now finds himself he knows not where. How like the half insane mumbling of a fever dream is the whole war part of his late message! At one time telling us that Mexico has nothing whatever that we can get—but territory; at another showing us how we can support the war by levying contributions on Mexico. At one time urging the national honor, the security of the future, the prevention of foreign interference, and even the good of Mexico herself as among the objects of the war; at another telling us that "to reject indemnity, by refusing to accept a cession of territory, would be to abandon all our just demands, and to wage the war, bearing all its expenses, without a purpose or definite object." So then this national honor, security of the future, and everything but territorial indemnity may be considered the no-purposes and indefinite objects of the war! But, having it now settled that territorial indemnity is the only object, we are urged to seize, by legislation here, all that he was content to take a few months ago, and the whole province of Lower California to boot, and to still carry on the war to take all we are fighting for, and still fight on. Again, the President is resolved under all circumstances to have full territorial indemnity for the expenses of the war; but he forgets to tell us how we are to get the excess after those expenses shall have surpassed the value of the whole of the Mexican territory. So again, he insists that the separate national existence of Mexico shall be maintained; but he does not tell us how this can be done, after we shall have taken all her territory. Lest the questions I have suggested be considered speculative merely, let me be indulged a moment in trying to show they are not. The war has gone on some twenty months; for the expenses of which, together with an inconsiderable old score, the President now claims about one half of the Mexican territory, and that by far the better half, so far as concerns our ability to make anything out of it. It is comparatively uninhabited; so that we could establish land-offices in it, and raise some money in that way. But the other half is already inhabited, as I understand it, tolerably densely for the nature of the country, and all its lands, or all that are valuable, already appropriated as private property. How then are we to make anything out of these lands with this encumbrance on them? or how remove the encumbrance? I suppose no one would say we should kill the people, or drive them out, or make slaves of them, or confiscate their property. How, then, can we make much out of this part of the territory? If the prosecution of the war has in expenses already equalled the better half of the country, how long its future prosecution will be in equalling the less valuable half is not a speculative, but a practical, question, pressing closely upon us. And yet it is a question which the President seems never to have thought of. As to the mode of terminating the war and securing peace, the President is equally wandering and indefinite. First, it is to be done by a more vigorous prosecution of the war in the vital parts of the enemy's country; and after apparently talking himself tired on this point, the President drops down into a half-despairing tone, and tells us that "with a people distracted and divided by contending factions, and a government subject to constant changes by successive revolutions, the continued success of our arms may fail to secure a satisfactory peace." Then he suggests the propriety of wheedling the Mexican people to desert the counsels of their own leaders, and, trusting in our protestations, to set up a government from which we can secure a satisfactory peace; telling us that "this may become the only mode of obtaining such a peace." But soon he falls into doubt of this too; and then drops back on to the already half-abandoned ground of "more vigorous prosecution." All this shows that the President is in nowise satisfied with his own positions. First he takes up one, and in attempting to argue us into it he argues himself out of it, then seizes another and goes through the same process, and then, confused at being able to think of nothing new, he snatches up the old one again, which he has some time before cast off. His mind, taxed beyond its power, is running hither and thither, like some tortured creature on a burning surface, finding no position on which it can settle down and be at ease.

Again, it is a singular omission in this message that it nowhere intimates when the President expects the war to terminate. At its beginning, General Scott was by this same President driven into disfavor if not disgrace, for intimating that peace could not be conquered in less than three or four months. But now, at the end of about twenty months, during which time our arms have given us the most splendid successes, every department and every part, land and water, officers and privates, regulars and volunteers, doing all that men could do, and hundreds of things which it had ever before been thought men could not do—after all this, this same President gives a long message, without showing us that as to the end he himself has even an imaginary conception. As I have before said, he knows not where he is. He is a bewildered, confounded, and miserably perplexed man. God grant he may be able to show there is not something about his conscience more painful than his mental perplexity.

The following is a copy of the so-called "treaty" referred to in the speech:

"Articles of Agreement entered into between his Excellency David G. Burnet, President of the Republic of Texas, of the one part, and his Excellency General Santa Anna, President-General-in-Chief of the Mexican army, of the other part:

"Article I. General Antonio Lopez de Santa Anna agrees that he will not take up arms, nor will he exercise his influence to cause them to be taken up, against the people of Texas during the present war of independence.

"Article II. All hostilities between the Mexican and Texan troops will cease immediately, both by land and water.

"Article III. The Mexican troops will evacuate the territory of Texas, passing to the other side of the Rio Grande Del Norte.

"Article IV. The Mexican army, in its retreat, shall not take the property of any person without his consent and just indemnification, using only such articles as may be necessary for its subsistence, in cases when the owner may not be present, and remitting to the commander of the army of Texas, or to the commissioners to be appointed for the adjustment of such matters, an account of the value of the property consumed, the place where taken, and the name of the owner, if it can be ascertained.

"Article V. That all private property, including cattle, horses, negro slaves, or indentured persons, of whatever denomination, that may have been captured by any portion of the Mexican army, or may have taken refuge in the said army, since the commencement of the late invasion, shall be restored to the commander of the Texan army, or to such other persons as may be appointed by the Government of Texas to receive them.

"Article VI. The troops of both armies will refrain from coming in contact with each other; and to this end the commander of the army of Texas will be careful not to approach within a shorter distance than five leagues.

"Article VII. The Mexican army shall not make any other delay on its march than that which is necessary to take up their hospitals, baggage, etc., and to cross the rivers; any delay not necessary to these purposes to be considered an infraction of this agreement.

"Article VIII. By an express, to be immediately despatched, this agreement shall be sent to General Vincente Filisola and to General T. J. Rusk, commander of the Texan army, in order that they may be apprised of its stipulations; and to this end they will exchange engagements to comply with the same.

"Article IX. That all Texan prisoners now in the possession of the Mexican army, or its authorities, be forthwith released, and furnished with free passports to return to their homes; in consideration of which a corresponding number of Mexican prisoners, rank and file, now in possession of the Government of Texas shall be immediately released; the remainder of the Mexican prisoners that continue in the possession of the Government of Texas to be treated with due humanity,—any extraordinary comforts that may be furnished them to be at the charge of the Government of Mexico.

"Article X. General Antonio Lopez de Santa Anna will be sent to Vera Cruz as soon as it shall be deemed proper.

"The contracting parties sign this instrument for the abovementioned purposes, in duplicate, at the port of Velasco, this fourteenth day of May, 1836.

"DAVID G. BURNET, *President,*
"JAS. COLLINGSWORTH, *Secretary of State,*
"ANTONIO LOPEZ DE SANTA ANNA,
"B. HARDIMAN, *Secretary of the Treasury,*
"P. W. GRAYSON, *Attorney-General.*"

SPEECH ON THE 1848 PRESIDENTIAL RACE,
WASHINGTON, DC, JULY 27, 1848.

General Taylor and the Veto.

Mr. Speaker, our Democratic friends seem to be in a great distress because they think our candidate for the Presidency don't suit us. Most of them cannot find out that General Taylor has any principles at all; some, however, have discovered that he has one, but that one is entirely wrong. This one principle is his position on the veto power. The gentleman from Tennessee [Mr. Stanton] who has just taken his seat, indeed, has said there is very little, if any, difference on this question between General Taylor and all the Presidents; and he seems to think it sufficient detraction from General Taylor's position on it that it has nothing new in it. But all others whom I have heard speak assail it furiously. A new member from Kentucky [Mr. Clark], of very considerable ability, was in particular concerned about it. He thought it altogether novel and unprecedented for a President or a Presidential candidate to think of approving bills whose constitutionality may not be entirely clear to his own mind. He thinks the ark of our safety is gone unless Presidents shall always veto such bills as in their judgment may be of doubtful constitutionality. However clear Congress may be on their authority to pass any particular act, the gentleman from Kentucky thinks the President must veto it if he has doubts about it. Now I have neither time nor inclination to argue with the gentleman on the veto power as an original question; but I wish to show that General Taylor, and not he, agrees with the earlier statesmen on this question. When the bill chartering the first Bank of the United States passed Congress, its constitutionality was questioned. Mr. Madison, then in the House of Representatives, as well as others, had opposed it on that ground. General Washington, as President, was called on to approve or reject it. He sought and obtained on the constitutionality question the separate written opinions of Jefferson, Hamilton, and Edmund Randolph,—they then being respectively Secretary of State, Secretary of the Treasury, and Attorney general. Hamilton's opinion was for the power; while Randolph's and Jefferson's were both against it. Mr. Jefferson, after giving his opinion deciding only against the constitutionality of the bill, closes his letter with the paragraph which I now read:

"It must be admitted, however, that unless the President's mind, on a view of everything which is urged for and against this bill, is tolerably clear that it is unauthorized by the Constitution,—if the pro and con hang so even as to balance his judgment, a just respect for the wisdom of the legislature would naturally decide the balance in favor of their opinion. It is chiefly for cases where they are clearly misled by error, ambition, or interest, that the Constitution has placed a check in the negative of the President.

"THOMAS JEFFERSON.

"February 15, 1791."

General Taylor's opinion, as expressed in his Allison letter, is as I now read:

"The power given by the veto is a high conservative power; but, in my opinion, should never be exercised except in cases of clear violation of the Constitution, or manifest haste and want of consideration by Congress."

It is here seen that, in Mr. Jefferson's opinion, if on the constitutionality of any given bill the President doubts, he is not to veto it, as the gentleman from Kentucky would have him do, but is to defer to Congress and approve it. And if we compare the opinion of Jefferson and Taylor, as expressed in these paragraphs, we shall find them more exactly alike than we can often find any two expressions having any literal difference. None but interested faultfinders, I think, can discover any substantial variation.

Taylor on Measures of Policy.

But gentlemen on the other side are unanimously agreed that General Taylor has no other principles. They are in utter darkness as to his opinions on any of the questions of policy which occupy the public attention. But is there any doubt as to what he will do on the prominent questions if elected? Not the least. It is not possible to know what he will or would do in every imaginable case, because many questions have passed away, and others doubtless will arise which none of us have yet thought of; but on the prominent questions of currency, tariff, internal improvements, and Wilmot Proviso, General Taylor's course is at least as well defined as is General Cass's. Why, in their eagerness to get at General Taylor, several Democratic members here have desired to know whether, in case of his election, a bankrupt law is to be established. Can they tell us General Cass's opinion on this question? [Some member answered, "He is against it."] Aye, how do you know he is? There is nothing about it in the platform, nor elsewhere, that I have seen. If the gentleman knows of anything which I do not know he can show it. But to return. General Taylor, in his Allison letter, says:

"Upon the subject of the tariff, the currency, the improvement of our great highways, rivers, lakes, and harbors, the will of the people, as expressed through their representatives in Congress, ought to be respected and carried out by the executive."

Now this is the whole matter. In substance, it is this: The people say to General Taylor, "If you are elected, shall we have a national bank?" He answers, "Your will, gentlemen, not mine." "What about the tariff?" "Say yourselves." "Shall our rivers and harbors be improved?" "Just as you please. If you desire a bank, an alteration of the tariff, internal improvements, any or all, I will not hinder you. If you do not desire them, I will not attempt to force them on you. Send up your members of Congress from the various districts, with opinions according to your own, and if they are for these measures, or any of them, I shall have nothing to oppose; if they are not for them, I shall not, by any appliances whatever, attempt to dragoon them into their adoption." Now can there be any difficulty in understanding this? To you Democrats it may not seem like principle; but surely you cannot fail to perceive the position plainly enough. The distinction between it and the position of your candidate is broad and obvious, and I admit you have a clear right to show it is wrong if you can; but you have no right to pretend you cannot see it at all. We see it, and to us it appears like principle, and the best sort of principle at that—the principle of allowing the people to do as they please with their own business. My friend from Indiana (C. B. Smith) has aptly asked, "Are you willing to trust the people?" Some of you answered substantially, "We are willing to trust the people; but the President is as much the representative of the people as Congress." In a certain sense, and to a certain extent, he is the representative of the people. He is elected by them, as well as Congress is; but can he, in the nature of things know the wants of the people as well as three hundred other men, coming from all the various localities of the nation? If so, where is the propriety of having a Congress? That the Constitution gives the President a negative on legislation, all know; but that this negative should be so combined with platforms and other appliances as to enable him, and in fact almost compel him, to take the whole of legislation into his own hands, is what we object to, is what General Taylor objects to, and is what constitutes the broad distinction between you and us. To thus transfer legislation is clearly to take it from those who understand with minuteness the interests of the people, and give it to one who does not and cannot so well understand it. I understand your idea that if a Presidential candidate avow his opinion upon a given question, or rather upon all questions, and the people, with full knowledge of this, elect him, they thereby distinctly approve all those opinions. By means of it, measures are adopted or rejected contrary to the wishes of the whole of one party, and often nearly half of the other. Three, four, or half a dozen questions are prominent at a given time; the party selects its candidate, and he takes his position on each of these questions. On all but one his positions have already been indorsed at former elections, and his party fully committed to them; but that one is new, and a large portion of them are against it. But what are they to do? The whole was strung together; and they must take all, or reject all. They cannot take what they like, and leave the rest. What they are already committed to being the majority, they shut their eyes, and gulp the whole. Next election, still another is introduced in the same way. If we run our eyes along the line of the past, we shall see that almost if not quite all the articles of the present Democratic creed have been at first forced upon the party in this very way. And just now, and just so, opposition to internal improvements is to be established if General Cass shall be elected. Almost half the Democrats here are for improvements; but they will vote for Cass, and if he succeeds, their vote will have aided in closing the doors against improvements. Now this is a process which we think is wrong. We prefer a candidate who, like General Taylor, will allow the people to have their own way, regardless of his private opinions; and I should think the internal-improvement Democrats, at least, ought to prefer such a candidate. He would force nothing on them which they don't want, and he would allow them to have improvements which their own candidate, if elected, will not.

Mr. Speaker, I have said General Taylor's position is as well defined as is that of General Cass. In saying this, I admit I do not certainly know what he would do on the Wilmot Proviso. I am a Northern man or rather a Western Free-State man, with a constituency I believe to be, and with personal feelings I know to be, against the extension of slavery. As such, and with what information I have, I hope and believe General Taylor, if elected, would not veto the proviso. But I do not know it. Yet if I knew he would, I still would vote for him. I should do so because, in my judgment, his election alone can defeat General Cass; and because, should slavery thereby go to the territory we now have, just so much will certainly happen by the election of Cass, and in addition a course of policy leading to new wars, new acquisitions of territory and still further extensions of slavery. One of the two is to be President. Which is preferable?

But there is as much doubt of Cass on improvements as there is of Taylor on the proviso. I have no doubt myself of General Cass on this question; but I know the Democrats differ among themselves as to his position. My internal-improvement colleague [Mr. Wentworth] stated on this floor the other day that he was satisfied Cass was for improvements, because he had voted for all the bills that he [Mr. Wentworth] had. So far so good. But Mr. Polk vetoed some of these very bills. The Baltimore convention passed a set of resolutions, among other things, approving these vetoes, and General Cass declares, in his letter accepting the nomination, that he has carefully read these resolutions, and that he adheres to them as firmly as he approves them cordially. In other words, General Cass voted for the bills, and thinks the President did right to veto them; and his friends here are amiable enough to consider him as being on one side or the other, just as one or the other may correspond with their own respective inclinations. My colleague admits that the platform declares against the constitutionality of a general system of improvements, and that General Cass indorses the platform; but he still thinks General Cass is in favor of some sort of improvements. Well, what are they? As he is against general objects, those he is for must be particular and local. Now this is taking the subject precisely by the wrong end. Particularity expending the money of the whole people for an object which will benefit only a portion of them—is the greatest real objection to improvements, and has been so held by General Jackson, Mr. Polk, and all others, I believe, till now. But now, behold, the objects most general—nearest free from this objection—are to be rejected, while those most liable to it are to be embraced. To return: I cannot help believing that General Cass, when he wrote his letter of acceptance, well understood he was to be claimed by the advocates of both sides of this question, and that he then closed the door against all further expressions of opinion purposely to retain the benefits of that double position. His subsequent equivocation at Cleveland, to my mind, proves such to have been the case.

One word more, and I shall have done with this branch of the subject. You Democrats, and your candidate, in the main are in favor of laying down in advance a platform—a set of party positions—as a unit, and then of forcing the people, by every sort of appliance, to ratify them, however unpalatable some of them may be. We and our candidate are in favor of making Presidential elections and the legislation of the country distinct matters; so that the people can elect whom they please, and afterward legislate just as they please, without any hindrance, save only so much as may guard against infractions of the Constitution, undue haste, and want of consideration. The difference between us is clear as noonday. That we are right we cannot doubt. We hold the true Republican position. In leaving the people's business in their hands, we cannot be wrong. We are willing, and even anxious, to go to the people on this issue.

Old Horses and Military Coat-tails.

But I suppose I cannot reasonably hope to convince you that we have any principles. The most I can expect is to assure you that we think we have and are quite contented with them. The other day one of the gentlemen from Georgia [Mr. Iverson], an eloquent man, and a man of learning, so far as I can judge, not being learned myself, came down upon us astonishingly. He spoke in what the 'Baltimore American' calls the "scathing and withering style." At the end of his second severe flash I was struck blind, and found myself feeling with my fingers for an assurance of my continued existence. A little of the bone was left, and I gradually revived. He eulogized Mr. Clay in high and beautiful terms, and then declared that we had deserted all our principles, and had turned Henry Clay out, like an old horse, to root. This is terribly severe. It cannot be answered by argument—at least I cannot so answer it. I merely wish to ask the gentleman if the Whigs are the only party he can think of who sometimes turn old horses out to root. Is not a certain Martin Van Buren an old horse which your own party have turned out to root? and is he not rooting a little to your discomfort about now? But in not nominating Mr. Clay we deserted our principles, you say. Ah! In what? Tell us, ye men of principle, what principle we violated. We say you did violate principle in discarding Van Buren, and we can tell you how. You violated the primary, the cardinal, the one great living principle of all democratic representative government—the principle that the representative is bound to carry out the known will of his constituents. A large majority of the Baltimore convention of 1844 were, by their constituents, instructed to procure Van Buren's nomination if they could. In violation—in utter glaring contempt of this, you rejected him; rejected him, as the gentleman from New York [Mr. Birdsall] the other day expressly admitted, for availability—that same "general availability" which you charge upon us, and daily chew over here, as something exceedingly odious and unprincipled. But the gentleman from Georgia [Mr. Iverson] gave us a second speech yesterday, all well considered and put down in writing, in which Van Buren was scathed and withered a "few" for his present position and movements. I cannot remember the gentleman's precise language; but I do remember he put Van Buren down, down, till he got him where he was finally to "stink" and "rot."

Mr. Speaker, it is no business or inclination of mine to defend Martin Van Buren in the war of extermination now waging between him and his old admirers. I say, "Devil take the hindmost"—and the foremost. But there is no mistaking the origin of the breach; and if the curse of "stinking" and "rotting" is to fall on the first and greatest violators of principle in the matter, I disinterestedly suggest that the gentleman from Georgia and his present co-workers are bound to take it upon themselves. But the gentleman from Georgia further says we have deserted all our principles, and taken shelter under General Taylor's military coat-tail, and he seems to think this is exceedingly degrading. Well, as his faith is, so be it unto him. But can he remember no other military coat-tail under which a certain other party have been sheltering for near a quarter of a century? Has he no acquaintance with the ample military coat tail of General Jackson? Does he not know that his own party have run the five last Presidential races under that coat-tail, and that they are now running the sixth under the same cover? Yes, sir, that coat-tail was used not only for General Jackson himself, but has been clung to, with the grip of death, by every Democratic candidate since. You have never ventured, and dare not now venture, from under it. Your campaign papers have constantly been "Old Hickories," with rude likenesses of the old general upon them; hickory poles and hickory brooms your never-ending emblems; Mr. Polk himself was "Young Hickory," or something so; and even now your campaign paper here is proclaiming that Cass and Butler are of the true "Hickory stripe." Now, sir, you dare not give it up. Like a horde of hungry ticks you have stuck to the tail of the Hermitage Lion to the end of his life; and you are still sticking to it, and drawing a loathsome sustenance from it, after he is dead. A fellow once advertised that he had made a discovery by which he could make a new man out of an old one, and have enough of the stuff left to make a little yellow dog. Just such a discovery has General Jackson's popularity been to you. You not only twice made President of him out of it, but you have had enough of the stuff left to make Presidents of several comparatively small men since; and it is your chief reliance now to make still another.

Mr. Speaker, old horses and military coat-tails, or tails of any sort, are not figures of speech such as I would be the first to introduce into discussions here; but as the gentleman from Georgia has thought fit to introduce them, he and you are welcome to all you have made, or can make by them. If you have any more old horses, trot them out; any more tails, just cock them and come at us. I repeat, I would not introduce this mode of discussion here; but I wish gentlemen on the other side to understand that the use of degrading figures is a game at which they may not find themselves able to take all the winnings. ["We give it up!"] Aye, you give it up, and well you may; but for a very different reason from that which you would have us understand. The point—the power to hurt—of all figures consists in the truthfulness of their application; and, understanding this, you may well give it up. They are weapons which hit you, but miss us.

Military Tail of the Great Michigander.

But in my hurry I was very near closing this subject of military tails before I was done with it. There is one entire article of the sort I have not discussed yet,—I mean the military tail you Democrats are now engaged in dovetailing into the great Michigander [Cass]. Yes, sir; all his biographies (and they are legion) have him in hand, tying him to a military tail, like so many mischievous boys tying a dog to a bladder of beans. True, the material they have is very limited, but they drive at it might and main. He invaded Canada without resistance, and he *out*vaded it without pursuit. As he did both under orders, I suppose there was to him neither credit nor discredit in them; but they constitute a large part of the tail. He was not at Hull's surrender, but he was close by; he was volunteer aid to General Harrison on the day of the battle of the Thames; and as you said in 1840 Harrison was picking huckleberries two miles off while the battle was fought, I suppose it is a just conclusion with you to say Cass was aiding Harrison to pick huckleberries. This is about all, except the mooted question of the broken sword. Some authors say he broke it, some say he threw it away, and some others, who ought to know, say nothing about it. Perhaps it would be a fair historical compromise to say, if he did not break it, he did not do anything else with it.

By the way, Mr. Speaker, did you know I am a military hero? Yes, sir; in the days of the Black Hawk war I fought, bled, and came away. Speaking of General Cass's career reminds me of my own. I was not at Stillman's defeat, but I was about as near it as Cass was to Hull's surrender; and, like him, I saw the place very soon afterward. It is quite certain I did not break my sword, for I had none to break; but I bent a musket pretty badly on one occasion. If Cass broke his sword, the idea is he broke it in desperation; I bent the musket by accident. If General Cass went in advance of me in picking huckleberries, I guess I surpassed him in charges upon the wild onions. If he saw any live, fighting Indians, it was more than I did; but I had a good many bloody struggles with the mosquitoes, and although I never fainted from the loss of blood, I can truly say I was often very hungry. Mr. Speaker, if I should ever conclude to doff whatever our Democratic friends may suppose there is of black-cockade federalism about me, and therefore they shall take me up as their candidate for the Presidency, I protest they shall not make fun of me, as they have of General Cass, by attempting to write me into a military hero.

Cass on the Wilmont Proviso.

While I have General Cass in hand, I wish to say a word about his political principles. As a specimen, I take the record of his progress in the Wilmot Proviso. In the Washington Union of March 2, 1847, there is a report of a speech of General Cass, made the day before in the Senate, on the Wilmot Proviso, during the delivery of which Mr. Miller of New Jersey is reported to have interrupted him as follows, to wit:

"Mr. Miller expressed his great surprise at the change in the sentiments of the Senator from Michigan, who had been regarded as the great champion of freedom in the Northwest, of which he was a distinguished ornament. Last year the Senator from Michigan was understood to be decidedly in favor of the Wilmot Proviso; and as no reason had been stated for the change, he [Mr. Miller] could not refrain from the expression of his extreme surprise."

To this General Cass is reported to have replied as follows, to wit:

"Mr. Cass said that the course of the Senator from New Jersey was most extraordinary. Last year he [Mr. Cass] should have voted for the proposition, had it come up. But circumstances had altogether changed. The honorable Senator then read several passages from the remarks, as given above, which he had committed to writing, in order to refute such a charge as that of the Senator from New Jersey."

In the "remarks above reduced to writing" is one numbered four, as follows, to wit:

"Fourth. Legislation now would be wholly inoperative, because no territory hereafter to be acquired can be governed without an act of Congress providing for its government; and such an act, on its passage, would open the whole subject, and leave the Congress called on to pass it free to exercise its own discretion, entirely uncontrolled by any declaration found on the statute-book."

In Niles's Register, vol. LXXIII., p. 293, there is a letter of General Cass to ——— Nicholson, of Nashville, Tennessee, dated December 24, 1847, from which the following are correct extracts:

"The Wilmot Proviso has been before the country some time. It has been repeatedly discussed in Congress and by the public press. I am strongly impressed with the opinion that a great change has been going on in the public mind upon this subject,—in my own as well as others',—and that doubts are resolving themselves into convictions that the principle it involves should be kept out of the national legislature, and left to the people of the confederacy in their respective local governments. . . . Briefly, then, I am opposed to the exercise of any jurisdiction by Congress over this matter; and I am in favor of leaving the people of any territory which may be hereafter acquired the right to regulate it themselves, under the general principles of the Constitution. Because—First. I do not see in the Constitution any grant of the requisite power to Congress; and I am not disposed to extend a doubtful precedent beyond its necessity,—the establishment of territorial governments when needed,—leaving to the inhabitants all the right compatible with the relations they bear to the confederation."

These extracts show that in 1846 General Cass was for the proviso at once; that in March, 1847, he was still for it, but not just then; and that in December, 1847, he was against it altogether. This is a true index to the whole man. When the question was raised in 1846, he was in a blustering hurry to take ground for it. He sought to be in advance, and to avoid the uninteresting position of a mere follower; but soon he began to see glimpses of the great Democratic ox-goad waving in his face, and to hear indistinctly a voice saying, "Back! Back, sir! Back a little!" He shakes his head, and bats his eyes, and blunders back to his position of March, 1847; but still the goad waves, and the voice grows more distinct and sharper still, "Back, sir! Back, I say! Further back!"—and back he goes to the position of December, 1847, at which the goad is still, and the voice soothingly says, "So! Stand at that!"

Have no fears, gentlemen, of your candidate. He exactly suits you, and we congratulate you upon it. However much you may be distressed about our candidate, you have all cause to be contented and happy with your own. If elected, he may not maintain all or even any of his positions previously taken; but he will be sure to do whatever the party exigency for the time being may require; and that is precisely what you want. He and Van Buren are the same "manner of men"; and, like Van Buren, he will never desert you till you first desert him.

Cass on Working and Eating.

Mr. Speaker, I adopt the suggestion of a friend, that General Cass is a general of splendidly successful charges—charges, to be sure, not upon the public enemy, but upon the public treasury. He was Governor of Michigan territory, and ex-officio Superintendent of Indian Affairs, from the 9th of October, 1813, till the 31st of July, 1831—a period of seventeen years, nine months, and twenty-two days. During this period he received from the United States treasury, for personal services and personal expenses, the aggregate sum of ninety-six thousand and twenty eight dollars, being an average of fourteen dollars and seventy-nine cents per day for every day of the time. This large sum was reached by assuming that he was doing service at several different places, and in several different capacities in the same place, all at the same time. By a correct analysis of his accounts during that period, the following propositions may be deduced:

First. He was paid in three different capacities during the whole of the time: that is to say—(1) As governor a salary at the rate per year of $2000. (2) As estimated for office rent, clerk hire, fuel, etc., in superintendence of Indian affairs in Michigan, at the rate per year of $1500. (3) As compensation and expenses for various miscellaneous items of Indian service out of Michigan, an average per year of $625.

Second. During part of the time—that is, from the 9th of October, 1813, to the 29th of May, 1822 he was paid in four different capacities; that is to say, the three as above, and, in addition thereto, the commutation of ten rations per day, amounting per year to $730.

Third. During another part of the time—that is, from the beginning of 1822 to the 31st of July, '83 he was also paid in four different capacities; that is to say, the first three, as above (the rations being dropped after the 29th of May, 1822), and, in addition thereto, for superintending Indian Agencies at Piqua, Ohio; Fort Wayne, Indiana; and Chicago, Illinois, at the rate per year of $1500. It should be observed here that the last item, commencing at the beginning of 1822, and the item of rations, ending on the 29th of May, 1822, lap on each other during so much of the time as lies between those two dates.

Fourth. Still another part of the time—that is, from the 31st of October, 1821, to the 29th of May, 1822—he was paid in six different capacities; that is to say, the three first, as above; the item of rations, as above; and, in addition thereto, another item of ten rations per day while at Washington settling his accounts, being at the rate per year of $730; and also an allowance for expenses traveling to and from Washington, and while there, of $1022, being at the rate per year of $1793.

Fifth. And yet during the little portion of the time which lies between the 1st of January, 1822, and the 29th of May, 1822, he was paid in seven different capacities; that is to say, the six last mentioned, and also, at the rate of $1500 per year, for the Piqua, Fort Wayne, and Chicago service, as mentioned above.

These accounts have already been discussed some here; but when we are amongst them, as when we are in the Patent Office, we must peep about a good deal before we can see all the curiosities. I shall not be tedious with them. As to the large item of $1500 per year— amounting in the aggregate to $26,715 for office rent, clerk hire, fuel, etc., I barely wish to remark that, so far as I can discover in the public documents, there is no evidence, by word or inference, either from any disinterested witness or of General Cass himself, that he ever rented or kept a separate office, ever hired or kept a clerk, or even used any extra amount of fuel, etc., in consequence of his Indian services. Indeed, General Cass's entire silence in regard to these items, in his two long letters urging his claims upon the government, is, to my mind, almost conclusive that no such claims had any real existence.

But I have introduced General Cass's accounts here chiefly to show the wonderful physical capacities of the man. They show that he not only did the labor of several men at the same time, but that he often did it at several places, many hundreds of miles apart, at the same time. And at eating, too, his capacities are shown to be quite as wonderful. From October, 1821, to May, 1822, he eat ten rations a day in Michigan, ten rations a day here in Washington, and near five dollars' worth a day on the road between the two places! And then there is an important discovery in his example—the art of being paid for what one eats, instead of having to pay for it. Hereafter if any nice young man should owe a bill which he cannot pay in any other way, he can just board it out. Mr. Speaker, we have all heard of the animal standing in doubt between two stacks of hay and starving to death. The like of that would never happen to General Cass. Place the stacks a thousand miles apart, he would stand stock-still midway between them, and eat them both at once, and the green grass along the line would be apt to suffer some, too, at the same time. By all means make him President, gentlemen. He will feed you bounteously—if—if there is any left after he shall have helped himself.

The Whigs and the War.

But, as General Taylor is, par excellence, the hero of the Mexican War, and as you Democrats say we Whigs have always opposed the war, you think it must be very awkward and embarrassing for us to go for General Taylor. The declaration that we have always opposed the war is true or false, according as one may understand the term "oppose the war." If to say "the war was unnecessarily and unconstitutionally commenced by the President" by opposing the war, then the Whigs have very generally opposed it. Whenever they have spoken at all, they have said this; and they have said it on what has appeared good reason to them. The marching an army into the midst of a peaceful Mexican settlement, frightening the inhabitants away, leaving their growing crops and other property to destruction, to you may appear a perfectly amiable, peaceful, unprovoking procedure; but it does not appear so to us. So to call such an act, to us appears no other than a naked, impudent absurdity, and we speak of it accordingly. But if, when the war had begun, and had become the cause of the country, the giving of our money and our blood, in common with yours, was support of the war, then it is not true that we have always opposed the war. With few individual exceptions, you have constantly had our votes here for all the necessary supplies. And, more than this, you have had the services, the blood, and the lives of our political brethren in every trial and on every field. The beardless boy and the mature man, the humble and the distinguished—you have had them. Through suffering and death, by disease and in battle they have endured and fought and fell with you. Clay and Webster each gave a son, never to be returned. From the State of my own residence, besides other worthy but less known Whig names, we sent Marshall, Morrison, Baker, and Hardin; they all fought, and one fell, and in the fall of that one we lost our best Whig man. Nor were the Whigs few in number, or laggard in the day of danger. In that fearful, bloody, breathless struggle at Buena Vista, where each man's hard task was to beat back five foes or die himself, of the five high officers who perished, four were Whigs.

In speaking of this, I mean no odious comparison between the lionhearted Whigs and the Democrats who fought there. On other occasions, and among the lower officers and privates on that occasion, I doubt not the proportion was different. I wish to do justice to all. I think of all those brave men as Americans, in whose proud fame, as an American, I too have a share. Many of them, Whigs and Democrats are my constituents and personal friends; and I thank them,—more than thank them,—one and all, for the high imperishable honor they have conferred on our common State.

But the distinction between the cause of the President in beginning the war, and the cause of the country after it was begun, is a distinction which you cannot perceive. To you the President and the country seem to be all one. You are interested to see no distinction between them; and I venture to suggest that probably your interest blinds you a little. We see the distinction, as we think, clearly enough; and our friends who have fought in the war have no difficulty in seeing it also. What those who have fallen would say, were they alive and here, of course we can never know; but with those who have returned there is no difficulty. Colonel Haskell and Major Gaines, members here, both fought in the war, and both of them underwent extraordinary perils and hardships; still they, like all other Whigs here, vote, on the record, that the war was unnecessarily and unconstitutionally commenced by the President. And even General Taylor himself, the noblest Roman of them all, has declared that as a citizen, and particularly as a soldier, it is sufficient for him to know that his country is at war with a foreign nation, to do all in his power to bring it to a speedy and honorable termination by the most vigorous and energetic operations, without inquiry about its justice, or anything else connected with it.

Mr. Speaker, let our Democratic friends be comforted with the assurance that we are content with our position, content with our company, and content with our candidate; and that although they, in their generous sympathy, think we ought to be miserable, we really are not, and that they may dismiss the great anxiety they have on our account.

Mr. Speaker, I see I have but three minutes left, and this forces me to throw out one whole branch of my subject. A single word on still another. The Democrats are keen enough to frequently remind us that we have some dissensions in our ranks. Our good friend from Baltimore immediately before me [Mr. McLane] expressed some doubt the other day as to which branch of our party General Taylor would ultimately fall into the hands of. That was a new idea to me. I knew we had dissenters, but I did not know they were trying to get our candidate away from us. I would like to say a word to our dissenters, but I have not the time. Some such we certainly have; have you none, gentlemen Democrats? Is it all union and harmony in your ranks? no bickerings? no divisions? If there be doubt as to which of our divisions will get our candidate, is there no doubt as to which of your candidates will get your party?

Divided Gangs of Hogs!

I have heard some things from New York; and if they are true, one might well say of your party there, as a drunken fellow once said when he heard the reading of an indictment for hog-stealing. The clerk read on till he got to and through the words, "did steal, take, and carry away ten boars, ten sows, ten shoats, and ten pigs," at which he exclaimed, "Well, by golly, that is the most equally divided gang of hogs I ever did hear of!" If there is any other gang of hogs more equally divided than the Democrats of New York are about this time, I have not heard of it.

CAMPAIGN SPEECH FOR ZACHARY TAYLOR, WORSECTER, MASSACHUSETTS, SEPTEMBER 12, 1848.

Mr. Kellogg then introduced to the meeting the Hon. Abram Lincoln, Whig member of Congress from Illinois, a representative of free soil.

Mr. Lincoln has a very tall and thin figure, with an intellectual face, showing a searching mind, and a cool judgment. He spoke in a clear and cool and very eloquent manner, for an hour and a half, carrying the audience with him in his able arguments and brilliant illustrations—only interrupted by warm and frequent applause. He began by expressing a real feeling of modesty in addressing an audience "this side of the mountains," a part of the country where, in the opinion of the people of his section, everybody was supposed to be instructed and wise. But he had devoted his attention to the question of the coming Presidential election, and was not unwilling to exchange with all whom he might the ideas to which he had arrived. He then began to show the fallacy of some of the arguments against Gen. Taylor, making his chief theme the fashionable statement of all those who oppose him ("the old Locofocos as well as the new") that he has no principles, and that the Whig party have abandoned their principles by adopting him as their candidate. He maintained that Gen. Taylor occupied a high and unexceptionable Whig ground, and took for his first instance and proof of this the statement in the Allison letter—with regard to the bank, tariff, rivers and harbors, etc.—that the will of the people should produce its own results, without executive influence. The principle that the people should do what—under the Constitution—as they please, is a Whig principle. All that Gen. Taylor is not only to consent to, but appeal to the people to judge and act for themselves. And this was no new doctrine for Whigs. It was the "platform" on which they had fought all their battles, the resistance of executive influence, and the principle of enabling the people to frame the government according to their will. Gen. Taylor consents to be the candidate, and to assist the people to do what they think to be their duty, and think to be best in their national affairs, but because he don't want to tell what we ought to do, he is accused of having no principles. The Whigs here maintained for years that neither the influence, the duress, or the prohibition of the executive should control the legitimately expressed will of the people; and now that, on that very ground, Gen. Taylor says that he should use the power given him by the people to do, to the best of his judgment, the will of the people, he is accused of want of principle, and of inconsistency in position.

Mr. Lincoln proceeded to examine the absurdity of an attempt to make a platform or creed for a national party, to all parts of which all must consent and agree, when it was clearly the intention and the true philosophy of our government, that in Congress all opinions and principles should be represented, and that when the wisdom of all had been compared and united, the will of the majority should be carried out. On this ground he conceived (and the audience seemed to go with him) that Gen. Taylor held correct, sound republican principles.

Mr. Lincoln then passed to the subject of slavery in the States, saying that the people of Illinois agreed entirely with the people of Massachusetts on this subject, except perhaps that they did not keep so constantly thinking about it. All agreed that slavery was an evil, but that we were not responsible for it and cannot affect it in States of this Union where we do not live. But the question of the extension of slavery to new territories of this country is a part of our responsibility and care, and is under our control. In opposition to this Mr. L. believed that the self-named "Free Soil" party was far behind the Whigs. Both parties opposed the extension. As he understood it the new party had no principle except this opposition. If their platform held any other, it was in such a general way that it was like the pair of pantaloons the Yankee peddler offered for sale, "large enough for any man, small enough for any boy." They therefore had taken a position calculated to break down their single important declared object. They were working for the election of either Gen. Cass or Gen. Taylor. The speaker then went on to show, clearly and eloquently, the danger of extension of slavery, likely to result from the election of Gen. Cass. To unite with those who annexed the new territory to prevent the extension of slavery in that territory seemed to him to be in the highest degree absurd and ridiculous. Suppose these gentlemen succeed in electing Mr. Van Buren, they had no specific means to prevent the extension of slavery to New Mexico and California, and Gen. Taylor, he confidently believed, would not encourage it, and would not prohibit its restriction. But if Gen. Cass was elected, he felt certain that the plans of farther extension of territory would be encouraged, and those of the extension of slavery would meet no check. The "Free Soil" mart in claiming that name indirectly attempts a deception, by implying that Whigs were not Free Soil men. Declaring that they would "do their duty and leave the consequences to God" merely gave an excuse for taking a course they were not able to maintain by a fair and full argument. To make this declaration did not show what their duty was. If it did we should have no use for judgment, we might as well be made without intellect; and when divine or human law does not clearly point out what is our duty, we have no means of finding out what it is but by using our most intelligent judgment of the consequences. If there were divine law or human law for voting for Martin Van Buren, or if a fair examination of the consequences and just reasoning would show that voting for him would bring about the ends they pretended to wish—then he would give up the argument. But since there was no fixed law on the subject, and since the whole probable result of their action would be an assistance in electing Gen. Cass, he must say that they were behind the Whigs in their advocacy of the freedom of the soil.

Mr. Lincoln proceeded to rally the Buffalo convention for forbearing to say anything—after all the previous declarations of those members who were formerly Whigs—on the subject of the Mexican War, because the Van Burens had been known to have supported it. He declared that of all the parties asking the confidence of the country, this new one had less of principle than any other.

He wondered whether it was still the opinion of these Free Soil gentlemen, as declared in the "whereas" at Buffalo, that the Whig and Democratic parties were both entirely dissolved and absorbed into their own body. Had the Vermont election given them any light? They had calculated on making as great an impression in that State as in any part of the Union, and there their attempts had been wholly ineffectual. Their failure was a greater success than they would find in any other part of the Union.

Mr. Lincoln went on to say that he honestly believed that all those who wished to keep up the character of the Union; who did not believe in enlarging our field, but in keeping our fences where they are and cultivating our present possessions, making it a garden, improving the morals and education of the people, devoting the administrations to this purpose; all real Whigs, friends of good honest government—the race was ours. He had opportunities of hearing from almost every part of the Union from reliable sources and had not heard of a county in which we had not received accessions from other parties. If the true Whigs come forward and join these new friends, they need not have a doubt. We had a candidate whose personal character and principles he had already described, whom he could not eulogize if he would. Gen. Taylor had been constantly, perseveringly, quietly standing up, doing his duty and asking no praise or reward for it. He was and must be just the man to whom the interests, principles, and prosperity of the country might be safely entrusted. He had never failed in anything he had undertaken, although many of his duties had been considered almost impossible.

Mr. Lincoln then went into a terse though rapid review of the origin of the Mexican War and the connection of the administration and General Taylor with it, from which he deduced a strong appeal to the Whigs present to do their duty in the support of General Taylor, and closed with the warmest aspirations for and confidence in a deserved success.

At the close of his truly masterly and convincing speech, the audience gave three enthusiastic cheers for Illinois, and three more for the eloquent Whig member from the State.

EULOGY ON HENRY CLAY, SPRINGFIELD, ILLINOIS, JULY 6, 1852.

On the fourth day of July, 1776, the people of a few feeble and oppressed colonies of Great Britain, inhabiting a portion of the Atlantic coast of North America, publicly declared their national independence, and made their appeal to the justice of their cause and to the God of battles for the maintenance of that declaration. That people were few in number and without resources, save only their wise heads and stout hearts. Within the first year of that declared independence, and while its maintenance was yet problematical, while the bloody struggle between those resolute rebels and their haughty would-be masters was still waging,—of undistinguished parents and in an obscure district of one of those colonies Henry Clay was born. The infant nation and the infant child began the race of life together. For three quarters of a century they have travelled hand in hand. They have been companions ever. The nation has passed its perils, and it is free, prosperous, and powerful. The child has reached his manhood, his middle age, his old age, and is dead. In all that has concerned the nation the man ever sympathized; and now the nation mourns the man.

The day after his death one of the public journals, opposed to him politically, held the following pathetic and beautiful language, which I adopt partly because such high and exclusive eulogy, originating with a political friend, might offend good taste, but chiefly because I could not in any language of my own so well express my thoughts:

"Alas, who can realize that Henry Clay is dead! Who can realize that never again that majestic form shall rise in the council-chambers of his country to beat back the storms of anarchy which may threaten, or pour the oil of peace upon the troubled billows as they rage and menace around! Who can realize that the workings of that mighty mind have ceased, that the throbbings of that gallant heart are stilled, that the mighty sweep of that graceful arm will be felt no more, and the magic of that eloquent tongue, which spake as spake no other tongue besides, is hushed—hushed for ever! Who can realize that freedom's champion, the champion of a civilized world and of all tongues and kindreds of people, has indeed fallen! Alas, in those dark hours of peril and dread which our land has experienced, and which she may be called to experience again, to whom now may her people look up for that counsel and advice which only wisdom and experience and patriotism can give, and which only the undoubting confidence of a nation will receive? Perchance in the whole circle of the great and gifted of our land there remains but one on whose shoulders the mighty mantle of the departed statesman may fall; one who while we now write is doubtless pouring his tears over the bier of his brother and friend brother, friend, ever, yet in political sentiment as far apart as party could make them. Ah, it is at times like these that the petty distinctions of mere party disappear. We see only the great, the grand, the noble features of the departed statesman; and we do not even beg permission to bow at his feet and mingle our tears with those who have ever been his political adherents—we do [not] beg this permission, we claim it as a right, though we feel it as a privilege. Henry Clay belonged to his country—to the world; mere party cannot claim men like him. His career has been national, his fame has filled the earth, his memory will endure to the last syllable of recorded time.

"Henry Clay is dead! He breathed his last on yesterday, at twenty minutes after eleven, in his chamber at Washington. To those who followed his lead in public affairs, it more appropriately belongs to pronounce his eulogy and pay specific honors to the memory of the illustrious dead. But all Americans may show the grief which his death inspires, for his character and fame are national property. As on a question of liberty he knew no North, no South, no East, no West, but only the Union which held them all in its sacred circle, so now his countrymen will know no grief that is not as wide-spread as the bounds of the confederacy. The career of Henry Clay was a public career. From his youth he has been devoted to the public service, at a period, too, in the world's history justly regarded as a remarkable era in human affairs. He witnessed in the beginning the throes of the French Revolution. He saw the rise and fall of Napoleon. He was called upon to legislate for America and direct her policy when all Europe was the battlefield of contending dynasties, and when the struggle for supremacy imperiled the rights of all neutral nations. His voice spoke war and peace in the contest with Great Britain.

"When Greece rose against the Turks and struck for liberty, his name was mingled with the battle-cry of freedom. When South America threw off the thraldom of Spain, his speeches were read at the head of her armies by Bolivar. His name has been, and will continue to be, hallowed in two hemispheres, for it is

"'One of the few, the immortal names
That were not born to die!'

"To the ardent patriot and profound statesman he added a quality possessed by few of the gifted on earth. His eloquence has not been surpassed. In the effective power to move the heart of man, Clay was without an equal, and the heaven-born endowment, in the spirit of its origin, has been most conspicuously exhibited against intestine feud. On at least three important occasions he has quelled our civil commotions by a power and influence which belonged to no other statesman of his age and times. And in our last internal discord, when this Union trembled to its centre, in old age he left the shades of private life, and gave the death-blow to fraternal strife, with the vigor of his earlier years, in a series of senatorial efforts which in themselves would bring immortality by challenging comparison with the efforts of any statesman in any age. He exorcised the demon which possessed the body politic, and gave peace to a distracted land. Alas! the achievement cost him his life. He sank day by day to the tomb his pale but noble brow bound with a triple wreath, put there by a grateful country. May his ashes rest in peace, while his spirit goes to take its station among the great and good men who preceded him."

While it is customary and proper upon occasions like the present to give a brief sketch of the life of the deceased, in the case of Mr. Clay it is less necessary than most others; for his biography has been written and rewritten and read and reread for the last twenty-five years; so that, with the exception of a few of the latest incidents of his life, all is as well known as it can be. The short sketch which I give is, therefore, merely to maintain the connection of this discourse.

Henry Clay was born on the twelfth day of April, 1777, in Hanover County, Virginia. Of his father, who died in the fourth or fifth year of Henry's age, little seems to be known, except that he was a respectable man and a preacher of the Baptist persuasion. Mr. Clay's education to the end of life was comparatively limited. I say "to the end of life," because I have understood that from time to time he added something to his education during the greater part of his whole life. Mr. Clay's lack of a more perfect early education, however it may be regretted generally, teaches at least one profitable lesson: it teaches that in this country one can scarcely be so poor but that, if he will, he can acquire sufficient education to get through the world respectably. In his twenty-third year Mr. Clay was licensed to practice law, and emigrated to Lexington, Kentucky. Here he commenced and continued the practice till the year 1803, when he was first elected to the Kentucky Legislature. By successive elections he was continued in the

Legislature till the latter part of 1806, when he was elected to fill a vacancy of a single session in the United States Senate. In 1807 he was again elected to the Kentucky House of Representatives, and by that body chosen Speaker. In 1808 he was re-elected to the same body. In 1809 he was again chosen to fill a vacancy of two years in the United States Senate. In 1811 he was elected to the United States House of Representatives, and on the first day of taking his seat in that body he was chosen its Speaker. In 1813 he was again elected Speaker. Early in 1814, being the period of our last British war, Mr. Clay was sent as commissioner, with others, to negotiate a treaty of peace, which treaty was concluded in the latter part of the same year. On his return from Europe he was again elected to the lower branch of Congress, and on taking his seat in December, 1815, was called to his old post-the Speaker's chair, a position in which he was retained by successive elections, with one brief intermission, till the inauguration of John Quincy Adams, in March, 1825. He was then appointed Secretary of State, and occupied that important station till the inauguration of General Jackson, in March, 1829. After this he returned to Kentucky, resumed the practice of law, and continued it till the autumn of 1831, when he was by the Legislature of Kentucky again placed in the United States Senate. By a reelection he was continued in the Senate till he resigned his seat and retired, in March, 1848. In December, 1849, he again took his seat in the Senate, which he again resigned only a few months before his death.

By the foregoing it is perceived that the period from the beginning of Mr. Clay's official life in 1803 to the end of 1852 is but one year short of half a century, and that the sum of all the intervals in it will not amount to ten years. But mere duration of time in office constitutes the smallest part of Mr. Clay's history. Throughout that long period he has constantly been the most loved and most implicitly followed by friends, and the most dreaded by opponents, of all living American politicians. In all the great questions which have agitated the country, and particularly in those fearful crises, the Missouri question, the nullification question, and the late slavery question, as connected with the newly acquired territory, involving and endangering the stability of the Union, his has been the leading and most conspicuous part. In 1824 he was first a candidate for the Presidency, and was defeated; and, although he was successively defeated for the same office in 1832 and in 1844, there has never been a moment since 1824 till after 1848 when a very large portion of the American people did not cling to him with an enthusiastic hope and purpose of still elevating him to the Presidency. With other men, to be defeated was to be forgotten; but with him defeat was but a trifling incident, neither changing him nor the world's estimate of him. Even those of both political parties who have been preferred to him for the highest office have run far briefer courses than he, and left him still shining high in the heavens of the political world. Jackson, Van Buren, Harrison, Polk, and Taylor all rose after, and set long before him. The spell—the long-enduring spell— with which the souls of men were bound to him is a miracle. Who can compass it? It is probably true he owed his pre-eminence to no one quality, but to a fortunate combination of several. He was surpassingly eloquent; but many eloquent men fail utterly, and they are not, as a class, generally successful. His judgment was excellent; but many men of good judgment live and die unnoticed. His will was indomitable; but this quality often secures to its owner nothing better than a character for useless obstinacy. These, then, were Mr. Clay's leading qualities. No one of them is very uncommon; but all together are rarely combined in a single individual, and this is probably the reason why such men as Henry Clay are so rare in the world.

Mr. Clay's eloquence did not consist, as many fine specimens of eloquence do, of types and figures, of antithesis and elegant arrangement of words and sentences, but rather of that deeply earnest and impassioned tone and manner which can proceed only from great sincerity, and a thorough conviction in the speaker of the justice and importance of his cause. This it is that truly touches the chords of sympathy; and those who heard Mr. Clay never failed to be moved by it, or ever afterward forgot the impression. All his efforts were made for practical effect. He never spoke merely to be heard. He never delivered a Fourth of July oration, or a eulogy on an occasion like this. As a politician or statesman, no one was so habitually careful to avoid all sectional ground. Whatever he did he did for the whole country. In the construction of his measures, he ever carefully surveyed every part of the field, and duly weighed every conflicting interest. Feeling as he did, and as the truth surely is, that the world's best hope depended on the continued union of these States, he was ever jealous of and watchful for whatever might have the slightest tendency to separate them.

Mr. Clay's predominant sentiment, from first to last, was a deep devotion to the cause of human liberty—a strong sympathy with the oppressed everywhere, and an ardent wish for their elevation. With him this was a primary and all-controlling passion. Subsidiary to this was the conduct of his whole life. He loved his country partly because it was his own country, and mostly because it was a free country; and he burned with a zeal for its advancement, prosperity, and glory, because he saw in such the advancement, prosperity, and glory of human liberty, human right, and human nature. He desired the prosperity of his countrymen, partly because they were his countrymen, but chiefly to show to the world that free men could be prosperous.

That his views and measures were always the wisest needs not to be affirmed; nor should it be on this occasion, where so many thinking differently join in doing honor to his memory. A free people in times of peace and quiet when pressed by no common danger-naturally divide into parties. At such times the man who is of neither party is not, cannot be, of any consequence. Mr. Clay therefore was of a party. Taking a prominent part, as he did, in all the great political questions of his country for the last half century, the wisdom of his course on many is doubted and denied by a large portion of his countrymen; and of such it is not now proper to speak particularly. But there are many others, about his course upon which there is little or no disagreement amongst intelligent and patriotic Americans. Of these last are the War of 1812, the Missouri question, nullification, and the now recent compromise measures. In 1812 Mr. Clay, though not unknown, was still a young man. Whether we should go to war with Great Britain being the question of the day, a minority opposed the declaration of war by Congress, while the majority, though apparently inclined to war, had for years wavered, and hesitated to act decisively. Meanwhile British aggressions multiplied, and grew more daring and aggravated. By Mr. Clay more than any other man the struggle was brought to a decision in Congress. The question, being now fully before Congress, came up in a variety of ways in rapid succession, on most of which occasions Mr. Clay spoke. Adding to all the logic of which the subject was susceptible that noble inspiration which came to him as it came to no other, he aroused and nerved and inspired his friends, and confounded and bore down all opposition. Several of his speeches on these occasions were reported and are still extant, but the best of them all never was. During its delivery the reporters forgot their vocation, dropped their pens, and sat enchanted from near the beginning to quite the close. The speech now lives only in the memory of a few old men, and the enthusiasm with which they cherish their recollection of it is absolutely astonishing. The precise language of this speech we shall never know; but we do know we cannot help knowing—that with deep pathos it pleaded the cause of the injured sailor, that it invoked the genius of the Revolution, that it apostrophized the names of Otis, of Henry, and of Washington, that it appealed to the interests, the pride, the honor, and the glory of the nation, that it shamed and taunted the timidity of friends, that it scorned and scouted and withered the temerity of domestic foes, that it bearded and defied the British lion, and, rising and swelling and maddening in its course, it sounded the onset, till the charge, the shock, the steady struggle, and the glorious victory all passed in vivid review before the entranced hearers.

Important and exciting as was the war question of 1812, it never so alarmed the sagacious statesmen of the country for the safety of the Republic as afterward did the Missouri question. This sprang from that unfortunate source of discord—negro slavery. When our Federal Constitution was adopted, we owned no territory beyond the limits or ownership of the States, except the territory northwest of the River

Ohio and east of the Mississippi. What has since been formed into the States of Maine, Kentucky and Tennessee, was, I believe, within the limits of or owned by Massachusetts, Virginia, and North Carolina. As to the Northwestern Territory, provision had been made even before the adoption of the Constitution that slavery should never go there. On the admission of States into the Union, carved from the territory we owned before the Constitution, no question, or at most no considerable question, arose about slavery—those which were within the limits of or owned by the old States following respectively the condition of the parent State, and those within the Northwest Territory following the previously made provision. But in 1803 we purchased Louisiana of the French, and it included with much more what has since been formed into the State of Missouri. With regard to it, nothing had been done to forestall the question of slavery. When, therefore, in 1819, Missouri, having formed a State constitution without excluding slavery, and with slavery already actually existing within its limits, knocked at the door of the Union for admission, almost the entire representation of the non-slaveholding States objected. A fearful and angry struggle instantly followed. This alarmed thinking men more than any previous question, because, unlike all the former, it divided the country by geographical lines. Other questions had their opposing partisans in all localities of the country and in almost every family, so that no division of the Union could follow such without a separation of friends to quite as great an extent as that of opponents. Not so with the Missouri question. On this a geographical line could be traced, which in the main would separate opponents only. This was the danger. Mr. Jefferson, then in retirement, wrote:

"I had for a long time ceased to read newspapers or to pay any attention to public affairs, confident they were in good hands and content to be a passenger in our bark to the shore from which I am not distant. But this momentous question, like a fire-bell in the night, awakened and filled me with terror. I considered it at once as the knell of the Union. It is hushed, indeed, for the moment. But this is a reprieve only, not a final sentence. A geographical line coinciding with a marked principle, moral and political, once conceived and held up to the angry passions of men, will never be obliterated, and every irritation will mark it deeper and deeper. I can say with conscious truth that there is not a man on earth who would sacrifice more than I would to relieve us from this heavy reproach in any practicable way. The cession of that kind of property—for it is so misnamed—is a bagatelle which would not cost me a second thought if in that way a general emancipation and expatriation could be effected, and gradually and with due sacrifices I think it might be. But as it is, we have the wolf by the ears, and we can neither hold him nor safely let him go. Justice is in one scale, and self-preservation in the other."

Mr. Clay was in Congress, and, perceiving the danger, at once engaged his whole energies to avert it. It began, as I have said, in 1819; and it did not terminate till 1821. Missouri would not yield the point; and Congress that is, a majority in Congress—by repeated votes showed a determination not to admit the State unless it should yield. After several failures, and great labor on the part of Mr. Clay to so present the question that a majority could consent to the admission, it was by a vote rejected, and, as all seemed to think, finally. A sullen gloom hung over the nation. All felt that the rejection of Missouri was equivalent to a dissolution of the Union, because those States which already had what Missouri was rejected for refusing to relinquish would go with Missouri. All deprecated and deplored this, but none saw how to avert it. For the judgment of members to be convinced of the necessity of yielding was not the whole difficulty; each had a constituency to meet and to answer to. Mr. Clay, though worn down and exhausted, was appealed to by members to renew his efforts at compromise. He did so, and by some judicious modifications of his plan, coupled with laborious efforts with individual members and his own overmastering eloquence upon that floor, he finally secured the admission of the State. Brightly and captivating as it had previously shown, it was now perceived that his great eloquence was a mere embellishment, or at most but a helping hand to his inventive genius and his devotion to his country in the day of her extreme peril.

After the settlement of the Missouri question, although a portion of the American people have differed with Mr. Clay, and a majority even appear generally to have been opposed to him on questions of ordinary administration, he seems constantly to have been regarded by all as the man for the crisis. Accordingly, in the days of nullification, and more recently in the reappearance of the slavery question connected with our territory newly acquired of Mexico, the task of devising a mode of adjustment seems to have been cast upon Mr. Clay by common consent—and his performance of the task in each case was little else than a literal fulfillment of the public expectation.

Mr. Clay's efforts in behalf of the South Americans, and afterward in behalf of the Greeks, in the times of their respective struggles for civil liberty, are among the finest on record, upon the noblest of all themes, and bear ample corroboration of what I have said was his ruling passion—a love of liberty and right, unselfishly, and for their own sakes.

Having been led to allude to domestic slavery so frequently already, I am unwilling to close without referring more particularly to Mr. Clay's views and conduct in regard to it. He ever was on principle and in feeling opposed to slavery. The very earliest, and one of the latest, public efforts of his life, separated by a period of more than fifty years, were both made in favor of gradual emancipation. He did not perceive that on a question of human right the negroes were to be excepted from the human race. And yet Mr. Clay was the owner of slaves. Cast into life when slavery was already widely spread and deeply seated, he did not perceive, as I think no wise man has perceived, how it could be at once eradicated without producing a greater evil even to the cause of human liberty itself. His feeling and his judgment, therefore, ever led him to oppose both extremes of opinion on the subject. Those who would shiver into fragments the Union of these States, tear to tatters its now venerated Constitution, and even burn the last copy of the Bible, rather than slavery should continue a single hour, together with all their more halting sympathizers, have received, and are receiving, their just execration; and the name and opinions and influence of Mr. Clay are fully and, as I trust, effectually and enduringly arrayed against them. But I would also, if I could, array his name, opinions, and influence against the opposite extreme— against a few but an increasing number of men who, for the sake of perpetuating slavery, are beginning to assail and to ridicule the white man's charter of freedom, the declaration that "all men are created free and equal." So far as I have learned, the first American of any note to do or attempt this was the late John C. Calhoun; and if I mistake not, it soon after found its way into some of the messages of the Governor of South Carolina. We, however, look for and are not much shocked by political eccentricities and heresies in South Carolina. But only last year I saw with astonishment what purported to be a letter of a very distinguished and influential clergyman of Virginia, copied, with apparent approbation, into a St. Louis newspaper, containing the following to me very unsatisfactory language:

"I am fully aware that there is a text in some Bibles that is not in mine. Professional abolitionists have made more use of it than of any passage in the Bible. It came, however, as I trace it, from Saint Voltaire, and was baptized by Thomas Jefferson, and since almost universally regarded as canonical authority 'All men are born free and equal.'

"This is a genuine coin in the political currency of our generation. I am sorry to say that I have never seen two men of whom it is true. But I must admit I never saw the Siamese Twins, and therefore will not dogmatically say that no man ever saw a proof of this sage aphorism."

This sounds strangely in republican America. The like was not heard in the fresher days of the republic. Let us contrast with it the language of that truly national man whose life and death we now commemorate and lament: I quote from a speech of Mr. Clay delivered before the American Colonization Society in 1827:

"We are reproached with doing mischief by the agitation of this question. The society goes into no household to disturb its domestic tranquility. It addresses itself to no slaves to weaken their obligations of obedience. It seeks to affect no man's property. It neither has the power nor the will to affect the property of any one contrary to his consent. The execution of its scheme would augment instead of diminishing the value of property left behind. The society, composed of free men, conceals itself only with the free. Collateral consequences we are not responsible for. It is not this society which has produced the great moral revolution which the age exhibits. What would they who thus reproach us have done? If they would repress all tendencies toward liberty and ultimate emancipation, they must do more than put down the benevolent efforts of this society. They must go back to the era of our liberty and independence, and muzzle the cannon which thunders its annual joyous return. They must renew the slave trade, with all its train of atrocities. They must suppress the workings of British philanthropy, seeking to meliorate the condition of the unfortunate West Indian slave. They must arrest the career of South American deliverance from thraldom. They must blow out the moral lights around us and extinguish that greatest torch of all which America presents to a benighted world—pointing the way to their rights, their liberties, and their happiness. And when they have achieved all those purposes their work will be yet incomplete. They must penetrate the human soul, and eradicate the light of reason and the love of liberty. Then, and not till then, when universal darkness and despair prevail, can you perpetuate slavery and repress all sympathy and all humane and benevolent efforts among free men in behalf of the unhappy portion of our race doomed to bondage."

The American Colonization Society was organized in 1816. Mr. Clay, though not its projector, was one of its earliest members; and he died, as for many preceding years he had been, its president. It was one of the most cherished objects of his direct care and consideration, and the association of his name with it has probably been its very greatest collateral support. He considered it no demerit in the society that it tended to relieve the slave-holders from the troublesome presence of the free negroes; but this was far from being its whole merit in his estimation. In the same speech from which we have quoted he says:

"There is a moral fitness in the idea of returning to Africa her children, whose ancestors have been torn from her by the ruthless hand of fraud and violence. Transplanted in a foreign land, they will carry back to their native soil the rich fruits of religion, civilization, law, and liberty. May it not be one of the great designs of the Ruler of the universe, whose ways are often inscrutable by short-sighted mortals, thus to transform an original crime into a signal blessing to that most unfortunate portion of the globe?"

This suggestion of the possible ultimate redemption of the African race and African continent was made twenty-five years ago. Every succeeding year has added strength to the hope of its realization. May it indeed be realized. Pharaoh's country was cursed with plagues, and his hosts were lost in the Red Sea, for striving to retain a captive people who had already served them more than four hundred years. May like disasters never befall us! If, as the friends of colonization hope, the present and coming generations of our countrymen shall by any means succeed in freeing our land from the dangerous presence of slavery, and at the same time in restoring a captive people to their long-lost fatherland with bright prospects for the future, and this too so gradually that neither races nor individuals shall have suffered by the change, it will indeed be a glorious consummation. And if to such a consummation the efforts of Mr. Clay shall have contributed, it will be what he most ardently wished, and none of his labors will have been more valuable to his country and his kind.

But Henry Clay is dead. His long and eventful life is closed. Our country is prosperous and powerful; but could it have been quite all it has been, and is, and is to be, without Henry Clay? Such a man the times have demanded, and such in the providence of God was given us. But he is gone. Let us strive to deserve, as far as mortals may, the continued care of Divine Providence, trusting that in future national emergencies He will not fail to provide us the instruments of safety and security.

SPEECH AT PEORIA, ILLINOIS, OCT 16, 1854.

I do not rise to speak now, if I can stipulate with the audience to meet me here at half-past six or at seven o'clock. It is now several minutes past five, and Judge Douglas has spoken over three hours. If you hear me at all, I wish you to hear me through. It will take me as long as it has taken him. That will carry us beyond eight o'clock at night. Now, every one of you who can remain that long can just as well get his supper, meet me at seven, and remain an hour or two later. The Judge has already informed you that he is to have an hour to reply to me. I doubt not but you have been a little surprised to learn that I have consented to give one of his high reputation and known ability this advantage of me. Indeed, my consenting to it, though reluctant, was not wholly unselfish, for I suspected, if it were understood that the Judge was entirely done, you Democrats would leave and not hear me; but by giving him the close, I felt confident you would stay for the fun of hearing him skin me.

The audience signified their assent to the arrangement, and adjourned to seven o'clock P.M., at which time they reassembled, and Mr. Lincoln spoke substantially as follows:

The repeal of the Missouri Compromise, and the propriety of its restoration, constitute the subject of what I am about to say. As I desire to present my own connected view of this subject, my remarks will not be specifically an answer to Judge Douglas; yet, as I proceed, the main points he has presented will arise, and will receive such respectful attention as I may be able to give them. I wish further to say that I do not propose to question the patriotism or to assail the motives of any man or class of men, but rather to confine myself strictly to the naked merits of the question. I also wish to be no less than national in all the positions I may take, and whenever I take ground which others have thought, or may think, narrow, sectional, and dangerous to the Union, I hope to give a reason which will appear sufficient, at least to some, why I think differently.

And as this subject is no other than part and parcel of the larger general question of domestic slavery, I wish to make and to keep the distinction between the existing institution and the extension of it so broad and so clear that no honest man can misunderstand me, and no dishonest one successfully misrepresent me.

In order to a clear understanding of what the Missouri Compromise is, a short history of the preceding kindred subjects will perhaps be proper.

When we established our independence, we did not own or claim the country to which this compromise applies. Indeed, strictly speaking, the Confederacy then owned no country at all; the States respectively owned the country within their limits, and some of them owned territory beyond their strict State limits. Virginia thus owned the Northwestern Territory—the country out of which the principal part of Ohio, all Indiana, all Illinois, all Michigan, and all Wisconsin have since been formed. She also owned (perhaps within her then limits) what has since been formed into the State of Kentucky. North Carolina thus owned what is now the State of Tennessee; and South Carolina and Georgia owned, in separate parts, what are now Mississippi and Alabama. Connecticut, I think, owned the little remaining part of Ohio, being the same where they now send Giddings to Congress and beat all creation in making cheese.

These territories, together with the States themselves, constitute all the country over which the Confederacy then claimed any sort of jurisdiction. We were then living under the Articles of Confederation, which were superseded by the Constitution several years afterward.

The question of ceding the territories to the General Government was set on foot. Mr. Jefferson,—the author of the Declaration of Independence, and otherwise a chief actor in the Revolution; then a delegate in Congress; afterward, twice President; who was, is, and perhaps will continue to be, the most distinguished politician of our history; a Virginian by birth and continued residence, and withal a slaveholder,—conceived the idea of taking that occasion to prevent slavery ever going into the Northwestern Territory. He prevailed on the Virginia Legislature to adopt his views, and to cede the Territory, making the prohibition of slavery therein a condition of the deed. (Jefferson got only an understanding, not a condition of the deed to this wish.) Congress accepted the cession with the condition; and the first ordinance (which the acts of Congress were then called) for the government of the Territory provided that slavery should never be permitted therein. This is the famed "Ordinance of '87," so often spoken of.

Thenceforward for sixty-one years, and until, in 1848, the last scrap of this Territory came into the Union as the State of Wisconsin, all parties acted in quiet obedience to this ordinance. It is now what Jefferson foresaw and intended—the happy home of teeming millions of free, white, prosperous people, and no slave among them.

Thus, with the author of the Declaration of Independence, the policy of prohibiting slavery in new territory originated. Thus, away back to the Constitution, in the pure, fresh, free breath of the Revolution, the State of Virginia and the national Congress put that policy into practice. Thus, through more than sixty of the best years of the republic, did that policy steadily work to its great and beneficent end. And thus, in those five States, and in five millions of free, enterprising people, we have before us the rich fruits of this policy.

But now new light breaks upon us. Now Congress declares this ought never to have been, and the like of it must never be again. The sacred right of self-government is grossly violated by it. We even find some men who drew their first breath—and every other breath of their lives—under this very restriction, now live in dread of absolute suffocation if they should be restricted in the "sacred right" of taking slaves to Nebraska. That perfect liberty they sigh for—the liberty of making slaves of other people, Jefferson never thought of, their own fathers never thought of, they never thought of themselves, a year ago. How fortunate for them they did not sooner become sensible of their great misery! Oh, how difficult it is to treat with respect such assaults upon all we have ever really held sacred!

But to return to history. In 1803 we purchased what was then called Louisiana, of France. It included the present States of Louisiana, Arkansas, Missouri, and Iowa; also the Territory of Minnesota, and the present bone of contention, Kansas and Nebraska. Slavery already existed among the French at New Orleans, and to some extent at St. Louis. In 1812 Louisiana came into the Union as a slave State, without controversy. In 1818 or '19, Missouri showed signs of a wish to come in with slavery. This was resisted by Northern members of Congress; and thus began the first great slavery agitation in the nation. This controversy lasted several months, and became very angry and exciting—the House of Representatives voting steadily for the prohibition of slavery in Missouri, and the Senate voting as steadily against it. Threats of the breaking up of the Union were freely made, and the ablest public men of the day became seriously alarmed. At length a compromise was made, in which, as in all compromises, both sides yielded something. It was a law, passed on the 6th of March, 1820, providing that Missouri might come into the Union with slavery, but that in all the remaining part of the territory purchased of France which lies north of thirty-six degrees and thirty minutes north latitude, slavery should never be permitted. This provision of law is the "Missouri Compromise." In excluding slavery north of the line, the same language is employed as in the Ordinance of 1787. It directly applied to Iowa, Minnesota, and to the present bone of contention, Kansas and Nebraska. Whether there should or should not be slavery south of that line, nothing was said in the law. But Arkansas constituted the principal remaining part south of the line; and it has since been admitted as a slave State, without serious controversy. More recently, Iowa, north of the line, came in as a free State without controversy. Still later, Minnesota, north of the line, had a territorial organization without controversy. Texas, principally south of the line, and west of Arkansas, though originally within the purchase from France, had, in 1819, been traded off to Spain in our treaty for the acquisition of Florida. It had thus become a part of Mexico. Mexico revolutionized and became independent of Spain. American citizens began settling rapidly with their slaves in the southern part of Texas. Soon they revolutionized against Mexico, and established an independent government of their own, adopting a constitution with slavery, strongly resembling the constitutions of our slave States. By still another rapid move, Texas, claiming a boundary much farther west than when we parted with her in 1819, was brought back to the United States, and admitted into the Union as a slave State. Then there was little or no settlement in the northern part of Texas, a considerable portion of which lay north of the Missouri line; and in the resolutions admitting her into the Union, the Missouri restriction was expressly extended westward across her territory. This was in 1845, only nine years ago.

Thus originated the Missouri Compromise; and thus has it been respected down to 1845. And even four years later, in 1849, our distinguished Senator, in a public address, held the following language in relation to it:

"The Missouri Compromise has been in practical operation for about a quarter of a century, and has received the sanction and approbation of men of all parties in every section of the Union. It has allayed all sectional jealousies and irritations growing out of this vexed question, and harmonized and tranquillized the whole country. It has given to Henry Clay, as its prominent champion, the proud sobriquet of the 'Great Pacificator,' and by that title, and for that service, his political friends had repeatedly appealed to the people to rally under his standard as a Presidential candidate, as the man who had exhibited the patriotism and power to suppress an unholy and treasonable agitation, and preserve the Union. He was not aware that any man or any party, from any section of the Union, had ever urged as an objection to Mr. Clay that he was the great champion of the Missouri Compromise. On the contrary, the effort was made by the opponents of Mr. Clay to prove that he was not entitled to the exclusive merit of that great patriotic measure, and that the honor was equally due to others, as well as to him, for securing its adoption; that it had its origin in the hearts of all patriotic men, who desired to preserve and perpetuate the blessings of our glorious Union—an origin akin to that of the Constitution of the United States, conceived in the same spirit of fraternal affection, and calculated to remove forever the only danger which seemed to threaten, at some distant day, to sever the social bond of union. All the evidences of public opinion at that day seemed to indicate that this compromise had been canonized in the hearts of the American people, as a sacred thing which no ruthless hand would ever be reckless enough to disturb."

I do not read this extract to involve Judge Douglas in an inconsistency. If he afterward thought he had been wrong, it was right for him to change. I bring this forward merely to show the high estimate placed on the Missouri Compromise by all parties up to so late as the year 1849.

But going back a little in point of time. Our war with Mexico broke out in 1846. When Congress was about adjourning that session, President Polk asked them to place two millions of dollars under his control, to be used by him in the recess, if found practicable and expedient, in negotiating a treaty of peace with Mexico, and acquiring some part of her territory. A bill was duly gotten up for the purpose, and was progressing swimmingly in the House of Representatives, when a member by the name of David Wilmot, a Democrat from Pennsylvania, moved as an amendment, "Provided, that in any territory thus acquired there never shall be slavery."

This is the origin of the far-famed Wilmot Proviso. It created a great flutter; but it stuck like wax, was voted into the bill, and the bill passed with it through the House. The Senate, however, adjourned without final action on it, and so both appropriation and proviso were lost for the time. The war continued, and at the next session the President renewed his request for the appropriation, enlarging the amount, I think, to three millions. Again came the proviso, and defeated the measure. Congress adjourned again, and the war went on. In December, 1847, the new Congress assembled. I was in the lower House that term. The Wilmot Proviso, or the principle of it, was constantly coming up in some shape or other, and I think I may venture to say I voted for it at least forty times during the short time I was there. The Senate, however, held it in check, and it never became a law. In the spring of 1848 a treaty of peace was made with Mexico, by which we obtained that portion of her country which now constitutes the Territories of New Mexico and Utah and the present State of California. By this treaty the Wilmot Proviso was defeated, in so far as it was intended to be a condition of the acquisition of territory. Its friends, however, were still determined to find some way to restrain slavery from getting into the new country. This new acquisition lay directly west of our old purchase from France, and extended west to the Pacific Ocean, and was so situated that if the Missouri line should be extended straight west, the new country would be divided by such extended line, leaving some north and some south of it. On Judge Douglas's motion, a bill, or provision of a bill, passed the Senate to so extend the Missouri line. The proviso men in the House, including myself, voted it down, because, by implication, it gave up the southern part to slavery, while we were bent on having it all free.

In the fall of 1848 the gold-mines were discovered in California. This attracted people to it with unprecedented rapidity, so that on, or soon after, the meeting of the new Congress in December, 1849, she already had a population of nearly a hundred thousand, had called a convention, formed a State constitution excluding slavery, and was knocking for admission into the Union. The proviso men, of course, were for letting her in, but the Senate, always true to the other side, would not consent to her admission, and there California stood, kept out of the Union because she would not let slavery into her borders. Under all the circumstances, perhaps, this was not wrong. There were other points of dispute connected with the general question of Slavery, which equally needed adjustment. The South clamored for a more efficient fugitive slave law. The North clamored for the abolition of a peculiar species of slave trade in the District of Columbia, in connection with which, in view from the windows of the Capitol, a sort of negro livery-stable, where droves of negroes were collected, temporarily kept, and finally taken to Southern markets, precisely like droves of horses, had been openly maintained for fifty years. Utah and New Mexico needed territorial governments; and whether slavery should or should not be prohibited within them was another question. The indefinite western boundary of Texas was to be settled. She was a slave State, and consequently the farther west the slavery men could push her boundary, the more slave country they secured; and the farther east the slavery opponents could thrust the boundary back, the less slave ground was secured. Thus this was just as clearly a slavery question as any of the others.

These points all needed adjustment, and they were held up, perhaps wisely, to make them help adjust one another. The Union now, as in 1820, was thought to be in danger, and devotion to the Union rightfully inclined men to yield somewhat in points where nothing else could have so inclined them. A compromise was finally affected. The South got their new fugitive slave law, and the North got California, (by far the best part of our acquisition from Mexico) as a free State. The South got a provision that New Mexico and Utah, when admitted as States, may come in with or without slavery as they may then choose; and the North got the slave trade abolished in the District of Columbia.. The North got the western boundary of Texas thrown farther back eastward than the South desired; but, in turn, they gave Texas ten millions of dollars with which to pay her old debts. This is the Compromise of 1850.

Preceding the Presidential election of 1852, each of the great political parties, Democrats and Whigs, met in convention and adopted resolutions indorsing the Compromise of '50, as a "finality," a final settlement, so far as these parties could make it so, of all slavery agitation. Previous to this, in 1851, the Illinois Legislature had indorsed it.

During this long period of time, Nebraska (the Nebraska Territory, not the State of as we know it now) had remained substantially an uninhabited country, but now emigration to and settlement within it began to take place. It is about one third as large as the present United States, and its importance, so long overlooked, begins to come into view. The restriction of slavery by the Missouri Compromise directly applies to it—in fact was first made, and has since been maintained expressly for it. In 1853, a bill to give it a territorial government passed the House of Representatives, and, in the hands of Judge Douglas, failed of passing only for want of time. This bill contained no repeal of the Missouri Compromise. Indeed, when it was assailed because it did not contain such repeal, Judge Douglas defended it in its existing form. On January 4, 1854, Judge Douglas introduces a new bill to give Nebraska territorial government. He accompanies this bill with a report, in which last he expressly recommends that the Missouri Compromise shall neither be affirmed nor repealed. Before long the bill is so modified as to make two territories instead of one, calling the southern one Kansas.

Also, about a month after the introduction of the bill, on the Judge's own motion it is so amended as to declare the Missouri Compromise inoperative and void; and, substantially, that the people who go and settle there may establish slavery, or exclude it, as they may see fit. In this shape the bill passed both branches of Congress and became a law.

This is the repeal of the Missouri Compromise. The foregoing history may not be precisely accurate in every particular, but I am sure it is sufficiently so for all the use I shall attempt to make of it, and in it we have before us the chief material enabling us to judge correctly whether the repeal of the Missouri Compromise is right or wrong. I think, and shall try to show, that it is wrong—wrong in its direct effect, letting slavery into Kansas and Nebraska, and wrong in its prospective principle, allowing it to spread to every other part of the wide world where men can be found inclined to take it.

This declared indifference, but, as I must think, covert real zeal, for the spread of slavery, I cannot but hate. I hate it because of the monstrous injustice of slavery itself. I hate it because it deprives our republican example of its just influence in the world; enables the enemies of free institutions with plausibility to taunt us as hypocrites; causes the real friends of freedom to doubt our sincerity; and especially because it forces so many good men among ourselves into an open war with the very fundamental principles of civil liberty, criticizing the Declaration of Independence, and insisting that there is no right principle of action but self-interest.

Before proceeding let me say that I think I have no prejudice against the Southern people. They are just what we would be in their situation. If slavery did not now exist among them, they would not introduce it. If it did now exist among us, we should not instantly give it up. This I believe of the masses North and South. Doubtless there are individuals on both sides who would not hold slaves under any circumstances, and others who would gladly introduce slavery anew if it were out of existence. We know that some Southern men do free their slaves, go North and become tip-top abolitionists, while some Northern ones go South and become most cruel slave masters.

When Southern people tell us that they are no more responsible for the origin of slavery than we are, I acknowledge the fact. When it is said that the institution exists, and that it is very difficult to get rid of it in any satisfactory way, I can understand and appreciate the saying. I surely will not blame them for not doing what I should not know how to do myself. If all earthly power were given me, I should not know what to do as to the existing institution. My first impulse would be to free all the slaves, and send them to Liberia, to their own native land. But a moment's reflection would convince me that whatever of high hope (as I think there is) there may be in this in the long run, its sudden execution is impossible. If they were all landed there in a day, they would all perish in the next ten days; and there are not surplus shipping and surplus money enough to carry them there in many times ten days. What then? Free them all, and keep them among us as underlings? Is it quite certain that this betters their condition? I think I would not hold one in slavery at any rate, yet the point is not clear enough for me to denounce people upon. What next? Free them, and make them politically and socially our equals? My own feelings will not admit of this, and if mine would, we well know that those of the great mass of whites will not. Whether this feeling accords with justice and sound judgment is not the sole question, if indeed it is any part of it. A universal feeling, whether well or ill founded, cannot be safely disregarded. We cannot then make them equals. It does seem to me that systems of gradual emancipation might be adopted, but for their tardiness in this I will not undertake to judge our brethren of the South.

When they remind us of their constitutional rights, I acknowledge them—not grudgingly, but fully and fairly; and I would give them any legislation for the reclaiming of their fugitives which should not in its stringency be more likely to carry a free man into slavery than our ordinary criminal laws are to hang an innocent one.

But all this, to my judgment, furnishes no more excuse for permitting slavery to go into our own free territory than it would for reviving the African slave trade by law. The law which forbids the bringing of slaves from Africa, and that which has so long forbidden the taking of them into Nebraska, can hardy be distinguished on any moral principle, and the repeal of the former could find quite as plausible excuses as that of the latter.

The arguments by which the repeal of the Missouri Compromise is sought to be justified are these: First. That the Nebraska country needed a territorial government. Second. That in various ways the public had repudiated that compromise and demanded the repeal, and therefore should not now complain of it. And, lastly, That the repeal establishes a principle which is intrinsically right.

I will attempt an answer to each of them in its turn. First, then: If that country was in need of a territorial organization, could it not have had it as well without as with a repeal? Iowa and Minnesota, to both of which the Missouri restriction applied, had, without its repeal, each in succession, territorial organizations. And even the year before, a bill for Nebraska itself was within an ace of passing without the repealing clause, and this in the hands of the same men who are now the champions of repeal. Why no necessity then for repeal? But still later, when this very bill was first brought in, it contained no repeal. But, say they, because the people had demanded, or rather commanded, the repeal, the repeal was to accompany the organization whenever that should occur.

Now, I deny that the public ever demanded any such thing—ever repudiated the Missouri Compromise, ever commanded its repeal. I deny it, and call for the proof. It is not contended, I believe, that any such command has ever been given in express terms. It is only said that it was done in principle. The support of the Wilmot Proviso is the first fact mentioned to prove that the Missouri restriction was repudiated in principle, and the second is the refusal to extend the Missouri line over the country acquired from Mexico. These are near enough alike to be treated together. The one was to exclude the chances of slavery from the whole new acquisition by the lump, and the other was to reject a division of it, by which one half was to be given up to those chances. Now, whether this was a repudiation of the Missouri line in principle depends upon whether the Missouri law contained any principle requiring the line to be extended over the country acquired from Mexico. I contend it did not. I insist that it contained no general principle, but that it was, in every sense, specific. That its terms limit it to the country purchased from France is undenied and undeniable. It could have no principle beyond the intention of those who made it. They did not intend to extend the line to country which they did not own. If they intended to extend it in the event of acquiring additional territory, why did they not say so? It was just as easy to say that "in all the country west of the Mississippi which we now own, or may hereafter acquire, there shall never be slavery," as to say what they did say; and they would have said it if they had meant it. An intention to extend the law is not only not mentioned in the law, but is not mentioned in any contemporaneous history. Both the law itself, and the history of the times, are a blank as to any principle of extension; and by neither the known rules of construing statutes and contracts, nor by common sense, can any such principle be inferred.

Another fact showing the specific character of the Missouri law— showing that it intended no more than it expressed, showing that the line was not intended as a universal dividing line between Free and Slave territory, present and prospective, north of which slavery could never go—is the fact that by that very law Missouri came in as a slave State, north of the line. If that law contained any prospective principle, the whole law must be looked to in order to ascertain what the principle was. And by this rule the South could fairly contend that, inasmuch as they got one slave State north of the line at the inception of the law, they have the right to have another given them north of it occasionally, now and then, in the indefinite westward extension of the line. This demonstrates the absurdity of attempting to deduce a prospective principle from the Missouri Compromise line.

When we voted for the Wilmot Proviso we were voting to keep slavery out of the whole Mexican acquisition, and little did we think we were thereby voting to let it into Nebraska lying several hundred miles distant. When we voted against extending the Missouri line, little did we think we were voting to destroy the old line, then of near thirty years' standing.

To argue that we thus repudiated the Missouri Compromise is no less absurd than it would be to argue that because we have so far forborne to acquire Cuba, we have thereby, in principle, repudiated our former acquisitions and determined to throw them out of the Union. No less absurd than it would be to say that because I may have refused to build an addition to my house, I thereby have decided to destroy the existing house! And if I catch you setting fire to my house, you will turn upon me and say I instructed you to do it!

The most conclusive argument, however, that while for the Wilmot Proviso, and while voting against the extension of the Missouri line, we never thought of disturbing the original Missouri Compromise, is found in the fact that there was then, and still is, an unorganized tract of fine country, nearly as large as the State of Missouri, lying immediately west of Arkansas and south of the Missouri Compromise line, and that we never attempted to prohibit slavery as to it. I wish particular attention to this. It adjoins the original Missouri Compromise line by its northern boundary, and consequently is part of the country into which by implication slavery was permitted to go by that compromise. There it has lain open ever s, and there it still lies, and yet no effort has been made at any time to wrest it from the South. In all our struggles to prohibit slavery within our Mexican acquisitions, we never so much as lifted a finger to prohibit it as to this tract. Is not this entirely conclusive that at all times we have held the Missouri Compromise as a sacred thing, even when against ourselves as well as when for us?

Senator Douglas sometimes says the Missouri line itself was in principle only an extension of the line of the Ordinance of '87—that is to say, an extension of the Ohio River. I think this is weak enough on its face. I will remark, however, that, as a glance at the map will show, the Missouri line is a long way farther south than the Ohio, and that if our Senator in proposing his extension had stuck to the principle of jogging southward, perhaps it might not have been voted down so readily.

But next it is said that the compromises of '50, and the ratification of them by both political parties in '52, established a new principle which required the repeal of the Missouri Compromise. This again I deny. I deny it, and demand the proof. I have already stated fully what the compromises of '50 are. That particular part of those measures from which the virtual repeal of the Missouri Compromise is sought to be inferred (for it is admitted they contain nothing about it in express terms) is the provision in the Utah and New Mexico laws which permits them when they seek admission into the Union as States to come in with or without slavery, as they shall then see fit. Now I insist this provision was made for Utah and New Mexico, and for no other place whatever. It had no more direct reference to Nebraska than it had to the territories of the moon. But, say they, it had reference to Nebraska in principle. Let us see. The North consented to this provision, not because they considered it right in itself, but because they were compensated—paid for it.

They at the same time got California into the Union as a free State. This was far the best part of all they had struggled for by the Wilmot Proviso. They also got the area of slavery somewhat narrowed in the settlement of the boundary of Texas. Also they got the slave trade abolished in the District of Columbia.

For all these desirable objects the North could afford to yield something; and they did yield to the South the Utah and New Mexico provision. I do not mean that the whole North, or even a majority, yielded, when the law passed; but enough yielded—when added to the vote of the South, to carry the measure. Nor can it be pretended that the principle of this arrangement requires us to permit the same provision to be applied to Nebraska, without any equivalent at all. Give us another free State; press the boundary of Texas still farther back; give us another step toward the destruction of slavery in the District, and you present us a similar case. But ask us not to repeat, for nothing, what you paid for in the first instance. If you wish the thing again, pay again. That is the principle of the compromises of '50, if, indeed, they had any principles beyond their specific terms—it was the system of equivalents.

Again, if Congress, at that time, intended that all future Territories should, when admitted as States, come in with or without slavery at their own option, why did it not say so? With such a universal provision, all know the bills could not have passed. Did they, then—could they establish a principle contrary to their own intention? Still further, if they intended to establish the principle that, whenever Congress had control, it should be left to the people to do as they thought fit with slavery, why did they not authorize the people of the District of Columbia, at their option, to abolish slavery within their limits?

I personally know that this has not been left undone because it was unthought of. It was frequently spoken of by members of Congress, and by citizens of Washington, six years ago; and I heard no one express a doubt that a system of gradual emancipation, with compensation to owners, would meet the approbation of a large majority of the white people of the District. But without the action of Congress they could say nothing; and Congress said "No." In the measures of 1850, Congress had the subject of slavery in the District expressly on hand. If they were then establishing the principle of allowing the people to do as they please with slavery, why did they not apply the principle to that people?

Again it is claimed that by the resolutions of the Illinois Legislature, passed in 1851, the repeal of the Missouri Compromise was demanded. This I deny also. Whatever may be worked out by a criticism of the language of those resolutions, the people have never understood them as being any more than an endorsement of the compromises of 1850, and a release of our senators from voting for the Wilmot Proviso. The whole people are living witnesses that this only was their view. Finally, it is asked, "If we did not mean to apply the Utah and New Mexico provision to all future territories, what did we mean when we, in 1852, indorsed the compromises of 1850?"

For myself I can answer this question most easily. I meant not to ask a repeal or modification of the Fugitive Slave law. I meant not to ask for the abolition of slavery in the District of Columbia. I meant not to resist the admission of Utah and New Mexico, even should they ask to come in as slave States. I meant nothing about additional Territories, because, as I understood, we then had no Territory whose character as to slavery was not already settled. As to Nebraska, I regarded its character as being fixed by the Missouri Compromise for thirty years—as unalterably fixed as that of my own home in Illinois. As to new acquisitions, I said, "Sufficient unto the day is the evil thereof." When we make new acquisitions, we will, as heretofore, try to manage them somehow. That is my answer; that is what I meant and said; and I appeal to the people to say each for himself whether that is not also the universal meaning of the free States.

And now, in turn, let me ask a few questions. If, by any or all these matters, the repeal of the Missouri Compromise was commanded, why was not the command sooner obeyed? Why was the repeal omitted in the Nebraska Bill of 1853? Why was it omitted in the original bill of 1854? Why in the accompanying report was such a repeal characterized as a departure from the course pursued in 1850 and its continued omission recommended?

I am aware Judge Douglas now argues that the subsequent express repeal is no substantial alteration of the bill. This argument seems wonderful to me. It is as if one should argue that white and black are not different. He admits, however, that there is a literal change in the bill, and that he made the change in deference to other senators who would not support the bill without. This proves that those other senators thought the change a substantial one, and that the Judge thought their opinions worth deferring to. His own opinions, therefore, seem not to rest on a very firm basis, even in his own mind; and I suppose the world believes, and will continue to believe, that precisely on the substance of that change this whole agitation has arisen.

I conclude, then, that the public never demanded the repeal of the Missouri Compromise.

I now come to consider whether the appeal with its avowed principles, is intrinsically right. I insist that it is not. Take the particular case. A controversy had arisen between the advocates and opponents of slavery, in relation to its establishment within the country we had purchased of France. The southern, and then best, part of the purchase was already in as a slave State. The controversy was settled by also letting Missouri in as a slave State; but with the agreement that within all the remaining part of the purchase, north of a certain line, there should never be slavery. As to what was to be done with the remaining part, south of the line, nothing was said; but perhaps the fair implication was, it should come in with slavery if it should so choose. The southern part, except a portion heretofore mentioned, afterward did come in with slavery, as the State of Arkansas. All these many years, since 1820, the northern part had remained a wilderness. At length settlements began in it also. In due course Iowa came in as a free State, and Minnesota was given a territorial government, without removing the slavery restriction. Finally, the sole remaining part north of the line—Kansas and Nebraska—was to be organized; and it is proposed, and carried, to blot out the old dividing line of thirty-four years' standing, and to open the whole of that country to the introduction of slavery. Now this, to my mind, is manifestly unjust. After an angry and dangerous controversy, the parties made friends by dividing the bone of contention. The one party first appropriates her own share, beyond all power to be disturbed in the possession of it, and then seizes the share of the other party. It is as if two starving men had divided their only loaf, the one had hastily swallowed his half, and then grabbed the other's half just as he was putting it to his mouth.

Let me here drop the main argument, to notice what I consider rather an inferior matter. It is argued that slavery will not go to Kansas and Nebraska, in any event. This is a palliation, a lullaby. I have some hope that it will not; but let us not be too confident. As to climate, a glance at the map shows that there are five slave States—Delaware, Maryland, Virginia, Kentucky, and Missouri, and also the District of Columbia, all north of the Missouri Compromise line. The census returns of 1850 show that within these there are eight hundred and sixty-seven thousand two hundred and seventy-six slaves, being more than one fourth of all the slaves in the nation.

It is not climate, then, that will keep slavery out of these Territories. Is there anything in the peculiar nature of the country? Missouri adjoins these Territories by her entire western boundary, and slavery is already within every one of her western counties. I have even heard it said that there are more slaves in proportion to whites in the northwestern county of Missouri than within any other county in the State. Slavery pressed entirely up to the old western boundary of the State, and when rather recently a part of that boundary at the northwest was moved out a little farther west, slavery followed on quite up to the new line. Now, when the restriction is removed, what is to prevent it from going still farther? Climate will not, no peculiarity of the country will, nothing in nature will. Will the disposition of the people prevent it? Those nearest the scene are all in favor of the extension. The Yankees who are opposed to it may be most numerous; but, in military phrase, the battlefield is too far from their base of operations.

But it is said there now is no law in Nebraska on the subject of slavery, and that, in such case, taking a slave there operates his freedom. That is good book-law, but it is not the rule of actual practice. Wherever slavery is it has been first introduced without law. The oldest laws we find concerning it are not laws introducing it, but regulating it as an already existing thing. A white man takes his slave to Nebraska now. Who will inform the negro that he is free? Who will take him before court to test the question of his freedom? In ignorance of his legal emancipation he is kept chopping, splitting, and plowing. Others are brought, and move on in the same track. At last, if ever the time for voting comes on the question of slavery the institution already, in fact, exists in the country, and cannot well be removed. The fact of its presence, and the difficulty of its removal, will carry the vote in its favor. Keep it out until a vote is taken, and a vote in favor of it cannot be got in any population of forty thousand on earth, who have been drawn together by the ordinary motives of emigration and settlement. To get slaves into the Territory simultaneously with the whites in the incipient stages of settlement is the precise stake played for and won in this Nebraska measure.

The question is asked us: "If slaves will go in notwithstanding the general principle of law liberates them, why would they not equally go in against positive statute law—go in, even if the Missouri restriction were maintained!" I answer, because it takes a much bolder man to venture in with his property in the latter case than in the former; because the positive Congressional enactment is known to and respected by all, or nearly all, whereas the negative principle that no law is free law is not much known except among lawyers. We have some experience of this practical difference. In spite of the Ordinance of '87, a few negroes were brought into Illinois, and held in a state of quasi-slavery, not enough, however, to carry a vote of the people in favor of the institution when they came to form a constitution. But into the adjoining Missouri country, where there was no Ordinance of '87,—was no restriction,—they were carried ten times, nay, a hundred times, as fast, and actually made a slave State. This is fact-naked fact.

Another lullaby argument is that taking slaves to new countries does not increase their number, does not make any one slave who would otherwise be free. There is some truth in this, and I am glad of it; but it is not wholly true. The African slave trade is not yet effectually suppressed; and, if we make a reasonable deduction for the white people among us who are foreigners and the descendants of foreigners arriving here since 1808, we shall find the increase of the black population outrunning that of the white to an extent unaccountable, except by supposing that some of them, too, have been coming from Africa. If this be so, the opening of new countries to the institution increases the demand for and augments the price of slaves, and so does, in fact, make slaves of freemen, by causing them to be brought from Africa and sold into bondage.

But however this may be, we know the opening of new countries to slavery tends to the perpetuation of the institution, and so does keep men in slavery who would otherwise be free. This result we do not feel like favoring, and we are under no legal obligation to suppress our feelings in this respect.

Equal justice to the South, it is said, requires us to consent to the extension of slavery to new countries. That is to say, inasmuch as you do not object to my taking my hog to Nebraska, therefore I must not object to your taking your slave. Now, I admit that this is perfectly logical if there is no difference between hogs and negroes. But while you thus require me to deny the humanity of the negro, I wish to ask whether you of the South, yourselves, have ever been willing to do as much? It is kindly provided that of all those who come into the world only a small percentage are natural tyrants. That percentage is no larger in the slave States than in the free. The great majority South, as well as North, have human sympathies, of which they can no more divest themselves than they can of their sensibility to physical pain. These sympathies in the bosoms of the Southern people manifest, in many ways, their sense of the wrong of slavery, and their consciousness that, after all, there is humanity in the negro. If they deny this, let me address them a few plain questions. In 1820 you (the South) joined the North, almost unanimously, in declaring the African slave trade piracy, and in annexing to it the punishment of death. Why did you do this? If you did not feel that it was wrong, why did you join in providing that men should be hung for it? The practice was no more than bringing wild negroes from Africa to such as would buy them. But you never thought of hanging men for catching and selling wild horses, wild buffaloes, or wild bears.

Again, you have among you a sneaking individual of the class of native tyrants known as the "slave-dealer." He watches your necessities, and crawls up to buy your slave, at a speculating price. If you cannot help it, you sell to him; but if you can help it, you drive him from your door. You despise him utterly. You do not recognize him as a friend, or even as an honest man. Your children must not play with his; they may rollick freely with the little negroes, but not with the slave-dealer's children. If you are obliged to deal with him, you try to get through the job without so much as touching him. It is common with you to join hands with the men you meet, but with the slave-dealer you avoid the ceremony—instinctively shrinking from the snaky contact. If he grows rich and retires from business, you still remember him, and still keep up the ban of non-intercourse upon him and his family. Now, why is this? You do not so treat the man who deals in corn, cotton, or tobacco.

And yet again: There are in the United States and Territories, including the District of Columbia, 433,643 free blacks. At five hundred dollars per head they are worth over two hundred millions of dollars. How comes this vast amount of property to be running about without owners? We do not see free horses or free cattle running at large. How is this? All these free blacks are the descendants of slaves, or have been slaves themselves; and they would be slaves now but for something which has operated on their white owners, inducing them at vast pecuniary sacrifice to liberate them. What is that something? Is there any mistaking it? In all these cases it is your sense of justice and human sympathy continually telling you that the poor negro has some natural right to himself—that those who deny it and make mere merchandise of him deserve kickings, contempt, and death.

And now why will you ask us to deny the humanity of the slave, and estimate him as only the equal of the hog? Why ask us to do what you will not do yourselves? Why ask us to do for nothing what two hundred millions of dollars could not induce you to do?

But one great argument in support of the repeal of the Missouri Compromise is still to come. That argument is "the sacred right of self-government." It seems our distinguished Senator has found great difficulty in getting his antagonists, even in the Senate, to meet him fairly on this argument. Some poet has said:

"Fools rush in where angels fear to tread."

At the hazard of being thought one of the fools of this quotation, I meet that argument—I rush in—I take that bull by the horns. I trust I understand and truly estimate the right of self-government. My faith in the proposition that each man should do precisely as he pleases with all which is exclusively his own lies at the foundation of the sense of justice there is in me. I extend the principle to communities of men as well as to individuals. I so extend it because it is politically wise, as well as naturally just; politically wise in saving us from broils about matters which do not concern us. Here, or at Washington, I would not trouble myself with the oyster laws of Virginia, or the cranberry laws of Indiana. The doctrine of self-government is right,—absolutely and eternally right,—but it has no just application as here attempted. Or perhaps I should rather say that whether it has such application depends upon whether a negro is or is not a man. If he is not a man, in that case he who is a man may as a matter of self-government do just what he pleases with him. But if the negro is a man, is it not to that extent a total destruction of self-government to say that he too shall not govern himself? When the white man governs himself, that is self-government; but when he governs himself and also governs another man, that is more than self-government—that is despotism. If the negro is a man, why, then, my ancient faith teaches me that "all men are created equal," and that there can be no moral right in connection with one man's making a slave of another.

Judge Douglas frequently, with bitter irony and sarcasm, paraphrases our argument by saying: "The white people of Nebraska are good enough to govern themselves, but they are not good enough to govern a few miserable negroes!"

Well, I doubt not that the people of Nebraska are and will continue to be as good as the average of people elsewhere. I do not say the contrary. What I do say is that no man is good enough to govern another man without that other's consent. I say this is the leading principle, the sheet-anchor of American republicanism. Our Declaration of Independence says:

"We hold these truths to be self-evident: That all men are created equal; that they are endowed by their Creator with certain inalienable rights; that among these are life, liberty, and the pursuit of happiness. That to secure these rights, governments are instituted among men, DERIVING THEIR JUST POWERS PROM THE CONSENT OF THE GOVERNED."

I have quoted so much at this time merely to show that, according to our ancient faith, the just powers of government are derived from the consent of the governed. Now the relation of master and slave is *pro tanto* a total violation of this principle. The master not only governs the slave without his consent, but he governs him by a set of rules altogether different from those which he prescribes for himself. Allow all the governed an equal voice in the government, and that, and that only, is self-government.

Let it not be said that I am contending for the establishment of political and social equality between the whites and blacks. I have already said the contrary. I am not combating the argument of necessity, arising from the fact that the blacks are already among us; but I am combating what is set up as moral argument for allowing them to be taken where they have never yet been—arguing against the extension of a bad thing, which, where it already exists, we must of necessity manage as we best can.

In support of his application of the doctrine of self-government, Senator Douglas has sought to bring to his aid the opinions and examples of our Revolutionary fathers. I am glad he has done this. I love the sentiments of those old-time men, and shall be most happy to abide by their opinions. He shows us that when it was in contemplation for the colonies to break off from Great Britain, and set up a new government for themselves, several of the States instructed their delegates to go for the measure, provided each State should be allowed to regulate its domestic concerns in its own way. I do not quote; but this in substance. This was right; I see nothing objectionable in it. I also think it probable that it had some reference to the existence of slavery among them. I will not deny that it had. But had it any reference to the carrying of slavery into new countries? That is the question, and we will let the fathers themselves answer it.

This same generation of men, and mostly the same individuals of the generation who declared this principle, who declared independence, who fought the war of the Revolution through, who afterward made the Constitution under which we still live—these same men passed the Ordinance of '87, declaring that slavery should never go to the Northwest Territory. I have no doubt Judge Douglas thinks they were very inconsistent in this. It is a question of discrimination between them and him. But there is not an inch of ground left for his claiming that their opinions, their example, their authority, are on his side in the controversy.

Again, is not Nebraska, while a Territory, a part of us? Do we not own the country? And if we surrender the control of it, do we not surrender the right of self-government? It is part of ourselves. If you say we shall not control it, because it is only part, the same is true of every other part; and when all the parts are gone, what has become of the whole? What is then left of us? What use for the General Government, when there is nothing left for it to govern?

But you say this question should be left to the people of Nebraska, because they are more particularly interested. If this be the rule, you must leave it to each individual to say for himself whether he will have slaves. What better moral right have thirty-one citizens of Nebraska to say that the thirty-second shall not hold slaves than the people of the thirty-one States have to say that slavery shall not go into the thirty-second State at all?

But if it is a sacred right for the people of Nebraska to take and hold slaves there, it is equally their sacred right to buy them where they can buy them cheapest; and that, undoubtedly, will be on the coast of Africa, provided you will consent not to hang them for going there to buy them. You must remove this restriction, too, from the sacred right of self-government. I am aware you say that taking slaves from the States to Nebraska does not make slaves of freemen; but the African slave-trader can say just as much. He does not catch free negroes and bring them here. He finds them already slaves in the hands of their black captors, and he honestly buys them at the rate of a red cotton handkerchief a head. This is very cheap, and it is a great abridgment of the sacred right of self-government to hang men for engaging in this profitable trade.

Another important objection to this application of the right of self-government is that it enables the first few to deprive the succeeding many of a free exercise of the right of self-government. The first few may get slavery in, and the subsequent many cannot easily get it out. How common is the remark now in the slave States, "If we were only clear of our slaves, how much better it would be for us." They are actually deprived of the privilege of governing themselves as they would, by the action of a very few in the beginning. The same thing was true of the whole nation at the time our Constitution was formed.

Whether slavery shall go into Nebraska, or other new Territories, is not a matter of exclusive concern to the people who may go there. The whole nation is interested that the best use shall be made of these Territories. We want them for homes of free white people. This they cannot be, to any considerable extent, if slavery shall be planted within them. Slave States are places for poor white people to remove from, not to remove to. New free States are the places for poor people to go to, and better their condition. For this use the nation needs these Territories.

Still further: there are constitutional relations between the slave and free States which are degrading to the latter. We are under legal obligations to catch and return their runaway slaves to them: a sort of dirty, disagreeable job, which, I believe, as a general rule, the slaveholders will not perform for one another. Then again, in the control of the government—the management of the partnership affairs—they have greatly the advantage of us. By the Constitution each State has two senators, each has a number of representatives in proportion to the number of its people, and each has a number of Presidential electors equal to the whole number of its senators and representatives together. But in ascertaining the number of the people for this purpose, five slaves are counted as being equal to three whites. The slaves do not vote; they are only counted and so used as to swell the influence of the white people's votes. The practical effect of this is more aptly shown by a comparison of the States of South Carolina and Maine. South Carolina has six representatives, and so has Maine; South Carolina has eight Presidential electors, and so has Maine. This is precise equality so far; and of course they are equal in senators, each having two. Thus in the control of the government the two States are equals precisely. But how are they in the number of their white people? Maine has 581,813, while South Carolina has 274,567; Maine has twice as many as South Carolina, and 32,679 over. Thus, each white man in South Carolina is more than the double of any man in Maine.

This is all because South Carolina, besides her free people, has 384,984 slaves. The South Carolinian has precisely the same advantage over the white man in every other free State as well as in Maine. He is more than the double of any one of us in this crowd. The same advantage, but not to the same extent, is held by all the citizens of the slave States over those of the free; and it is an absolute truth, without an exception, that there is no voter in any slave State but who has more legal power in the government than any voter in any free State. There is no instance of exact equality; and the disadvantage is against us the whole chapter through. This principle, in the aggregate, gives the slave States in the present Congress twenty additional representatives, being seven more than the whole majority by which they passed the Nebraska Bill.

Now all this is manifestly unfair; yet I do not mention it to complain of it, in so far as it is already settled. It is in the Constitution, and I do not for that cause, or any other cause, propose to destroy, or alter, or disregard the Constitution. I stand to it, fairly, fully, and firmly.

But when I am told I must leave it altogether to other people to say whether new partners are to be bred up and brought into the firm, on the same degrading terms against me, I respectfully demur. I insist that whether I shall be a whole man or only the half of one, in comparison with others is a question in which I am somewhat concerned, and one which no other man can have a sacred right of deciding for me. If I am wrong in this, if it really be a sacred right of self-government in the man who shall go to Nebraska to decide whether he will be the equal of me or the double of me, then, after he shall have exercised that right, and thereby shall have reduced me to a still smaller fraction of a man than I already am, I should like for some gentleman, deeply skilled in the mysteries of sacred rights, to provide himself with a microscope, and peep about, and find out, if he can, what has become of my sacred rights. They will surely be too small for detection with the naked eye.

Finally, I insist that if there is anything which it is the duty of the whole people to never entrust to any hands but their own, that thing is the preservation and perpetuity of their own liberties and institutions. And if they shall think as I do, that the extension of slavery endangers them more than any or all other causes, how recreant to themselves if they submit The question, and with it the fate of their country, to a mere handful of men bent only on self-interest. If this question of slavery extension were an insignificant one, one having no power to do harm—it might be shuffled aside in this way; and being, as it is, the great Behemoth of danger, shall the strong grip of the nation be loosened upon him, to entrust him to the hands of such feeble keepers?

I have done with this mighty argument of self-government. Go, sacred thing! Go in peace.

But Nebraska is urged as a great Union-saving measure. Well, I too go for saving the Union. Much as I hate slavery, I would consent to the extension of it rather than see the Union dissolved, just as I would consent to any great evil to avoid a greater one. But when I go to Union-saving, I must believe, at least, that the means I employ have some adaptation to the end. To my mind, Nebraska has no such adaptation.

"It hath no relish of salvation in it."

It is an aggravation, rather, of the only one thing which ever endangers the Union. When it came upon us, all was peace and quiet. The nation was looking to the forming of new bends of union, and a long course of peace and prosperity seemed to lie before us. In the whole range of possibility, there scarcely appears to me to have been anything out of which the slavery agitation could have been revived, except the very project of repealing the Missouri Compromise. Every inch of territory we owned already had a definite settlement of the slavery question, by which all parties were pledged to abide. Indeed, there was no uninhabited country on the continent which we could acquire, if we except some extreme northern regions which are wholly out of the question.

In this state of affairs the Genius of Discord himself could scarcely have invented a way of again setting us by the ears but by turning back and destroying the peace measures of the past. The counsels of that Genius seem to have prevailed. The Missouri Compromise was repealed; and here we are in the midst of a new slavery agitation, such, I think, as we have never seen before. Who is responsible for this? Is it those who resist the measure, or those who causelessly brought it forward, and pressed it through, having reason to know, and in fact knowing, it must and would be so resisted? It could not but be expected by its author that it would be looked upon as a measure for the extension of slavery, aggravated by a gross breach of faith.

Argue as you will and long as you will, this is the naked front and aspect of the measure. And in this aspect it could not but produce agitation. Slavery is founded in the selfishness of man's nature— opposition to it in his love of justice. These principles are at eternal antagonism, and when brought into collision so fiercely as slavery extension brings them, shocks and throes and convulsions must ceaselessly follow. Repeal the Missouri Compromise, repeal all compromises, repeal the Declaration of Independence, repeal all past history, you still cannot repeal human nature. It still will be the abundance of man's heart that slavery extension is wrong, and out of the abundance of his heart his mouth will continue to speak.

The structure, too, of the Nebraska Bill is very peculiar. The people are to decide the question of slavery for themselves; but when they are to decide, or how they are to decide, or whether, when the question is once decided, it is to remain so or is to be subject to an indefinite succession of new trials, the law does not say. Is it to be decided by the first dozen settlers who arrive there, or is it to await the arrival of a hundred? Is it to be decided by a vote of the people or a vote of the Legislature, or, indeed, by a vote of any sort? To these questions the law gives no answer. There is a mystery about this; for when a member proposed to give the Legislature express authority to exclude slavery, it was hooted down by the friends of the bill. This fact is worth remembering. Some Yankees in the East are sending emigrants to Nebraska to exclude slavery from it; and, so far as I can judge, they expect the question to be decided by voting in some way or other. But the Missourians are awake, too. They are within a stone's-throw of the contested ground. They hold meetings and pass resolutions, in which not the slightest allusion to voting is made. They resolve that slavery already exists in the Territory; that more shall go there; that they, remaining in Missouri, will protect it, and that abolitionists shall be hung or driven away. Through all this bowie knives and six-shooters are seen plainly enough, but never a glimpse of the ballot-box.

And, really, what is the result of all this? Each party within having numerous and determined backers without, is it not probable that the contest will come to blows and bloodshed? Could there be a more apt invention to bring about collision and violence on the slavery question than this Nebraska project is? I do not charge or believe that such was intended by Congress; but if they had literally formed a ring and placed champions within it to fight out the controversy, the fight could be no more likely to come off than it is. And if this fight should begin, is it likely to take a very peaceful, Union-saving turn? Will not the first drop of blood so shed be the real knell of the Union?

The Missouri Compromise ought to be restored. For the sake of the Union, it ought to be restored. We ought to elect a House of Representatives which will vote its restoration. If by any means we omit to do this, what follows? Slavery may or may not be established in Nebraska. But whether it be or not, we shall have repudiated—discarded from the councils of the nation—the spirit of compromise; for who, after this, will ever trust in a national compromise? The spirit of mutual concession—that spirit which first gave us the Constitution, and which has thrice saved the Union—we shall have strangled and cast from us forever. And what shall we have in lieu of it? The South flushed with triumph and tempted to excess; the North, betrayed as they believe, brooding on wrong and burning for revenge. One side will provoke, the other resent. The one will taunt, the other defy; one aggresses, the other retaliates. Already a few in the North defy all constitutional restraints, resist the execution of the Fugitive Slave law, and even menace the institution of slavery in the States where it exists. Already a few in the South claim the constitutional right to take and to hold slaves in the free States, demand the revival of the slave trade, and demand a treaty with Great Britain by which fugitive slaves may be reclaimed from Canada. As yet they are but few on either side. It is a grave question for lovers of the union whether the final destruction of the Missouri Compromise, and with it the spirit of all compromise, will or will not embolden and embitter each of these, and fatally increase the number of both.

But restore the compromise, and what then? We thereby restore the national faith, the national confidence, the national feeling of brotherhood. We thereby reinstate the spirit of concession and compromise, that spirit which has never failed us in past perils, and which may be safely trusted for all the future. The South ought to join in doing this. The peace of the nation is as dear to them as to us. In memories of the past and hopes of the future, they share as largely as we. It would be on their part a great act—great in its spirit, and great in its effect. It would be worth to the nation a hundred years purchase of peace and prosperity. And what of sacrifice would they make? They only surrender to us what they gave us for a consideration long, long ago; what they have not now asked for, struggled or cared for; what has been thrust upon them, not less to their astonishment than to ours.

But it is said we cannot restore it; that though we elect every member of the lower House, the Senate is still against us. It is quite true that of the senators who passed the Nebraska Bill a majority of the whole Senate will retain their seats in spite of the elections of this and the next year. But if at these elections their several constituencies shall clearly express their will against Nebraska, will these senators disregard their will? Will they neither obey nor make room for those who will?

But even if we fail to technically restore the compromise, it is still a great point to carry a popular vote in favor of the restoration. The moral weight of such a vote cannot be estimated too highly. The authors of Nebraska are not at all satisfied with the destruction of the compromise—an endorsement of this principle they proclaim to be the great object. With them, Nebraska alone is a small matter—to establish a principle for future use is what they particularly desire.

The future use is to be the planting of slavery wherever in the wide world local and unorganized opposition cannot prevent it. Now, if you wish to give them this endorsement, if you wish to establish this principle, do so. I shall regret it, but it is your right. On the contrary, if you are opposed to the principle,—intend to give it no such endorsement, let no wheedling, no sophistry, divert you from throwing a direct vote against it.

Some men, mostly Whigs, who condemn the repeal of the Missouri Compromise, nevertheless hesitate to go for its restoration, lest they be thrown in company with the abolitionists. Will they allow me, as an old

Whig, to tell them, good-humoredly, that I think this is very silly? Stand with anybody that stands right. Stand with him while he is right, and part with him when he goes wrong. Stand with the abolitionist in restoring the Missouri Compromise, and stand against him when he attempts to repeal the Fugitive Slave law. In the latter case you stand with the Southern disunionist. What of that? You are still right. In both cases you are right. In both cases you oppose the dangerous extremes. In both you stand on middle ground, and hold the ship level and steady. In both you are national, and nothing less than national. This is the good old Whig ground. To desert such ground because of any company is to be less than a Whig—less than a man—less than an American.

I particularly object to the new position which the avowed principle of this Nebraska law gives to slavery in the body politic. I object to it because it assumes that there can be moral right in the enslaving of one man by another. I object to it as a dangerous dalliance for a free people—a sad evidence that, feeling prosperity, we forget right; that liberty, as a principle, we have ceased to revere. I object to it because the fathers of the republic eschewed and rejected it. The argument of "necessity" was the only argument they ever admitted in favor of slavery; and so far, and so far only, as it carried them did they ever go. They found the institution existing among us, which they could not help, and they cast blame upon the British king for having permitted its introduction. Before the Constitution they prohibited its introduction into the Northwestern Territory, the only country we owned then free from it. At the framing and adoption of the Constitution, they forbore to so much as mention the word "slave" or "slavery" in the whole instrument. In the provision for the recovery of fugitives, the slave is spoken of as a "person held to service or labor." In that prohibiting the abolition of the African slave trade for twenty years, that trade is spoken of as "the migration or importation of such persons as any of the States now existing shall think proper to admit," etc. These are the only provisions alluding to slavery. Thus the thing is hid away in the Constitution, just as an afflicted man hides away a wen or cancer which he dares not cut out at once, lest he bleed to death,— with the promise, nevertheless, that the cutting may begin at a certain time. Less than this our fathers could not do, and more they would not do. Necessity drove them so far, and farther they would not go. But this is not all. The earliest Congress under the Constitution took the same view of slavery. They hedged and hemmed it in to the narrowest limits of necessity.

In 1794 they prohibited an outgoing slave trade—that is, the taking of slaves from the United States to sell. In 1798 they prohibited the bringing of slaves from Africa into the Mississippi Territory, this Territory then comprising what are now the States of Mississippi and Alabama. This was ten years before they had the authority to do the same thing as to the States existing at the adoption of the Constitution. In 1800 they prohibited American citizens from trading in slaves between foreign countries, as, for instance, from Africa to Brazil. In 1803 they passed a law in aid of one or two slave-State laws in restraint of the internal slave trade. In 1807, in apparent hot haste, they passed the law, nearly a year in advance,—to take effect the first day of 1808, the very first day the Constitution would permit, prohibiting the African slave trade by heavy pecuniary and corporal penalties. In 1820, finding these provisions ineffectual, they declared the slave trade piracy, and annexed to it the extreme penalty of death. While all this was passing in the General Government, five or six of the original slave States had adopted systems of gradual emancipation, by which the institution was rapidly becoming extinct within their limits. Thus we see that the plain, unmistakable spirit of that age toward slavery was hostility to the principle and toleration only by necessity.

But now it is to be transformed into a "sacred right." Nebraska brings it forth, places it on the highroad to extension and perpetuity, and with a pat on its back says to it, "Go, and God speed you." Henceforth it is to be the chief jewel of the nation the very figure-head of the ship of state. Little by little, but steadily as man's march to the grave, we have been giving up the old for the new faith. Near eighty years ago we began by declaring that all men are created equal; but now from that beginning we have run down to the other declaration, that for some men to enslave others is a "sacred right of self-government." These principles cannot stand together. They are as opposite as God and Mammon; and who ever holds to the one must despise the other. When Pettit, in connection with his support of the Nebraska Bill, called the Declaration of Independence "a self-evident lie," he only did what consistency and candor require all other Nebraska men to do. Of the forty-odd Nebraska senators who sat present and heard him, no one rebuked him. Nor am I apprised that any Nebraska newspaper, or any Nebraska orator, in the whole nation has ever yet rebuked him. If this had been said among Marion's men, Southerners though they were, what would have become of the man who said it? If this had been said to the men who captured Andre, the man who said it would probably have been hung sooner than Andre was. If it had been said in old Independence Hall seventy-eight years ago, the very doorkeeper would have throttled the man and thrust him into the street. Let no one be deceived. The spirit of seventy-six and the spirit of Nebraska are utter antagonisms; and the former is being rapidly displaced by the latter.

Fellow-countrymen, Americans, South as well as North, shall we make no effort to arrest this? Already the liberal party throughout the world express the apprehension that "the one retrograde institution in America is undermining the principles of progress, and fatally violating the noblest political system the world ever saw." This is not the taunt of enemies, but the warning of friends. Is it quite safe to disregard it—to despise it? Is there no danger to liberty itself in discarding the earliest practice and first precept of our ancient faith? In our greedy chase to make profit of the negro, let us beware lest we "cancel and tear in pieces" even the white man's charter of freedom.

Our republican robe is soiled and trailed in the dust. Let us repurify it. Let us turn and wash it white in the spirit, if not the blood, of the Revolution. Let us turn slavery from its claims of "moral right," back upon its existing legal rights and its arguments of "necessity." Let us return it to the position our fathers gave it, and there let it rest in peace. Let us readopt the Declaration of Independence, and with it the practices and policy which harmonize with it. Let North and South, let all Americans—let all lovers of liberty everywhere join in the great and good work. If we do this, we shall not only have saved the Union, but we shall have so saved it as to make and to keep it forever worthy of the saving. We shall have so saved it that the succeeding millions of free happy people the world over shall rise up and call us blessed to the latest generations.

At Springfield, twelve days ago, where I had spoken substantially as I have here, Judge Douglas replied to me; and as he is to reply to me here, I shall attempt to anticipate him by noticing some of the points he made there. He commenced by stating I had assumed all the way through that the principle of the Nebraska Bill would have the effect of extending slavery. He denied that this was intended or that this effect would follow.

I will not reopen the argument upon this point. That such was the intention the world believed at the start, and will continue to believe. This was the countenance of the thing, and both friends and enemies instantly recognized it as such. That countenance cannot now be changed by argument. You can as easily argue the color out of the negro's skin. Like the "bloody hand," you may wash it and wash it, the red witness of guilt still sticks and stares horribly at you.

Next he says that Congressional intervention never prevented slavery anywhere; that it did not prevent it in the Northwestern Territory, nor in Illinois; that, in fact, Illinois came into the Union as a slave State; that the principle of the Nebraska Bill expelled it from Illinois, from several old States, from everywhere.

Now this is mere quibbling all the way through. If the Ordinance of '87 did not keep slavery out of the Northwest Territory, how happens it that the northwest shore of the Ohio River is entirely free from it, while the southeast shore, less than a mile distant, along nearly the whole length of the river, is entirely covered with it?

If that ordinance did not keep it out of Illinois, what was it that made the difference between Illinois and Missouri? They lie side by side, the Mississippi River only dividing them, while their early settlements were within the same latitude. Between 1810 and 1820 the number of slaves in Missouri increased 7211, while in Illinois in the same ten years they decreased 51. This appears by the census returns. During nearly all of that ten years both were Territories, not States. During this time the ordinance forbade slavery to go into Illinois, and nothing forbade it to go into Missouri. It did go into Missouri, and did not go into Illinois. That is the fact. Can any one doubt as to the reason of it? But he says Illinois came into the Union as a slave State. Silence, perhaps, would be the best answer to this flat contradiction of the known history of the country. What are the facts upon which this bold assertion is based? When we first acquired the country, as far back as 1787, there were some slaves within it held by the French inhabitants of Kaskaskia. The territorial legislation admitted a few negroes from the slave States as indentured servants. One year after the adoption of the first State constitution, the whole number of them was—what do you think? Just one hundred and seventeen, while the aggregate free population was 55,094,—about four hundred and seventy to one. Upon this state of facts the people framed their constitution prohibiting the further introduction of slavery, with a sort of guaranty to the owners of the few indentured servants, giving freedom to their children to be born thereafter, and making no mention whatever of any supposed slave for life. Out of this small matter the Judge manufactures his argument that Illinois came into the Union as a slave State. Let the facts be the answer to the argument.

The principles of the Nebraska Bill, he says, expelled slavery from Illinois. The principle of that bill first planted it here—that is, it first came because there was no law to prevent it, first came before we owned the country; and finding it here, and having the Ordinance of '87 to prevent its increasing, our people struggled along, and finally got rid of it as best they could.

But the principle of the Nebraska Bill abolished slavery in several of the old States. Well, it is true that several of the old States, in the last quarter of the last century, did adopt systems of gradual emancipation by which the institution has finally become extinct within their limits; but it may or may not be true that the principle of the Nebraska Bill was the cause that led to the adoption of these measures. It is now more than fifty years since the last of these States adopted its system of emancipation.

If the Nebraska Bill is the real author of the benevolent works, it is rather deplorable that it has for so long a time ceased working altogether. Is there not some reason to suspect that it was the principle of the Revolution, and not the principle of the Nebraska Bill, that led to emancipation in these old States? Leave it to the people of these old emancipating States, and I am quite certain they will decide that neither that nor any other good thing ever did or ever will come of the Nebraska Bill.

In the course of my main argument, Judge Douglas interrupted me to say that the principle of the Nebraska Bill was very old; that it originated when God made man, and placed good and evil before him, allowing him to choose for himself, being responsible for the choice he should make. At the time I thought this was merely playful, and I answered it accordingly. But in his reply to me he renewed it as a serious argument. In seriousness, then, the facts of this proposition are not true as stated. God did not place good and evil before man, telling him to make his choice. On the contrary, he did tell him there was one tree of the fruit of which he should not eat, upon pain of certain death. I should scarcely wish so strong a prohibition against slavery in Nebraska.

But this argument strikes me as not a little remarkable in another particular—in its strong resemblance to the old argument for the "divine right of kings." By the latter, the king is to do just as he pleases with his white subjects, being responsible to God alone. By the former, the white man is to do just as he pleases with his black slaves, being responsible to God alone. The two things are precisely alike, and it is but natural that they should find similar arguments to sustain them.

I had argued that the application of the principle of self-government, as contended for, would require the revival of the African slave trade; that no argument could be made in favor of a man's right to take slaves to Nebraska which could not be equally well made in favor of his right to bring them from the coast of Africa. The Judge replied that the Constitution requires the suppression of the foreign slave trade, but does not require the prohibition of slavery in the Territories. That is a mistake in point of fact. The Constitution does not require the action of Congress in either case, and it does authorize it in both. And so there is still no difference between the cases.

In regard to what I have said of the advantage the slave States have over the free in the matter of representation, the Judge replied that we in the free States count five free negroes as five white people, while in the slave States they count five slaves as three whites only; and that the advantage, at last, was on the side of the free States.

Now, in the slave States they count free negroes just as we do; and it so happens that, besides their slaves, they have as many free negroes as we have, and thirty thousand over. Thus, their free negroes more than balance ours; and their advantage over us, in consequence of their slaves, still remains as I stated it.

In reply to my argument that the compromise measures of 1850 were a system of equivalents, and that the provisions of no one of them could fairly be carried to other subjects without its corresponding equivalent being carried with it, the Judge denied outright that these measures had any connection with or dependence upon each other. This is mere desperation. If they had no connection, why are they always spoken of in connection? Why has he so spoken of them a thousand times? Why has he constantly called them a series of measures? Why does everybody call them a compromise? Why was California kept out of the Union six or seven months, if it was not because of its connection with the other measures? Webster's leading definition of the verb "to compromise" is "to adjust and settle a difference, by mutual agreement, with concessions of claims by the parties." This conveys precisely the popular understanding of the word "compromise."

We knew, before the Judge told us, that these measures passed separately, and in distinct bills, and that no two of them were passed by the votes of precisely the same members. But we also know, and so does he know, that no one of them could have passed both branches of Congress but for the understanding that the others were to pass also. Upon this understanding, each got votes which it could have got in no other way. It is this fact which gives to the measures their true character; and it is the universal knowledge of this fact that has given them the name of "compromises," so expressive of that true character.

I had asked: "If, in carrying the Utah and New Mexico laws to Nebraska, you could clear away other objection, how could you leave Nebraska 'perfectly free' to introduce slavery before she forms a constitution, during her territorial government, while the Utah and New Mexico laws only authorize it when they form constitutions and are admitted into the Union?" To this Judge Douglas answered that the Utah and New Mexico laws also authorized it before; and to prove this he read from one of their laws, as follows: "That the legislative power of said Territory shall extend to all rightful subjects of legislation, consistent with the Constitution of the United States and the provisions of this act."

Now it is perceived from the reading of this that there is nothing express upon the subject, but that the authority is sought to be implied merely for the general provision of "all rightful subjects of legislation." In reply to this I insist, as a legal rule of construction, as well as the plain, popular view of the matter, that the express provision for Utah and New Mexico coming in with slavery, if they choose, when they shall form constitutions, is an exclusion of all implied authority on the same subject; that Congress having the subject distinctly in their minds when they made the express provision, they therein expressed their whole meaning on that subject.

The Judge rather insinuated that I had found it convenient to forget the Washington territorial law passed in 1853. This was a division of Oregon, organizing the northern part as the Territory of Washington. He asserted that by this act the Ordinance of '87, theretofore existing in Oregon, was repealed; that nearly all the members of Congress voted for it, beginning in the House of Representatives with Charles Allen of Massachusetts, and ending with Richard Yates of Illinois; and that he could not understand how those who now opposed the Nebraska Bill so voted there, unless it was because it was then too soon after both the great political parties had ratified the compromises of 1850, and the ratification therefore was too fresh to be then repudiated.

Now I had seen the Washington act before, and I have carefully examined it since; and I aver that there is no repeal of the Ordinance of '87, or of any prohibition of slavery, in it. In express terms, there is absolutely nothing in the whole law upon the subject—in fact, nothing to lead a reader to think of the subject. To my judgment it is equally free from everything from which repeal can be legally implied; but, however this may be, are men now to be entrapped by a legal implication, extracted from covert language, introduced perhaps for the very purpose of entrapping them? I sincerely wish every man could read this law quite through, carefully watching every sentence and every line for a repeal of the Ordinance of '87, or anything equivalent to it.

Another point on the Washington act: If it was intended to be modeled after the Utah and New Mexico acts, as Judge Douglas insists, why was it not inserted in it, as in them, that Washington was to come in with or without slavery as she may choose at the adoption of her constitution? It has no such provision in it; and I defy the ingenuity of man to give a reason for the omission, other than that it was not intended to follow the Utah and New Mexico laws in regard to the question of slavery.

The Washington act not only differs vitally from the Utah and New Mexico acts, but the Nebraska act differs vitally from both. By the latter act the people are left "perfectly free" to regulate their own domestic concerns, etc.; but in all the former, all their laws are to be submitted to Congress, and if disapproved are to be null. The Washington act goes even further; it absolutely prohibits the territorial Legislature, by very strong and guarded language, from establishing banks or borrowing money on the faith of the Territory. Is this the sacred right of self-government we hear vaunted so much? No, sir; the Nebraska Bill finds no model in the acts of '50 or the Washington act. It finds no model in any law from Adam till to-day. As Phillips says of Napoleon, the Nebraska act is grand, gloomy and peculiar, wrapped in the solitude of its own originality, without a model and without a shadow upon the earth.

In the course of his reply Senator Douglas remarked in substance that he had always considered this government was made for the white people and not for the negroes. Why, in point of mere fact, I think so too. But in this remark of the Judge there is a significance which I think is the key to the great mistake (if there is any such mistake) which he has made in this Nebraska measure. It shows that the Judge has no very vivid impression that the negro is human, and consequently has no idea that there can be any moral question in legislating about him. In his view the question of whether a new country shall be slave or free is a matter of as utter indifference as it is whether his neighbor shall plant his farm with tobacco or stock it with horned cattle. Now, whether this view is right or wrong, it is very certain that the great mass of mankind take a totally different view. They consider slavery a great moral wrong, and their feeling against it is not evanescent, but eternal. It lies at the very foundation of their sense of justice, and it cannot be trifled with. It is a great and durable element of popular action, and I think no statesman can safely disregard it.

Our Senator also objects that those who oppose him in this matter do not entirely agree with one another. He reminds me that in my firm adherence to the constitutional rights of the slave States I differ widely from others who are cooperating with me in opposing the Nebraska Bill, and he says it is not quite fair to oppose him in this variety of ways. He should remember that he took us by surprise—astounded us by this measure. We were thunderstruck and stunned, and we reeled and fell in utter confusion. But we rose, each fighting, grasping whatever he could first reach—a scythe, a pitchfork, a chopping-ax, or a butcher's cleaver. We struck in the direction of the sound, and we were rapidly closing in upon him. He must not think to divert us from our purpose by showing us that our drill, our dress, and our weapons are not entirely perfect and uniform. When the storm shall be past he shall find us still Americans, no less devoted to the continued union and prosperity of the country than heretofore.

Finally, the Judge invokes against me the memory of Clay and Webster, They were great men, and men of great deeds. But where have I assailed them? For what is it that their lifelong enemy shall now make profit by assuming to defend them against me, their lifelong friend? I go against the repeal of the Missouri Compromise; did they ever go for it? They went for the Compromise of 1850; did I ever go against them? They were greatly devoted to the Union; to the small measure of my ability was I ever less so? Clay and Webster were dead before this question arose; by what authority shall our Senator say they would espouse his side of it if alive? Mr. Clay was the leading spirit in making the Missouri Compromise; is it very credible that if now alive he would take the lead in the breaking of it? The truth is that some support from Whigs is now a necessity with the Judge, and for this it is that the names of Clay and Webster are invoked. His old friends have deserted him in such numbers as to leave too few to live by. He came to his own, and his own received him not; and lo! he turns unto the Gentiles.

A word now as to the Judge's desperate assumption that the

compromises of 1850 had no connection with one another; that Illinois came into the Union as a slave State, and some other similar ones. This is no other than a bold denial of the history of the country. If we do not know that the compromises of 1850 were dependent on each other; if we do not know that Illinois came into the Union as a free State,—we do not know anything. If we do not know these things, we do not know that we ever had a Revolutionary War or such a chief as Washington. To deny these things is to deny our national axioms,—or dogmas, at least,—and it puts an end to all argument. If a man will stand up and assert, and repeat and reassert, that two and two do not make four, I know nothing in the power of argument that can stop him. I think I can answer the Judge so long as he sticks to the premises; but when he flies from them, I cannot work any argument into the consistency of a mental gag and actually close his mouth with it. In such a case I can only commend him to the seventy thousand answers just in from Pennsylvania, Ohio, and Indiana.

SPEECH DELIVERED AT SPRINGFIELD, ILLINOIS, AT THE CLOSE
OF THE REPUBLICAN STATE CONVENTION, JUNE 16, 1858.

MR. PRESIDENT AND GENTLEMEN OF THE CONVENTION:—If we could first know where we are, and whither we are tending, we could better judge what to do, and how to do it. We are now far into the fifth year since a policy was initiated with the avowed object and confident promise of putting an end to slavery agitation. Under the operation of that policy, that agitation has not only not ceased, but has constantly augmented. In my opinion, it will not cease until a crisis shall have been reached and passed. "A house divided against itself cannot stand." I believe this government cannot endure permanently half slave and half free. I do not expect the Union to be dissolved; I do not expect the house to fall; but I do expect it will cease to be divided. It will become all one thing, or all the other. Either the opponents of slavery will arrest the further spread of it, and place it where the public mind shall rest in the belief that it is in the course of ultimate extinction, or its advocates will push it forward till it shall become alike lawful in all the States, old as well as new, North as well as South.

Have we no tendency to the latter condition? Let any one who doubts, carefully contemplate that now almost complete legal combination-piece of machinery, so to speak compounded of the Nebraska doctrine and the Dred Scott decision. Let him consider, not only what work the machinery is adapted to do, and how well adapted, but also let him study the history of its construction, and trace, if he can, or rather fail, if he can, to trace the evidences of design, and concert of action, among its chief architects, from the beginning.

The new year of 1854 found slavery excluded from more than half the States by State Constitutions, and from most of the National territory by Congressional prohibition. Four days later, commenced the struggle which ended in repealing that Congressional prohibition. This opened all the National territory to slavery, and was the first point gained.

But, so far, Congress only had acted, and an endorsement by the people, real or apparent, was indispensable to save the point already gained, and give chance for more.

This necessity had not been overlooked, but had been provided for, as well as might be, in the notable argument of "squatter sovereignty," otherwise called "sacred right of self-government," which latter phrase, though expressive of the only rightful basis of any government, was so perverted in this attempted use of it as to amount to just this: That if any one man choose to enslave another, no third man shall be allowed to object. That argument was incorporated into the Nebraska Bill itself, in the language which follows: "It being the true intent and meaning of this Act not to legislate slavery into any Territory or State, nor to exclude it therefrom, but to leave the people thereof perfectly free to form and regulate their domestic institutions in their own way, subject only to the Constitution of the United States." Then opened the roar of loose declamation in favor of "squatter sovereignty," and "sacred right of self-government." "But," said opposition members, "let us amend the bill so as to expressly declare that the people of the Territory may exclude slavery." "Not we," said the friends of the measure, and down they voted the amendment.

While the Nebraska Bill was passing through Congress, a law case, involving the question of a negro's freedom, by reason of his owner having voluntarily taken him first into a free State, and then into a territory covered by the Congressional Prohibition, and held him as a slave for a long time in each, was passing through the United States Circuit Court for the District of Missouri; and both Nebraska Bill and lawsuit were brought to a decision in the same month of May, 1854. The negro's name was "Dred Scott," which name now designates the decision finally made in the case. Before the then next Presidential election, the law case came to, and was argued in, the Supreme Court of the United States; but the decision of it was deferred until after the election. Still, before the election, Senator Trumbull, on the floor of the Senate, requested the leading advocate of the Nebraska Bill to state his opinion whether the people of a territory can constitutionally exclude slavery from their limits; and the latter answers: "That is a question for the Supreme Court."

The election came. Mr. Buchanan was elected, and the endorsement, such as it was, secured. That was the second point gained. The endorsement, however, fell short of a clear popular majority by nearly four hundred thousand votes,(approximately 10% of the vote) and so, perhaps, was not overwhelmingly reliable and satisfactory. The outgoing President, in his last annual message, as impressively as possible echoed back upon the people the weight and authority of the endorsement. The Supreme Court met again, did not announce their decision, but ordered a reargument. The Presidential inauguration came, and still no decision of the court; but the incoming President, in his inaugural address, fervently exhorted the people to abide by the forth-coming decision, whatever it might be. Then, in a few days, came the decision.

The reputed author of the Nebraska Bill finds an early occasion to make a speech at this capital indorsing the Dred Scott decision, and vehemently denouncing all opposition to it. The new President, too, seizes the early occasion of the Silliman letter to indorse and strongly construe that decision, and to express his astonishment that any different view had ever been entertained!

At length a squabble springs up between the President and the author of the Nebraska Bill, on the mere question of fact, whether the Lecompton Constitution was or was not in any just sense made by the people of Kansas; and in that quarrel the latter declares that all he wants is a fair vote for the people, and that he cares not whether slavery be voted down or voted up. I do not understand his declaration, that he cares not whether slavery be voted down or voted up, to be intended by him other than as an apt definition of the policy he would impress upon the public mind,—the principle for which he declares he has suffered so much, and is ready to suffer to the end. And well may he cling to that principle! If he has any parental feeling, well may he cling to it. That principle is the only shred left of his original Nebraska doctrine. Under the Dred Scott decision "squatter sovereignty" squatted out of existence, tumbled down like temporary scaffolding; like the mould at the foundry, served through one blast, and fell back into loose sand; helped to carry an election, and then was kicked to the winds. His late joint struggle with the Republicans, against the Lecompton Constitution, involves nothing of the original Nebraska doctrine. That struggle was made on a point—the right of a people to make their own constitution—upon which he and the Republicans have never differed.

The several points of the Dred Scott decision, in connection with Senator Douglas's "care not" policy, constitute the piece of machinery, in its present state of advancement. This was the third point gained. The working points of that machinery are:

Firstly, That no negro slave, imported as such from Africa, and no descendant of such slave, can ever be a citizen of any State, in the sense of that term as used in the Constitution of the United States. This point is made in order to deprive the negro, in every possible event, of the benefit of that provision of the United States Constitution which declares that "The citizens of each State shall be entitled to all privileges and immunities of citizens in the several States."

Secondly, That, "subject to the Constitution of the United States," neither Congress nor a Territorial Legislature can exclude slavery from any United States Territory. This point is made in order that individual men may fill up the Territories with slaves, without danger of losing them as property, and thus to enhance the chances of permanency to the institution through all the future.

Thirdly, That whether the holding a negro in actual slavery in a free State makes him free, as against the holder, the United States courts will not decide, but will leave to be decided by the courts of any slave State the negro may be forced into by the master. This point is made, not to be pressed immediately; but, if acquiesced in for a while, and apparently indorsed by the people at an election, then to sustain the logical conclusion that what Dred Scott's master might lawfully do with Dred Scott, in the free State of Illinois, every other master may lawfully do with any other one, or one thousand slaves, in Illinois, or in any other free State.

Auxiliary to all this, and working hand in hand with it, the Nebraska doctrine, or what is left of it, is to educate and mould public opinion, at least Northern public opinion, not to care whether slavery is voted down or voted up. This shows exactly where we now are; and partially, also, wither we are tending.

It will throw additional light on the latter, to go back and run the mind over the string of historical facts already stated. Several things will now appear less dark and mysterious than they did when they were transpiring. The people were to be left "perfectly free," "subject only to the Constitution." What the Constitution had to do with it, outsiders could not then see. Plainly enough now,—it was an exactly fitted niche, for the Dred Scott decision to afterward come in, and declare the perfect freedom of the people to be just no freedom at all. Why was the amendment, expressly declaring the right of the people, voted down? Plainly enough now,—the adoption of it would have spoiled the niche for the Dred Scott decision. Why was the court decision held up? Why even a Senator's individual opinion withheld, till after the Presidential election? Plainly enough now,—the speaking out then would have damaged the "perfectly free" argument upon which the election was to be carried. Why the outgoing President's felicitation on the endorsement? Why the delay of a reargument? Why the incoming President's advance exhortation in favor of the decision? These things look like the cautious patting and petting of a spirited horse preparatory to mounting him, when it is dreaded that he may give the rider a fall. And why the hasty after-endorsement of the decision by the President and others?

We cannot absolutely know that all these exact adaptations are the result of preconcert. But when we see a lot of framed timbers, different portions of which we know have been gotten out at different times and places and by different workmen, Stephen, Franklin, Roger, and James, for instance, and when we see these timbers joined together, and see they exactly make the frame of a house or a mill, all the tenons and mortises exactly fitting, and all the lengths and proportions of the different pieces exactly adapted to their respective places, and not a piece too many or too few,—not omitting even scaffolding,—or, if a single piece be lacking, we see the place in the frame exactly fitted and prepared yet to bring such piece in,—in such a case, we find it impossible not to believe that Stephen and Franklin and Roger and James all understood one another from the beginning, and all worked upon a common plan or draft drawn up before the first blow was struck.

It should not be overlooked that by the Nebraska Bill the people of a State as well as Territory were to be left "perfectly free," "subject only to the Constitution." Why mention a State? They were legislating for Territories, and not for or about States. Certainly the people of a State are and ought to be subject to the Constitution of the United States; but why is mention of this lugged into this merely Territorial law? Why are the people of a Territory and the people of a State therein lumped together, and their relation to the Constitution therefore treated as being precisely the same? While the opinion of the court, by Chief Justice Taney, in the Dred Scott case, and the separate opinions of all the concurring Judges, expressly declare that the Constitution of the United States neither permits Congress nor a Territorial Legislature to exclude slavery from any United States Territory, they all omit to declare whether or not the same Constitution permits a State, or the people of a State, to exclude it. Possibly, this is a mere omission; but who can be quite sure, if McLean or Curtis had sought to get into the opinion a declaration of unlimited power in the people of a State to exclude slavery from their limits, just as Chase and Mace sought to get such declaration, in behalf of the people of a Territory, into the Nebraska Bill,—I ask, who can be quite sure that it would not have been voted down in the one case as it had been in the other? The nearest approach to the point of declaring the power of a State over slavery is made by Judge Nelson. He approaches it more than once, Using the precise idea, and almost the language, too, of the Nebraska Act. On one occasion, his exact language is, "Except in cases where the power is restrained by the Constitution of the United States, the law of the State is supreme over the subject of slavery within its jurisdiction." In what cases the power of the States is so restrained by the United States Constitution, is left an open question, precisely as the same question, as to the restraint on the power of the Territories, was left open in the Nebraska Act. Put this and that together, and we have another nice little niche, which we may, ere long, see filled with another Supreme Court decision, declaring that the Constitution of the

United States does not permit a State to exclude slavery from its limits. And this may especially be expected if the doctrine of "care not whether slavery be voted down or voted up" shall gain upon the public mind sufficiently to give promise that such a decision can be maintained when made.

Such a decision is all that slavery now lacks of being alike lawful in all the States. Welcome or unwelcome, such decision is probably coming, and will soon be upon us, unless the power of the present political dynasty shall be met and overthrown. We shall lie down pleasantly dreaming that the people of Missouri are on the verge of making their State free, and we shall awake to the reality instead that the Supreme Court has made Illinois a slave State. To meet and overthrow the power of that dynasty is the work now before all those who would prevent that consummation. That is what we have to do. How can we best do it?

There are those who denounce us openly to their friends, and yet whisper to us softly that Senator Douglas is the aptest instrument there is with which to effect that object. They wish us to infer all, from the fact that he now has a little quarrel with the present head of the dynasty, and that he has regularly voted with us on a single point, upon which he and we have never differed. They remind us that he is a great man, and that the largest of us are very small ones. Let this be granted. But "a living dog is better than a dead lion." Judge Douglas, if not a dead lion, for this work is at least a caged and toothless one. How can he oppose the advances of slavery? He don't care anything about it. His avowed mission is impressing the "public heart" to care nothing about it. A leading Douglas Democratic newspaper thinks Douglas's superior talent will be needed to resist the revival of the African slave trade. Does Douglas believe an effort to revive that trade is approaching? He has not said so. Does he really think so? But if it is, how can he resist it? For years he has labored to prove it a sacred right of white men to take negro slaves into the new Territories. Can he possibly show that it is less a sacred right to buy them where they can be bought cheapest? And unquestionably they can be bought cheaper in Africa than in Virginia. He has done all in his power to reduce the whole question of slavery to one of a mere right of property; and, as such, how can he oppose the foreign slave trade, how can he refuse that trade in that "property" shall be "perfectly free,"—unless he does it as a protection to the home production? And as the home producers will probably not ask the protection, he will be wholly without a ground of opposition.

Senator Douglas holds, we know, that a man may rightfully be wiser to-day than he was yesterday; that he may rightfully change when he finds himself wrong. But can we, for that reason, run ahead, and infer that he will make any particular change, of which he himself has given no intimation? Can we safely base our action upon any such vague inference? Now, as ever, I wish not to misrepresent Judge Douglas's position, question his motives, or do aught that can be personally offensive to him. Whenever, if ever, he and we can come together on principle so that our cause may have assistance from his great ability, I hope to have interposed no adventitious obstacles. But clearly he is not now with us; he does not pretend to be,—he does not promise ever to be.

Our cause, then, must be entrusted to, and conducted by, its own undoubted friends,—those whose hands are free, whose hearts are in the work, who do care for the result. Two years ago the Republicans of the nation mustered over thirteen hundred thousand strong. We did this under the single impulse of resistance to a common danger, with every external circumstance against us. Of strange, discordant, and even hostile elements we gathered from the four winds, and formed and fought the battle through, under the constant hot fire of a disciplined, proud, and pampered enemy. Did we brave all then to falter now,— now, when that same enemy is wavering, dissevered, and belligerent? The result is not doubtful. We shall not fail; if we stand firm, we shall not fail. Wise counsels may accelerate, or mistakes delay it, but, sooner or later, the victory is sure to come.

SPEECH AT CHICAGO, ILLINOIS, JULY 10, 1858.

MY FELLOW-CITIZENS:—On yesterday evening, upon the occasion of the reception given to Senator Douglas, I was furnished with a seat very convenient for hearing him, and was otherwise very courteously treated by him and his friends, and for which I thank him and them. During the course of his remarks my name was mentioned in such a way as, I suppose, renders it at least not improper that I should make some sort of reply to him. I shall not attempt to follow him in the precise order in which he addressed the assembled multitude upon that occasion, though I shall perhaps do so in the main.

There was one question to which he asked the attention of the crowd, which I deem of somewhat less importance—at least of propriety—for me to dwell upon than the others, which he brought in near the close of his speech, and which I think it would not be entirely proper for me to omit attending to, and yet if I were not to give some attention to it now, I should probably forget it altogether. While I am upon this subject, allow me to say that I do not intend to indulge in that inconvenient mode sometimes adopted in public speaking, of reading from documents; but I shall depart from that rule so far as to read a little scrap from his speech, which notices this first topic of which I shall speak,—that is, provided I can find it in the paper:

"I have made up my mind to appeal to the people against the combination that has been made against me; the Republican leaders having formed an alliance, an unholy and unnatural alliance, with a portion of unscrupulous Federal office-holders. I intend to fight that allied army wherever I meet them. I know they deny the alliance; but yet these men who are trying to divide the Democratic party for the purpose of electing a Republican Senator in my place are just as much the agents and tools of the supporters of Mr. Lincoln. Hence I shall deal with this allied army just as the Russians dealt with the Allies at Sebastopol,—that is, the Russians did not stop to inquire, when they fired a broadside, whether it hit an Englishman, a Frenchman, or a Turk. Nor will I stop to inquire, nor shall I hesitate, whether my blows shall hit the Republican leaders or their allies, who are holding the Federal offices, and yet acting in concert with them."

Well, now, gentlemen, is not that very alarming? Just to think of it! right at the outset of his canvass, I, a poor, kind, amiable, intelligent gentleman,—I am to be slain in this way! Why, my friend the Judge is not only, as it turns out, not a dead lion, nor even a living one,—he is the rugged Russian Bear!

But if they will have it—for he says that we deny it—that there is any such alliance, as he says there is,—and I don't propose hanging very much upon this question of veracity,—but if he will have it that there is such an alliance, that the Administration men and we are allied, and we stand in the attitude of English, French, and Turk, he occupying the position of the Russian, in that case I beg that he will indulge us while we barely suggest to him that these allies took Sebastopol.

Gentlemen, only a few more words as to this alliance. For my part, I have to say that whether there be such an alliance depends, so far as I know, upon what may be a right definition of the term alliance. If for the Republican party to see the other great party to which they are opposed divided among themselves, and not try to stop the division, and rather be glad of it,—if that is an alliance, I confess I am in; but if it is meant to be said that the Republicans had formed an alliance going beyond that, by which there is contribution of money or sacrifice of principle on the one side or the other, so far as the Republican party is concerned,—if there be any such thing, I protest that I neither know anything of it, nor do I believe it. I will, however, say,—as I think this branch of the argument is lugged in,—I would before I leave it state, for the benefit of those concerned, that one of those same Buchanan men did once tell me of an argument that he made for his opposition to Judge Douglas. He said that a friend of our Senator Douglas had been talking to him, and had, among other things, said to him: "Why, you don't want to beat Douglas?" "Yes," said he, "I do want to beat him, and I will tell you why. I believe his original Nebraska Bill was right in the abstract, but it was wrong in the time that it was brought forward. It was wrong in the application to a Territory in regard to which the question had been settled; it was brought forward at a time when nobody asked him; it was tendered to the South when the South had not asked for it, but when they could not well refuse it; and for this same reason he forced that question upon our party. It has sunk the best men all over the nation, everywhere; and now, when our President, struggling with the difficulties of this man's getting up, has reached the very hardest point to turn in the case, he deserts him and I am for putting him where he will trouble us no more."

Now, gentlemen, that is not my argument; that is not my argument at all. I have only been stating to you the argument of a Buchanan man. You will judge if there is any force in it.

Popular sovereignty! Everlasting popular sovereignty! Let us for a moment inquire into this vast matter of popular sovereignty. What is popular sovereignty? We recollect that at an early period in the history of this struggle there was another name for the same thing,—"squatter sovereignty." It was not exactly popular sovereignty, but squatter sovereignty. What do those terms mean? What do those terms mean when used now? And vast credit is taken by our friend the Judge in regard to his support of it, when he declares the last years of his life have been, and all the future years of his life shall be, devoted to this matter of popular sovereignty. What is it? Why, it is the sovereignty of the people! What was squatter sovereignty? I suppose, if it had any significance at all, it was the right of the people to govern themselves, to be sovereign in their own affairs while they were squatted down in a country not their own, while they had squatted on a Territory that did not belong to them, in the sense that a State belongs to the people who inhabit it, when it belonged to the nation; such right to govern themselves was called "squatter sovereignty."

Now, I wish you to mark: What has become of that squatter sovereignty? what has become of it? Can you get anybody to tell you now that the people of a Territory have any authority to govern themselves, in regard to this mooted question of slavery, before they form a State constitution? No such thing at all; although there is a general running fire, and although there has been a hurrah made in every speech on that side, assuming that policy had given the people of a Territory the right to govern themselves upon this question, yet the point is dodged. To-day it has been decided—no more than a year ago it was decided—by the Supreme Court of the United States, and is insisted upon to-day that the people of a Territory have no right to exclude slavery from a Territory; that if any one man chooses to take slaves into a Territory, all the rest of the people have no right to keep them out. This being so, and this decision being made one of the points that the Judge approved, and one in the approval of which he says he means to keep me down,—put me down I should not say, for I have never been up,—he says he is in favor of it, and sticks to it, and expects to win his battle on that decision, which says that there is no such thing as squatter sovereignty, but that any one man may take slaves into a Territory, and all the other men in the Territory may be opposed to it, and yet by reason of the Constitution they cannot prohibit it. When that is so, how much is left of this vast matter of squatter sovereignty, I should like to know?

When we get back, we get to the point of the right of the people to make a constitution. Kansas was settled, for example, in 1854. It was a Territory yet, without having formed a constitution, in a very regular way, for three years. All this time negro slavery could be taken in by any few individuals, and by that decision of the Supreme Court, which the Judge approves, all the rest of the people cannot keep it out; but when they come to make a constitution, they may say they will not have slavery. But it is there; they are obliged to tolerate it some way, and all experience shows it will be so, for they will not take the negro slaves and absolutely deprive the owners of them. All experience shows this to be so. All that space of time that runs from the beginning of the settlement of the Territory until there is sufficiency of people to make a State constitution,—all that portion of time popular sovereignty is given up. The seal is absolutely put down upon it by the court decision, and Judge Douglas puts his own upon the top of that; yet he is appealing to the people to give him vast credit for his devotion to popular sovereignty.

Again, when we get to the question of the right of the people to form a State constitution as they please, to form it with slavery or without slavery, if that is anything new, I confess I don't know it. Has there ever been a time when anybody said that any other than the people of a Territory itself should form a constitution? What is now in it that Judge Douglas should have fought several years of his life, and pledge himself to fight all the remaining years of his life for? Can Judge Douglas find anybody on earth that said that anybody else should form a constitution for a people? [A voice, "Yes."] Well, I should like you to name him; I should like to know who he was. [Same voice, "John Calhoun."]

No, sir, I never heard of even John Calhoun saying such a thing. He insisted on the same principle as Judge Douglas; but his mode of applying it, in fact, was wrong. It is enough for my purpose to ask this crowd whenever a Republican said anything against it. They never said anything against it, but they have constantly spoken for it; and whoever will undertake to examine the platform, and the speeches of responsible men of the party, and of irresponsible men, too, if you please, will be unable to find one word from anybody in the Republican ranks opposed to that popular sovereignty which Judge Douglas thinks that he has invented. I suppose that Judge Douglas will claim, in a little while, that he is the inventor of the idea that the people should govern themselves; that nobody ever thought of such a thing until he brought it forward. We do not remember that in that old Declaration of Independence it is said that: "We hold these truths to be self-evident, that all men are created equal; that they are endowed by their Creator with certain inalienable rights; that among these are life, liberty, and the pursuit of happiness; that to secure these rights, governments are instituted among men, deriving their just powers from the consent of the governed." There is the origin of popular sovereignty. Who, then, shall come in at this day and claim that he invented it?

The Lecompton Constitution connects itself with this question, for it is in this matter of the Lecompton Constitution that our friend Judge Douglas claims such vast credit. I agree that in opposing the Lecompton Constitution, so far as I can perceive, he was right. I do not deny that at all; and, gentlemen, you will readily see why I could not deny it, even if I wanted to. But I do not wish to; for all the Republicans in the nation opposed it, and they would have opposed it just as much without Judge Douglas's aid as with it. They had all taken ground against it long before he did. Why, the reason that he urges against that constitution I urged against him a year before. I have the printed speech in my hand. The argument that he makes, why that constitution should not be adopted, that the people were not fairly represented nor allowed to vote, I pointed out in a speech a year ago, which I hold in my hand now, that no fair chance was to be given to the people. ["Read it, Read it."] I shall not waste your time by trying to read it. ["Read it, Read it."] Gentlemen, reading from speeches is a very tedious business, particularly for an old man that has to put on spectacles, and more so if the man be so tall that he has to bend over to the light.

A little more, now, as to this matter of popular sovereignty and the Lecompton Constitution. The Lecompton Constitution, as the Judge tells us, was defeated. The defeat of it was a good thing or it was not. He thinks the defeat of it was a good thing, and so do I, and we agree in that. Who defeated it? [A voice: Judge Douglas.] Yes, he furnished himself, and if you suppose he controlled the other Democrats that went with him, he furnished three votes; while the Republicans furnished twenty.

That is what he did to defeat it. In the House of Representatives he and his friends furnished some twenty votes, and the Republicans furnished ninety odd. Now, who was it that did the work? [A voice: Douglas.] Why, yes, Douglas did it! To be sure he did.

Let us, however, put that proposition another way. The Republicans could not have done it without Judge Douglas. Could he have done it without them? Which could have come the nearest to doing it without the other? [A voice: Who killed the bill?] [Another voice: Douglas.] Ground was taken against it by the Republicans long before Douglas did it. The proportion of opposition to that measure is about five to one. [A voice: Why don't they come out on it?] You don't know what you are talking about, my friend. I am quite willing to answer any gentleman in the crowd who asks an intelligent question.

Now, who in all this country has ever found any of our friends of Judge Douglas's way of thinking, and who have acted upon this main question, that has ever thought of uttering a word in behalf of Judge Trumbull? [A voice: We have.] I defy you to show a printed resolution passed in a Democratic meeting—I take it upon myself to defy any man to show a printed resolution of a Democratic meeting, large or small— in favor of Judge Trumbull, or any of the five to one Republicans who beat that bill. Everything must be for the Democrats! They did everything, and the five to the one that really did the thing they snub over, and they do not seem to remember that they have an existence upon the face of the earth.

Gentlemen, I fear that I shall become tedious. I leave this branch of the subject to take hold of another. I take up that part of Judge Douglas's speech in which he respectfully attended to me.

Judge Douglas made two points upon my recent speech at Springfield. He says they are to be the issues of this campaign. The first one of these points he bases upon the language in a speech which I delivered at Springfield, which I believe I can quote correctly from memory. I said there that "we are now far into the fifth year since a policy was instituted for the avowed object, and with the confident promise, of putting an end to slavery agitation; under the operation of that policy, that agitation has not only not ceased, but has constantly augmented." "I believe it will not cease until a crisis shall have been reached and passed. 'A house divided against itself cannot stand.' I believe this government cannot endure permanently half slave and half free." "I do not expect the Union to be dissolved,"—I am quoting from my speech, "—I do not expect the house to fall, but I do expect it will cease to be divided. It will become all one thing or all the other. Either the opponents of slavery will arrest the spread of it and place it where the public mind shall rest in the belief that it is in the course of ultimate extinction, or its advocates will push it forward until it shall become alike lawful in all the States, north as well as south."

That is the paragraph! In this paragraph, which I have quoted in your hearing, and to which I ask the attention of all, Judge Douglas thinks he discovers great political heresy. I want your attention particularly to what he has inferred from it. He says I am in favor of making all the States of this Union uniform in all their internal regulations; that in all their domestic concerns I am in favor of making them entirely uniform. He draws this inference from the language I have quoted to you. He says that I am in favor of making war by the North upon the South for the extinction of slavery; that I am also in favor of inviting (as he expresses it) the South to a war upon the North for the purpose of nationalizing slavery. Now, it is singular enough, if you will carefully read that passage over, that I did not say that I was in favor of anything in it. I only said what I expected would take place. I made a prediction only,—it may have been a foolish one, perhaps. I did not even say that I desired that slavery should be put in course of ultimate extinction. I do say so now, however, so there need be no longer any difficulty about that. It may be written down in the great speech.

Gentlemen, Judge Douglas informed you that this speech of mine was probably carefully prepared. I admit that it was. I am not master of language; I have not a fine education; I am not capable of entering into a disquisition upon dialectics, as I believe you call it; but I do not believe the language I employed bears any such construction as Judge Douglas puts upon it. But I don't care about a quibble in regard to words. I know what I meant, and I will not leave this crowd in doubt, if I can explain it to them, what I really meant in the use of that paragraph.

I am not, in the first place, unaware that this government has endured eighty-two years half slave and half free. I know that. I am tolerably well acquainted with the history of the country, and I know that it has endured eighty-two years half slave and half free. I believe— and that is what I meant to allude to there—I believe it has endured because during all that time, until the introduction of the Nebraska Bill, the public mind did rest all the time in the belief that slavery was in course of ultimate extinction. That was what gave us the rest that we had through that period of eighty-two years,—at least, so I believe. I have always hated slavery, I think, as much as any Abolitionist,—I have been an Old Line Whig,—I have always hated it; but I have always been quiet about it until this new era of the introduction of the Nebraska Bill began. I always believed that everybody was against it, and that it was in course of ultimate extinction. [Pointing to Mr. Browning, who stood near by.] Browning thought so; the great mass of the nation have rested in the belief that slavery was in course of ultimate extinction. They had reason so to believe.

The adoption of the Constitution and its attendant history led the people to believe so; and that such was the belief of the framers of the Constitution itself, why did those old men, about the time of the adoption of the Constitution, decree that slavery should not go into the new Territory, where it had not already gone? Why declare that within twenty years the African slave trade, by which slaves are supplied, might be cut off by Congress? Why were all these acts? I might enumerate more of these acts; but enough. What were they but a clear indication that the framers of the Constitution intended and expected the ultimate extinction of that institution? And now, when I say, as I said in my speech that Judge Douglas has quoted from, when I say that I think the opponents of slavery will resist the farther spread of it, and place it where the public mind shall rest with the belief that it is in course of ultimate extinction, I only mean to say that they will place it where the founders of this government originally placed it.

I have said a hundred times, and I have now no inclination to take it back, that I believe there is no right, and ought to be no inclination, in the people of the free States to enter into the slave States and interfere with the question of slavery at all. I have said that always; Judge Douglas has heard me say it, if not quite a hundred times, at least as good as a hundred times; and when it is said that I am in favor of interfering with slavery where it exists, I know it is unwarranted by anything I have ever intended, and, as I believe, by anything I have ever said. If, by any means, I have ever used language which could fairly be so construed (as, however, I believe I never have), I now correct it.

So much, then, for the inference that Judge Douglas draws, that I am in favor of setting the sections at war with one another. I know that I never meant any such thing, and I believe that no fair mind can infer any such thing from anything I have ever said.

Now, in relation to his inference that I am in favor of a general consolidation of all the local institutions of the various States. I will attend to that for a little while, and try to inquire, if I can, how on earth it could be that any man could draw such an inference from anything I said. I have said, very many times, in Judge Douglas's hearing, that no man believed more than I in the principle of self-government; that it lies at the bottom of all my ideas of just government, from beginning to end. I have denied that his use of that term applies properly. But for the thing itself, I deny that any man has ever gone ahead of me in his devotion to the principle, whatever he may have done in efficiency in advocating it. I think that I have said it in your hearing, that I believe each individual is naturally entitled to do as he pleases with himself and the fruit of his labor, so far as it in no wise interferes with any other man's rights; that each community as a State has a right to do exactly as it pleases with all the concerns within that State that interfere with the right of no other State; and that the General Government, upon principle, has no right to interfere with anything other than that general class of things that does concern the whole. I have said that at all times. I have said, as illustrations, that I do not believe in the right of Illinois to interfere with the cranberry laws of Indiana, the oyster laws of Virginia, or the liquor laws of Maine. I have said these things over and over again, and I repeat them here as my sentiments.

How is it, then, that Judge Douglas infers, because I hope to see slavery put where the public mind shall rest in the belief that it is in the course of ultimate extinction, that I am in favor of Illinois going over and interfering with the cranberry laws of Indiana? What can authorize him to draw any such inference? I suppose there might be one thing that at least enabled him to draw such an inference that would not be true with me or many others: that is, because he looks upon all this matter of slavery as an exceedingly little thing,—this matter of keeping one sixth of the population of the whole nation in a state of oppression and tyranny unequaled in the world. He looks upon it as being an exceedingly little thing,—only equal to the question of the cranberry laws of Indiana; as something having no moral question in it; as something on a par with the question of whether a man shall pasture his land with cattle, or plant it with tobacco; so little and so small a thing that he concludes, if I could desire that anything should be done to bring about the ultimate extinction of that little thing, I must be in favor of bringing about an amalgamation of all the other little things in the Union. Now, it so happens—and there, I presume, is the foundation of this mistake—that the Judge thinks thus; and it so happens that there is a vast portion of the American people that do not look upon that matter as being this very little thing. They look upon it as a vast moral evil; they can prove it as such by the writings of those who gave us the blessings of liberty which we enjoy, and that they so looked upon it, and not as an evil merely confining itself to the States where it is situated; and while we agree that, by the Constitution we assented to, in the States where it exists, we have no right to interfere with it, because it is in the Constitution; and we are by both duty and inclination to stick by that Constitution, in all its letter and spirit, from beginning to end.

So much, then, as to my disposition—my wish to have all the State legislatures blotted out, and to have one consolidated government, and a uniformity of domestic regulations in all the States, by which I suppose it is meant, if we raise corn here, we must make sugar-cane grow here too, and we must make those which grow North grow in the South. All this I suppose he understands I am in favor of doing. Now, so much for all this nonsense; for I must call it so. The Judge can have no issue with me on a question of establishing uniformity in the domestic regulations of the States.

A little now on the other point,—the Dred Scott decision. Another of the issues he says that is to be made with me is upon his devotion to the Dred Scott decision, and my opposition to it.

I have expressed heretofore, and I now repeat, my opposition to the Dred Scott decision; but I should be allowed to state the nature of that opposition, and I ask your indulgence while I do so. What is fairly implied by the term Judge Douglas has used, "resistance to the decision"? I do not resist it. If I wanted to take Dred Scott from his master, I would be interfering with property, and that terrible difficulty that Judge Douglas speaks of, of interfering with property, would arise. But I am doing no such thing as that, but all that I am doing is refusing to obey it as a political rule. If I were in Congress, and a vote should come up on a question whether slavery should be prohibited in a new Territory, in spite of the Dred Scott decision, I would vote that it should.

That is what I should do. Judge Douglas said last night that before the decision he might advance his opinion, and it might be contrary to the decision when it was made; but after it was made he would abide by it until it was reversed. Just so! We let this property abide by the decision, but we will try to reverse that decision. We will try to put it where Judge Douglas would not object, for he says he will obey it until it is reversed. Somebody has to reverse that decision, since it is made, and we mean to reverse it, and we mean to do it peaceably.

What are the uses of decisions of courts? They have two uses. As rules of property they have two uses. First, they decide upon the question before the court. They decide in this case that Dred Scott is a slave. Nobody resists that, not only that, but they say to everybody else that persons standing just as Dred Scott stands are as he is. That is, they say that when a question comes up upon another person, it will be so decided again, unless the court decides in another way, unless the court overrules its decision. Well, we mean to do what we can to have the court decide the other way. That is one thing we mean to try to do.

The sacredness that Judge Douglas throws around this decision is a degree of sacredness that has never been before thrown around any other decision. I have never heard of such a thing. Why, decisions apparently contrary to that decision, or that good lawyers thought were contrary to that decision, have been made by that very court before. It is the first of its kind; it is an astonisher in legal history. It is a new wonder of the world. It is based upon falsehood in the main as to the facts; allegations of facts upon which it stands are not facts at all in many instances, and no decision made on any question—the first instance of a decision made under so many unfavorable circumstances—thus placed, has ever been held by the profession as law, and it has always needed confirmation before the lawyers regarded it as settled law. But Judge Douglas will have it that all hands must take this extraordinary decision, made under these extraordinary circumstances, and give their vote in Congress in accordance with it, yield to it, and obey it in every possible sense. Circumstances alter cases. Do not gentlemen here remember the case of that same Supreme Court some twenty-five or thirty years ago deciding that a National Bank was constitutional? I ask, if somebody does not remember that a National Bank was declared to be constitutional? Such is the truth, whether it be remembered or not. The Bank charter ran out, and a recharter was granted by Congress. That recharter was laid before General Jackson. It was urged upon him, when he denied the constitutionality of the Bank, that the Supreme Court had decided that it was constitutional; and General Jackson then said that the Supreme Court had no right to lay down a rule to govern a coordinate branch of the government, the members of which had sworn to support the Constitution; that each member had sworn to support that Constitution as he understood it. I will venture here to say that I have heard Judge Douglas say that he approved of General Jackson for that act. What has now become of all his tirade about "resistance of the Supreme Court"?

My fellow-citizens, getting back a little,—for I pass from these points,—when Judge Douglas makes his threat of annihilation upon the "alliance," he is cautious to say that that warfare of his is to fall upon the leaders of the Republican party. Almost every word he utters, and every distinction he makes, has its significance. He means for the Republicans who do not count themselves as leaders, to be his friends; he makes no fuss over them; it is the leaders that he is making war upon. He wants it understood that the mass of the Republican party are really his friends. It is only the leaders that are doing something that are intolerant, and that require extermination at his hands. As this is dearly and unquestionably the light in which he presents that matter, I want to ask your attention, addressing myself to the Republicans here, that I may ask you some questions as to where you, as the Republican party, would be placed if you sustained Judge Douglas in his present position by a re-election? I do not claim, gentlemen, to be unselfish; I do not pretend that I would not like to go to the United States Senate,—I make no such hypocritical pretense; but I do say to you that in this mighty issue it is nothing to you—nothing to the mass of the people of the nation,—whether or not Judge Douglas or myself shall ever be heard of after this night; it may be a trifle to either of us, but in connection with this mighty question, upon which hang the destinies of the nation, perhaps, it is absolutely nothing: but where will you be placed if you re-endorse Judge Douglas? Don't you know how apt he is, how exceedingly anxious he is at all times, to seize upon anything and everything to persuade you that something he has done you did yourselves? Why, he tried to persuade you last night that our Illinois Legislature instructed him to introduce the Nebraska Bill. There was nobody in that Legislature ever thought of such a thing; and when he first introduced the bill, he never thought of it; but still he fights furiously for the proposition, and that he did it because there was a standing instruction to our Senators to be always introducing Nebraska bills. He tells you he is for the Cincinnati platform, he tells you he is for the Dred Scott decision. He tells you, not in his speech last night, but substantially in a former speech, that he cares not if slavery is voted up or down; he tells you the struggle on Lecompton is past; it may come up again or not, and if it does, he stands where he stood when, in spite of him and his opposition, you built up the Republican party. If you indorse him, you tell him you do not care whether slavery be voted up or down, and he will close or try to close your mouths with his declaration, repeated by the day, the week, the month, and the year. Is that what you mean? [Cries of "No," one voice "Yes."] Yes, I have no doubt you who have always been for him, if you mean that. No doubt of that, soberly I have said, and I repeat it. I think, in the position in which Judge Douglas stood in opposing the Lecompton Constitution, he was right; he does not know that it will return, but if it does we may know where to find him, and if it does not, we may know where to look for him, and that is on the Cincinnati platform. Now, I could ask the Republican party, after all the hard names that Judge Douglas has called them by all his repeated charges of their inclination to marry with and hug negroes; all his declarations of Black Republicanism,—by the way, we are improving, the black has got rubbed off,—but with all that, if he be indorsed by Republican votes, where do you stand? Plainly, you stand ready saddled, bridled, and harnessed, and waiting to be driven over to the slavery extension camp of the nation,—just ready to be driven over, tied together in a lot, to be driven over, every man with a rope around his neck, that halter being held by Judge Douglas. That is the question. If Republican men have been in earnest in what they have done, I think they had better not do it; but I think that the Republican party is made up of those who, as far as they can peaceably, will oppose the extension of slavery, and who will hope for its ultimate extinction. If they believe it is wrong in grasping up the new lands of the continent and keeping them from the settlement of free white laborers, who want the land to bring up their families upon; if they are in earnest, although they may make a mistake, they will grow restless, and the time will come when they will come back again and reorganize, if not by the same name, at least upon the same principles as their party now has. It is better, then, to save the work while it is begun. You have done the labor; maintain it, keep it. If men choose to serve you, go with them; but as you have made up your organization upon principle, stand by it; for, as surely as God reigns over you, and has inspired your mind, and given you a sense of propriety, and continues to give you hope, so surely will you still cling to these ideas, and you will at last come back again after your wanderings, merely to do your work over again.

We were often,—more than once, at least,—in the course of Judge Douglas's speech last night, reminded that this government was made for white men; that he believed it was made for white men. Well, that is putting it into a shape in which no one wants to deny it; but the Judge then goes into his passion for drawing inferences that are not warranted. I protest, now and forever, against that counterfeit logic which presumes that because I did not want a negro woman for a slave,

I do necessarily want her for a wife. My understanding is that I need not have her for either, but, as God made us separate, we can leave one another alone, and do one another much good thereby. There are white men enough to marry all the white women, and enough black men to marry all the black women; and in God's name let them be so married. The Judge regales us with the terrible enormities that take place by the mixture of races; that the inferior race bears the superior down. Why, Judge, if we do not let them get together in the Territories, they won't mix there. [A voice: "Three cheers for Lincoln".—The cheers were given with a hearty good-will.] I should say at least that that is a self-evident truth.

Now, it happens that we meet together once every year, sometimes about the 4th of July, for some reason or other. These 4th of July gatherings I suppose have their uses. If you will indulge me, I will state what I suppose to be some of them.

We are now a mighty nation; we are thirty or about thirty millions of people, and we own and inhabit about one fifteenth part of the dry land of the whole earth. We run our memory back over the pages of history for about eighty-two years, and we discover that we were then a very small people in point of numbers, vastly inferior to what we are now, with a vastly less extent of country, with vastly less of everything we deem desirable among men; we look upon the change as exceedingly advantageous to us and to our posterity, and we fix upon something that happened away back, as in some way or other being connected with this rise of prosperity. We find a race of men living in that day whom we claim as our fathers and grandfathers; they were iron men; they fought for the principle that they were contending for; and we understood that by what they then did it has followed that the degree of prosperity which we now enjoy has come to us. We hold this annual celebration to remind ourselves of all the good done in this process of time, of how it was done and who did it, and how we are historically connected with it; and we go from these meetings in better humor with ourselves, we feel more attached the one to the other, and more firmly bound to the country we inhabit. In every way we are better men in the age and race and country in which we live, for these celebrations. But after we have done all this we have not yet reached the whole. There is something else connected with it. We have— besides these, men descended by blood from our ancestors—among us perhaps half our people who are not descendants at all of these men; they are men who have come from Europe, German, Irish, French, and Scandinavian,—men that have come from Europe themselves, or whose ancestors have come hither and settled here, finding themselves our equals in all things. If they look back through this history to trace their connection with those days by blood, they find they have none, they cannot carry themselves back into that glorious epoch and make themselves feel that they are part of us; but when they look through that old Declaration of Independence, they find that those old men say that "We hold these truths to be self-evident, that all men are created equal"; and then they feel that that moral sentiment, taught in that day, evidences their relation to those men, that it is the father of all moral principle in them, and that they have a right to claim it as though they were blood of the blood, and flesh of the flesh, of the men who wrote that Declaration; and so they are. That is the electric cord in that Declaration that Clinks the hearts of patriotic and liberty-loving men together, that will link those patriotic hearts as long as the love of freedom exists in the minds of men throughout the world.

Now, sirs, for the purpose of squaring things with this idea of "don't care if slavery is voted up or voted down," for sustaining the Dred Scott decision, for holding that the Declaration of Independence did not mean anything at all, we have Judge Douglas giving his exposition of what the Declaration of Independence means, and we have him saying that the people of America are equal to the people of England. According to his construction, you Germans are not connected with it. Now, I ask you in all soberness if all these things, if indulged in, if ratified, if confirmed and indorsed, if taught to our children, and repeated to them, do not tend to rub out the sentiment of liberty in the country, and to transform this government into a government of some other form. Those arguments that are made, that the inferior race are to be treated with as much allowance as they are capable of enjoying; that as much is to be done for them as their condition will allow,—what are these arguments? They are the arguments that kings have made for enslaving the people in all ages of the world. You will find that all the arguments in favor of kingcraft were of this class; they always bestrode the necks of the people not that they wanted to do it, but because the people were better off for being ridden. That is their argument, and this argument of the Judge is the same old serpent that says, You work, and I eat; you toil, and I will enjoy the fruits of it. Turn in whatever way you will, whether it come from the mouth of a king, an excuse for enslaving the people of his country, or from the mouth of men of one race as a reason for enslaving the men of another race, it is all the same old serpent; and I hold, if that course of argumentation that is made for the purpose of convincing the public mind that we should not care about this should be granted, it does not stop with the negro. I should like to know, if taking this old Declaration of Independence, which declares that all men are equal upon principle, and making exceptions to it, where will it stop? If one man says it does not mean a negro, why not another say it does not mean some other man? If that Declaration is not the truth, let us get the statute book, in which we find it, and tear it out! Who is so bold as to do it? If it is not true, let us tear it out! [Cries of "No, no."] Let us stick to it, then; let us stand firmly by it, then.

It may be argued that there are certain conditions that make necessities and impose them upon us; and to the extent that a necessity is imposed upon a man, he must submit to it. I think that was the condition in which we found ourselves when we established this government. We had slavery among us, we could not get our Constitution unless we permitted them to remain in slavery, we could not secure the good we did secure if we grasped for more; and having by necessity submitted to that much, it does not destroy the principle that is the charter of our liberties. Let that charter stand as our standard.

My friend has said to me that I am a poor hand to quote Scripture. I will try it again, however. It is said in one of the admonitions of our Lord, "As your Father in heaven is perfect, be ye also perfect." The Savior, I suppose, did not expect that any human creature could be perfect as the Father in heaven; but he said, "As your Father in heaven is perfect, be ye also perfect." He set that up as a standard; and he who did most towards reaching that standard attained the highest degree of moral perfection. So I say in relation to the principle that all men are created equal, let it be as nearly reached as we can. If we cannot give freedom to every creature, let us do nothing that will impose slavery upon any other creature. Let us then turn this government back into the channel in which the framers of the Constitution originally placed it. Let us stand firmly by each other. If we do not do so, we are turning in the contrary direction, that our friend Judge Douglas proposes—not intentionally—as working in the traces tends to make this one universal slave nation. He is one that runs in that direction, and as such I resist him.

My friends, I have detained you about as long as I desired to do, and I have only to say: Let us discard all this quibbling about this man and the other man, this race and that race and the other race being inferior, and therefore they must be placed in an inferior position; discarding our standard that we have left us. Let us discard all these things, and unite as one people throughout this land, until we shall once more stand up declaring that all men are created equal.

My friends, I could not, without launching off upon some new topic, which would detain you too long, continue to-night. I thank you for this most extensive audience that you have furnished me to-night. I leave you, hoping that the lamp of liberty will burn in your bosoms until there shall no longer be a doubt that all men are created free and equal.

SPEECH AT LEWISTON, ILLINOIS, AUGUST 17, 1858.

"The Declaration of Independence was formed by the representatives of American liberty from thirteen States of the confederacy—twelve of which were slaveholding communities. We need not discuss the way or the reason of their becoming slaveholding communities. It is sufficient for our purpose that all of them greatly deplored the evil and that they placed a provision in the Constitution which they supposed would gradually remove the disease by cutting off its source. This was the abolition of the slave trade. So general was conviction—the public determination—to abolish the African slave trade, that the provision which I have referred to as being placed in the Constitution, declared that it should not be abolished prior to the year 1808. A constitutional provision was necessary to prevent the people, through Congress, from putting a stop to the traffic immediately at the close of the war. Now, if slavery had been a good thing, would the Fathers of the Republic have taken a step calculated to diminish its beneficent influences among themselves, and snatch the boon wholly from their posterity? These communities, by their representatives in old Independence Hall, said to the whole world of men: "We hold these truths to be self evident: that all men are created equal; that they are endowed by their Creator with certain unalienable rights; that among these are life, liberty and the pursuit of happiness." This was their majestic interpretation of the economy of the Universe. This was their lofty, and wise, and noble understanding of the justice of the Creator to His creatures. Yes, gentlemen, to all His creatures, to the whole great family of man. In their enlightened belief, nothing stamped with the Divine image and likeness was sent into the world to be trodden on, and degraded, and imbruted by its fellows. They grasped not only the whole race of man then living, but they reached forward and seized upon the farthest posterity. They erected a beacon to guide their children and their children's children, and the countless myriads who should inhabit the earth in other ages. Wise statesmen as they were, they knew the tendency of prosperity to breed tyrants, and so they established these great self-evident truths, that when in the distant future some man, some faction, some interest, should set up the doctrine that none but rich men, or none but white men, were entitled to life, liberty and the pursuit of happiness, their posterity might look up again to the Declaration of Independence and take courage to renew the battle which their fathers began—so that truth, and justice, and mercy, and all the humane and Christian virtues might not be extinguished from the land; so that no man would hereafter dare to limit and circumscribe the great principles on which the temple of liberty was being built.

"Now, my countrymen, if you have been taught doctrines conflicting with the great landmarks of the Declaration of Independence; if you have listened to suggestions which would take away from its grandeur, and mutilate the fair symmetry of its proportions; if you have been inclined to believe that all men are not created equal in those inalienable rights enumerated by our chart of liberty, let me entreat you to come back. Return to the fountain whose waters spring close by the blood of the Revolution. Think nothing of me—take no thought for the political fate of any man whomsoever—but come back to the truths that are in the Declaration of Independence. "You may do anything with me you choose, if you will but heed these sacred principles. You may not only defeat me for the Senate, but you may take me and put me to death. While pretending no indifference to earthly honors, I do claim to be actuated in this contest by something higher than an anxiety for office. I charge you to drop every paltry and insignificant thought for any man's success. It is nothing; I am nothing; Judge Douglas is nothing. But do not destroy that immortal emblem of Humanity, the Declaration of American Independence."

FIFTH DEBATE WITH STEPHEN A. DOUGLAS,
GALESBURG, ILLINOIS, OCTOBER 7, 1858.

Mr. Lincoln's Reply in the Galesburg Joint Debate.

MY FELLOW-CITIZENS: A very large portion of the speech which Judge Douglas has addressed to you has previously been delivered and put in print. I do not mean that for a hit upon the Judge at all.—If I had not been interrupted, I was going to say that such an answer as I was able to make to a very large portion of it had already been more than once made and published. There has been an opportunity afforded to the public to see our respective views upon the topics discussed in a large portion of the speech which he has just delivered. I make these remarks for the purpose of excusing myself for not passing over the entire ground that the Judge has traversed. I however desire to take up some of the points that he has attended to, and ask your attention to them, and I shall follow him backwards upon some notes which I have taken, reversing the order, by beginning where he concluded.

The Judge has alluded to the Declaration of Independence, and insisted that negroes are not included in that Declaration; and that it is a slander upon the framers of that instrument to suppose that negroes were meant therein; and he asks you: Is it possible to believe that Mr. Jefferson, who penned the immortal paper, could have supposed himself applying the language of that instrument to the negro race, and yet held a portion of that race in slavery? Would he not at once have freed them? I only have to remark upon this part of the Judge's speech (and that, too, very briefly, for I shall not detain myself, or you, upon that point for any great length of time), that I believe the entire records of the world, from the date of the Declaration of Independence up to within three years ago, may be searched in vain for one single affirmation, from one single man, that the negro was not included in the Declaration of Independence; I think I may defy Judge Douglas to show that he ever said so, that Washington ever said so, that any President ever said so, that any member of Congress ever said so, or that any living man upon the whole earth ever said so, until the necessities of the present policy of the Democratic party, in regard to slavery, had to invent that affirmation. And I will remind Judge Douglas and this audience that while Mr. Jefferson was the owner of slaves, as undoubtedly he was, in speaking upon this very subject he used the strong language that "he trembled for his country when he remembered that God was just"; and I will offer the highest premium in my power to Judge Douglas if he will show that he, in all his life, ever uttered a sentiment at all akin to that of Jefferson.

The next thing to which I will ask your attention is the Judge's comments upon the fact, as he assumes it to be, that we cannot call our public meetings as Republican meetings; and he instances Tazewell County as one of the places where the friends of Lincoln have called a public meeting and have not dared to name it a Republican meeting. He instances Monroe County as another, where Judge Trumbull and Jehu Baker addressed the persons whom the Judge assumes to be the friends of Lincoln calling them the "Free Democracy." I have the honor to inform Judge Douglas that he spoke in that very county of Tazewell last Saturday, and I was there on Tuesday last; and when he spoke there, he spoke under a call not venturing to use the word "Democrat." [Turning to Judge Douglas.] what think you of this?

So, again, there is another thing to which I would ask the Judge's attention upon this subject. In the contest of 1856 his party delighted to call themselves together as the "National Democracy"; but now, if there should be a notice put up anywhere for a meeting of the "National Democracy," Judge Douglas and his friends would not come. They would not suppose themselves invited. They would understand that it was a call for those hateful postmasters whom he talks about.

Now a few words in regard to these extracts from speeches of mine which Judge Douglas has read to you, and which he supposes are in very great contrast to each other. Those speeches have been before the public for a considerable time, and if they have any inconsistency in them, if there is any conflict in them, the public have been able to detect it. When the Judge says, in speaking on this subject, that I make speeches of one sort for the people of the northern end of the State, and of a different sort for the southern people, he assumes that I do not understand that my speeches will be put in print and read north and south. I knew all the while that the speech that I made at Chicago, and the one I made at Jonesboro and the one at Charleston, would all be put in print, and all the reading and intelligent men in the community would see them and know all about my opinions. And I have not supposed, and do not now suppose, that there is any conflict whatever between them. But the Judge will have it that if we do not confess that there is a sort of inequality between the white and black races which justifies us in making them slaves, we must then insist that there is a degree of equality that requires us to make them our wives. Now, I have all the while taken a broad distinction in regard to that matter; and that is all there is in these different speeches which he arrays here; and the entire reading of either of the speeches will show that that distinction was made. Perhaps by taking two parts of the same speech he could have got up as much of a conflict as the one he has found. I have all the while maintained that in so far as it should be insisted that there was an equality between the white and black races that should produce a perfect social and political equality, it was an impossibility. This you have seen in my printed speeches, and with it I have said that in their right to "life, liberty, and the pursuit of happiness," as proclaimed in that old Declaration, the inferior races are our equals. And these declarations I have constantly made in reference to the abstract moral question, to contemplate and consider when we are legislating about any new country which is not already cursed with the actual presence of the evil,—slavery. I have never manifested any impatience with the necessities that spring from the actual presence of black people amongst us, and the actual existence of slavery amongst us where it does already exist; but I have insisted that, in legislating for new countries where it does not exist there is no just rule other than that of moral and abstract right! With reference to those new countries, those maxims as to the right of a people to "life, liberty, and the pursuit of happiness" were the just rules to be constantly referred to. There is no misunderstanding this, except by men interested to misunderstand it. I take it that I have to address an intelligent and reading community, who will peruse what I say, weigh it, and then judge whether I advanced improper or unsound views, or whether I advanced hypocritical, and deceptive, and contrary views in different portions of the country. I believe myself to be guilty of no such thing as the latter, though, of course, I cannot claim that I am entirely free from all error in the opinions I advance.

The Judge has also detained us awhile in regard to the distinction between his party and our party. His he assumes to be a national party, ours a sectional one. He does this in asking the question whether this country has any interest in the maintenance of the Republican party. He assumes that our party is altogether sectional, that the party to which he adheres is national; and the argument is, that no party can be a rightful party—and be based upon rightful principles—unless it can announce its principles everywhere. I presume that Judge Douglas could not go into Russia and announce the doctrine of our national Democracy; he could not denounce the doctrine of kings and emperors and monarchies in Russia; and it may be true of this country that in some places we may not be able to proclaim a doctrine as clearly true as the truth of democracy, because there is a section so directly opposed to it that they will not tolerate us in doing so. Is it the true test of the soundness of a doctrine that in some places people won't let you proclaim it? Is that the way to test the truth of any doctrine? Why, I understood that at one time the people of Chicago would not let Judge Douglas preach a certain favorite doctrine of his. I commend to his consideration the question whether he takes that as a test of the unsoundness of what he wanted to preach.

There is another thing to which I wish to ask attention for a little while on this occasion. What has always been the evidence brought forward to prove that the Republican party is a sectional party? The main one was that in the Southern portion of the Union the people did not let the Republicans proclaim their doctrines amongst them. That has been the main evidence brought forward,—that they had no supporters, or substantially none, in the Slave States. The South have not taken hold of our principles as we announce them; nor does Judge Douglas now grapple with those principles. We have a Republican State Platform, laid down in Springfield in June last stating our position all the way through the questions before the country. We are now far advanced in this canvass. Judge Douglas and I have made perhaps forty speeches apiece, and we have now for the fifth time met face to face in debate, and up to this day I have not found either Judge Douglas or any friend of his taking hold of the Republican platform, or laying his finger upon anything in it that is wrong. I ask you all to recollect that. Judge Douglas turns away from the platform of principles to the fact that he can find people somewhere who will not allow us to announce those principles. If he had great confidence that our principles were wrong, he would take hold of them and demonstrate them to be wrong. But he does not do so. The only evidence he has of their being wrong is in the fact that there are people who won't allow us to preach them. I ask again, is that the way to test the soundness of a doctrine?

I ask his attention also to the fact that by the rule of nationality he is himself fast becoming sectional. I ask his attention to the fact that his speeches would not go as current now south of the Ohio River as they have formerly gone there I ask his attention to the fact that he felicitates himself to-day that all the Democrats of the free States are agreeing with him, while he omits to tell us that the Democrats of any slave State agree with him. If he has not thought of this, I commend to his consideration the evidence in his own declaration, on this day, of his becoming sectional too. I see it rapidly approaching. Whatever may be the result of this ephemeral contest between Judge Douglas and myself, I see the day rapidly approaching when his pill of sectionalism, which he has been thrusting down the throats of Republicans for years past, will be crowded down his own throat.

Now, in regard to what Judge Douglas said (in the beginning of his speech) about the Compromise of 1850 containing the principles of the Nebraska Bill, although I have often presented my views upon that subject, yet as I have not done so in this canvass, I will, if you please, detain you a little with them. I have always maintained, so far as I was able, that there was nothing of the principle of the Nebraska Bill in the Compromise of 1850 at all,—nothing whatever. Where can you find the principle of the Nebraska Bill in that Compromise? If anywhere, in the two pieces of the Compromise organizing the Territories of New Mexico and Utah. It was expressly provided in these two acts that when they came to be admitted into the Union they should be admitted with or without slavery, as they should choose, by their own constitutions. Nothing was said in either of those acts as to what was to be done in relation to slavery during the Territorial existence of those Territories, while Henry Clay constantly made the declaration (Judge Douglas recognizing him as a leader) that, in his opinion, the old Mexican laws would control that question during the Territorial existence, and that these old Mexican laws excluded slavery. How can that be used as a principle for declaring that during the Territorial existence as well as at the time of framing the constitution the people, if you please, might have slaves if they wanted them? I am not discussing the question whether it is right or wrong; but how are the New Mexican and Utah laws patterns for the Nebraska Bill? I maintain that the organization of Utah and New Mexico did not establish a general principle at all. It had no feature of establishing a general principle. The acts to which I have referred were a part of a general system of Compromises. They did not lay down what was proposed as a regular policy for the Territories, only an agreement in this particular case to do in that way, because other things were done that were to be a compensation for it. They were allowed to come in in that shape, because in another way it was paid for, considering that as a part of that system of measures called the Compromise of 1850, which finally included half-a-dozen acts. It included the admission of California as a free State, which was kept out of the Union for half a year because it had formed a free constitution. It included the settlement of the boundary of Texas, which had been undefined before, which was in itself a slavery question; for if you pushed the line farther west, you made Texas larger, and made more slave territory; while, if you drew the line toward the east, you narrowed the boundary and diminished the domain of slavery, and by so much increased free territory. It included the abolition of the slave trade in the District of Columbia. It included the passage of a new Fugitive Slave law. All these things were put together, and, though passed in separate acts, were nevertheless, in legislation (as the speeches at the time will show), made to depend upon each other. Each got votes with the understanding that the other measures were to pass, and by this system of compromise, in that series of measures, those two bills—the New Mexico and Utah bills—were passed: and I say for that reason they could not be taken as models, framed upon their own intrinsic principle, for all future Territories. And I have the evidence of this in the fact that Judge Douglas, a year afterward, or more than a year afterward, perhaps, when he first introduced bills for the purpose of framing new Territories, did not attempt to follow these bills of New Mexico and Utah; and even when he introduced this Nebraska Bill, I think you will discover that he did not exactly follow them. But I do not wish to dwell at great length upon this branch of the discussion. My own opinion is, that a thorough investigation will show most plainly that the New Mexico and Utah bills were part of a system of compromise, and not designed as patterns for future Territorial legislation; and that this Nebraska Bill did not follow them as a pattern at all.

The Judge tells, in proceeding, that he is opposed to making any odious distinctions between free and slave States. I am altogether unaware that the Republicans are in favor of making any odious distinctions between the free and slave States. But there is still a difference, I think, between Judge Douglas and the Republicans in this. I suppose that the real difference between Judge Douglas and his friends, and the Republicans on the contrary, is, that the Judge is not in favor of making any difference between slavery and liberty; that he is in favor of eradicating, of pressing out of view, the questions of preference in this country for free or slave institutions; and consequently every sentiment he utters discards the idea that there is any wrong in slavery. Everything that emanates from him or his coadjutors in their course of policy carefully excludes the thought that there is anything wrong in slavery. All their arguments, if you will consider them, will be seen to exclude the thought that there is anything whatever wrong in slavery. If you will take the Judge's speeches, and select the short and pointed sentences expressed by him,—as his declaration that he "don't care whether slavery is voted up or down,"—you will see at once that this is perfectly logical, if you do not admit that slavery is wrong. If you do admit that it is wrong, Judge Douglas cannot logically say he don't care whether a wrong is voted up or voted down. Judge Douglas declares that if any community wants slavery they have a right to have it. He can say that logically, if he says that there is no wrong in slavery; but if you admit that there is a wrong in it, he cannot logically say that anybody has a right to do wrong. He insists that upon the score of equality the owners of slaves and owners of property—of horses and every other sort of property—should be alike, and hold them alike in a new Territory. That is perfectly logical if the two species of property are alike and are equally founded in right. But if you admit that one of them is wrong, you cannot institute any equality between right and wrong. And from this difference of sentiment,—the belief on the part of one that the institution is wrong, and a policy springing from that belief which looks to the arrest of the enlargement of that wrong, and this other sentiment, that it is no wrong, and a policy sprung from that sentiment, which will tolerate no idea of preventing the wrong from growing larger, and looks to there never being an end to it through all the existence of things,—arises the real difference between Judge Douglas and his friends on the one hand and the Republicans on the other. Now, I confess myself as belonging to that class in the country who contemplate slavery as a moral, social, and political evil, having due regard for its actual existence amongst us and the difficulties of getting rid of it in any satisfactory way, and to all the constitutional obligations which have been thrown about it; but, nevertheless, desire a policy that looks to the prevention of it as a wrong, and looks hopefully to the time when as a wrong it may come to an end.

Judge Douglas has again, for, I believe, the fifth time, if not the seventh, in my presence, reiterated his charge of a conspiracy or combination between the National Democrats and Republicans. What evidence Judge Douglas has upon this subject I know not, inasmuch as he never favors us with any. I have said upon a former occasion, and I do not choose to suppress it now, that I have no objection to the division in the Judge's party. He got it up himself. It was all his and their work. He had, I think, a great deal more to do with the steps that led to the Lecompton Constitution than Mr. Buchanan had; though at last, when they reached it, they quarreled over it, and their friends divided upon it. I am very free to confess to Judge Douglas that I have no objection to the division; but I defy the Judge to show any evidence that I have in any way promoted that division, unless he insists on being a witness himself in merely saying so. I can give all fair friends of Judge Douglas here to understand exactly the view that Republicans take in regard to that division. Don't you remember how two years ago the opponents of the Democratic party were divided between Fremont and Fillmore? I guess you do. Any Democrat who remembers that division will remember also that he was at the time very glad of it, and then he will be able to see all there is between the National Democrats and the Republicans. What we now think of the two divisions of Democrats, you then thought of the Fremont and Fillmore divisions. That is all there is of it.

But if the Judge continues to put forward the declaration that there is an unholy and unnatural alliance between the Republicans and the National Democrats, I now want to enter my protest against receiving him as an entirely competent witness upon that subject. I want to call to the Judge's attention an attack he made upon me in the first one of these debates, at Ottawa, on the 21st of August. In order to fix extreme Abolitionism upon me, Judge Douglas read a set of resolutions which he declared had been passed by a Republican State Convention, in October, 1854, at Springfield, Illinois, and he declared I had taken part in that Convention. It turned out that although a few men calling themselves an anti-Nebraska State Convention had sat at Springfield about that time, yet neither did I take any part in it, nor did it pass the resolutions or any such resolutions as Judge Douglas read. So apparent had it become that the resolutions which he read had not been passed at Springfield at all, nor by a State Convention in which I had taken part, that seven days afterward, at Freeport, Judge Douglas declared that he had been misled by Charles H. Lanphier, editor of the State Register, and Thomas L. Harris, member of Congress in that district, and he promised in that speech that when he went to Springfield he would investigate the matter. Since then Judge Douglas has been to Springfield, and I presume has made the investigation; but a month has passed since he has been there, and, so far as I know, he has made no report of the result of his investigation. I have waited as I think sufficient time for the report of that investigation, and I have some curiosity to see and hear it. A fraud, an absolute forgery was committed, and the perpetration of it was traced to the three,— Lanphier, Harris, and Douglas. Whether it can be narrowed in any way so as to exonerate any one of them, is what Judge Douglas's report would probably show.

It is true that the set of resolutions read by Judge Douglas were published in the Illinois State Register on the 16th of October, 1854, as being the resolutions of an anti-Nebraska Convention which had sat in that same month of October, at Springfield. But it is also true that the publication in the Register was a forgery then, and the question is still behind, which of the three, if not all of them, committed that forgery. The idea that it was done by mistake is absurd. The article in the Illinois State Register contains part of the real proceedings of that Springfield Convention, showing that the writer of the article had the real proceedings before him, and purposely threw out the genuine resolutions passed by the Convention and fraudulently substituted the others. Lanphier then, as now, was the editor of the Register, so that there seems to be but little room for his escape. But then it is to be borne in mind that Lanphier had less interest in the object of that forgery than either of the other two. The main object of that forgery at that time was to beat Yates and elect Harris to Congress, and that object was known to be exceedingly dear to Judge Douglas at that time. Harris and Douglas were both in Springfield when the Convention was in session, and although they both left before the fraud appeared in the Register, subsequent events show that they have both had their eyes fixed upon that Convention.

The fraud having been apparently successful upon the occasion, both Harris and Douglas have more than once since then been attempting to put it to new uses. As the fisherman's wife, whose drowned husband was brought home with his body full of eels, said when she was asked what was to be done with him, "Take the eels out and set him again," so Harris and Douglas have shown a disposition to take the eels out of that stale fraud by which they gained Harris's election, and set the fraud again more than once. On the 9th of July, 1856, Douglas attempted a repetition of it upon Trumbull on the floor of the Senate of the United States, as will appear from the appendix of the Congressional Globe of that date. On the 9th of August, Harris attempted it again upon Norton in the House of Representatives, as will appear by the same documents,—the appendix to the Congressional Globe of that date. On the 21st of August last, all three—Lanphier, Douglas, and Harris—reattempted it upon me at Ottawa. It has been clung to and played out again and again as an exceedingly high trump by this blessed trio. And now that it has been discovered publicly to be a fraud we find that Judge Douglas manifests no surprise at it at all. He makes no complaint of Lanphier, who must have known it to be a fraud from the beginning. He, Lanphier, and Harris are just as cozy now and just as active in the concoction of new schemes as they were before the general discovery of this fraud. Now, all this is very natural if they are all alike guilty in that fraud, and it is very unnatural if any one of them is innocent. Lanphier perhaps insists that the rule of honor among thieves does not quite require him to take all upon himself, and consequently my friend Judge Douglas finds it difficult to make a satisfactory report upon his investigation. But meanwhile the three are agreed that each is "a most honorable man."

Judge Douglas requires an endorsement of his truth and honor by a re-election to the United States Senate, and he makes and reports against me and against Judge Trumbull, day after day, charges which we know to be utterly untrue, without for a moment seeming to think that this one unexplained fraud, which he promised to investigate, will be the least drawback to his claim to belief. Harris ditto. He asks a re-election to the lower House of Congress without seeming to remember at all that he is involved in this dishonorable fraud! The Illinois State Register, edited by Lanphier, then, as now, the central organ of both Harris and Douglas, continues to din the public ear with this assertion, without seeming to suspect that these assertions are at all lacking in title to belief.

After all, the question still recurs upon us, How did that fraud originally get into the State Register? Lanphier then, as now, was the editor of that paper. Lanphier knows. Lanphier cannot be ignorant of how and by whom it was originally concocted. Can he be induced to tell, or, if he has told, can Judge Douglas be induced to tell how it originally was concocted? It may be true that Lanphier insists that the two men for whose benefit it was originally devised shall at least bear their share of it! How that is, I do not know, and while it remains unexplained I hope to be pardoned if I insist that the mere fact of Judge Douglas making charges against Trumbull and myself is not quite sufficient evidence to establish them!

While we were at Freeport, in one of these joint discussions, I answered certain interrogatories which Judge Douglas had propounded to me, and then in turn propounded some to him, which he in a sort of way answered. The third one of these interrogatories I have with me, and wish now to make some comments upon it. It was in these words: "If the Supreme Court of States cannot exclude slavery from their limits, are you in favor of acquiescing in, adhering to, and following such decision as a rule of political action?"

To this interrogatory Judge Douglas made no answer in any just sense of the word. He contented himself with sneering at the thought that it was possible for the Supreme Court ever to make such a decision. He sneered at me for propounding the interrogatory. I had not propounded it without some reflection, and I wish now to address to this audience some remarks upon it.

In the second clause of the sixth article, I believe it is, of the Constitution of the United States, we find the following language: "This Constitution and the laws of the United States which shall be made in pursuance thereof, and all treaties made, or which shall be made, under the authority of the United States, shall be the supreme law of the land; and the judges in every State shall be bound thereby, anything in the Constitution or laws of any State to the contrary notwithstanding."

The essence of the Dred Scott case is compressed into the sentence which I will now read: "Now, as we have already said in an earlier part of this opinion, upon a different point, the right of property in a slave is distinctly and expressly affirmed in the Constitution." I repeat it, "The right of property in a slave is distinctly and expressly affirmed in the Constitution"! What is it to be "affirmed" in the Constitution? Made firm in the Constitution, so made that it cannot be separated from the Constitution without breaking the Constitution; durable as the Constitution, and part of the Constitution. Now, remembering the provision of the Constitution which I have read—affirming that that instrument is the supreme law of the land; that the judges of every State shall be bound by it, any law or constitution of any State to the contrary notwithstanding; that the right of property in a slave is affirmed in that

Constitution, is made, formed into, and cannot be separated from it without breaking it; durable as the instrument; part of the instrument;— what follows as a short and even syllogistic argument from it? I think it follows, and I submit to the consideration of men capable of arguing whether, as I state it, in syllogistic form, the argument has any fault in it:

Nothing in the Constitution or laws of any State can destroy a right distinctly and expressly affirmed in the Constitution of the United States.

The right of property in a slave is distinctly and expressly affirmed in the Constitution of the United States.

Therefore, nothing in the Constitution or laws of any State can destroy the right of property in a slave.

I believe that no fault can be pointed out in that argument; assuming the truth of the premises, the conclusion, so far as I have capacity at all to understand it, follows inevitably. There is a fault in it as I think, but the fault is not in the reasoning; but the falsehood in fact is a fault of the premises. I believe that the right of property in a slave is not distinctly and expressly affirmed in the Constitution, and Judge Douglas thinks it is. I believe that the Supreme Court and the advocates of that decision may search in vain for the place in the Constitution where the right of property in a slave is distinctly and expressly affirmed I say, therefore, that I think one of the premises is not true in fact. But it is true with Judge Douglas. It is true with the Supreme Court who pronounced it. They are estopped from denying it, and being estopped from denying it, the conclusion follows that, the Constitution of the United States being the supreme law, no constitution or law can interfere with it. It being affirmed in the decision that the right of property in a slave is distinctly and expressly affirmed in the Constitution, the conclusion inevitably follows that no State law or constitution can destroy that right. I then say to Judge Douglas and to all others that I think it will take a better answer than a sneer to show that those who have said that the right of property in a slave is distinctly and expressly affirmed in the Constitution, are not prepared to show that no constitution or law can destroy that right. I say I believe it will take a far better argument than a mere sneer to show to the minds of intelligent men that whoever has so said is not prepared, whenever public sentiment is so far advanced as to justify it, to say the other.

This is but an opinion, and the opinion of one very humble man; but it is my opinion that the Dred Scott decision, as it is, never would have been made in its present form if the party that made it had not been sustained previously by the elections. My own opinion is, that the new Dred Scott decision, deciding against the right of the people of the States to exclude slavery, will never be made if that party is not sustained by the elections. I believe, further, that it is just as sure to be made as to-morrow is to come, if that party shall be sustained. I have said, upon a former occasion, and I repeat it now, that the course of argument that Judge Douglas makes use of upon this subject (I charge not his motives in this), is preparing the public mind for that new Dred Scott decision. I have asked him again to point out to me the reasons for his first adherence to the Dred Scott decision as it is. I have turned his attention to the fact that General Jackson differed with him in regard to the political obligation of a Supreme Court decision. I have asked his attention to the fact that Jefferson differed with him in regard to the political obligation of a Supreme Court decision. Jefferson said that "Judges are as honest as other men, and not more so." And he said, substantially, that whenever a free people should give up in absolute submission to any department of government, retaining for themselves no appeal from it, their liberties were gone. I have asked his attention to the fact that the Cincinnati platform, upon which he says he stands, disregards a time-honored decision of the Supreme Court, in denying the power of Congress to establish a National Bank. I have asked his attention to the fact that he himself was one of the most active instruments at one time in breaking down the Supreme Court of the State of Illinois because it had made a decision distasteful to him,—a struggle ending in the remarkable circumstance of his sitting down as one of the new Judges who were to overslaugh that decision; getting his title of Judge in that very way.

So far in this controversy I can get no answer at all from Judge Douglas upon these subjects. Not one can I get from him, except that he swells himself up and says, "All of us who stand by the decision of the Supreme Court are the friends of the Constitution; all you fellows that dare question it in any way are the enemies of the Constitution." Now, in this very devoted adherence to this decision, in opposition to all the great political leaders whom he has recognized as leaders, in opposition to his former self and history, there is something very marked. And the manner in which he adheres to it,—not as being right upon the merits, as he conceives (because he did not discuss that at all), but as being absolutely obligatory upon every one simply because of the source from whence it comes, as that which no man can gainsay, whatever it may be,—this is another marked feature of his adherence to that decision. It marks it in this respect, that it commits him to the next decision, whenever it comes, as being as obligatory as this one, since he does not investigate it, and won't inquire whether this opinion is right or wrong. So he takes the next one without inquiring whether it is right or wrong. He teaches men this doctrine, and in so doing prepares the public mind to take the next decision when it comes, without any inquiry. In this I think I argue fairly (without questioning motives at all) that Judge Douglas is most ingeniously and powerfully preparing the public mind to take that decision when it comes; and not only so, but he is doing it in various other ways. In these general maxims about liberty, in his assertions that he "don't care whether slavery is voted up or voted down,"; that "whoever wants slavery has a right to have it"; that "upon principles of equality it should be allowed to go everywhere"; that "there is no inconsistency between free and slave institutions"—in this he is also preparing (whether purposely or not) the way for making the institution of slavery national! I repeat again, for I wish no misunderstanding, that I do not charge that he means it so; but I call upon your minds to inquire, if you were going to get the best instrument you could, and then set it to work in the most ingenious way, to prepare the public mind for this movement, operating in the free States, where there is now an abhorrence of the institution of slavery, could you find an instrument so capable of doing it as Judge Douglas, or one employed in so apt a way to do it?

I have said once before, and I will repeat it now, that Mr. Clay, when he was once answering an objection to the Colonization Society, that it had a tendency to the ultimate emancipation of the slaves, said that: "Those who would repress all tendencies to liberty and ultimate emancipation must do more than put down the benevolent efforts of the Colonization Society: they must go back to the era of our liberty and independence, and muzzle the cannon that thunders its annual joyous return; they must blow out the moral lights around us; they must penetrate the human soul, and eradicate the light of reason and the love of liberty!" And I do think—I repeat, though I said it on a former occasion—that Judge Douglas and whoever, like him, teaches that the negro has no share, humble though it may be, in the Declaration of Independence, is going back to the era of our liberty and independence, and, so far as in him lies, muzzling the cannon that thunders its annual joyous return; that he is blowing out the moral lights around us, when he contends that whoever wants slaves has a right to hold them; that he is penetrating, so far as lies in his power, the human soul, and eradicating the light of reason and the love of liberty, when he is in every possible way preparing the public mind, by his vast influence, for making the institution of slavery perpetual and national.

There is, my friends, only one other point to which I will call your attention for the remaining time that I have left me, and perhaps I shall not occupy the entire time that I have, as that one point may not take me clear through it.

Among the interrogatories that Judge Douglas propounded to me at Freeport, there was one in about this language: "Are you opposed to the acquisition of any further territory to the United States, unless slavery shall first be prohibited therein?" I answered, as I thought, in this way: that I am not generally opposed to the acquisition of additional territory, and that I would support a proposition for the acquisition of additional territory according as my supporting it was or was not calculated to aggravate this slavery question amongst us. I then proposed to Judge Douglas another interrogatory, which was correlative to that: "Are you in favor of acquiring additional territory, in disregard of how it may affect us upon the slavery question?" Judge Douglas answered,—that is, in his own way he answered it. I believe that, although he took a good many words to answer it, it was a little more fully answered than any other. The substance of his answer was that this country would continue to expand; that it would need additional territory; that it was as absurd to suppose that we could continue upon our present territory, enlarging in population as we are, as it would be to hoop a boy twelve years of age, and expect him to grow to man's size without bursting the hoops. I believe it was something like that. Consequently, he was in favor of the acquisition of further territory as fast as we might need it, in disregard of how it might affect the slavery question. I do not say this as giving his exact language, but he said so substantially; and he would leave the question of slavery, where the territory was acquired, to be settled by the people of the acquired territory. ["That's the doctrine."] May be it is; let us consider that for a while. This will probably, in the run of things, become one of the concrete manifestations of this slavery question. If Judge Douglas's policy upon this question succeeds, and gets fairly settled down, until all opposition is crushed out, the next thing will be a grab for the territory of poor Mexico, an invasion of the rich lands of South America, then the adjoining islands will follow, each one of which promises additional slave-fields. And this question is to be left to the people of those countries for settlement. When we get Mexico, I don't know whether the Judge will be in favor of the Mexican people that we get with it settling that question for themselves and all others; because we know the Judge has a great horror for mongrels, and I understand that the people of Mexico are most decidedly a race of mongrels. I understand that there is not more than one person there out of eight who is pure white, and I suppose from the Judge's previous declaration that when we get Mexico, or any considerable portion of it, that he will be in favor of these mongrels settling the question, which would bring him somewhat into collision with his horror of an inferior race.

It is to be remembered, though, that this power of acquiring additional territory is a power confided to the President and the Senate of the United States. It is a power not under the control of the representatives of the people any further than they, the President and the Senate, can be considered the representatives of the people. Let me illustrate that by a case we have in our history. When we acquired the territory from Mexico in the Mexican War, the House of Representatives, composed of the immediate representatives of the people, all the time insisted that the territory thus to be acquired should be brought in upon condition that slavery should be forever prohibited therein, upon the terms and in the language that slavery had been prohibited from coming into this country. That was insisted upon constantly and never failed to call forth an assurance that any territory thus acquired should have that prohibition in it, so far as the House of Representatives was concerned. But at last the President and Senate acquired the territory without asking the House of Representatives anything about it, and took it without that prohibition. They have the power of acquiring territory without the immediate representatives of the people being called upon to say anything about it, and thus furnishing a very apt and powerful means of bringing new territory into the Union, and, when it is once brought into the country, involving us anew in this slavery agitation. It is therefore, as I think, a very important question for due consideration of the American people, whether the policy of bringing in additional territory, without considering at all how it will operate upon the safety of the Union in reference to this one great disturbing element in our national politics, shall be adopted as the policy of the country. You will bear in mind that it is to be acquired, according to the Judge's view, as fast as it is needed, and the indefinite part of this proposition is that we have only Judge Douglas and his class of men to decide how fast it is needed. We have no clear and certain way of determining or demonstrating how fast territory is needed by the necessities of the country. Whoever wants to go out filibustering, then, thinks that more territory is needed. Whoever wants wider slave-fields feels sure that some additional territory is needed as slave territory. Then it is as easy to show the necessity of additional slave-territory as it is to assert anything that is incapable of absolute demonstration. Whatever motive a man or a set of men may have for making annexation of property or territory, it is very easy to assert, but much less easy to disprove, that it is necessary for the wants of the country.

And now it only remains for me to say that I think it is a very grave question for the people of this Union to consider, whether, in view of the fact that this slavery question has been the only one that has ever endangered our Republican institutions, the only one that has ever threatened or menaced a dissolution of the Union, that has ever disturbed us in such a way as to make us fear for the perpetuity of our liberty,—in view of these facts, I think it is an exceedingly interesting and important question for this people to consider whether we shall engage in the policy of acquiring additional territory, discarding altogether from our consideration, while obtaining new territory, the question how it may affect us in regard to this, the only endangering element to our liberties and national greatness. The Judge's view has been expressed. I, in my answer to his question, have expressed mine. I think it will become an important and practical question. Our views are before the public. I am willing and anxious that they should consider them fully; that they should turn it about and consider the importance of the question, and arrive at a just conclusion as to whether it is or is not wise in the people of this Union, in the acquisition of new territory, to consider whether it will add to the disturbance that is existing amongst us—whether it will add to the one only danger that has ever threatened the perpetuity of the Union or our own liberties. I think it is extremely important that they shall decide, and rightly decide, that question before entering upon that policy.

And now, my friends, having said the little I wish to say upon this head, whether I have occupied the whole of the remnant of my time or not, I believe I could not enter upon any new topic so as to treat it fully, without transcending my time, which I would not for a moment think of doing. I give way to Judge Douglas.

SIXTH DEBATE WITH STEPHEN A. DOUGLAS, QUINCY, ILLINOIS, OCTOBER 13, 1858.

LADIES AND GENTLEMEN: I have had no immediate conference with Judge Douglas, but I will venture to say that he and I will perfectly agree that your entire silence, both when I speak and when he speaks, will be most agreeable to us.

In the month of May, 1856, the elements in the State of Illinois which have since been consolidated into the Republican party assembled together in a State Convention at Bloomington. They adopted at that time what, in political language, is called a platform. In June of the same year the elements of the Republican party in the nation assembled together in a National Convention at Philadelphia. They adopted what is called the National Platform. In June, 1858,—the present year,—the Republicans of Illinois reassembled at Springfield, in State Convention, and adopted again their platform, as I suppose not differing in any essential particular from either of the former ones, but perhaps adding something in relation to the new developments of political progress in the country.

The Convention that assembled in June last did me the honor, if it be one, and I esteem it such, to nominate me as their candidate for the United States Senate. I have supposed that, in entering upon this canvass, I stood generally upon these platforms. We are now met together on the 13th of October of the same year, only four months from the adoption of the last platform, and I am unaware that in this canvass, from the beginning until to-day, any one of our adversaries has taken hold of our platforms, or laid his finger upon anything that he calls wrong in them.

In the very first one of these joint discussions between Senator Douglas and myself, Senator Douglas, without alluding at all to these platforms, or any one of them, of which I have spoken, attempted to hold me responsible for a set of resolutions passed long before the meeting of either one of these conventions of which I have spoken. And as a ground for holding me responsible for these resolutions, he assumed that they had been passed at a State Convention of the Republican party, and that I took part in that Convention. It was discovered afterward that this was erroneous, that the resolutions which he endeavored to hold me responsible for had not been passed by any State Convention anywhere, had not been passed at Springfield, where he supposed they had, or assumed that they had, and that they had been passed in no convention in which I had taken part. The Judge, nevertheless, was not willing to give up the point that he was endeavoring to make upon me, and he therefore thought to still hold me to the point that he was endeavoring to make, by showing that the resolutions that he read had been passed at a local convention in the northern part of the State, although it was not a local convention that embraced my residence at all, nor one that reached, as I suppose, nearer than one hundred and fifty or two hundred miles of where I was when it met, nor one in which I took any part at all. He also introduced other resolutions, passed at other meetings, and by combining the whole, although they were all antecedent to the two State Conventions and the one National Convention I have mentioned, still he insisted, and now insists, as I understand, that I am in some way responsible for them.

At Jonesboro, on our third meeting, I insisted to the Judge that I was in no way rightfully held responsible for the proceedings of this local meeting or convention, in which I had taken no part, and in which I was in no way embraced; but I insisted to him that if he thought I was responsible for every man or every set of men everywhere, who happen to be my friends, the rule ought to work both ways, and he ought to be responsible for the acts and resolutions of all men or sets of men who were or are now his supporters and friends, and gave him a pretty long string of resolutions, passed by men who are now his friends, and announcing doctrines for which he does not desire to be held responsible.

This still does not satisfy Judge Douglas. He still adheres to his proposition, that I am responsible for what some of my friends in different parts of the State have done, but that he is not responsible for what his have done. At least, so I understand him. But in addition to that, the Judge, at our meeting in Galesburg, last week, undertakes to establish that I am guilty of a species of double dealing with the public; that I make speeches of a certain sort in the north, among the Abolitionists, which I would not make in the south, and that I make speeches of a certain sort in the south which I would not make in the north. I apprehend, in the course I have marked out for myself, that I shall not have to dwell at very great length upon this subject.

As this was done in the Judge's opening speech at Galesburg, I had an opportunity, as I had the middle speech then, of saying something in answer to it. He brought forward a quotation or two from a speech of mine delivered at Chicago, and then, to contrast with it, he brought forward an extract from a speech of mine at Charleston, in which he insisted that I was greatly inconsistent, and insisted that his conclusion followed, that I was playing a double part, and speaking in one region one way, and in another region another way. I have not time now to dwell on this as long as I would like, and wish only now to requote that portion of my speech at Charleston which the Judge quoted, and then make some comments upon it. This he quotes from me as being delivered at Charleston, and I believe correctly:

"I will say, then, that I am not, nor ever have been, in favor of bringing about in any way the social and political equality of the white and black races; that I am not, nor ever have been, in favor of making voters or jurors of negroes, nor of qualifying them to hold office, nor to intermarry with white people; and I will say, in addition to this, that there is a physical difference between the white and black races which will forever forbid the two races living together on terms of social and political equality. And inasmuch as they cannot so live while they do remain together, there must be the position of superior and inferior. I am as much as any other man in favor of having the superior position assigned to the white race."

This, I believe, is the entire quotation from Charleston speech, as Judge Douglas made it his comments are as follows:

"Yes, here you find men who hurrah for Lincoln, and say he is right when he discards all distinction between races, or when he declares that he discards the doctrine that there is such a thing as a superior and inferior race; and Abolitionists are required and expected to vote for Mr. Lincoln because he goes for the equality of races, holding that in the Declaration of Independence the white man and negro were declared equal, and endowed by divine law with equality. And down South, with the old-line Whigs, with the Kentuckians, the Virginians and the Tennesseeans, he tells you that there is a physical difference between the races, making the one superior, the other inferior, and he is in favor of maintaining the superiority of the white race over the negro."

Those are the Judges comments. Now, I wish to show you that a month, or only lacking three days of a month, before I made the speech at Charleston, which the Judge quotes from, he had himself heard me say substantially the same thing It was in our first meeting, at Ottawa—

and I will say a word about where it was, and the atmosphere it was in, after a while—but at our first meeting, at Ottawa, I read an extract from an old speech of mine, made nearly four years ago, not merely to show my sentiments, but to show that my sentiments were long entertained and openly expressed; in which extract I expressly declared that my own feelings would not admit a social and political equality between the white and black races, and that even if my own feelings would admit of it, I still knew that the public sentiment of the country would not, and that such a thing was an utter impossibility, or substantially that. That extract from my old speech the reporters by some sort of accident passed over, and it was not reported. I lay no blame upon anybody. I suppose they thought that I would hand it over to them, and dropped reporting while I was giving it, but afterward went away without getting it from me. At the end of that quotation from my old speech, which I read at Ottawa, I made the comments which were reported at that time, and which I will now read, and ask you to notice how very nearly they are the same as Judge Douglas says were delivered by me down in Egypt. After reading, I added these words:

"Now, gentlemen, I don't want to read at any great length; but this is the true complexion of all I have ever said in regard to the institution of slavery or the black race, and this is the whole of it: anything that argues me into his idea of perfect social and political equality with the negro, is but a specious and fantastical arrangement of words by which a man can prove a horse-chestnut to be a chestnut horse. I will say here, while upon this subject, that I have no purpose, directly or indirectly, to interfere with the institution in the States where it exists. I believe I have no right to do so. I have no inclination to do so. I have no purpose to introduce political and social equality between the white and black races. There is a physical difference between the two which, in my judgment, will probably forever forbid their living together on the footing of perfect equality; and inasmuch as it becomes a necessity that there must be a difference, I, as well as Judge Douglas, am in favor of the race to which I belong having the superior position. I have never said anything to the contrary, but I hold that, notwithstanding all this, there is no reason in the world why the negro is not entitled to all the rights enumerated in the Declaration of Independence,—the right of life, liberty, and the pursuit of happiness. I hold that he is as much entitled to these as the white man. I agree with Judge Douglas that he is not my equal in many respects, certainly not in color, perhaps not in intellectual and moral endowments; but in the right to eat the bread, without the leave of anybody else, which his own hand earns, he is my equal and the equal of Judge Douglas, and the equal of every other man."

I have chiefly introduced this for the purpose of meeting the Judge's charge that the quotation he took from my Charleston speech was what I would say down South among the Kentuckians, the Virginians, etc., but would not say in the regions in which was supposed to be more of the Abolition element. I now make this comment: That speech from which I have now read the quotation, and which is there given correctly—perhaps too much so for good taste—was made away up North in the Abolition District of this State par excellence, in the Lovejoy District, in the personal presence of Lovejoy, for he was on the stand with us when I made it. It had been made and put in print in that region only three days less than a month before the speech made at Charleston, the like of which Judge Douglas thinks I would not make where there was any Abolition element. I only refer to this matter to say that I am altogether unconscious of having attempted any double-dealing anywhere; that upon one occasion I may say one thing, and leave other things unsaid, and *vice versa*, but that I have said anything on one occasion that is inconsistent with what I have said elsewhere, I deny, at least I deny it so far as the intention is concerned. I find that I have devoted to this topic a larger portion of my time than I had intended. I wished to show, but I will pass it upon this occasion, that in the sentiment I have occasionally advanced upon the Declaration of Independence I am entirely borne out by the sentiments advanced by our old Whig leader, Henry Clay, and I have the book here to show it from but because I have already occupied more time than I intended to do on that topic, I pass over it.

At Galesburg, I tried to show that by the Dred Scott decision, pushed to its legitimate consequences, slavery would be established in all the States as well as in the Territories. I did this because, upon a former occasion, I had asked Judge Douglas whether, if the Supreme Court should make a decision declaring that the States had not the power to exclude slavery from their limits, he would adopt and follow that decision as a rule of political action; and because he had not directly answered that question, but had merely contented himself with sneering at it, I again introduced it, and tried to show that the conclusion that I stated followed inevitably and logically from the proposition already decided by the court. Judge Douglas had the privilege of replying to me at Galesburg, and again he gave me no direct answer as to whether he would or would not sustain such a decision if made. I give him his third chance to say yes or no. He is not obliged to do either, probably he will not do either; but I give him the third chance. I tried to show then that this result, this conclusion, inevitably followed from the point already decided by the court. The Judge, in his reply, again sneers at the thought of the court making any such decision, and in the course of his remarks upon this subject uses the language which I will now read. Speaking of me, the Judge says:

"He goes on and insists that the Dred Scott decision would carry slavery into the free States, notwithstanding the decision itself says the contrary." And he adds: "Mr. Lincoln knows that there is no member of the Supreme Court that holds that doctrine. He knows that every one of them in their opinions held the reverse."

I especially introduce this subject again for the purpose of saying that I have the Dred Scott decision here, and I will thank Judge Douglas to lay his finger upon the place in the entire opinions of the court where any one of them "says the contrary." It is very hard to affirm a negative with entire confidence. I say, however, that I have examined that decision with a good deal of care, as a lawyer examines a decision and, so far as I have been able to do so, the court has nowhere in its opinions said that the States have the power to exclude slavery, nor have they used other language substantially that, I also say, so far as I can find, not one of the concurring judges has said that the States can exclude slavery, nor said anything that was substantially that. The nearest approach that any one of them has made to it, so far as I can find, was by Judge Nelson, and the approach he made to it was exactly, in substance, the Nebraska Bill,—that the States had the exclusive power over the question of slavery, so far as they are not limited by the Constitution of the United States. I asked the question, therefore, if the non-concurring judges, McLean or Curtis, had asked to get an express declaration that the States could absolutely exclude slavery from their limits, what reason have we to believe that it would not have been voted down by the majority of the judges, just as Chase's amendment was voted down by Judge Douglas and his compeers when it was offered to the Nebraska Bill.

Also, at Galesburg, I said something in regard to those Springfield resolutions that Judge Douglas had attempted to use upon me at Ottawa, and commented at some length upon the fact that they were, as presented, not genuine. Judge Douglas in his reply to me seemed to be somewhat exasperated. He said he would never have believed that Abraham Lincoln, as he kindly called me, would have attempted such a thing as I had attempted upon that occasion; and among other expressions which he used toward me, was that I dared to say forgery, that I had dared to say forgery [turning to Judge Douglas]. Yes, Judge, I did dare to say forgery. But in this political canvass the Judge ought to remember that I was not the first who dared to say forgery. At Jacksonville, Judge Douglas made a speech in answer to something said by Judge Trumbull, and at the close of what he said upon that subject, he dared to say that Trumbull had forged his evidence. He said, too, that he should not concern himself with Trumbull any more, but thereafter he should hold Lincoln responsible for the slanders upon him. When I met him at Charleston after that, although I think that I should not have noticed the subject if he had not said he would hold me responsible for it, I spread out before him the statements of the evidence that Judge Trumbull had used, and I asked Judge Douglas, piece by piece, to put his finger upon one piece of all that evidence that he would say was a forgery! When I went through with each and every piece, Judge Douglas did not dare then to say that any piece of it was a forgery. So it seems that there are some things that Judge Douglas dares to do, and some that he dares not to do. [A voice: It is the same thing with you.] Yes, sir, it is the same thing with me. I do dare to say forgery when it is true, and don't dare to say forgery when it is false. Now I will say here to this audience and to Judge Douglas I have not dared to say he committed a forgery, and I never shall until I know it; but I did dare to say—just to suggest to the Judge—that a forgery had been committed, which by his own showing had been traced to him and two of his friends. I dared to suggest to him that he had expressly promised in one of his public speeches to investigate that matter, and I dared to suggest to him that there was an implied promise that when he investigated it he would make known the result. I dared to suggest to the Judge that he could not expect to be quite clear of suspicion of that fraud, for since the time that promise was made he had been with those friends, and had not kept his promise in regard to the investigation and the report upon it. I am not a very daring man, but I dared that much, Judge, and I am not much scared about it yet. When the Judge says he would n't have believed of Abraham Lincoln that he would have made such an attempt as that he reminds me of the fact that he entered upon this canvass with the purpose to treat me courteously; that touched me somewhat. It sets me to thinking. I was aware, when it was first agreed that Judge Douglas and I were to have these seven joint discussions, that they were the successive acts of a drama, perhaps I should say, to be enacted, not merely in the face of audiences like this, but in the face of the nation, and to some extent, by my relation to him, and not from anything in myself, in the face of the world; and I am anxious that they should be conducted with dignity and in the good temper which would be befitting the vast audiences before which it was conducted. But when Judge Douglas got home from Washington and made his first speech in Chicago, the evening afterward I made some sort of a reply to it. His second speech was made at Bloomington, in which he commented upon my speech at Chicago and said that I had used language ingeniously contrived to conceal my intentions, or words to that effect. Now, I understand that this is an imputation upon my veracity and my candor. I do not know what the Judge understood by it, but in our first discussion, at Ottawa, he led off by charging a bargain, somewhat corrupt in its character, upon Trumbull and myself,—that we had entered into a bargain, one of the terms of which was that Trumbull was to Abolitionize the old Democratic party, and I (Lincoln) was to Abolitionize the old Whig party; I pretending to be as good an old-line

Whig as ever. Judge Douglas may not understand that he implicated my truthfulness and my honor when he said I was doing one thing and pretending another; and I misunderstood him if he thought he was treating me in a dignified way, as a man of honor and truth, as he now claims he was disposed to treat me. Even after that time, at Galesburg, when he brings forward an extract from a speech made at Chicago and an extract from a speech made at Charleston, to prove that I was trying to play a double part, that I was trying to cheat the public, and get votes upon one set of principles at one place, and upon another set of principles at another place,—I do not understand but what he impeaches my honor, my veracity, and my candor; and because he does this, I do not understand that I am bound, if I see a truthful ground for it, to keep my hands off of him. As soon as I learned that Judge Douglas was disposed to treat me in this way, I signified in one of my speeches that I should be driven to draw upon whatever of humble resources I might have,—to adopt a new course with him. I was not entirely sure that I should be able to hold my own with him, but I at least had the purpose made to do as well as I could upon him; and now I say that I will not be the first to cry "Hold." I think it originated with the Judge, and when he quits, I probably will. But I shall not ask any favors at all. He asks me, or he asks the audience, if I wish to push this matter to the point of personal difficulty. I tell him, no. He did not make a mistake, in one of his early speeches, when he called me an "amiable" man, though perhaps he did when he called me an "intelligent" man. It really hurts me very much to suppose that I have wronged anybody on earth. I again tell him, no! I very much prefer, when this canvass shall be over, however it may result, that we at least part without any bitter recollections of personal difficulties.

The Judge, in his concluding speech at Galesburg, says that I was pushing this matter to a personal difficulty, to avoid the responsibility for the enormity of my principles. I say to the Judge and this audience, now, that I will again state our principles, as well as I hastily can, in all their enormity, and if the Judge hereafter chooses to confine himself to a war upon these principles, he will probably not find me departing from the same course.

We have in this nation this element of domestic slavery. It is a matter of absolute certainty that it is a disturbing element. It is the opinion of all the great men who have expressed an opinion upon it, that it is a dangerous element. We keep up a controversy in regard to it. That controversy necessarily springs from difference of opinion; and if we can learn exactly—can reduce to the lowest elements—what that difference of opinion is, we perhaps shall be better prepared for discussing the different systems of policy that we would propose in regard to that disturbing element. I suggest that the difference of opinion, reduced to its lowest of terms, is no other than the difference between the men who think slavery a wrong and those who do not think it wrong. The Republican party think it wrong; we think it is a moral, a social, and a political wrong. We think it as a wrong not confining itself merely to the persons or the States where it exists, but that it is a wrong in its tendency, to say the least, that extends itself to the existence of the whole nation. Because we think it wrong, we propose a course of policy that shall deal with it as a wrong. We deal with it as with any other wrong, in so far as we can prevent its growing any larger, and so deal with it that in the run of time there may be some promise of an end to it. We have a due regard to the actual presence of it amongst us, and the difficulties of getting rid of it in any satisfactory way, and all the constitutional obligations thrown about it. I suppose that in reference both to its actual existence in the nation, and to our constitutional obligations, we have no right at all to disturb it in the States where it exists, and we profess that we have no more inclination to disturb it than we have the right to do it. We go further than that: we don't propose to disturb it where, in one instance, we think the Constitution would permit us. We think the Constitution would permit us to disturb it in the District of Columbia. Still, we do not propose to do that, unless it should be in terms which I don't suppose the nation is very likely soon to agree to,—the terms of making the emancipation gradual, and compensating the unwilling owners. Where we suppose we have the constitutional right, we restrain ourselves in reference to the actual existence of the institution and the difficulties thrown about it. We also oppose it as an evil so far as it seeks to spread itself. We insist on the policy that shall restrict it to its present limits. We don't suppose that in doing this we violate anything due to the actual presence of the institution, or anything due to the constitutional guaranties thrown around it.

We oppose the Dred Scott decision in a certain way, upon which I ought perhaps to address you a few words. We do not propose that when Dred Scott has been decided to be a slave by the court, we, as a mob, will decide him to be free. We do not propose that, when any other one, or one thousand, shall be decided by that court to be slaves, we will in any violent way disturb the rights of property thus settled; but we nevertheless do oppose that decision as a political rule which shall be binding on the voter to vote for nobody who thinks it wrong, which shall be binding on the members of Congress or the President to favor no measure that does not actually concur with the principles of that decision. We do not propose to be bound by it as a political rule in that way, because we think it lays the foundation, not merely of enlarging and spreading out what we consider an evil, but it lays the foundation for spreading that evil into the States themselves. We propose so resisting it as to have it reversed if we can, and a new judicial rule established upon this subject.

I will add this: that if there be any man who does not believe that slavery is wrong in the three aspects which I have mentioned, or in any one of them, that man is misplaced, and ought to leave us; while on the other hand, if there be any man in the Republican party who is impatient over the necessity springing from its actual presence, and is impatient of the constitutional guaranties thrown around it, and would act in disregard of these, he too is misplaced, standing with us. He will find his place somewhere else; for we have a due regard, so far as we are capable of understanding them, for all these things. This, gentlemen, as well as I can give it, is a plain statement of our principles in all their enormity.

I will say now that there is a sentiment in the country contrary to me,—a sentiment which holds that slavery is not wrong, and therefore it goes for the policy that does not propose dealing with it as a wrong. That policy is the Democratic policy, and that sentiment is the Democratic sentiment. If there be a doubt in the mind of any one of this vast audience that this is really the central idea of the Democratic party in relation to this subject, I ask him to bear with me while I state a few things tending, as I think, to prove that proposition. In the first place, the leading man—I think I may do my friend Judge Douglas the honor of calling him such advocating the present Democratic policy never himself says it is wrong. He has the high distinction, so far as I know, of never having said slavery is either right or wrong. Almost everybody else says one or the other, but the Judge never does. If there be a man in the Democratic party who thinks it is wrong, and yet clings to that party, I suggest to him, in the first place, that his leader don't talk as he does, for he never says that it is wrong. In the second place, I suggest to him that if he will examine the policy proposed to be carried forward, he will find that he carefully excludes the idea that there is anything wrong in it. If you will examine the arguments that are made on it, you will find that every one carefully excludes the idea that there is anything wrong in slavery. Perhaps that Democrat who says he is as much opposed to slavery as I am will tell me that I am wrong about this. I wish him to examine his own course in regard to this matter a moment, and then see if his opinion will not be changed a little. You say it is wrong; but don't you constantly object to anybody else saying so? Do you not constantly argue that this is not the right place to oppose it? You say it must not be opposed in the free States, because slavery is not here; it must not be opposed in the slave States, because it is there; it must not be opposed in politics, because that will make a fuss; it must not be opposed in the pulpit, because it is not religion. Then where is the place to oppose it? There is no suitable place to oppose it. There is no place in the country to oppose this evil overspreading the continent, which you say yourself is coming. Frank Blair and Gratz Brown tried to get up a system of gradual emancipation in Missouri, had an election in August, and got beat, and you, Mr. Democrat, threw up your hat, and hallooed "Hurrah for Democracy!" So I say, again, that in regard to the arguments that are made, when Judge Douglas Says he "don't care whether slavery is voted up or voted down," whether he means that as an individual expression of sentiment, or only as a sort of statement of his views on national policy, it is alike true to say that he can thus argue logically if he don't see anything wrong in it; but he cannot say so logically if he admits that slavery is wrong. He cannot say that he would as soon see a wrong voted up as voted down. When Judge Douglas says that whoever or whatever community wants slaves, they have a right to have them, he is perfectly logical, if there is nothing wrong in the institution; but if you admit that it is wrong, he cannot logically say that anybody has a right to do wrong. When he says that slave property and horse and hog property are alike to be allowed to go into the Territories, upon the principles of equality, he is reasoning truly, if there is no difference between them as property; but if the one is property held rightfully, and the other is wrong, then there is no equality between the right and wrong; so that, turn it in anyway you can, in all the arguments sustaining the Democratic policy, and in that policy itself, there is a careful, studied exclusion of the idea that there is anything wrong in slavery. Let us understand this. I am not, just here, trying to prove that we are right, and they are wrong. I have been stating where we and they stand, and trying to show what is the real difference between us; and I now say that whenever we can get the question distinctly stated, can get all these men who believe that slavery is in some of these respects wrong to stand and act with us in treating it as a wrong,—then, and not till then, I think we will in some way come to an end of this slavery agitation.

Mr. Lincoln's Rejoinder.

MY FRIENDS:—Since Judge Douglas has said to you in his conclusion that he had not time in an hour and a half to answer all I had said in an hour, it follows of course that I will not be able to answer in half an hour all that he said in an hour and a half.

I wish to return to Judge Douglas my profound thanks for his public annunciation here to-day, to be put on record, that his system of policy in regard to the institution of slavery contemplates that it shall last forever. We are getting a little nearer the true issue of this controversy, and I am profoundly grateful for this one sentence. Judge Douglas asks you, Why cannot the institution of slavery, or rather, why cannot the nation, part slave and part free, continue as our fathers made it, forever? In the first place, I insist that our fathers did not make this nation half slave and half free, or part slave and part free. I insist that they found the institution of slavery existing here. They did not make it so but they left it so because they knew of no way to get rid of it at that time. When Judge Douglas undertakes to say that, as a matter of choice, the fathers of the government made this nation part slave and part free, he assumes what is historically a falsehood. More than that: when the fathers of the government cut off the source of slavery by the abolition of the slave-trade, and adopted a system of restricting it from the new Territories where it had not existed, I maintain that they placed it where they understood, and all sensible men understood, it was in the course of ultimate extinction; and when Judge Douglas asks me why it cannot continue as our fathers made it, I ask him why he and his friends could not let it remain as our fathers made it?

It is precisely all I ask of him in relation to the institution of slavery, that it shall be placed upon the basis that our fathers placed it upon. Mr. Brooks, of South Carolina, once said, and truly said, that when this government was established, no one expected the institution of slavery to last until this day, and that the men who formed this government were wiser and better than the men of these days; but the men of these days had experience which the fathers had not, and that experience had taught them the invention of the cotton-gin, and this had made the perpetuation of the institution of slavery a necessity in this country. Judge Douglas could not let it stand upon the basis which our fathers placed it, but removed it, and put it upon the cotton-gin basis. It is a question, therefore, for him and his friends to answer, why they could not let it remain where the fathers of the government originally placed it.

I hope nobody has understood me as trying to sustain the doctrine that we have a right to quarrel with Kentucky, or Virginia, or any of the slave States, about the institution of slavery,—thus giving the Judge an opportunity to be eloquent and valiant against us in fighting for their rights. I expressly declared in my opening speech that I had neither the inclination to exercise, nor the belief in the existence of, the right to interfere with the States of Kentucky or Virginia in doing as they pleased with slavery Or any other existing institution. Then what becomes of all his eloquence in behalf of the rights of States, which are assailed by no living man?

But I have to hurry on, for I have but a half hour. The Judge has informed me, or informed this audience, that the Washington Union is laboring for my election to the United States Senate. This is news to me,—not very ungrateful news either. [Turning to Mr. W. H. Carlin, who was on the stand]—I hope that Carlin will be elected to the State Senate, and will vote for me. [Mr. Carlin shook his head.] Carlin don't fall in, I perceive, and I suppose he will not do much for me; but I am glad of all the support I can get, anywhere, if I can get it without practicing any deception to obtain it. In respect to this large portion of Judge Douglas's speech in which he tries to show that in the controversy between himself and the Administration party he is in the right, I do not feel myself at all competent or inclined to answer him. I say to him, "Give it to them,—give it to them just all you can!" and, on the other hand, I say to Carlin, and Jake Davis, and to this man Wogley up here in Hancock, "Give it to Douglas, just pour it into him!"

Now, in regard to this matter of the Dred Scott decision, I wish to say a word or two. After all, the Judge will not say whether, if a decision is made holding that the people of the States cannot exclude slavery, he will support it or not. He obstinately refuses to say what he will do in that case. The judges of the Supreme Court as obstinately refused to say what they would do on this subject. Before this I reminded him that at Galesburg he said the judges had expressly declared the contrary, and you remember that in my Opening speech I told him I had the book containing that decision here, and I would thank him to lay his finger on the place where any such thing was said. He has occupied his hour and a half, and he has not ventured to try to sustain his assertion. He never will. But he is desirous of knowing how we are going to reverse that Dred Scott decision. Judge Douglas ought to know how. Did not he and his political friends find a way to reverse the decision of that same court in favor of the constitutionality of the National Bank? Didn't they find a way to do it so effectually that they have reversed it as completely as any decision ever was reversed, so far as its practical operation is concerned? And let me ask you, didn't Judge Douglas find a way to reverse the decision of our Supreme Court when it decided that Carlin's father—old Governor Carlin had not the constitutional power to remove a Secretary of State? Did he not appeal to the "MOBS," as he calls them? Did he not make speeches in the lobby to show how villainous that decision was, and how it ought to be overthrown? Did he not succeed, too, in getting an act passed by the Legislature to have it overthrown? And didn't he himself sit down on that bench as one of the five added judges, who were to overslaugh the four old ones, getting his name of "judge" in that way, and no other? If there is a villainy in using disrespect or making opposition to Supreme Court decisions, I commend it to Judge Douglas's earnest consideration. I know of no man in the State of Illinois who ought to know so well about how much villainy it takes to oppose a decision of the Supreme Court as our honorable friend Stephen A. Douglas.

Judge Douglas also makes the declaration that I say the Democrats are bound by the Dred Scott decision, while the Republicans are not. In the sense in which he argues, I never said it; but I will tell you what I have said and what I do not hesitate to repeat to-day. I have said that as the Democrats believe that decision to be correct, and that the extension of slavery is affirmed in the National Constitution, they are bound to support it as such; and I will tell you here that General Jackson once said each man was bound to support the Constitution "as he understood it." Now, Judge Douglas understands the Constitution according to the Dred Scott decision, and he is bound to support it as he understands it. I understand it another way, and therefore I am bound to support it in the way in which I understand it. And as Judge Douglas believes that decision to be correct, I will remake that argument if I have time to do so. Let me talk to some gentleman down there among you who looks me in the face. We will say you are a member of the Territorial Legislature, and, like Judge Douglas, you believe that the right to take and hold slaves there is a constitutional right The first thing you do is to swear you will support the Constitution, and all rights guaranteed therein; that you will, whenever your neighbor needs your legislation to support his constitutional rights, not withhold that legislation. If you withhold that necessary legislation for the support of the Constitution and constitutional rights, do you not commit perjury? I ask every sensible man if that is not so? That is undoubtedly just so, say what you please. Now, that is precisely what Judge Douglas says, that this is a constitutional right. Does the Judge mean to say that the Territorial Legislature in legislating may, by withholding necessary laws, or by passing unfriendly laws, nullify that constitutional right? Does he mean to say that? Does he mean to ignore the proposition so long and well established in law, that what you cannot do directly, you cannot do indirectly? Does he mean that? The truth about the matter is this: Judge Douglas has sung paeans to his "Popular Sovereignty" doctrine until his Supreme Court, co-operating with him, has squatted his Squatter Sovereignty out. But he will keep up this species of humbuggery about Squatter Sovereignty. He has at last invented this sort of do-nothing sovereignty,—that the people may exclude slavery by a sort of "sovereignty" that is exercised by doing nothing at all. Is not that running his Popular Sovereignty down awfully? Has it not got down as thin as the homeopathic soup that was made by boiling the shadow of a pigeon that had starved to death? But at last, when it is brought to the test of close reasoning, there is not even that thin decoction of it left. It is a presumption impossible in the domain of thought. It is precisely no other than the putting of that most unphilosophical proposition, that two bodies can occupy the same space at the same time. The Dred Scott decision covers the whole ground, and while it occupies it, there is no room even for the shadow of a starved pigeon to occupy the same ground.

Judge Douglas, in reply to what I have said about having upon a previous occasion made the speech at Ottawa as the one he took an extract from at Charleston, says it only shows that I practiced the deception twice. Now, my friends, are any of you obtuse enough to swallow that? Judge Douglas had said I had made a speech at Charleston that I would not make up north, and I turned around and answered him by showing I had made that same speech up north,—had made it at Ottawa; made it in his hearing; made it in the Abolition District,—in Lovejoy's District,—in the personal presence of Lovejoy himself,—in the same atmosphere exactly in which I had made my Chicago speech, of which he complains so much.

Now, in relation to my not having said anything about the quotation from the Chicago speech: he thinks that is a terrible subject for me to handle. Why, gentlemen, I can show you that the substance of the Chicago speech I delivered two years ago in "Egypt," as he calls it. It was down at Springfield. That speech is here in this book, and I could turn to it and read it to you but for the lack of time. I have not now the time to read it. ["Read it, read it."] No, gentlemen, I am obliged to use discretion in disposing most advantageously of my brief time. The Judge has taken great exception to my adopting the heretical statement in the Declaration of Independence, that "all men are created equal," and he has a great deal to say about negro equality. I want to say that in sometimes alluding to the Declaration of Independence, I have only uttered the sentiments that Henry Clay used to hold. Allow me to occupy your time a moment with what he said. Mr. Clay was at one time called upon in Indiana, and in a way that I suppose was very insulting, to liberate his slaves; and he made a written reply to that application, and one portion of it is in these words:

"What is the foundation of this appeal to me in Indiana to liberate the slaves under my care in Kentucky? It is a general declaration in the act announcing to the world the independence of the thirteen American colonies, that 'men are created equal.' Now, as an abstract principle, there is no doubt of the truth of that declaration, and it is desirable in the original construction of society, and in organized societies, to keep it in view as a great fundamental principle."

When I sometimes, in relation to the organization of new societies in new countries, where the soil is clean and clear, insisted that we should keep that principle in view, Judge Douglas will have it that I want a negro wife. He never can be brought to understand that there is any middle ground on this subject. I have lived until my fiftieth year, and have never had a negro woman either for a slave or a wife, and I think I can live fifty centuries, for that matter, without having had one for either. I maintain that you may take Judge Douglas's quotations from my Chicago speech, and from my Charleston speech, and the Galesburg speech,—in his speech of to-day,—and compare them over, and I am willing to trust them with you upon his proposition that they show rascality or double-dealing. I deny that they do.

The Judge does not seem at all disposed to have peace, but I find he is disposed to have a personal warfare with me. He says that my oath would not be taken against the bare word of Charles H. Lanphier or

Thomas L. Harris. Well, that is altogether a matter of opinion. It is certainly not for me to vaunt my word against oaths of these gentlemen, but I will tell Judge Douglas again the facts upon which I "dared" to say they proved a forgery. I pointed out at Galesburg that the publication of these resolutions in the Illinois State Register could not have been the result of accident, as the proceedings of that meeting bore unmistakable evidence of being done by a man who knew it was a forgery; that it was a publication partly taken from the real proceedings of the Convention, and partly from the proceedings of a convention at another place, which showed that he had the real proceedings before him, and taking one part of the resolutions, he threw out another part, and substituted false and fraudulent ones in their stead. I pointed that out to him, and also that his friend Lanphier, who was editor of the Register at that time and now is, must have known how it was done. Now, whether he did it, or got some friend to do it for him, I could not tell, but he certainly knew all about it. I pointed out to Judge Douglas that in his Freeport speech he had promised to investigate that matter. Does he now say that he did not make that promise? I have a right to ask why he did not keep it. I call upon him to tell here to-day why he did not keep that promise? That fraud has been traced up so that it lies between him, Harris, and Lanphier. There is little room for escape for Lanphier. Lanphier is doing the Judge good service, and Douglas desires his word to be taken for the truth. He desires Lanphier to be taken as authority in what he states in his newspaper. He desires Harris to be taken as a man of vast credibility; and when this thing lies among them, they will not press it to show where the guilt really belongs. Now, as he has said that he would investigate it, and implied that he would tell us the result of his investigation, I demand of him to tell why he did not investigate it, if he did not; and if he did, why he won't tell the result. I call upon him for that.

This is the third time that Judge Douglas has assumed that he learned about these resolutions by Harris's attempting to use them against Norton on the floor of Congress. I tell Judge Douglas the public records of the country show that he himself attempted it upon Trumbull a month before Harris tried them on Norton; that Harris had the opportunity of learning it from him, rather than he from Harris. I now ask his attention to that part of the record on the case. My friends, I am not disposed to detain you longer in regard to that matter.

I am told that I still have five minutes left. There is another matter I wish to call attention to. He says, when he discovered there was a mistake in that case, he came forward magnanimously, without my calling his attention to it, and explained it. I will tell you how he became so magnanimous. When the newspapers of our side had discovered and published it, and put it beyond his power to deny it, then he came forward and made a virtue of necessity by acknowledging it. Now he argues that all the point there was in those resolutions, although never passed at Springfield, is retained by their being passed at other localities. Is that true? He said I had a hand in passing them, in his opening speech, that I was in the convention and helped to pass them. Do the resolutions touch me at all? It strikes me there is some difference between holding a man responsible for an act which he has not done and holding him responsible for an act that he has done. You will judge whether there is any difference in the "spots." And he has taken credit for great magnanimity in coming forward and acknowledging what is proved on him beyond even the capacity of Judge Douglas to deny; and he has more capacity in that way than any other living man.

Then he wants to know why I won't withdraw the charge in regard to a conspiracy to make slavery national, as he has withdrawn the one he made. May it please his worship, I will withdraw it when it is proven false on me as that was proven false on him. I will add a little more than that, I will withdraw it whenever a reasonable man shall be brought to believe that the charge is not true. I have asked Judge Douglas's attention to certain matters of fact tending to prove the charge of a conspiracy to nationalize slavery, and he says he convinces me that this is all untrue because Buchanan was not in the country at that time, and because the Dred Scott case had not then got into the Supreme Court; and he says that I say the Democratic owners of Dred Scott got up the case. I never did say that I defy Judge Douglas to show that I ever said so, for I never uttered it. [One of Mr. Douglas's reporters gesticulated affirmatively at Mr. Lincoln.] I don't care if your hireling does say I did, I tell you myself that I never said the "Democratic" owners of Dred Scott got up the case. I have never pretended to know whether Dred Scott's owners were Democrats, or Abolitionists, or Free-soilers or Border Ruffians. I have said that there is evidence about the case tending to show that it was a made-up case, for the purpose of getting that decision. I have said that that evidence was very strong in the fact that when Dred Scott was declared to be a slave, the owner of him made him free, showing that he had had the case tried and the question settled for such use as could be made of that decision; he cared nothing about the property thus declared to be his by that decision. But my time is out, and I can say no more.

SEVENTH DEBATE WITH STEPHEN A. DOUGLAS,
ALTON, ILLINOIS, OCTOBER 15, 1858.

LADIES AND GENTLEMEN:—I have been somewhat, in my own mind, complimented by a large portion of Judge Douglas's speech,—I mean that portion which he devotes to the controversy between himself and the present Administration. This is the seventh time Judge Douglas and myself have met in these joint discussions, and he has been gradually improving in regard to his war with the Administration. At Quincy, day before yesterday, he was a little more severe upon the Administration than I had heard him upon any occasion, and I took pains to compliment him for it. I then told him to give it to them with all the power he had; and as some of them were present, I told them I would be very much obliged if they would give it to him in about the same way. I take it he has now vastly improved upon the attack he made then upon the Administration. I flatter myself he has really taken my advice on this subject. All I can say now is to re-commend to him and to them what I then commended,—to prosecute the war against one another in the most vigorous manner. I say to them again: "Go it, husband!—Go it, bear!"

There is one other thing I will mention before I leave this branch of the discussion,—although I do not consider it much of my business, anyway. I refer to that part of the Judge's remarks where he undertakes to involve Mr. Buchanan in an inconsistency. He reads something from Mr. Buchanan, from which he undertakes to involve him in an inconsistency; and he gets something of a cheer for having done so. I would only remind the Judge that while he is very valiantly fighting for the Nebraska Bill and the repeal of the Missouri Compromise, it has been but a little while since he was the valiant advocate of the Missouri Compromise. I want to know if Buchanan has not as much right to be inconsistent as Douglas has? Has Douglas the exclusive right, in this country, of being on all sides of all questions? Is nobody allowed that high privilege but himself? Is he to have an entire monopoly on that subject?

So far as Judge Douglas addressed his speech to me, or so far as it was about me, it is my business to pay some attention to it. I have heard the Judge state two or three times what he has stated to-day, that in a speech which I made at Springfield, Illinois, I had in a very especial manner complained that the Supreme Court in the Dred Scott case had decided that a negro could never be a citizen of the United States. I have omitted by some accident heretofore to analyze this statement, and it is required of me to notice it now. In point of fact it is untrue. I never have complained especially of the Dred Scott decision because it held that a negro could not be a citizen, and the Judge is always wrong when he says I ever did so complain of it. I have the speech here, and I will thank him or any of his friends to show where I said that a negro should be a citizen, and complained especially of the Dred Scott decision because it declared he could not be one. I have done no such thing; and Judge Douglas, so persistently insisting that I have done so, has strongly impressed me with the belief of a predetermination on his part to misrepresent me. He could not get his foundation for insisting that I was in favor of this negro equality anywhere else as well as he could by assuming that untrue proposition.

Let me tell this audience what is true in regard to that matter; and the means by which they may correct me if I do not tell them truly is by a recurrence to the speech itself. I spoke of the Dred Scott decision in my Springfield speech, and I was then endeavoring to prove that the Dred Scott decision was a portion of a system or scheme to make slavery national in this country. I pointed out what things had been decided by the court. I mentioned as a fact that they had decided that a negro could not be a citizen; that they had done so, as I supposed, to deprive the negro, under all circumstances, of the remotest possibility of ever becoming a citizen and claiming the rights of a citizen of the United States under a certain clause of the Constitution. I stated that, without making any complaint of it at all. I then went on and stated the other points decided in the case; namely, that the bringing of a negro into the State of Illinois and holding him in slavery for two years here was a matter in regard to which they would not decide whether it would make him free or not; that they decided the further point that taking him into a United States Territory where slavery was prohibited by Act of Congress did not make him free, because that Act of Congress, as they held, was unconstitutional. I mentioned these three things as making up the points decided in that case. I mentioned them in a lump, taken in connection with the introduction of the Nebraska Bill, and the amendment of Chase, offered at the time, declaratory of the right of the people of the Territories to exclude slavery, which was voted down by the friends of the bill. I mentioned all these things together, as evidence tending to prove a combination and conspiracy to make the institution of slavery national. In that connection and in that way I mentioned the decision on the point that a negro could not be a citizen, and in no other connection.

Out of this Judge Douglas builds up his beautiful fabrication of my purpose to introduce a perfect social and political equality between the white and black races. His assertion that I made an "especial objection" (that is his exact language) to the decision on this account is untrue in point of fact.

Now, while I am upon this subject, and as Henry Clay has been alluded to, I desire to place myself, in connection with Mr. Clay, as nearly right before this people as may be. I am quite aware what the

Judge's object is here by all these allusions. He knows that we are before an audience having strong sympathies southward, by relationship, place of birth, and so on. He desires to place me in an extremely Abolition attitude. He read upon a former occasion, and alludes, without reading, to-day to a portion of a speech which I delivered in Chicago. In his quotations from that speech, as he has made them upon former occasions, the extracts were taken in such a way as, I suppose, brings them within the definition of what is called garbling,—taking portions of a speech which, when taken by themselves, do not present the entire sense of the speaker as expressed at the time. I propose, therefore, out of that same speech, to show how one portion of it which he skipped over (taking an extract before and an extract after) will give a different idea, and the true idea I intended to convey. It will take me some little time to read it, but I believe I will occupy the time that way.

You have heard him frequently allude to my controversy with him in regard to the Declaration of Independence. I confess that I have had a struggle with Judge Douglas on that matter, and I will try briefly to place myself right in regard to it on this occasion. I said—and it is between the extracts Judge Douglas has taken from this speech, and put in his published speeches:

"It may be argued that there are certain conditions that make necessities and impose them upon us, and to the extent that a necessity is imposed upon a man he must submit to it. I think that was the condition in which we found ourselves when we established this government. We had slaves among us, we could not get our Constitution unless we permitted them to remain in slavery, we could not secure the good we did secure if we grasped for more; and having by necessity submitted to that much, it does not destroy the principle that is the charter of our liberties. Let the charter remain as our standard."

Now, I have upon all occasions declared as strongly as Judge Douglas against the disposition to interfere with the existing institution of slavery. You hear me read it from the same speech from which he takes garbled extracts for the purpose of proving upon me a disposition to interfere with the institution of slavery, and establish a perfect social and political equality between negroes and white people.

Allow me while upon this subject briefly to present one other extract from a speech of mine, more than a year ago, at Springfield, in discussing this very same question, soon after Judge Douglas took his ground that negroes were, not included in the Declaration of Independence:

"I think the authors of that notable instrument intended to include all men, but they did not mean to declare all men equal in all respects. They did not mean to say all men were equal in color, size, intellect, moral development, or social capacity. They defined with tolerable distinctness in what they did consider all men created equal,—equal in certain inalienable rights, among which are life, liberty, and the pursuit of happiness. This they said, and this they meant. They did not mean to assert the obvious untruth that all were then actually enjoying that equality, or yet that they were about to confer it immediately upon them. In fact they had no power to confer such a boon. They meant simply to declare the right, so that the enforcement of it might follow as fast as circumstances should permit.

"They meant to set up a standard maxim for free society which should be familiar to all,—constantly looked to, constantly labored for, and even, though never perfectly attained, constantly approximated, and thereby constantly spreading and deepening its influence, and augmenting the happiness and value of life to all people, of all colors, everywhere."

There again are the sentiments I have expressed in regard to the Declaration of Independence upon a former occasion,—sentiments which have been put in print and read wherever anybody cared to know what so humble an individual as myself chose to say in regard to it.

At Galesburg, the other day, I said, in answer to Judge Douglas, that three years ago there never had been a man, so far as I knew or believed, in the whole world, who had said that the Declaration of Independence did not include negroes in the term "all men." I reassert it to-day. I assert that Judge Douglas and all his friends may search the whole records of the country, and it will be a matter of great astonishment to me if they shall be able to find that one human being three years ago had ever uttered the astounding sentiment that the term "all men" in the Declaration did not include the negro.

Do not let me be misunderstood. I know that more than three years ago there were men who, finding this assertion constantly in the way of their schemes to bring about the ascendency and perpetuation of slavery, denied the truth of it. I know that Mr. Calhoun and all the politicians of his school denied the truth of the Declaration. I know that it ran along in the mouth of some Southern men for a period of years, ending at last in that shameful, though rather forcible, declaration of Pettit of Indiana, upon the floor of the United States Senate, that the Declaration of Independence was in that respect "a self-evident lie," rather than a self-evident truth. But I say, with a perfect knowledge of all this hawking at the Declaration without directly attacking it, that three years ago there never had lived a man who had ventured to assail it in the sneaking way of pretending to believe it, and then asserting it did not include the negro. I believe the first man who ever said it was Chief Justice Taney in the Dred Scott case, and the next to him was our friend Stephen A. Douglas. And now it has become the catchword of the entire party. I would like to call upon his friends everywhere to consider how they have come in so short a time to view this matter in a way so entirely different from their former belief; to ask whether they are not being borne along by an irresistible current,—whither, they know not.

In answer to my proposition at Galesburg last week, I see that some man in Chicago has got up a letter, addressed to the Chicago *Times*, to show, as he professes, that somebody had said so before; and he signs himself "An Old-Line Whig," if I remember correctly. In the first place, I would say he was not an old-line Whig. I am somewhat acquainted with old-line Whigs from the origin to the end of that party; I became pretty well acquainted with them, and I know they always had some sense, whatever else you could ascribe to them. I know there never was one who had not more sense than to try to show by the evidence he produces that some men had, prior to the time I named, said that negroes were not included in the term "all men" in the Declaration of Independence. What is the evidence he produces? I will bring forward his evidence, and let you see what he offers by way of showing that somebody more than three years ago had said negroes were not included in the Declaration. He brings forward part of a speech from Henry Clay,—the part of the speech of Henry Clay which I used to bring forward to prove precisely the contrary. I guess we are surrounded to some extent to-day by the old friends of Mr. Clay, and they will be glad to hear anything from that authority. While he was in Indiana a man presented a petition to liberate his negroes, and he (Mr. Clay) made a speech in answer to it, which I suppose he carefully wrote out himself and caused to be published. I have before me an extract from that speech which constitutes the evidence this pretended "Old-Line Whig" at Chicago brought forward to show that Mr. Clay didn't suppose the negro was included in the Declaration of Independence. Hear what Mr. Clay said:

"And what is the foundation of this appeal to me in Indiana to liberate the slaves under my care in Kentucky? It is a general declaration in the act announcing to the world the independence of the thirteen American colonies, that all men are created equal. Now, as an abstract principle, there is no doubt of the truth of that declaration; and it is desirable, in the original construction of society and in organized societies, to keep it in view as a great fundamental principle. But, then, I apprehend that in no society that ever did exist, or ever shall be formed, was or can the equality asserted among the members of the human race be practically enforced and carried out. There are portions, large portions, women, minors, insane, culprits, transient sojourners, that will always probably remain subject to the government of another portion of the community.

"That declaration, whatever may be the extent of its import, was made by the delegations of the thirteen States. In most of them slavery existed, and had long existed, and was established by law. It was introduced and forced upon the colonies by the paramount law of England. Do you believe that in making that declaration the States that concurred in it intended that it should be tortured into a virtual emancipation of all the slaves within their respective limits? Would Virginia and other Southern States have ever united in a declaration which was to be interpreted into an abolition of slavery among them? Did any one of the thirteen colonies entertain such a design or expectation? To impute such a secret and unavowed purpose, would be to charge a political fraud upon the noblest band of patriots that ever assembled in council,—a fraud upon the Confederacy of the Revolution; a fraud upon the union of those States whose Constitution not only recognized the lawfulness of slavery, but permitted the importation of slaves from Africa until the year 1808."

This is the entire quotation brought forward to prove that somebody previous to three years ago had said the negro was not included in the term "all men" in the Declaration. How does it do so? In what way has it a tendency to prove that? Mr. Clay says it is true as an abstract principle that all men are created equal, but that we cannot practically apply it in all eases. He illustrates this by bringing forward the cases of females, minors, and insane persons, with whom it cannot be enforced; but he says it is true as an abstract principle in the organization of society as well as in organized society and it should be kept in view as a fundamental principle. Let me read a few words more before I add some comments of my own. Mr. Clay says, a little further on:

"I desire no concealment of my opinions in regard to the institution of slavery. I look upon it as a great evil, and deeply lament that we have derived it from the parental government and from our ancestors. I wish every slave in the United States was in the country of his ancestors. But here they are, and the question is, How can they be best dealt with? If a state of nature existed, and we were about to lay the foundations of society, no man would be more strongly opposed than I should be to incorporate the institution of slavery amongst its elements."

Now, here in this same book, in this same speech, in this same extract, brought forward to prove that Mr. Clay held that the negro was not included in the Declaration of Independence, is no such statement on his part, but the declaration that it is a great fundamental truth which should be constantly kept in view in the organization of society and in societies already organized. But if I say a word about it; if I attempt, as Mr. Clay said all good men ought to do, to keep it in view; if, in this "organized society," I ask to have the public eye turned upon it; if I ask, in relation to the organization of new Territories, that the public eye should be turned upon it, forthwith I am vilified as you hear me to-day. What have I done that I have not the license of Henry Clay's illustrious example here in doing? Have I done aught that I have not his authority for, while maintaining that in organizing new Territories and societies this fundamental principle should be regarded, and in organized society holding it up to the public view and recognizing what he recognized as the great principle of free government?

And when this new principle—this new proposition that no human being ever thought of three years ago—is brought forward, I combat it as having an evil tendency, if not an evil design. I combat it as having a tendency to dehumanize the negro, to take away from him the right of ever striving to be a man. I combat it as being one of the thousand things constantly done in these days to prepare the public mind to make property, and nothing but property, of the negro in all the States of this Union.

But there is a point that I wish, before leaving this part of the discussion, to ask attention to. I have read and I repeat the words of Henry Clay:

"I desire no concealment of my opinions in regard to the institution of slavery. I look upon it as a great evil, and deeply lament that we have derived it from the parental government and from our ancestors. I wish every slave in the United States was in the country of his ancestors. But here they are, and the question is, How can they be best dealt with? If a state of nature existed, and we were about to lay the foundations of society, no man would be more strongly opposed than I should be to incorporate the institution of slavery amongst its elements."

The principle upon which I have insisted in this canvass is in relation to laying the foundations of new societies. I have never sought to apply these principles to the old States for the purpose of abolishing slavery in those States. It is nothing but a miserable perversion of what I have said, to assume that I have declared Missouri, or any other slave State, shall emancipate her slaves; I have proposed no such thing. But when Mr. Clay says that in laying the foundations of society in our Territories where it does not exist, he would be opposed to the introduction of slavery as an element, I insist that we have his warrant—his license—for insisting upon the exclusion of that element which he declared in such strong and emphatic language was most hurtful to him.

Judge Douglas has again referred to a Springfield speech in which I said "a house divided against itself cannot stand." The Judge has so often made the entire quotation from that speech that I can make it from memory. I used this language:

"We are now far into the fifth year since a policy was initiated with the avowed object and confident promise of putting an end to the slavery agitation. Under the operation of this policy, that agitation has not only not ceased, but has constantly augmented. In my opinion it will not cease until a crisis shall have been reached and passed. 'A house divided against itself cannot stand.' I believe this government cannot endure permanently, half slave and half free. I do not expect the house to fall, but I do expect it will cease to be divided. It will become all one thing, or all the other. Either the opponents of slavery will arrest the further spread of it, and place it where the public mind shall rest in the belief that it is in the course of ultimate extinction, or its advocates will push it forward till it shall become alike lawful in all the States, old as well as new, North as well as South."

That extract and the sentiments expressed in it have been extremely offensive to Judge Douglas. He has warred upon them as Satan wars upon the Bible. His perversions upon it are endless. Here now are my views upon it in brief:

I said we were now far into the fifth year since a policy was initiated with the avowed object and confident promise of putting an end to the slavery agitation. Is it not so? When that Nebraska Bill was brought forward four years ago last January, was it not for the "avowed object" of putting an end to the slavery agitation? We were to have no more agitation in Congress; it was all to be banished to the Territories.

By the way, I will remark here that, as Judge Douglas is very fond of complimenting Mr. Crittenden in these days, Mr. Crittenden has said there was a falsehood in that whole business, for there was no slavery agitation at that time to allay. We were for a little while quiet on the troublesome thing, and that very allaying plaster of Judge Douglas's stirred it up again. But was it not understood or intimated with the "confident promise" of putting an end to the slavery agitation? Surely it was. In every speech you heard Judge Douglas make, until he got into this "imbroglio," as they call it, with the Administration about the Lecompton Constitution, every speech on that Nebraska Bill was full of his felicitations that we were just at the end of the slavery agitation. The last tip of the last joint of the old serpent's tail was just drawing out of view. But has it proved so? I have asserted that under that policy that agitation "has not only not ceased, but has constantly augmented." When was there ever a greater agitation in Congress than last winter?

When was it as great in the country as to-day?

There was a collateral object in the introduction of that Nebraska policy, which was to clothe the people of the Territories with a superior degree of self-government, beyond what they had ever had before. The first object and the main one of conferring upon the people a higher degree of "self-government" is a question of fact to be determined by you in answer to a single question. Have you ever heard or known of a people anywhere on earth who had as little to do as, in the first instance of its use, the people of Kansas had with this same right of "self-government "? In its main policy and in its collateral object, it has been nothing but a living, creeping lie from the time of its introduction till to-day.

I have intimated that I thought the agitation would not cease until a crisis should have been reached and passed. I have stated in what way I thought it would be reached and passed. I have said that it might go one way or the other. We might, by arresting the further spread of it, and placing it where the fathers originally placed it, put it where the public mind should rest in the belief that it was in the course of ultimate extinction. Thus the agitation may cease. It may be pushed forward until it shall become alike lawful in all the States, old as well as new, North as well as South. I have said, and I repeat, my wish is that the further spread of it may be arrested, and that it may be where the public mind shall rest in the belief that it is in the course of ultimate extinction—I have expressed that as my wish I entertain the opinion, upon evidence sufficient to my mind, that the fathers of this government placed that institution where the public mind did rest in the belief that it was in the course of ultimate extinction. Let me ask why they made provision that the source of slavery—the African slave-trade—should be cut off at the end of twenty years? Why did they make provision that in all the new territory we owned at that time slavery should be forever inhibited? Why stop its spread in one direction, and cut off its source in another, if they did not look to its being placed in the course of its ultimate extinction?

Again: the institution of slavery is only mentioned in the Constitution of the United States two or three times, and in neither of these cases does the word "slavery" or "negro race" occur; but covert language is used each time, and for a purpose full of significance. What is the language in regard to the prohibition of the African slave-trade? It runs in about this way: "The migration or importation of such persons as any of the States now existing shall think proper to admit, shall not be prohibited by the Congress prior to the year one thousand eight hundred and eight."

The next allusion in the Constitution to the question of slavery and the black race is on the subject of the basis of representation, and there the language used is:

"Representatives and direct taxes shall be apportioned among the several States which may be included within this Union, according to their respective numbers, which shall be determined by adding to the whole number of free persons, including those bound to service for a term of years, and excluding Indians not taxed, three-fifths of all other persons."

It says "persons," not slaves, not negroes; but this "three-fifths" can be applied to no other class among us than the negroes.

Lastly, in the provision for the reclamation of fugitive slaves, it is said: "No person held to service or labor in one State, under the laws thereof, escaping into another, shall in consequence of any law or regulation therein be discharged from such service or labor, but shall be delivered up, on claim of the party to whom such service or labor may be due." There again there is no mention of the word "negro" or of slavery. In all three of these places, being the only allusions to slavery in the instrument, covert language is used. Language is used not suggesting that slavery existed or that the black race were among us. And I understand the contemporaneous history of those times to be that covert language was used with a purpose, and that purpose was that in our Constitution, which it was hoped and is still hoped will endure forever,—when it should be read by intelligent and patriotic men, after the institution of slavery had passed from among us,—there should be nothing on the face of the great charter of liberty suggesting that such a thing as negro slavery had ever existed among us. This is part of the evidence that the fathers of the government expected and intended the institution of slavery to come to an end. They expected and intended that it should be in the course of ultimate extinction. And when I say that I desire to see the further spread of it arrested, I only say I desire to see that done which the fathers have first done. When I say I desire to see it placed where the public mind will rest in the belief that it is in the course of ultimate extinction, I only say I desire to see it placed where they placed it.

It is not true that our fathers, as Judge Douglas assumes, made this government part slave and part free. Understand the sense in which he puts it. He assumes that slavery is a rightful thing within itself,—was introduced by the framers of the Constitution. The exact truth is, that they found the institution existing among us, and they left it as they found it. But in making the government they left this institution with many clear marks of disapprobation upon it. They found slavery among them, and they left it among them because of the difficulty—the absolute impossibility—of its immediate removal. And when Judge Douglas asks me why we cannot let it remain part slave and part free, as the fathers of the government made it, he asks a question based upon an assumption which is itself a falsehood; and I turn upon him and ask him the question, when the policy that the fathers of the government had adopted in relation to this element among us was the best policy in the world, the only wise policy, the only policy that we can ever safely continue upon that will ever give us peace, unless this dangerous element masters us all and becomes a national institution,—I turn upon him and ask him why he could not leave it alone. I turn and ask him why he was driven to the necessity of introducing a new policy in regard to it.

He has himself said he introduced a new policy. He said so in his speech on the 22d of March of the present year, 1858. I ask him why he could not let it remain where our fathers placed it. I ask, too, of Judge Douglas and his friends why we shall not again place this institution upon the basis on which the fathers left it. I ask you, when he infers that I am in favor of setting the free and slave States at war, when the institution was placed in that attitude by those who made the Constitution, did they make any war? If we had no war out of it when thus placed, wherein is the ground of belief that we shall have war out of it if we return to that policy? Have we had any peace upon this matter springing from any other basis? I maintain that we have not. I have proposed nothing more than a return to the policy of the fathers.

I confess, when I propose a certain measure of policy, it is not enough for me that I do not intend anything evil in the result, but it is incumbent on me to show that it has not a tendency to that result. I have met Judge Douglas in that point of view. I have not only made the declaration that I do not mean to produce a conflict between the States, but I have tried to show by fair reasoning, and I think I have shown to the minds of fair men, that I propose nothing but what has a most peaceful tendency. The quotation that I happened to make in that Springfield Speech, that "a house divided against itself cannot stand," and which has proved so offensive to the judge, was part and parcel of the same thing. He tries to show that variety in the democratic institutions of the different States is necessary and indispensable. I do not dispute it. I have no controversy with Judge Douglas about that.

I shall very readily agree with him that it would be foolish for us to insist upon having a cranberry law here in Illinois, where we have no cranberries, because they have a cranberry law in Indiana, where they have cranberries. I should insist that it would be exceedingly wrong in us to deny to Virginia the right to enact oyster laws, where they have oysters, because we want no such laws here. I understand, I hope, quite as well as Judge Douglas or anybody else, that the variety in the soil and climate and face of the country, and consequent variety in the industrial pursuits and productions of a country, require systems of law conforming to this variety in the natural features of the country. I understand quite as well as Judge Douglas that if we here raise a barrel of flour more than we want, and the Louisianians raise a barrel of sugar more than they want, it is of mutual advantage to exchange. That produces commerce, brings us together, and makes us better friends. We like one another the more for it. And I understand as well as Judge Douglas, or anybody else, that these mutual accommodations are the cements which bind together the different parts of this Union; that instead of being a thing to "divide the house,"—figuratively expressing the Union,—they tend to sustain it; they are the props of the house, tending always to hold it up.

But when I have admitted all this, I ask if there is any parallel between these things and this institution of slavery? I do not see that there is any parallel at all between them. Consider it. When have we had any difficulty or quarrel amongst ourselves about the cranberry laws of Indiana, or the oyster laws of Virginia, or the pine-lumber laws of Maine, or the fact that Louisiana produces sugar, and Illinois flour? When have we had any quarrels over these things? When have we had perfect peace in regard to this thing which I say is an element of discord in this Union? We have sometimes had peace, but when was it? It was when the institution of slavery remained quiet where it was. We have had difficulty and turmoil whenever it has made a struggle to spread itself where it was not. I ask, then, if experience does not speak in thunder-tones telling us that the policy which has given peace to the country heretofore, being returned to, gives the greatest promise of peace again.

You may say, and Judge Douglas has intimated the same thing, that all this difficulty in regard to the institution of slavery is the mere agitation of office-seekers and ambitious Northern politicians. He thinks we want to get "his place," I suppose. I agree that there are office-seekers amongst us. The Bible says somewhere that we are desperately selfish. I think we would have discovered that fact without the Bible. I do not claim that I am any less so than the average of men, but I do claim that I am not more selfish than Judge Douglas. But is it true that all the difficulty and agitation we have in regard to this institution of slavery spring from office-seeking, from the mere ambition of politicians? Is that the truth? How many times have we had danger from this question? Go back to the day of the Missouri Compromise. Go back to the nullification question, at the bottom of which lay this same slavery question. Go back to the time of the annexation of Texas. Go back to the troubles that led to the Compromise of 1850. You will find that every time, with the single exception of the Nullification question, they sprung from an endeavor to spread this institution.

There never was a party in the history of this country, and there probably never will be, of sufficient strength to disturb the general peace of the country. Parties themselves may be divided and quarrel on minor questions, yet it extends not beyond the parties themselves. But does not this question make a disturbance outside of political circles? Does it not enter into the churches and rend them asunder? What divided the great Methodist Church into two parts, North and South? What has raised this constant disturbance in every Presbyterian General Assembly that meets? What disturbed the Unitarian Church in this very city two years ago? What has jarred and shaken the great American Tract Society recently, not yet splitting it, but sure to divide it in the end? Is it not this same mighty, deep-seated power that somehow operates on the minds of men, exciting and stirring them up in every avenue of society,—in politics, in religion, in literature, in morals, in all the manifold relations of life?

Is this the work of politicians? Is that irresistible power, which for fifty years has shaken the government and agitated the people, to be stifled and subdued by pretending that it is an exceedingly simple thing, and we ought not to talk about it? If you will get everybody else to stop talking about it, I assure you I will quit before they have half done so. But where is the philosophy or statesmanship which assumes that you can quiet that disturbing element in our society which has disturbed us for more than half a century, which has been the only serious danger that has threatened our institutions,—I say, where is the philosophy or the statesmanship based on the assumption that we are to quit talking about it, and that the public mind is all at once to cease being agitated by it? Yet this is the policy here in the North that Douglas is advocating, that we are to care nothing about it! I ask you if it is not a false philosophy. Is it not a false statesmanship that undertakes to build up a system of policy upon the basis of caring nothing about the very thing that everybody does care the most about?—a thing which all experience has shown we care a very great deal about?

The Judge alludes very often in the course of his remarks to the exclusive right which the States have to decide the whole thing for themselves. I agree with him very readily that the different States have that right. He is but fighting a man of straw when he assumes that I am contending against the right of the States to do as they please about it. Our controversy with him is in regard to the new Territories. We agree that when the States come in as States they have the right and the power to do as they please. We have no power as citizens of the free-States, or in our Federal capacity as members of the Federal Union through the General Government, to disturb slavery in the States where it exists. We profess constantly that we have no more inclination than belief in the power of the government to disturb it; yet we are driven constantly to defend ourselves from the assumption that we are warring upon the rights of the States. What I insist upon is, that the new Territories shall be kept free from it while in the Territorial condition. Judge Douglas assumes that we have no interest in them,—that we have no right whatever to interfere. I think we have some interest. I think that as white men we have.

Do we not wish for an outlet for our surplus population, if I may so express myself? Do we not feel an interest in getting to that outlet with such institutions as we would like to have prevail there? If you go to the Territory opposed to slavery, and another man comes upon the same ground with his slave, upon the assumption that the things are equal, it turns out that he has the equal right all his way, and you have no part of it your way. If he goes in and makes it a slave Territory, and by consequence a slave State, is it not time that those who desire to have it a free State were on equal ground? Let me suggest it in a different way. How many Democrats are there about here ["A thousand"] who have left slave States and come into the free State of Illinois to get rid of the institution of slavery? [Another voice: "A thousand and one."] I reckon there are a thousand and one. I will ask you, if the policy you are now advocating had prevailed when this country was in a Territorial condition, where would you have gone to get rid of it? Where would you have found your free State or Territory to go to? And when hereafter, for any cause, the people in this place shall desire to find new homes, if they wish to be rid of the institution, where will they find the place to go to?

Now, irrespective of the moral aspect of this question as to whether there is a right or wrong in enslaving a negro, I am still in favor of our new Territories being in such a condition that white men may find a home,—may find some spot where they can better their condition; where they can settle upon new soil and better their condition in life. I am in favor of this, not merely (I must say it here as I have elsewhere) for our own people who are born amongst us, but as an outlet for free white people everywhere, the world over—in which Hans, and Baptiste, and Patrick, and all other men from all the world, may find new homes and better their conditions in life.

I have stated upon former occasions, and I may as well state again, what I understand to be the real issue in this controversy between Judge Douglas and myself. On the point of my wanting to make war between the free and the slave States, there has been no issue between us. So, too, when he assumes that I am in favor of producing a perfect social and political equality between the white and black races. These are false issues, upon which Judge Douglas has tried to force the controversy. There is no foundation in truth for the charge that I maintain either of these propositions. The real issue in this controversy—the one pressing upon every mind—is the sentiment on the part of one class that looks upon the institution of slavery as a wrong, and of another class that does not look upon it as a wrong.

The sentiment that contemplates the institution of slavery in this country as a wrong is the sentiment of the Republican party. It is the sentiment around which all their actions, all their arguments, circle, from which all their propositions radiate. They look upon it as being a moral, social, and political wrong; and while they contemplate it as such, they nevertheless have due regard for its actual existence among us, and the difficulties of getting rid of it in any satisfactory way, and to all the constitutional obligations thrown about it. Yet, having a due regard for these, they desire a policy in regard to it that looks to its not creating any more danger. They insist that it should, as far as may be, be treated as a wrong; and one of the methods of treating it as a wrong is to make provision that it shall grow no larger. They also desire a policy that looks to a peaceful end of slavery at some time, as being wrong.

These are the views they entertain in regard to it as I understand them; and all their sentiments, all their arguments and propositions, are brought within this range. I have said, and I repeat it here, that if there be a man amongst us who does not think that the institution of slavery is wrong in any one of the aspects of which I have spoken, he is misplaced, and ought not to be with us. And if there be a man amongst us who is so impatient of it as a wrong as to disregard its actual presence among us and the difficulty of getting rid of it suddenly in a satisfactory way, and to disregard the constitutional obligations thrown about it, that man is misplaced if he is on our platform. We disclaim sympathy with him in practical action. He is not placed properly with us.

On this subject of treating it as a wrong, and limiting its spread, let me say a word. Has anything ever threatened the existence of this Union save and except this very institution of slavery? What is it that we hold most dear amongst us? Our own liberty and prosperity. What has ever threatened our liberty and prosperity, save and except this institution of slavery? If this is true, how do you propose to improve the condition of things by enlarging slavery, by spreading it out and making it bigger? You may have a wen or cancer upon your person, and not be able to cut it out, lest you bleed to death; but surely it is no way to cure it, to engraft it and spread it over your whole body. That is no proper way of treating what you regard a wrong. You see this peaceful way of dealing with it as a wrong, restricting the spread of it, and not allowing it to go into new countries where it has not already existed. That is the peaceful way, the old-fashioned way, the way in which the fathers themselves set us the example.

On the other hand, I have said there is a sentiment which treats it as not being wrong. That is the Democratic sentiment of this day. I do not mean to say that every man who stands within that range positively asserts that it is right. That class will include all who positively assert that it is right, and all who, like Judge Douglas, treat it as indifferent and do not say it is either right or wrong. These two classes of men fall within the general class of those who do not look upon it as a wrong. And if there be among you anybody who supposes that he, as a Democrat, can consider himself "as much opposed to slavery as anybody," I would like to reason with him. You never treat it as a wrong. What other thing that you consider as a wrong do you deal with as you deal with that? Perhaps you say it is wrong—but your leader never does, and you quarrel with anybody who says it is wrong. Although you pretend to say so yourself, you can find no fit place to deal with it as a wrong. You must not say anything about it in the free States, because it is not here. You must not say anything about it in the slave States, because it is there. You must not say anything about it in the pulpit, because that is religion, and has nothing to do with it. You must not say anything about it in politics, because that will disturb the security of "my place." There is no place to talk about it as being a wrong, although you say yourself it is a wrong.

But, finally, you will screw yourself up to the belief that if the people of the slave States should adopt a system of gradual emancipation on the slavery question, you would be in favor of it. You would be in favor of it. You say that is getting it in the right place, and you would be glad to see it succeed. But you are deceiving yourself. You all know that Frank Blair and Gratz Brown, down there in St. Louis, undertook to introduce that system in Missouri. They fought as valiantly as they could for the system of gradual emancipation which you pretend you would be glad to see succeed. Now, I will bring you to the test. After a hard fight they were beaten, and when the news came over here, you threw up your hats and hurrahed for Democracy. More than that, take all the argument made in favor of the system you have proposed, and it carefully excludes the idea that there is anything wrong in the institution of slavery. The arguments to sustain that policy carefully exclude it. Even here to-day you heard Judge Douglas quarrel with me because I uttered a wish that it might sometime come to an end. Although Henry Clay could say he wished every slave in the United States was in the country of his ancestors, I am denounced by those pretending to respect Henry Clay for uttering a wish that it might sometime, in some peaceful way, come to an end. The Democratic policy in regard to that institution will not tolerate the merest breath, the slightest hint, of the least degree of wrong about it.

Try it by some of Judge Douglas's arguments. He says he "don't care whether it is voted up or voted down" in the Territories. I do not care myself, in dealing with that expression, whether it is intended to be expressive of his individual sentiments on the subject, or only of the national policy he desires to have established. It is alike valuable for my purpose. Any man can say that who does not see anything wrong in slavery; but no man can logically say it who does see a wrong in it, because no man can logically say he don't care whether a wrong is voted up or voted down. He may say he don't care whether an indifferent thing is voted up or down, but he must logically have a choice between a right thing and a wrong thing. He contends that whatever community wants slaves has a right to have them. So they have, if it is not a wrong. But if it is a wrong, he cannot say people have a right to do wrong. He says that upon the score of equality slaves should be allowed to go in a new Territory, like other property. This is strictly logical if there is no difference between it and other property. If it and other property are equal, this argument is entirely logical. But if you insist that one is wrong and the other right, there is no use to institute a comparison between right and wrong. You may turn over everything in the Democratic policy from beginning to end, whether in the shape it takes on the statute book, in the shape it takes in the Dred Scott decision, in the shape it takes in conversation, or the shape it takes in short maxim-like arguments,—it everywhere carefully excludes the idea that there is anything wrong in it.

That is the real issue. That is the issue that will continue in this country when these poor tongues of Judge Douglas and myself shall be silent. It is the eternal struggle between these two principles—right and wrong—throughout the world. They are the two principles that have stood face to face from the beginning of time, and will ever continue to struggle. The one is the common right of humanity, and the other the divine right of kings. It is the same principle in whatever shape it develops itself. It is the same spirit that says, "You work and toil and earn bread, and I'll eat it." No matter in what shape it comes, whether from the mouth of a king who seeks to bestride the people of his own nation and live by the fruit of their labor, or from one race of men as an apology for enslaving another race, it is the same tyrannical principle.

I was glad to express my gratitude at Quincy, and I re-express it here, to Judge Douglas,—that he looks to no end of the institution of slavery. That will help the people to see where the struggle really is. It will hereafter place with us all men who really do wish the wrong may have an end. And whenever we can get rid of the fog which obscures the real question, when we can get Judge Douglas and his friends to avow a policy looking to its perpetuation,—we can get out from among that class of men and bring them to the side of those who treat it as a wrong. Then there will soon be an end of it, and that end will be its "ultimate extinction." Whenever the issue can be distinctly made, and all extraneous matter thrown out so that men can fairly see the real difference between the parties, this controversy will soon be settled, and it will be done peaceably too. There will be no war, no violence. It will be placed again where the wisest and best men of the world placed it. Brooks of South Carolina once declared that when this Constitution was framed its framers did not look to the institution existing until this day. When he said this, I think he stated a fact that is fully borne out by the history of the times. But he also said they were better and wiser men than the men of these days, yet the men of these days had experience which they had not, and by the invention of the cotton-gin it became a necessity in this country that slavery should be perpetual. I now say that, willingly or unwillingly—purposely or without purpose, Judge Douglas has been the most prominent instrument in changing the position of the institution of slavery,—which the fathers of the government expected to come to an end ere this,—and putting it upon Brooks's cotton-gin basis; placing it where he openly confesses he has no desire there shall ever be an end of it.

I understand I have ten minutes yet. I will employ it in saying something about this argument Judge Douglas uses, while he sustains the Dred Scott decision, that the people of the Territories can still somehow exclude slavery. The first thing I ask attention to is the fact that Judge Douglas constantly said, before the decision, that whether they could or not, was a question for the Supreme Court. But after the court had made the decision he virtually says it is not a question for the Supreme Court, but for the people. And how is it he tells us they can exclude it? He says it needs "police regulations," and that admits of "unfriendly legislation." Although it is a right established by the Constitution of the United States to take a slave into a Territory of the United States and hold him as property, yet unless the Territorial Legislature will give friendly legislation, and more especially if they adopt unfriendly legislation, they can practically exclude him.

Now, without meeting this proposition as a matter of fact, I pass to consider the real constitutional obligation. Let me take the gentleman who looks me in the face before me, and let us suppose that he is a member of the Territorial Legislature. The first thing he will do will be to swear that he will support the Constitution of the United States. His neighbor by his side in the Territory has slaves and needs Territorial legislation to enable him to enjoy that constitutional right. Can he withhold the legislation which his neighbor needs for the enjoyment of a right which is fixed in his favor in the Constitution of the United States which he has sworn to support? Can he withhold it without violating his oath? And, more especially, can he pass unfriendly legislation to violate his oath?

Why, this is a monstrous sort of talk about the Constitution of the United States! There has never been as outlandish or lawless a doctrine from the mouth of any respectable man on earth. I do not believe it is a constitutional right to hold slaves in a Territory of the United States. I believe the decision was improperly made and I go for reversing it. Judge Douglas is furious against those who go for reversing a decision. But he is for legislating it out of all force while the law itself stands. I repeat that there has never been so monstrous a doctrine uttered from the mouth of a respectable man.

I suppose most of us (I know it of myself) believe that the people of the Southern States are entitled to a Congressional Fugitive Slave law,—that is a right fixed in the Constitution. But it cannot be made available to them without Congressional legislation. In the Judge's language, it is a "barren right," which needs legislation before it can become efficient and valuable to the persons to whom it is guaranteed. And as the right is constitutional, I agree that the legislation shall be granted to it, and that not that we like the institution of slavery. We profess to have no taste for running and catching niggers, at least, I profess no taste for that job at all. Why then do I yield support to a Fugitive Slave law? Because I do not understand that the Constitution, which guarantees that right, can be supported without it. And if I believed that the right to hold a slave in a Territory was equally fixed in the Constitution with the right to reclaim fugitives, I should be bound to give it the legislation necessary to support it. I say that no man can deny his obligation to give the necessary legislation to support slavery in a Territory, who believes it is a constitutional right to have it there. No man can, who does not give the Abolitionists an argument to deny the obligation enjoined by the Constitution to enact a Fugitive State law. Try it now. It is the strongest Abolition argument ever made. I say if that Dred Scott decision is correct, then the right to hold slaves in a Territory is equally a constitutional right with the right of a slaveholder to have his runaway returned. No one can show the distinction between them. The one is express, so that we cannot deny it. The other is construed to be in the Constitution, so that he who believes the decision to be correct believes in the right. And the man who argues that by unfriendly legislation, in spite of that constitutional right, slavery may be driven from the Territories, cannot avoid furnishing an argument by which Abolitionists may deny the obligation to return fugitives, and claim the power to pass laws unfriendly to the right of the slaveholder to reclaim his fugitive.

I do not know how such an argument may strike a popular assembly like this, but I defy anybody to go before a body of men whose minds are educated to estimating evidence and reasoning, and show that there is an iota of difference between the constitutional right to reclaim a fugitive and the constitutional right to hold a slave, in a Territory, provided this Dred Scott decision is correct, I defy any man to make an argument that will justify unfriendly legislation to deprive a slaveholder of his right to hold his slave in a Territory, that will not equally, in all its length, breadth, and thickness, furnish an argument for nullifying the Fugitive Slave law. Why, there is not such an Abolitionist in the nation as Douglas, after all!

LAST SPEECH IN SPRINGFIELD, ILLINOIS, IN THE
1858 CAMPAIGN, OCTOBER 30, 1858.

My friends, to-day closes the discussions of this canvass. The planting and the culture are over; and there remains but the preparation, and the harvest.

I stand here surrounded by friends—some political, all personal friends, I trust. May I be indulged, in this closing scene, to say a few words of myself. I have borne a laborious, and, in some respects to myself, a painful part in the contest. Through all, I have neither assailed, nor wrestled with any part of the constitution. The legal right of the Southern people to reclaim their fugitives I have constantly admitted. The legal right of Congress to interfere with their institutions in the States, I have constantly denied. In resisting the spread of slavery to new territory, and with that, what appears to me to be a tendency to subvert the first principle of free government itself my whole effort has consisted. To the best of my judgment I have labored for, and not against, the Union. As I have not felt, so I have not expressed any harsh sentiment towards our Southern brethren. I have constantly declared, as I have really believed, the only difference between them and us, is the difference of circumstances.

I have meant to assail the motives of no party, or individual; and if I have, in any instance (of which I am not conscious) departed from my purpose, I regret it.

I have said that in some respects the contest has been painful to me. Myself, and those with whom I act, have been constantly accused of a purpose to destroy the Union; and bespattered with every imaginable odious epithet; and some who were friends, as it were but yesterday have made themselves most active in this. I have cultivated patience, and made no attempt at a retort.

Ambition has been ascribed to me. God knows how sincerely I prayed from the first that this field of ambition might not be opened. I claim no insensibility to political honors; but to-day could the Missouri restriction be restored, and the whole slavery question replaced on the old ground of "toleration" by necessity where it exists, with unyielding hostility to the spread of it, on principle, I would, in consideration, gladly agree, that Judge Douglas should never be out, and I never in, an office, so long as we both, or either, live.

ADDRESS BEFORE THE WISCONSIN STATE AGRICULTURAL SOCIETY, MILWAUKEE, WISCONSIN, SEPTEMBER 30, 1859.

MEMBERS OF THE AGRICULTURAL SOCIETY AND CITIZENS OF WISCONSIN: Agricultural fairs are becoming an institution of the country. They are useful in more ways than one. They bring us together, and thereby make us better acquainted and better friends than we otherwise would be. From the first appearance of man upon the earth down to very recent times, the words "stranger" and "enemy" were quite or almost synonymous. Long after civilized nations had defined robbery and murder as high crimes, and had affixed severe punishments to them, when practiced among and upon their own people respectively, it was deemed no offense, but even meritorious, to rob and murder and enslave strangers, whether as nations or as individuals. Even yet, this has not totally disappeared. The man of the highest moral cultivation, in spite of all which abstract principle can do, likes him whom he does know much better than him whom he does not know. To correct the evils, great and small, which spring from want of sympathy and from positive enmity among strangers, as nations or as individuals, is one of the highest functions of civilization. To this end our agricultural fairs contribute in no small degree. They render more pleasant, and more strong, and more durable the bond of social and political union among us. Again, if, as Pope declares, "happiness is our being's end and aim," our fairs contribute much to that end and aim, as occasions of recreation, as holidays. Constituted as man is, he has positive need of occasional recreation, and whatever can give him this associated with virtue and advantage, and free from vice and disadvantage, is a positive good. Such recreation our fairs afford. They are a present pleasure, to be followed by no pain as a consequence; they are a present pleasure, making the future more pleasant.

But the chief use of agricultural fairs is to aid in improving the great calling of agriculture in all its departments and minute divisions; to make mutual exchange of agricultural discovery, information, and knowledge; so that, at the end, all may know everything which may have been known to but one or to but few, at the beginning; to bring together especially all which is supposed to be not generally known because of recent discovery or invention.

And not only to bring together and to impart all which has been accidentally discovered and invented upon ordinary motive, but by exciting emulation for premiums, and for the pride and honor of success,—of triumph, in some sort,—to stimulate that discovery and invention into extraordinary activity. In this these fairs are kindred to the patent clause in the Constitution of the United States, and to the department and practical system based upon that clause.

One feature, I believe, of every fair is a regular address. The Agricultural Society of the young, prosperous, and soon to be great State of Wisconsin has done me the high honor of selecting me to make that address upon this occasion—an honor for which I make my profound and grateful acknowledgment.

I presume I am not expected to employ the time assigned me in the mere flattery of the farmers as a class. My opinion of them is that, in proportion to numbers, they are neither better nor worse than other people. In the nature of things they are more numerous than any other class; and I believe there really are more attempts at flattering them than any other, the reason of which I cannot perceive, unless it be that they can cast more votes than any other. On reflection, I am not quite sure that there is not cause of suspicion against you in selecting me, in some sort a politician and in no sort a farmer, to address you.

But farmers being the most numerous class, it follows that their interest is the largest interest. It also follows that that interest is most worthy of all to be cherished and cultivated—that if there be inevitable conflict between that interest and any other, that other should yield.

Again, I suppose it is not expected of me to impart to you much specific information on agriculture. You have no reason to believe, and do not believe, that I possess it; if that were what you seek in this address, any one of your own number or class would be more able to furnish it. You, perhaps, do expect me to give some general interest to the occasion, and to make some general suggestions on practical matters. I shall attempt nothing more. And in such suggestions by me, quite likely very little will be new to you, and a large part of the rest will be possibly already known to be erroneous.

My first suggestion is an inquiry as to the effect of greater thoroughness in all the departments of agriculture than now prevails in the Northwest—perhaps I might say in America. To speak entirely within bounds, it is known that fifty bushels of wheat, or one hundred bushels of Indian corn, can be produced from an acre. Less than a year ago I saw it stated that a man, by extraordinary care and labor, had produced of wheat what was equal to two hundred bushels from an acre. But take fifty of wheat, and one hundred of corn, to be the possibility, and compare it with the actual crops of the country. Many years ago I saw it stated, in a patent-office report, that eighteen bushels was the average crop throughout the United States; and this year an intelligent farmer of Illinois assured me that he did not believe the land harvested in that State this season had yielded more than an average of eight bushels to the acre; much was cut, and then abandoned as not worth threshing, and much was abandoned as not worth cutting. As to Indian corn, and indeed, most other crops, the case has not been much better. For the last four years I do not believe the ground planted with corn in Illinois has produced an average of twenty bushels to the acre.

It is true that heretofore we have had better crops with no better cultivation, but I believe it is also true that the soil has never been pushed up to one half of its capacity.

What would be the effect upon the farming interest to push the soil up to something near its full capacity! Unquestionably it will take more labor to produce fifty bushels from an acre than it will to produce ten bushels from the same acre; but will it take more labor to produce fifty bushels from one acre than from five? Unquestionably thorough cultivation will require more labor to the acre; but will it require more to the bushel? If it should require just as much to the bushel, there are some probable, and several certain, advantages in favor of the thorough practice. It is probable it would develop those unknown causes which of late years have cut down our crops below their former average. It is almost certain, I think, that by deeper plowing, analysis of the soils, experiments with manures and varieties of seeds, observance of seasons, and the like, these causes would be discovered and remedied. It is certain that thorough cultivation would spare half, or more than half, the cost of land, simply because the same product would be got from half, or from less than half, the quantity of land. This proposition is self-evident, and can be made no plainer by repetitions or illustrations. The cost of land is a great item, even in new countries, and it constantly grows greater and greater, in comparison with other items, as the country grows older.

It also would spare the making and maintaining of enclosures for the same, whether these enclosures should be hedges, ditches, or fences, This again is a heavy item—heavy at first, and heavy in its continual demand for repairs. I remember once being greatly astonished by an apparently authentic exhibition of the proportion the cost of an enclosure bears to all the other expenses of the farmer, though I cannot remember exactly what that proportion was. Any farmer, if he will, can ascertain it in his own case for himself.

Again, a great amount of locomotion is spared by thorough cultivation. Take fifty bushels of wheat ready for harvest, standing upon a single acre, and it can be harvested in any of the known ways with less than half the labor which would be required if it were spread over five acres. This would be true if cut by the old hand-sickle; true, to a greater extent, if by the scythe and cradle; and to a still greater extent, if by the machines now in use. These machines are chiefly valuable as a means of substituting animal-power for the power of men in this branch of farm-work. In the highest degree of perfection yet reached in applying the horse-power to harvesting, fully nine tenths of the power is expended by the animal in carrying himself and dragging the machine over the field, leaving certainly not more than one tenth to be applied directly to the only end of the whole operation—the gathering in of the grain, and clipping of the straw. When grain is very thin on the ground, it is always more or less intermingled with weeds, chess, and the like, and a large part of the power is expended in cutting these. It is plain that when the crop is very thick upon the ground, a larger proportion of the power is directly applied to gathering in and cutting it; and the smaller to that which is totally useless as an end. And what I have said of harvesting is true in a greater or less degree of mowing, plowing, gathering in of crops generally, and indeed of almost all farm-work.

The effect of thorough cultivation upon the farmer's own mind, and in reaction through his mind back upon his business, is perhaps quite equal to any other of its effects. Every man is proud of what he does well, and no man is proud of that he does not well. With the former his heart is in his work, and he will do twice as much of it with less fatigue; the latter he performs a little imperfectly, looks at it in disgust, turns from it, and imagines himself exceedingly tired—the little he has done comes to nothing for want of finishing.

The man who produces a good full crop will scarcely ever let any part of it go to waste; he will keep up the enclosure about it, and allow neither man nor beast to trespass upon it; he will gather it in due season, and store it in perfect security. Thus he labors with satisfaction, and saves himself the whole fruit of his labor. The other, starting with no purpose for a full crop, labors less, and with less satisfaction, allows his fences to fall, and cattle to trespass, gathers not in due season, or not at all. Thus the labor he has performed is wasted away, little by little, till in the end he derives scarcely anything from it.

The ambition for broad acres leads to poor farming, even with men of energy. I scarcely ever knew a mammoth farm to sustain itself, much less to return a profit upon the outlay. I have more than once known a man to spend a respectable fortune upon one, fail, and leave it, and then some man of modest aims get a small fraction of the ground, and make a good living upon it. Mammoth farms are like tools or weapons which are too heavy to be handled; ere long they are thrown aside at a great loss.

The successful application of steam-power to farm-work is a desideratum—especially a steam-plow. It is not enough that a machine operated by steam will really plow. To be successful, it must, all things considered, plow better than can be done with animal-power. It must do all the work as well, and cheaper; or more rapidly, so as to get through more perfectly in season; or in some way afford an advantage over plowing with animals, else it is no success. I have never seen a machine intended for a steam-plow. Much praise and admiration are bestowed upon some of them, and they may be, for aught I know, already successful; but I have not perceived the demonstration of it. I have thought a good deal, in an abstract way, about a steam-plow. That one which shall be so contrived as to apply the larger proportion of its power to the cutting and turning the soil, and the smallest, to the moving itself over the field, will be the best one. A very small stationary-engine would draw a large gang of plows through the ground from a short distance to itself; but when it is not stationary, but has to move along like a horse, dragging the plows after it, it must have additional power to carry itself; and the difficulty grows by what is intended to overcome it; for what adds power also adds size and weight to the machine, thus increasing again the demand for power. Suppose you construct the machine so as to cut a succession of short furrows, say a rod in length, transversely to the course the machine is locomoting, something like the shuttle in weaving. In such case the whole machine would move north only the width of a furrow, while in length the furrow would be a rod from east to west. In such case a very large proportion of the power would be applied to the actual plowing. But in this, too, there would be difficulty, which would be the getting of the plow into and out of the ground, at the end of all these short furrows.

I believe, however, ingenious men will, if they have not already, overcome the difficulty I have suggested. But there is still another, about which I am less sanguine. It is the supply of fuel, and especially water, to make steam. Such supply is clearly practicable; but can the expense of it be borne? Steamboats live upon the water, and find their fuel at stated places. Steam-mills and other stationary steam-machinery have their stationary supplies of fuel and water. Railroad-locomotives have their regular wood and water stations. But the steam-plow is less fortunate. It does not live upon the water, and if it be once at a water-station, it will work away from it, and when it gets away cannot return without leaving its work, at a great expense of its time and strength. It will occur that a wagon-and-horse team might be employed to supply it with fuel and water; but this, too, is expensive; and the question recurs, "Can the expense be borne?" When this is added to all other expenses, will not plowing cost more than in the old way!

It is to be hoped that the steam-plow will be finally successful, and if it shall be, "thorough cultivation"—putting the soil to the top of its capacity, producing the largest crop possible from a given quantity of ground—will be most favorable for it. Doing a large amount of work upon a small quantity of ground, it will be as nearly as possible stationary while working, and as free as possible from locomotion, thus expending its strength as much as possible upon its work, and as little as possible in traveling. Our thanks, and something more substantial than thanks, are due to every man engaged in the effort to produce a successful steam-plow. Even the unsuccessful will bring something to light which, in the hands of others, will contribute to the final success. I have not pointed out difficulties in order to discourage, but in order that, being seen, they may be the more readily overcome.

The world is agreed that labor is the source from which human wants are mainly supplied. There is no dispute upon this point. From this point, however, men immediately diverge. Much disputation is maintained as to the best way of applying and controlling the labor element. By some it is assumed that labor is available only in connection with capital—that nobody labors, unless somebody else owning capital, somehow, by the use of it, induces him to do it. Having assumed this, they proceed to consider whether it is best that capital shall hire laborers, and thus induce them to work by their own consent, or buy them, and drive them to it, without their consent. Having proceeded so far, they naturally conclude that all laborers are naturally either hired laborers or slaves. They further assume that whoever is once a hired laborer, is fatally fixed in that condition for life; and thence again, that his condition is as bad as, or worse than, that of a slave. This is the "mud-sill" theory. But another class of reasoners hold the opinion that there is no such relation between capital and labor as assumed; that there is no such thing as a free man being fatally fixed for life in the condition of a hired laborer; that both these assumptions are false, and all inferences from them groundless. They hold that labor is prior to, and independent of, capital; that, in fact, capital is the fruit of labor, and could never have existed if labor had not first existed; that labor can exist without capital, but that capital could never have existed without labor. Hence they hold that labor is the superior—greatly the superior—of capital.

They do not deny that there is, and probably always will be, a relation between labor and capital. The error, as they hold, is in assuming that the whole labor of the world exists within that relation. A few men own capital; and that few avoid labor themselves, and with their capital hire or buy another few to labor for them. A large majority belong to neither class—neither work for others, nor have others working for them. Even in all our slave States except South Carolina, a majority of the whole people of all colors are neither slaves nor masters. In these free States, a large majority are neither hirers nor hired. Men, with their families—wives, sons, and daughters—work for themselves, on their farms, in their houses, and in their shops, taking the whole product to themselves, and asking no favors of capital on the one hand, nor of hirelings or slaves on the other. It is not forgotten that a considerable number of persons mingle their own labor with capital—that is, labor with their own hands, and also buy slaves or hire free men to labor for them; but this is only a mixed, and not a distinct, class. No principle stated is disturbed by the existence of this mixed class. Again, as has already been said, the opponents of the "mud-sill" theory insist that there is not, of necessity, any such thing as the free hired laborer being fixed to that condition for life. There is demonstration for saying this. Many independent men in this assembly doubtless a few years ago were hired laborers. And their case is almost, if not quite, the general rule.

The prudent, penniless beginner in the world labors for wages awhile, saves a surplus with which to buy tools or land for himself, then labors on his own account another while, and at length hires another new beginner to help him. This, say its advocates, is free labor—the just, and generous, and prosperous system, which opens the way for all, gives hope to all, and energy, and progress, and improvement of condition to all. If any continue through life in the condition of the hired laborer, it is not the fault of the system, but because of either a dependent nature which prefers it, or improvidence, folly, or singular misfortune. I have said this much about the elements of labor generally, as introductory to the consideration of a new phase which that element is in process of assuming. The old general rule was that educated people did not perform manual labor. They managed to eat their bread, leaving the toil of producing it to the uneducated. This was not an insupportable evil to the working bees, so long as the class of drones remained very small. But now, especially in these free States, nearly all are educated—quite too nearly all to leave the labor of the uneducated in any wise adequate to the support of the whole. It follows from this that henceforth educated people must labor. Otherwise, education itself would become a positive and intolerable evil. No country can sustain in idleness more than a small percentage of its numbers. The great majority must labor at something productive. From these premises the problem springs, "How can labor and education be the most satisfactorily combined?"

By the "mud-sill" theory it is assumed that labor and education are incompatible, and any practical combination of them impossible. According to that theory, a blind horse upon a tread-mill is a perfect illustration of what a laborer should be—all the better for being blind, that he could not kick understandingly. According to that theory, the education of laborers is not only useless but pernicious and dangerous. In fact, it is, in some sort, deemed a misfortune that laborers should have heads at all. Those same heads are regarded as explosive materials, only to be safely kept in damp places, as far as possible from that peculiar sort of fire which ignites them. A Yankee who could invent a strong-handed man without a head would receive the everlasting gratitude of the "mud-sill" advocates.

But free labor says, "No." Free labor argues that as the Author of man makes every individual with one head and one pair of hands, it was probably intended that heads and hands should cooperate as friends, and that that particular head should direct and control that pair of hands. As each man has one mouth to be fed, and one pair of hands to furnish food, it was probably intended that that particular pair of hands should feed that particular mouth—that each head is the natural guardian, director, and protector of the hands and mouth inseparably connected with it; and that being so, every head should be cultivated and improved by whatever will add to its capacity for performing its charge. In one word, free labor insists on universal education.

I have so far stated the opposite theories of "mud-sill" and "free labor," without declaring any preference of my own between them. On an occasion like this, I ought not to declare any. I suppose, however, I shall not be mistaken in assuming as a fact that the people of Wisconsin prefer free labor, with its natural companion, education.

This leads to the further reflection that no other human occupation opens so wide a field for the profitable and agreeable combination of labor with cultivated thought, as agriculture. I know nothing so pleasant to the mind as the discovery of anything that is at once new and valuable—nothing that so lightens and sweetens toil as the hopeful pursuit of such discovery. And how vast and how varied a field is agriculture for such discovery! The mind, already trained to thought in the country school, or higher school, cannot fail to find there an exhaustless source of enjoyment. Every blade of grass is a study; and to produce two where there was but one is both a profit and a pleasure. And not grass alone, but soils, seeds, and seasons—hedges, ditches, and fences—draining, droughts, and irrigation—plowing, hoeing, and harrowing—reaping, mowing, and threshing—saving crops, pests of crops, diseases of crops, and what will prevent or cure them—implements, utensils, and machines, their relative merits, and how to improve them—hogs, horses, and cattle—sheep, goats, and poultry—trees, shrubs, fruits, plants, and flowers—the thousand things of which these are specimens—each a world of study within itself.

In all this, book-learning is available. A capacity and taste for reading gives access to whatever has already been discovered by others. It is the key, or one of the keys, to the already solved problems. And not only so: it gives a relish and facility for successfully pursuing the unsolved ones. The rudiments of science are available, and highly available. Some knowledge of botany assists in dealing with the vegetable world—with all growing crops. Chemistry assists in the analysis of soils, selection and application of manures, and in numerous other ways. The mechanical branches of natural philosophy are ready help in almost everything, but especially in reference to implements and machinery.

The thought recurs that education—cultivated thought—can best be combined with agricultural labor, or any labor, on the principle of thorough work; that careless, half performed, slovenly work makes no place for such combination; and thorough work, again, renders sufficient the smallest quantity of ground to each man; and this, again, conforms to what must occur in a world less inclined to wars and more devoted to the arts of peace than heretofore. Population must increase rapidly, more rapidly than in former times, and ere long the most valuable of all arts will be the art of deriving a comfortable subsistence from the smallest area of soil. No community whose every member possesses this art, can ever be the victim of oppression in any of its forms. Such community will be alike independent of crowned kings, money kings, and land kings.

But, according to your program, the awarding of premiums awaits the closing of this address. Considering the deep interest necessarily pertaining to that performance, it would be no wonder if I am already heard with some impatience. I will detain you but a moment longer. Some of you will be successful, and such will need but little philosophy to take them home in cheerful spirits; others will be disappointed, and will be in a less happy mood. To such let it be said, "Lay it not too much to heart." Let them adopt the maxim, "Better luck next time," and then by renewed exertion make that better luck for themselves.

And by the successful and unsuccessful let it be remembered that while occasions like the present bring their sober and durable benefits, the exultations and mortifications of them are but temporary; that the victor will soon be vanquished if he relax in his exertion; and that the vanquished this year may be victor the next, in spite of all competition.

It is said an Eastern monarch once charged his wise men to invent him a sentence to be ever in view, and which should be true and appropriate in all times and situations. They presented him the words, "And this, too, shall pass away." How much it expresses! How chastening in the hour of pride! How consoling in the depths of affliction! "And this, too, shall pass away." And yet, let us hope, it is not quite true. Let us hope, rather, that by the best cultivation of the physical world beneath and around us, and the intellectual and moral world within us, we shall secure an individual, social, and political prosperity and happiness, whose course shall be onward and upward, and which, while the earth endures, shall not pass away.

ADDRESS AT COOPER INSTITUTE, NEW YORK
CITY, FEBRUARY 27, 1860.

MR. PRESIDENT AND FELLOW-CITIZENS OF NEW YORK:—The facts with which I shall deal this evening are mainly old and familiar; nor is there anything new in the general use I shall make of them. If there shall be any novelty, it will be in the mode of presenting the facts, and the inferences and observations following that presentation.

In his speech last autumn at Columbus, Ohio, as reported in the New York *Times*, Senator Douglas said:

"Our fathers, when they framed the Government under which we live, understood this question just as well, and even better than we do now."

I fully indorse this, and I adopt it as a text for this discourse. I so adopt it because it furnishes a precise and an agreed starting-point for a discussion between Republicans and that wing of the Democracy headed by Senator Douglas. It simply leaves the inquiry: "What was the understanding those fathers had of the question mentioned?"

What is the frame of Government under which we live? The answer must be: "The Constitution of the United States." That Constitution consists of the original, framed in 1787 (and under which the present Government first went into operation), and twelve subsequently framed amendments, the first ten of which were framed in 1789.

Who were our fathers that framed the Constitution? I suppose the "thirty-nine" who signed the original instrument may be fairly called our fathers who framed that part of the present Government. It is almost exactly true to say they framed it, and it is altogether true to say they fairly represented the opinion and sentiment of the whole nation at that time. Their names, being familiar to nearly all, and accessible to quite all, need not now be repeated. I take these "thirty-nine," for the present, as being "our fathers who framed the Government under which we live."

What is the question which, according to the text, those fathers understood just as well, and even better than we do now? It is this: Does the proper division of local from Federal authority, or anything in the Constitution, forbid our Federal Government to control as to slavery in our Federal Territories?

Upon this Senator Douglas holds the affirmative, and Republicans the negative. This affirmation and denial form an issue, and this issue— this question—is precisely what the text declares our fathers understood better than we. Let us now inquire whether the "thirty-nine," or any of them, acted upon this question; and if they did—how they acted upon it—how they expressed that better understanding.

In 1784—three years before the Constitution—the United States then owning the Northwestern Territory, and no other—the Congress of the Confederation had before them the question of prohibiting slavery in that Territory; and four of the "thirty nine" who afterward framed the Constitution were in that Congress and voted on that question. Of these, Roger Sherman, Thomas Mifflin, and Hugh Williamson voted for the prohibition, thus showing that, in their understanding, no line dividing local from Federal authority, nor anything else, properly forbade the Federal Government to control as to slavery in Federal territory. The other of the four—James McHenry voted against the prohibition, showing that, for some cause, he thought it improper to vote for it.

In 1787, still before the Constitution, but while the convention was in session framing it, and while the Northwestern Territory still was the only Territory owned by the United States—the same question of prohibiting slavery in the Territory again came before the Congress of the Confederation; and two more of the "thirty-nine" who afterward signed the Constitution were in that Congress, and voted on the question. They were William Blount and William Few; and they both voted for the prohibition thus showing that, in their understanding, no line dividing local from Federal authority, nor anything else, properly forbade the Federal Government to control as to slavery in Federal territory. This time the prohibition became a law, being part of what is now well known as the Ordinance of '87.

The question of Federal control of slavery in the Territories seems not to have been directly before the convention which framed the original Constitution; and hence it is not recorded that the "thirty-nine," or any of them, while engaged on that instrument, expressed any opinion on that precise question.

In 1789, by the first Congress which sat under the Constitution, an act was passed to enforce the Ordinance of '87, including the prohibition of slavery in the Northwestern Territory. The bill for this act was reported by one of the "thirty-nine," Thomas Fitzsimmons, then a member of the House of Representatives from Pennsylvania. It went through all its stages without a word of opposition, and finally passed both branches without yeas and nays, which is equivalent to a unanimous passage. In this Congress there were sixteen of the thirty-nine fathers who framed the original Constitution. They were: John Langdon, Nicholas Gilman, Wm. S. Johnnson, Roger Sherman, Robert Morris, Thos. Fitzsimmons, William Few, Abraham Baldwin, Rufus King, William Paterson, George Claimer, Richard Bassett, George Read, Pierce Butler, Daniel Carroll, James Madison.

This shows that, in their understanding, no line dividing local from Federal authority, nor anything in the Constitution, properly forbade Congress to prohibit slavery in the Federal territory; else both their fidelity to correct principles and their oath to support the Constitution would have constrained them to oppose the prohibition.

Again: George Washington, another of the "thirty nine," was then President of the United States, and, as such, approved and signed the bill; thus completing its validity as a law, and thus showing that, in his understanding, no line dividing local from Federal authority, nor anything in the Constitution, forbade the Federal Government to control as to slavery in Federal territory.

No great while after the adoption of the original Constitution, North Carolina ceded to the Federal Government the country now constituting the State of Tennessee; and, a few years later, Georgia ceded that which now constitutes the States of Mississippi and

Alabama. In both deeds of cession it was made a condition by the ceding States that the Federal Government should not prohibit slavery in the ceded country. Besides this, slavery was then actually in the ceded country. Under these circumstances, Congress, on taking charge of these countries, did not absolutely prohibit slavery within them. But they did interfere with it—take control of it—even there, to a certain extent. In 1798, Congress organized the Territory of Mississippi: In the act of organization they prohibited the bringing of slaves into the Territory from any place without the United States, by fine and giving freedom to slaves so brought. This act passed both branches of Congress without yeas and nays. In that Congress were three of the "thirty-nine" who framed the original Constitution. They were John Langdon, George Read, and Abraham Baldwin. They all, probably, voted for it. Certainly they would have placed their opposition to it upon record, if, in their understanding, any line dividing local from Federal authority, or anything in the Constitution, properly forbade the Federal Government to control as to slavery in Federal territory.

In 1803, the Federal Government purchased the Louisiana country. Our former territorial acquisitions came from certain of our own States; but this Louisiana country was acquired from a foreign nation. In 1804, Congress gave a territorial organization to that part of it which now constitutes the State of Louisiana. New Orleans, lying within that part, was an old and comparatively large city. There were other considerable towns and settlements, and slavery was extensively and thoroughly intermingled with the people. Congress did not, in the Territorial Act, prohibit slavery; but they did interfere with it take control of it—in a more marked and extensive way than they did in the case of Mississippi. The substance of the provision therein made in relation to slaves was:

First. That no slave should be imported into the Territory from foreign parts.

Second. That no slave should be carried into it who had been imported into the United States since the first day of May, 1798.

Third. That no slave should be carried into it except by the owner, and for his own use as a settler; the penalty in all the cases being a fine upon the violator of the law, and freedom to the slave.

This act also was passed without yeas and nays. In the Congress which passed it there were two of the "thirty-nine." They were Abraham Baldwin and Jonathan Dayton. As stated in the case of Mississippi, it is probable they both voted for it. They would not have allowed it to pass without recording their opposition to it, if, in their understanding, it violated either the line properly dividing local from Federal authority, or any provision of the Constitution.

In 1819-20 came and passed the Missouri question. Many votes were taken, by yeas and nays, in both branches of Congress, upon the various phases of the general question. Two of the "thirty-nine"—Rufus King and Charles Pinckney were members of that Congress. Mr. King steadily voted for slavery prohibition and against all compromises, while Mr. Pinckney as steadily voted against slavery prohibition, and against all compromises. By this, Mr. King showed that, in his understanding, no line dividing local from Federal authority, nor anything in the Constitution, was violated by Congress prohibiting slavery in Federal territory; while Mr. Pinckney, by his vote, showed that in his understanding there was some sufficient reason for opposing such prohibition in that case.

The cases I have mentioned are the only acts of the "thirty-nine," or of any of them, upon the direct issue, which I have been able to discover.

To enumerate the persons who thus acted, as being four in 1784, two in 1787, seventeen in 1789, three in 1798, two in 1804, and two in 1819-20—there would be thirty of them. But this would be counting, John Langdon, Roger Sherman, William Few, Rufus King, and George Read, each twice, and Abraham Baldwin three times. The true number of those of the "thirty-nine" whom I have shown to have acted upon the question which, by the text, they understood better than we, is twenty-three, leaving sixteen not shown to have acted upon it in any way.

Here, then, we have twenty-three out of our thirty-nine fathers "who framed the Government under which we live," who have, upon their official responsibility and their corporal oaths, acted upon the very question which the text affirms they "understood just as well, and even better than we do now"; and twenty-one of them—a clear majority of the whole "thirty-nine"—so acting upon it as to make them guilty of gross political impropriety and willful perjury, if, in their understanding, any proper division between local and Federal authority, or anything in the Constitution they had made themselves, and sworn to support, forbade the Federal Government to control as to slavery in the Federal Territories. Thus the twenty-one acted; and, as actions speak louder than words, so actions under such responsibilities speak still louder.

Two of the twenty-three voted against Congressional prohibition of slavery in the Federal Territories, in the instances in which they acted upon the question. But for what reasons they so voted is not known. They may have done so because they thought a proper division of local from Federal authority, or some provision or principle of the Constitution, stood in the way; or they may, without any such question, have voted against the prohibition on what appeared to them to be sufficient grounds of expediency. No one who has sworn to support the Constitution can conscientiously vote for what he understands to be an unconstitutional measure, however expedient he may think it; but one may and ought to vote against a measure which he deems constitutional, if, at the same time, he deems it inexpedient. It therefore would be unsafe to set down even the two who voted against the prohibition as having done so because, in their understanding, any proper division of local from Federal authority, or anything in the Constitution, forbade the Federal Government to control as to slavery in Federal territory.

The remaining sixteen of the "thirty-nine," so far as I have discovered, have left no record of their understanding upon the direct question of Federal control on slavery in the Federal Territories. But there is much reason to believe that their understanding upon that question would not have appeared different from that of their twenty-three compeers, had it been manifested at all.

For the purpose of adhering rigidly to the text, I have purposely omitted whatever understanding may have been manifested by any person, however distinguished, other than the thirty-nine fathers who framed the original Constitution; and, for the same reason, I have also omitted whatever understanding may have been manifested by any of the "thirty tine" even on any other phase of the general question of slavery. If we should look into their acts and declarations on those other phases, as the foreign slave trade, and the morality and policy of slavery generally, it would appear to us that on the direct question of Federal control of slavery in Federal Territories, the sixteen, if they had acted at all, would probably have acted just as the twenty-three did. Among that sixteen were several of the most noted anti-slavery men of those times—as Dr. Franklin, Alexander Hamilton, and Governor Morris while there was not one now known to have been otherwise, unless it may be John Rutledge, of South Carolina.

The sum of the whole is, that of our thirty-nine fathers who framed the original Constitution, twenty-one—a clear majority of the whole— certainly understood that no proper division of local from Federal authority, nor any part of the Constitution, forbade the Federal Government to control slavery in the Federal Territories; whilst all the rest probably had the same understanding. Such, unquestionably, was the understanding of our fathers who framed the original Constitution; and the text affirms that they understood the question "better than we."

But, so far, I have been considering the understanding of the question manifested by the framers of the original Constitution. In and by the original instrument, a mode was provided for amending it; and, as I have already stated, the present frame of "the Government under which we live" consists of that original, and twelve amendatory articles framed and adopted since. Those who now insist that Federal control of slavery in Federal Territories violates the Constitution, point us to the provisions which they suppose it thus violates; and, as I understand, they all fix upon provisions in these amendatory articles, and not in the original instrument. The Supreme Court, in the Dred Scott case, plant themselves upon the fifth amendment, which provides that no person shall be deprived of "life, liberty, or property without due process of law"; while Senator Douglas and his peculiar adherents plant themselves upon the tenth amendment, providing that "the powers not delegated to the United States by the Constitution" "are reserved to the States respectively, or to the people."

Now, it so happens that these amendments were framed by the first Congress which sat under the Constitution—the identical Congress which passed the act already mentioned, enforcing the prohibition of slavery in the Northwestern Territory. Not only was it the same Congress, but they were the identical same individual men who, at the same session, and at the same time within the session, had under consideration, and in progress toward maturity, these Constitutional amendments, and this act prohibiting slavery in all the territory the nation then owned. The Constitutional amendments were introduced before and passed after the act enforcing the Ordinance of '87; so that, during the whole pendency of the act to enforce the Ordinance, the Constitutional amendments were also pending.

That Congress, consisting in all of seventy-six members, including sixteen of the framers of the original Constitution, as before stated, were pre-eminently our fathers who framed that part of "the Government under which we live," which is now claimed as forbidding the Federal Government to control slavery in the Federal Territories.

Is it not a little presumptuous in any one at this day to affirm that the two things which that Congress deliberately framed, and carried to maturity at the same time, are absolutely inconsistent with each other? And does not such affirmation become impudently absurd when coupled with the other affirmation from the same mouth, that those who did the two things alleged to be inconsistent understood whether they really were inconsistent better than we—better than he who affirms that they are inconsistent?

It is surely safe to assume that the thirty-nine framers of the original Constitution, and the seventy-six members of the Congress which framed the amendments thereto, taken together, do certainly include those who may be fairly called "our fathers who framed the Government under which we live." And, so assuming, I defy any man to show that any one of them ever, in his whole life, declared that, in his understanding, any proper division of local from Federal authority, or any part of the Constitution, forbade the Federal Government to control as to slavery in the Federal Territories. I go a step further. I defy any one to show that any living man in the world ever did, prior to the beginning of the present century (and I might almost say prior to the beginning of the last half of the present century), declare that, in his understanding, any proper division of local from Federal authority, or any part of the Constitution, forbade the Federal Government to control as to slavery in the Federal Territories. To those who now so declare, I give not only "our fathers who framed the Government under which we live," but with them all other living men within the century in which it was framed, among whom to search, and they shall not be able to find the evidence of a single man agreeing with them.

Now and here let me guard a little against being misunderstood. I do not mean to say we are bound to follow implicitly in whatever our fathers did. To do so would be to discard all the lights of current experience to reject all progress, all improvement. What I do say is that, if we would supplant the opinions and policy of our fathers in any case, we should do so upon evidence so conclusive, and argument so clear, that even their great authority, fairly considered and weighed, cannot stand; and most surely not in a case whereof we ourselves declare they understood the question better than we.

If any man at this day sincerely believes that proper division of local from Federal authority, or any part of the Constitution, forbids the Federal Government to control as to slavery in the Federal Territories, he is right to say so, and to enforce his position by all truthful evidence and fair argument which he can. But he has no right to mislead others who have less access to history, and less leisure to study it, into the false belief that "our fathers who framed the Government under which we live" were of the same opinion thus substituting falsehood and deception for truthful evidence and fair argument. If any man at this day sincerely believes "our fathers, who framed the Government under which we live," used and applied principles, in other cases, which ought to have led them to understand that a proper division of local from Federal authority, or some part of the Constitution, forbids the Federal Government to control as to slavery in the Federal Territories, he is right to say so. But he should, at the same time, brave the responsibility of declaring that, in his opinion, he understands their principles better than they did themselves; and especially should he not shirk that responsibility by asserting that they "understood the question just as well, and even better than we do now."

But enough! Let all who believe that "our fathers, who framed the Government under which we live, understood this question just as well, and even better than we do now," speak as they spoke, and act as they acted upon it. This is all Republicans ask—all Republicans desire—in relation to slavery. As those fathers marked it, so let it be again marked, as an evil not to be extended, but to be tolerated and protected only because of, and so far as, its actual presence among us makes that toleration and protection a necessity. Let all the guaranties those fathers gave it be not grudgingly, but fully and fairly maintained. For this Republicans contend, and with this, so far as I know or believe, they will be content.

And now, if they would listen—as I suppose they will not—I

would address a few words to the Southern people.

I would say to them: You consider yourselves a reasonable and a just people; and I consider that in the general qualities of reason and justice you are not inferior to any other people. Still, when you speak of us Republicans, you do so only to denounce us as reptiles, or, at the best, as no better than outlaws. You will grant a hearing to pirates or murderers, but nothing like it to "Black Republicans." In all your contentions with one another, each of you deems an unconditional condemnation of "Black Republicanism" as the first thing to be attended to. Indeed, such condemnation of us seems to be an indispensable prerequisite license, so to speak among you, to be admitted or permitted to speak at all.

Now; can you, or not, be prevailed upon to pause, and to consider whether this is quite just to us, or even to yourselves? Bring forward your charges and specifications, and then be patient long enough to hear us deny or justify. You say we are sectional. We deny it. That makes an issue; and the burden of proof is upon you. You produce your proof; and what is it? Why, that our party has no existence in your section—gets no votes in your section. The fact is substantially true; but does it prove the issue? If it does, then in case we should, without change of principle, begin to get votes in your section, we should thereby cease to be sectional. You cannot escape this conclusion; and yet, are you willing to abide by it? If you are, you will probably soon find that we have ceased to be sectional, for we shall get votes in your section this very year. You will then begin to discover, as the truth plainly is, that your proof, does not touch the issue.

The fact that we get no votes in your section is a fact of your making, and not of ours. And if there be fault in that fact, that fault is primarily yours, and remains so until you show that we repel you by, some wrong principle or practice. If we do repel you by any wrong principle or practice, the fault is ours; but this brings you to where you ought to have started to a discussion of the right or wrong of our principle. If our principle, put in practice, would wrong your section for the benefit of ours, or for any other object, then our principle, and we with it, are sectional, and are justly opposed and denounced as such.

Meet us, then, on the question of whether our principle, put in practice, would wrong your section; and so meet us as if it were possible that something may be said on our side. Do you accept the challenge? No! Then you really believe that the principle which "our fathers who framed the Government under which we live" thought so clearly right as to adopt it, and indorse it again and again, upon their official oaths, is in fact so clearly wrong as to demand your condemnation without a moment's consideration.

Some of you delight to flaunt in our faces the warning against sectional parties given by Washington in his Farewell Address. Less than eight years before Washington gave that warning, he had, as President of the United States, approved and signed an act of Congress enforcing the prohibition of slavery in the Northwestern Territory, which act embodied the policy of the Government upon that subject up to, and at, the very moment he penned that warning; and about one year after he penned it, he wrote La Fayette that he considered that prohibition a wise measure, expressing in the same connection his hope that we should at some time have a confederacy of free States.

Bearing this in mind, and seeing that sectionalism has since arisen upon this same subject, is that warning a weapon in your hands against us, or in our hands against you? Could Washington himself speak, would he cast the blame of that sectionalism upon us, who sustain his policy, or upon you, who repudiate it? We respect that warning of Washington, and we commend it to you, together with his example pointing to the right application of it.

But you say you are conservative—eminently conservative—while we are revolutionary, destructive, or something, of the sort. What is conservatism? Is it not adherence to the old and tried, against a new and untried? We stick to, contend for, the identical old policy on the point in controversy which was adopted by "our fathers who framed the Government under which we live"; while you with one accord reject, and scout, and spit upon that old policy and insist upon substituting something new. True, you disagree among yourselves as to what that substitute shall be. You are divided on new propositions and plans, but you are unanimous in rejecting and denouncing the old policy of the fathers.

Some of you are for reviving the foreign slave trade; some for a Congressional slave code for the Territories; some for Congress forbidding the Territories to prohibit slavery within their limits; some for maintaining slavery in the Territories through the judiciary; some for the "gur-reat pur-rinciple" that "if one man would enslave another, no third man should object," fantastically called "popular sovereignty"; but never a man among you in favor of Federal prohibition of slavery in Federal Territories, according to the practice of "our fathers who framed the Government under which we live." Not one of all your various plans can show a precedent or an advocate in the century within which our Government originated. Consider, then, whether your claim of conservatism for yourselves, and your charge of destructiveness against us, are based on the most clear and stable foundations.

Again: You say we have made the slavery question more prominent than it formerly was. We deny it. We admit that it is more prominent, but we deny that we made it so. It was not we, but you, who discarded the old policy of the fathers. We resisted and still resist your innovation; and thence comes the greater prominence of the question. Would you have that question reduced to its former proportions? Go back to that old policy. What has been will be again, under the same conditions. If you would have the peace of the old times, readopt the precepts and policy of the old times.

You charge that we stir up insurrections among your slaves. We deny it; and what is your proof? Harper's Ferry! John Brown!! John Brown was no Republican; and you have failed to implicate a single Republican in his Harper's Ferry enterprise. If any member of our party is guilty in that matter you know it or you do not know it. If you do know it, you are inexcusable for not designating the man and proving the fact. If you do not know it, you are inexcusable for asserting it, and especially for persisting in the assertion after you have tried and failed to make the proof. You need not be told that persisting in a charge which one does not know to be true is simply malicious slander.

Some of you admit that no Republican designedly aided or encouraged the Harper's Ferry affair, but still insist that our doctrines and declarations necessarily lead to such results. We do not believe it. We know we hold to no doctrine, and make no declaration, which were not held to and made by our fathers who framed the Government under which we live. You never dealt fairly by us in relation to this affair. When it occurred, some important State elections were near at hand, and you were in evident glee with the belief that, by charging the blame upon us, you could get an advantage of us in those elections. The elections came, and your expectations were not quite fulfilled. Every Republican man knew that, as to himself at least, your charge was a slander, and he was not much inclined by it to cast his vote in your favor.

Republican doctrines and declarations are accompanied with a continued protest against any interference whatever with your slaves, or with you about your slaves. Surely, this does not encourage them to revolt. True, we do, in common with "our fathers, who framed the Government under which we live," declare our belief that slavery is wrong; but the slaves do not hear us declare even this. For any thing we say or do, the slaves would scarcely know there is a Republican party. I believe they would not, in fact, generally know it but for your misrepresentations of us in their hearing. In your political contests among yourselves, each faction charges the other with sympathy with Black Republicanism; and then, to give point to the charge, defines Black Republicanism to simply be insurrection, blood, and thunder among the slaves.

Slave insurrections are no more common now than they were before the Republican party was organized. What induced the Southampton insurrection, twenty-eight years ago, in which, at least, three times as many lives were lost as at Harper's Ferry? You can scarcely stretch your very elastic fancy to the conclusion that Southampton was "got up by Black Republicanism." In the present state of things in the United States, I do not think a general or even a very extensive slave insurrection is possible. The indispensable concert of action cannot be attained. The slaves have no means of rapid communication; nor can incendiary freemen, black or white, supply it. The explosive materials are everywhere in parcels; but there neither are, nor can be supplied the indispensable connecting trains.

Much is said by Southern people about the affection of slaves for their masters and mistresses; and a part of it, at least, is true. A plot for an uprising could scarcely be devised and communicated to twenty individuals before some one of them, to save the life of a favorite master or mistress, would divulge it. This is the rule; and the slave revolution in Haiti was not an exception to it, but a case occurring under peculiar circumstances. The gunpowder plot of British history, though not connected with slaves, was more in point. In that case, only about twenty were admitted to the secret; and yet one of them, in his anxiety to save a friend, betrayed the plot to that friend, and, by consequence, averted the calamity. Occasional poisonings from the kitchen, and open or stealthy assassinations in the field, and local revolts, extending to a score or so, will continue to occur as the natural results of slavery; but no general insurrection of slaves, as I think, can happen in this country for a long time. Whoever much fears or much hopes for such an event will be alike disappointed.

In the language of Mr. Jefferson, uttered many years ago, "It is still in our power to direct the process of emancipation and deportation peaceably, and in such slow degrees as that the evil will wear off insensibly, and their places be, *pari passu,* filled up by free white laborers. If, on the contrary, it is left to force itself on, human nature must shudder at the prospect held up."

Mr. Jefferson did not mean to say, nor do I, that the power of emancipation is in the Federal Government. He spoke of Virginia; and, as to the power of emancipation, I speak of the slave holding States only. The Federal Government, however, as we insist, has the power of restraining the extension of the institution—the power to insure that a slave insurrection shall never occur on any American soil which is now free from slavery.

John Brown's effort was peculiar. It was not a slave insurrection. It was an attempt by white men to get up a revolt among slaves, in which the slaves refused to participate. In fact, it was so absurd that the slaves, with all their ignorance, saw plainly enough it could not succeed. That affair, in its philosophy, corresponds with the many attempts related in history at the assassination of kings and emperors. An enthusiast broods over the oppression of a people till he fancies himself commissioned by Heaven to liberate them. He ventures the attempt, which ends in little else than his own execution. Orsini's attempt on Louis Napoleon and John Brown's attempt at Harper's Ferry were, in their philosophy, precisely the same. The eagerness to cast blame on old England in the one case, and on New England in the other, does not disprove the sameness of the two things.

And how much would it avail you, if you could, by the use of John Brown, Helper's Book, and the like, break up the Republican organization? Human action can be modified to some extent, but human nature cannot be changed. There is a judgment and a feeling against slavery in this nation, which cast at least a million and a half of votes. You cannot destroy that judgment and feeling—that sentiment— by breaking up the political organization which rallies around it. You can scarcely scatter and disperse an army which has been formed into order in the face of your heaviest fire; but if you could, how much would you gain by forcing the sentiment which created it out of the peaceful channel of the ballot-box, into some other channel? What would that other channel probably be? Would the number of John Browns be lessened or enlarged by the operation?

But you will break up the Union rather than submit to a denial of your constitutional rights.

That has a somewhat reckless sound; but it would be palliated, if not fully justified, were we proposing, by the mere force of numbers, to deprive you of some right plainly written down in the Constitution. But we are proposing no such thing.

When you make these declarations, you have a specific and well-understood allusion to an assumed constitutional right of yours to take slaves into the Federal Territories, and to hold them there as property. But no such right is specifically written in the Constitution. That instrument is literally silent about any such right. We, on the contrary, deny that such a right has any existence in the Constitution, even by implication.

Your purpose, then, plainly stated, is that you will destroy the Government unless you be allowed to construe and enforce the Constitution as you please on all points in dispute between you and us. You will rule or ruin, in all events. This, plainly stated, is your language to us.

Perhaps you will say the Supreme Court has decided the disputed constitutional question in your favor. Not quite so. But, waiving the lawyer's distinction between dictum and decision, the court have decided the question for you in a sort of way. The court have substantially said it is your constitutional right to take slaves into the Federal Territories, and to hold them there as property.

When I say, the decision was made in a sort of way, I mean it was made in a divided court, by a bare majority of the judges, and they not quite agreeing with one another in the reasons for making it; that it is so made as that its avowed supporters disagree with one another about its meaning, and that it was mainly based upon a mistaken statement of fact—the statement in the opinion that "the right of property in a slave is distinctly and expressly affirmed in the Constitution."

An inspection of the Constitution will show that the right of property in a slave is not "distinctly and expressly affirmed" in it. Bear in mind, the judges do not pledge their judicial opinion that such right is impliedly affirmed in the Constitution; but they pledge their veracity that it is "distinctly and expressly" affirmed there—"distinctly," that is, not mingled with anything else; "expressly," that is, in words meaning just that, without the aid of any inference, and susceptible of no other meaning.

If they had only pledged their judicial opinion that such right is affirmed in the instrument by implication, it would be open to others to show that neither the word "slave" nor "slavery" is to be found in the Constitution, nor the word "property" even, in any connection with language alluding to the things slave or slavery; and that wherever in that instrument the slave is alluded to, he is called a "person"; and wherever his master's legal right in relation to him is alluded to, it is spoken of as "service or labor which may be due," as a debt payable in service or labor. Also, it would be open to show, by contemporaneous history, that this mode of alluding to slaves and slavery, instead of speaking of them, was employed on purpose to exclude from the Constitution the idea that there could be property in man.

To show all this, is easy and certain.

When this obvious mistake of the judges shall be brought to their notice, is it not reasonable to expect that they will withdraw the mistaken statement, and reconsider the conclusion based upon it?

And then it is to be remembered that "our fathers; who framed the Government under which we live",—the men who made the Constitution—decided this same constitutional question in our favor, long ago; decided it without division among themselves, when making the decision, without division among themselves about the meaning of it after it was made, and, so far as any evidence is left, without basing it upon any mistaken statement of facts.

Under all these circumstances, do you really feel yourselves justified to break up this Government unless such a court decision as yours is shall be at once submitted to as a conclusive and final rule of political action? But you will not abide the election of a Republican President! In that supposed event, you say, you will destroy the Union; and then, you say, the great crime of having destroyed it will be upon us! That is cool. A highwayman holds a pistol to my ear, and mutters through his teeth, "stand and deliver, or I shall kill you, and then you'll be a murderer!" To be sure, what the robber demanded of me-my money was my own, and I had a clear right to keep it; but it was no more my own than my vote is my own; and the threat of death to me, to extort my money, and the threat of destruction to the Union, to extort my vote, can scarcely be distinguished in principle.

A few words now to Republicans: It is exceedingly desirable that all parts of this great confederacy shall be at peace and in harmony one with another. Let us Republicans do our part to have it so. Even though much provoked, let us do nothing through passion and ill temper. Even though the Southern people will not so much as listen to us, let us calmly consider their demands, and yield to them if, in our deliberate view of our duty, we possibly can. Judging by all they say and do, and by the subject and nature of their controversy with us, let us determine, if we can, what will satisfy them.

Will they be satisfied if the Territories be unconditionally surrendered to them? We know they will not. In all their present complaints against us, the Territories are scarcely mentioned. Invasions and insurrections are the rage now. Will it satisfy them if, in the future, we have nothing to do with invasions and, insurrections? We know it will not. We so know because we know we never had anything to do with invasions and insurrections; and yet this total abstaining does not exempt us from the charge and the denunciation.

The question recurs, what will satisfy them? Simply this: We must not only let them alone, but we must, somehow, convince them that we do let them alone. This, we know by experience, is no easy task. We have been so trying to convince them from the very beginning of our organization, but with no success. In all our platforms and speeches we have constantly protested our purpose to let them alone; but this has had no tendency to convince them. Alike unavailing to convince them is the fact that they have never detected a man of us in any attempt to disturb them.

These natural and apparently adequate means all failing, what will convince them? This, and this only: cease to call slavery wrong, and join them in calling it right. And this must be done thoroughly—done in acts as well as in words. Silence will not be tolerated—we must place ourselves avowedly with them. Senator Douglas's new sedition law must be enacted and enforced, suppressing all declarations that slavery is wrong, whether made in politics, in presses, in pulpits; or in private. We must arrest and return their fugitive slaves with greedy pleasure. We must pull down our free State constitutions. The whole atmosphere must be disinfected from all taint of opposition to slavery, before they will cease to believe that all their troubles proceed from us.

I am quite aware they do not state their case precisely in this way. Most of them would probably say to us, "Let us alone, do nothing to us, and say what you please about slavery." But we do let them alone have never disturbed them—so that after all it is what we say which dissatisfies them. They will continue to accuse us of doing, until we cease saying.

I am also aware they have not as yet, in terms, demanded the overthrow of our free State constitutions. Yet those constitutions declare the wrong of slavery, with more solemn emphasis than do all other sayings against it; and when all these other sayings shall have been silenced, the overthrow of these constitutions will be demanded, and nothing be left to resist the demand. It is nothing to the contrary, that they do not demand the whole of this just now. Demanding what they do, and for the reason they do, they can voluntarily stop nowhere short of this consummation. Holding, as they do, that slavery is morally right, and socially elevating, they cannot cease to demand a full national recognition of it, as a legal right and a social blessing.

Nor can we justifiably withhold this on any ground save our conviction that slavery is wrong. If slavery is right, all words, acts, laws, and constitutions against it are themselves wrong, and should be silenced and swept away. If it is right, we cannot justly object to its nationality its universality; if it is wrong, they cannot justly insist upon its extension—its enlargement. All they ask we could readily grant if we thought slavery right; all we ask they could as readily grant, if they thought it wrong.

Their thinking it right and our thinking it wrong is the precise fact upon which depends the whole controversy. Thinking it right, as they do, they are not to blame for desiring its full recognition, as being right; but thinking it wrong, as we do, can we yield to them? Can we cast our votes with their view, and against our own? In view of our moral, social, and political responsibilities, can we do this?

Wrong as we think slavery is, we can yet afford to let it alone where it is, because that much is due to the necessity arising from its actual presence in the nation; but can we, while our votes will prevent it, allow it to spread into the national Territories, and to overrun us here in these free States?

If our sense of duty forbids this, then let us stand by our duty, fearlessly and effectively. Let us be diverted by none of those sophistical contrivances wherewith we are so industriously plied and belabored-contrivances such as groping for some middle ground between the right and the wrong, vain as the search for a man who should be neither a living man nor a dead man-such as a policy of "don't care" on a question about which all true men do care—such as Union appeals beseeching true Union men to yield to Disunionists, reversing the divine rule, and calling, not the sinners, but the righteous to repentance—such as invocations to Washington, imploring men to unsay what Washington said, and undo what Washington did.

Neither let us be slandered from our duty by false accusations against us, nor frightened from it by menaces of destruction to the Government nor of dungeons to ourselves.

Let us have faith that right makes might, and in that faith let us, to the end, dare to do our duty as we understand it.

SPEECH AT NEW HAVEN, CONNECTICUT, MARCH 6, 1860.

MR. PRESIDENT, AND FELLOW-CITIZENS OF NEW HAVEN:—If the Republican party of this nation shall ever have the national House entrusted to its keeping, it will be the duty of that party to attend to all the affairs of national housekeeping. Whatever matters of importance may come up, whatever difficulties may arise in its way of administration of the Government, that party will then have to attend to. It will then be compelled to attend to other questions, besides this question which now assumes an overwhelming importance—the question of slavery. It is true that in the organization of the Republican party this question of slavery was more important than any other: indeed, so much more important has it become that no more national question can even get a hearing just at present. The old question of tariff—a matter that will remain one of the chief affairs of national house-keeping to all time; the question of the management of financial affairs; the question of the disposition of the public domain how shall it be managed for the purpose of getting it well settled, and of making there the homes of a free and happy people? these will remain open and require attention for a great while yet, and these questions will have to be attended to by whatever party has the control of the Government. Yet, just now, they cannot even obtain a hearing, and I do not propose to detain you upon these topics or what sort of hearing they should have when opportunity shall come.

For, whether we will or not, the question of slavery is the question, the all-absorbing topic of the day. It is true that all of us—and by that I mean, not the Republican party alone, but the whole American people, here and elsewhere—all of us wish this question settled, wish it out of the way. It stands in the way, and prevents the adjustment, and the giving of necessary attention to other questions of national house-keeping. The people of the whole nation agree that this question ought to be settled, and yet it is not settled. And the reason is that they are not yet agreed how it shall be settled. All wish it done, but some wish one way and some another, and some a third, or fourth, or fifth; different bodies are pulling in different directions, and none of them, having a decided majority, are able to accomplish the common object.

In the beginning of the year 1854, a new policy was inaugurated with the avowed object and confident promise that it would entirely and forever put an end to the slavery agitation. It was again and again declared that under this policy, when once successfully established, the country would be forever rid of this whole question. Yet under the operation of that policy this agitation has not only not ceased, but it has been constantly augmented. And this too, although, from the day of its introduction, its friends, who promised that it would wholly end all agitation, constantly insisted, down to the time that the Lecompton Bill was introduced, that it was working admirably, and that its inevitable tendency was to remove the question forever from the politics of the country. Can you call to mind any Democratic speech, made after the repeal of the Missouri Compromise, down to the time of the Lecompton Bill, in which it was not predicted that the slavery agitation was just at an end, that "the abolition excitement was played out," "the Kansas question was dead," "they have made the most they can out of this question and it is now forever settled"? But since the Lecompton Bill no Democrat, within my experience, has ever pretended that he could see the end. That cry has been dropped. They themselves do not pretend, now, that the agitation of this subject has come to an end yet.

The truth is that this question is one of national importance, and we cannot help dealing with it; we must do something about it, whether we will or not. We cannot avoid it; the subject is one we cannot avoid considering; we can no more avoid it than a man can live without eating. It is upon us; it attaches to the body politic as much and closely as the natural wants attach to our natural bodies. Now I think it important that this matter should be taken up in earnest, and really settled: And one way to bring about a true settlement of the question is to understand its true magnitude.

There have been many efforts made to settle it. Again and again it has been fondly hoped that it was settled; but every time it breaks out afresh, and more violently than ever. It was settled, our fathers hoped, by the Missouri Compromise, but it did not stay settled. Then the compromises of 1850 were declared to be a full and final settlement of the question. The two great parties, each in national convention, adopted resolutions declaring that the settlement made by the Compromise of 1850 was a finality that it would last forever. Yet how long before it was unsettled again? It broke out again in 1854, and blazed higher and raged more furiously than ever before, and the agitation has not rested since.

These repeated settlements must have some faults about them. There must be some inadequacy in their very nature to the purpose to which they were designed. We can only speculate as to where that fault, that inadequacy, is, but we may perhaps profit by past experiences.

I think that one of the causes of these repeated failures is that our best and greatest men have greatly underestimated the size of this question. They have constantly brought forward small cures for great sores—plasters too small to cover the wound. That is one reason that all settlements have proved temporary—so evanescent.

Look at the magnitude of this subject: One sixth of our population, in round numbers—not quite one sixth, and yet more than a seventh,— about one sixth of the whole population of the United States are slaves.

The owners of these slaves consider them property. The effect upon the minds of the owners is that of property, and nothing else it induces them to insist upon all that will favorably affect its value as property, to demand laws and institutions and a public policy that shall increase and secure its value, and make it durable, lasting, and universal. The effect on the minds of the owners is to persuade them that there is no wrong in it. The slaveholder does not like to be considered a mean fellow for holding that species of property, and hence, he has to struggle within himself and sets about arguing himself into the belief that slavery is right. The property influences his mind. The dissenting minister who argued some theological point with one of the established church was always met with the reply, "I can't see it so." He opened a Bible and pointed him a passage, but the orthodox minister replied, "I can't see it so." Then he showed him a single word—"Can you see that?" "Yes, I see it," was the reply. The dissenter laid a guinea over the word and asked, "Do you see it now?" So here. Whether the owners of this species of property do really see it as it is, it is not for me to say, but if they do, they see it as it is through two thousand millions of dollars, and that is a pretty thick coating. Certain it is that they do not see it as we see it. Certain it is that this two thousand millions of dollars, invested in this species of property, all so concentrated that the mind can grasp it at once—this immense pecuniary interest—has its influence upon their minds.

But here in Connecticut and at the North slavery does not exist, and we see it through no such medium. To us it appears natural to think that slaves are human beings; men, not property; that some of the things, at least, stated about men in the Declaration of Independence apply to them as well as to us. I say we think, most of us, that this charter of freedom applies to the slaves as well as to ourselves; that the class of arguments put forward to batter down that idea are also calculated to break down the very idea of a free government, even for white men, and to undermine the very foundations of free society. We think slavery a great moral wrong, and, while we do not claim the right to touch it where it exists, we wish to treat it as a wrong in the Territories, where our votes will reach it. We think that a respect for ourselves, a regard for future generations and for the God that made us, require that we put down this wrong where our votes will properly reach it. We think that species of labor an injury to free white men—in short, we think slavery a great moral, social, and political evil, tolerable only because, and so far as, its actual existence makes it necessary to tolerate it, and that beyond that it ought to be treated as a wrong.

Now these two ideas, the property idea that slavery is right, and the idea that it is wrong, come into collision, and do actually produce that irrepressible conflict which Mr. Seward has been so roundly abused for mentioning. The two ideas conflict, and must conflict.

Again, in its political aspect, does anything in any way endanger the perpetuity of this Union but that single thing, slavery? Many of our adversaries are anxious to claim that they are specially devoted to the Union, and take pains to charge upon us hostility to the Union. Now we claim that we are the only true Union men, and we put to them this one proposition: Whatever endangers this Union, save and except slavery? Did any other thing ever cause a moment's fear? All men must agree that this thing alone has ever endangered the perpetuity of the Union. But if it was threatened by any other influence, would not all men say that the best thing that could be done, if we could not or ought not to destroy it, would be at least to keep it from growing any larger? Can any man believe, that the way to save the Union is to extend and increase the only thing that threatens the Union, and to suffer it to grow bigger and bigger?

Whenever this question shall be settled, it must be settled on some philosophical basis. No policy that does not rest upon some philosophical opinion can be permanently maintained. And hence there are but two policies in regard to slavery that can be at all maintained. The first, based on the property view that slavery is right, conforms to that idea throughout, and demands that we shall do everything for it that we ought to do if it were right. We must sweep away all opposition, for opposition to the right is wrong; we must agree that slavery is right, and we must adopt the idea that property has persuaded the owner to believe that slavery is morally right and socially elevating. This gives a philosophical basis for a permanent policy of encouragement.

The other policy is one that squares with the idea that slavery is wrong, and it consists in doing everything that we ought to do if it is wrong. Now, I don't wish to be misunderstood, nor to leave a gap down to be misrepresented, even. I don't mean that we ought to attack it where it exists. To me it seems that if we were to form a government anew, in view of the actual presence of slavery we should find it necessary to frame just such a government as our fathers did—giving to the slaveholder the entire control where the system was established, while we possessed the power to restrain it from going outside those limits. From the necessities of the case we should be compelled to form just such a government as our blessed fathers gave us; and, surely, if they have so made it, that adds another reason why we should let slavery alone where it exists.

If I saw a venomous snake crawling in the road, any man would say I might seize the nearest stick and kill it; but if I found that snake in bed with my children, that would be another question. I might hurt the children more than the snake, and it might bite them. Much more if I found it in bed with my neighbor's children, and I had bound myself by a solemn compact not to meddle with his children under any circumstances, it would become me to let that particular mode of getting rid of the gentleman alone. But if there was a bed newly made up, to which the children were to be taken, and it was proposed to take a batch of young snakes and put them there with them, I take it no man would say there was any question how I ought to decide!

That is just the case. The new Territories are the newly made bed to which our children are to go, and it lies with the nation to say whether they shall have snakes mixed up with them or not. It does not seem as if there could be much hesitation what our policy should be!

Now I have spoken of a policy based on the idea that slavery is wrong, and a policy based on the idea that it is right. But an effort has been made for a policy that shall treat it as neither right nor wrong. It is based upon utter indifference. Its leading advocate [Douglas] has said, "I don't care whether it be voted up or down." "It is merely a matter of dollars and cents." "The Almighty has drawn a line across this continent, on one side of which all soil must forever be cultivated by slave labor, and on the other by free." "When the struggle is between the white man and the negro, I am for the white man; when it is between the negro and the crocodile, I am for the negro." Its central idea is indifference. It holds that it makes no more difference to us whether the Territories become free or slave States than whether my neighbor stocks his farm with horned cattle or puts in tobacco. All recognize this policy, the plausible sugar-coated name of which is "popular sovereignty."

This policy chiefly stands in the way of a permanent settlement of the question. I believe there is no danger of its becoming the permanent policy of the country, for it is based on a public indifference. There is nobody that "don't care." All the people do care one way or the other! I do not charge that its author, when he says he "don't care," states his individual opinion; he only expresses his policy for the government. I understand that he has never said as an individual whether he thought slavery right or wrong—and he is the only man in the nation that has not! Now such a policy may have a temporary run; it may spring up as necessary to the political prospects of some gentleman; but it is utterly baseless: the people are not indifferent, and it can therefore have no durability or permanence.

But suppose it could: Then it could be maintained only by a public opinion that shall say, "We don't care." There must be a change in public opinion; the public mind must be so far debauched as to square with this policy of caring not at all. The people must come to consider this as "merely a question of dollars and cents," and to believe that in some places the Almighty has made slavery necessarily eternal. This policy can be brought to prevail if the people can be brought round to say honestly, "We don't care"; if not, it can never be maintained. It is for you to say whether that can be done.

You are ready to say it cannot, but be not too fast! Remember what a long stride has been taken since the repeal of the Missouri Compromise! Do you know of any Democrat, of either branch of the party—do you know one who declares that he believes that the Declaration of Independence has any application to the negro? Judge Taney declares that it has not, and Judge Douglas even vilifies me personally and scolds me roundly for saying that the Declaration applies to all men, and that negroes are men. Is there a Democrat here who does not deny that the Declaration applies to the negro? Do any of you know of one? Well, I have tried before perhaps fifty audiences, some larger and some smaller than this, to find one such Democrat, and never yet have I found one who said I did not place him right in that. I must assume that Democrats hold that, and now, not one of these Democrats can show that he said that five years ago! I venture to defy the whole party to produce one man that ever uttered the belief that the Declaration did not apply to negroes, before the repeal of the Missouri Compromise! Four or five years ago we all thought negroes were men, and that when "all men" were named, negroes were included. But the whole Democratic party has deliberately taken negroes from the class of men and put them in the class of brutes. Turn it as you will it is simply the truth! Don't be too hasty, then, in saying that the people cannot be brought to this new doctrine, but note that long stride. One more as long completes the journey from where negroes are estimated as men to where they are estimated as mere brutes—as rightful property!

That saying "In the struggle between white men and the negro," etc., which I know came from the same source as this policy—that saying marks another step. There is a falsehood wrapped up in that statement. "In the struggle between the white man and the negro" assumes that there is a struggle, in which either the white man must enslave the negro or the negro must enslave the white. There is no such struggle! It is merely the ingenious falsehood to degrade and brutalize the negro. Let each let the other alone, and there is no struggle about it. If it was like two wrecked seamen on a narrow plank, when each must push the other off or drown himself, I would push the negro off or a white man either, but it is not; the plank is large enough for both. This good earth is plenty broad enough for white man and negro both, and there is no need of either pushing the other off.

So that saying, "In the struggle between the negro and the crocodile," etc., is made up from the idea that down where the crocodile inhabits, a white man can't labor; it must be nothing else but crocodile or negro; if the negro does not the crocodile must possess the earth; in that case he declares for the negro. The meaning of the whole is just this: As a white man is to a negro, so is a negro to a crocodile; and as the negro may rightfully treat the crocodile, so may the white man rightfully treat the negro. This very dear phrase coined by its author, and so dear that he deliberately repeats it in many speeches, has a tendency to still further brutalize the negro, and to bring public opinion to the point of utter indifference whether men so brutalized are enslaved or not. When that time shall come, if ever, I think that policy to which I refer may prevail. But I hope the good freemen of this country will never allow it to come, and until then the policy can never be maintained.

Now consider the effect of this policy. We in the States are not to care whether freedom or slavery gets the better, but the people in the Territories may care. They are to decide, and they may think what they please; it is a matter of dollars and cents! But are not the people of the Territories detailed from the States? If this feeling of indifference this absence of moral sense about the question prevails in the States, will it not be carried into the Territories? Will not every man say, "I don't care, it is nothing to me"? If any one comes that wants slavery, must they not say, "I don't care whether freedom or slavery be voted up or voted down"? It results at last in nationalizing the institution of slavery. Even if fairly carried out, that policy is just as certain to nationalize slavery as the doctrine of Jeff Davis himself. These are only two roads to the same goal, and "popular sovereignty" is just as sure and almost as short as the other.

What we want, and all we want, is to have with us the men who think slavery wrong. But those who say they hate slavery, and are opposed to it, but yet act with the Democratic party—where are they? Let us apply a few tests. You say that you think slavery is wrong, but you denounce all attempts to restrain it. Is there anything else that you think wrong that you are not willing to deal with as wrong? Why are you so careful, so tender, of this one wrong and no other? You will not let us do a single thing as if it was wrong; there is no place where you will even allow it to be called wrong! We must not call it wrong in the free States, because it is not there, and we must not call it wrong in the slave States, because it is there; we must not call it wrong in politics because that is bringing morality into politics, and we must not call it wrong in the pulpit because that is bringing politics into religion; we must not bring it into the Tract Society or the other societies, because those are such unsuitable places—and there is no single place, according to you, where this wrong thing can properly be called wrong!

Perhaps you will plead that if the people of the slave States should themselves set on foot an effort for emancipation, you would wish them success, and bid them God-speed. Let us test that: In 1858 the emancipation party of Missouri, with Frank Blair at their head, tried to get up a movement for that purpose, and having started a party contested the State. Blair was beaten, apparently if not truly, and when the news came to Connecticut, you, who knew that Frank Blair was taking hold of this thing by the right end, and doing the only thing that you say can properly be done to remove this wrong—did you bow your heads in sorrow because of that defeat? Do you, any of you, know one single Democrat that showed sorrow over that result? Not one! On the contrary every man threw up his hat, and hallooed at the top of his lungs, "Hooray for Democracy!"

Now, gentlemen, the Republicans desire to place this great question of slavery on the very basis on which our fathers placed it, and no other. It is easy to demonstrate that "our fathers, who framed this Government under which we live," looked on slavery as wrong, and so framed it and everything about it as to square with the idea that it was wrong, so far as the necessities arising from its existence permitted. In forming the Constitution they found the slave trade existing, capital invested in it, fields depending upon it for labor, and the whole system resting upon the importation of slave labor. They therefore did not prohibit the slave trade at once, but they gave the power to prohibit it after twenty years. Why was this? What other foreign trade did they treat in that way? Would they have done this if they had not thought slavery wrong?

Another thing was done by some of the same men who framed the Constitution, and afterwards adopted as their own the act by the first Congress held under that Constitution, of which many of the framers were members, that prohibited the spread of slavery into Territories. Thus the same men, the framers of the Constitution, cut off the supply and prohibited the spread of slavery, and both acts show conclusively that they considered that the thing was wrong.

If additional proof is wanted it can be found in the phraseology of the Constitution. When men are framing a supreme law and chart of government, to secure blessings and prosperity to untold generations yet to come, they use language as short and direct and plain as can be found, to express their meaning In all matters but this of slavery the framers of the Constitution used the very clearest, shortest, and most direct language. But the Constitution alludes to slavery three times without mentioning it once The language used becomes ambiguous, roundabout, and mystical. They speak of the "immigration of persons," and mean the importation of slaves, but do not say so. In establishing a basis of representation they say "all other persons," when they mean to say slaves—why did they not use the shortest phrase? In providing for the return of fugitives they say "persons held to service or labor." If they had said slaves it would have been plainer, and less liable to misconstruction. Why did n't they do it? We cannot doubt that it was done on purpose. Only one reason is possible, and that is supplied us by one of the framers of the Constitution—and it is not possible for man to conceive of any other—they expected and desired that the system would come to an end, and meant that when it did, the Constitution should not show that there ever had been a slave in this good free country of ours.

I will dwell on that no longer. I see the signs of approaching triumph of the Republicans in the bearing of their political adversaries. A great deal of their war with us nowadays is mere bushwhacking. At the battle of Waterloo, when Napoleon's cavalry had charged again and again upon the unbroken squares of British infantry, at last they were giving up the attempt, and going off in disorder, when some of the officers in mere vexation and complete despair fired their pistols at those solid squares. The Democrats are in that sort of extreme desperation; it is nothing else. I will take up a few of these arguments.

There is "the irrepressible conflict." How they rail at Seward for that saying! They repeat it constantly; and, although the proof has been thrust under their noses again and again that almost every good man since the formation of our Government has uttered that same sentiment, from General Washington, who "trusted that we should yet have a confederacy of free States," with Jefferson, Jay, Monroe, down to the latest days, yet they refuse to notice that at all, and persist in railing at Seward for saying it. Even Roger A. Pryor, editor of the Richmond Enquirer, uttered the same sentiment in almost the same language, and yet so little offence did it give the Democrats that he was sent for to Washington to edit the States—the Douglas organ there—while Douglas goes into hydrophobia and spasms of rage because Seward dared to repeat it. This is what I call bushwhacking, a sort of argument that they must know any child can see through.

Another is John Brown: "You stir up insurrections, you invade the South; John Brown! Harper's Ferry!" Why, John Brown was not a Republican! You have never implicated a single Republican in that Harper's Ferry enterprise. We tell you that if any member of the Republican party is guilty in that matter, you know it or you do not know it. If you do know it, you are inexcusable not to designate the man and prove the fact. If you do not know it, you are inexcusable to assert it, and especially to persist in the assertion after you have tried and failed to make the proof. You need not be told that persisting in a charge which one does not know to be true is simply malicious slander. Some of you admit that no Republican designedly aided or encouraged the Harper's Ferry affair, but still insist that our doctrines and declarations necessarily lead to such results. We do not believe it. We know we hold to no doctrines, and make no declarations, which were not held to and made by our fathers who framed the Government under which we live, and we cannot see how declarations that were patriotic when they made them are villainous when we make them. You never dealt fairly by us in relation to that affair—and I will say frankly that I know of nothing in your character that should lead us to suppose that you would. You had just been soundly thrashed in elections in several

States, and others were soon to come. You rejoiced at the occasion, and only were troubled that there were not three times as many killed in the affair. You were in evident glee; there was no sorrow for the killed nor for the peace of Virginia disturbed; you were rejoicing that by charging Republicans with this thing you might get an advantage of us in New York, and the other States. You pulled that string as tightly as you could, but your very generous and worthy expectations were not quite fulfilled. Each Republican knew that the charge was a slander as to himself at least, and was not inclined by it to cast his vote in your favor. It was mere bushwhacking, because you had nothing else to do. You are still on that track, and I say, go on! If you think you can slander a woman into loving you or a man into voting for you, try it till you are satisfied!

Another specimen of this bushwhacking, that "shoe strike." Now be it understood that I do not pretend to know all about the matter. I am merely going to speculate a little about some of its phases. And at the outset, I am glad to see that a system of labor prevails in New England under which laborers can strike when they want to, where they are not obliged to work under all circumstances, and are not tied down and obliged to labor whether you pay them or not! I like the system which lets a man quit when he wants to, and wish it might prevail everywhere. One of the reasons why I am opposed to slavery is just here. What is the true condition of the laborer? I take it that it is best for all to leave each man free to acquire property as fast as he can. Some will get wealthy. I don't believe in a law to prevent a man from getting rich; it would do more harm than good. So, while we do not propose any war upon capital, we do wish to allow the humblest man an equal chance to get rich with everybody else. When one starts poor, as most do in the race of life, free society is such that he knows he can better his condition; he knows that there is no fixed condition of labor for his whole life. I am not ashamed to confess that twenty-five years ago I was a hired laborer, mauling rails, at work on a flatboat—just what might happen to any poor man's son! I want every man to have a chance—and I believe a Black man is entitled to it—in which he can better his condition; when he may look forward and hope to be a hired laborer this year and the next, work for himself afterward, and finally to hire men to work for him! That is the system. Up here in New England, you have a soil that scarcely sprouts black-eyed beans, and yet where will you find wealthy men so wealthy, and poverty so rarely in extremity? There is not another such place on earth! I desire that if you get too thick here, and find it hard to better your condition on this soil, you may have a chance to strike and go somewhere else, where you may not be degraded, nor have your families corrupted, by forced rivalry with negro slaves. I want you to have a clean bed and no snakes in it! Then you can better your condition, and so it may go on and on in one endless round so long as man exists on the face of the earth!

Now, to come back to this shoe strike,—if, as the senator from Illinois asserts, this is caused by withdrawal of Southern votes, consider briefly how you will meet the difficulty. You have done nothing, and have protested that you have done nothing, to injure the South. And yet, to get back the shoe trade, you must leave off doing something which you are now doing. What is it? You must stop thinking slavery wrong! Let your institutions be wholly changed; let your State constitutions be subverted; glorify slavery, and so you will get back the shoe trade—for what? You have brought owned labor with it, to compete with your own labor, to underwork you, and to degrade you! Are you ready to get back the trade on those terms?

But the statement is not correct. You have not lost that trade; orders were never better than now! Senator Mason, a Democrat, comes into the Senate in homespun, a proof that the dissolution of the Union has actually begun! but orders are the same. Your factories have not struck work, neither those where they make anything for coats, nor for pants nor for shirts, nor for ladies' dresses. Mr. Mason has not reached the manufacturers who ought to have made him a coat and pants! To make his proof good for anything he should have come into the Senate barefoot!

Another bushwhacking contrivance; simply that, nothing else! I find a good many people who are very much concerned about the loss of Southern trade. Now either these people are sincere or they are not. I will speculate a little about that. If they are sincere, and are moved by any real danger of the loss of Southern trade, they will simply get their names on the white list, and then, instead of persuading Republicans to do likewise, they will be glad to keep you away! Don't you see that they cut off competition? They would not be whispering around to Republicans to come in and share the profits with them. But if they are not sincere, and are merely trying to fool Republicans out of their votes, they will grow very anxious about your pecuniary prospects; they are afraid you are going to get broken up and ruined; they do not care about Democratic votes, oh, no, no, no! You must judge which class those belong to whom you meet: I leave it to you to determine from the facts.

Let us notice some more of the stale charges against Republicans. You say we are sectional. We deny it. That makes an issue; and the burden of proof is upon you. You produce your proof; and what is it? Why, that our party has no existence in your section—gets no votes in your section. The fact is substantially true; but does it prove the issue? If it does, then in case we should, without change of principle, begin to get votes in your section, we should thereby cease to be sectional. You cannot escape this conclusion; and yet, are you willing to abide by it? If you are, you will probably soon find that we have ceased to be sectional, for we shall get votes in your section this very year. The fact that we get no votes in your section is a fact of your making and not of ours. And if there be fault in that fact, that fault is primarily yours, and remains so until you show that we repel you by some wrong principle or practice. If we ours; but this brings you to where you ought to have started—to a discussion of the right or wrong of our principle. If our principle, put in practice, would wrong your section for the benefit of ours, or for any other object, then our principle, and we with it, are sectional, and are justly opposed and denounced as such. Meet us, then, on the question of whether our principle put in practice would wrong your section; and so meet it as if it were possible that something may be said on our side. Do you accept the challenge? No? Then you really believe that the principle which our fathers who framed the Government under which we live thought so clearly right as to adopt it, and indorse it again and again, upon their official oaths, is in fact so clearly wrong as to demand our condemnation without a moment's consideration. Some of you delight to flaunt in our faces the warning against sectional parties given by Washington in his Farewell Address. Less than eight years before Washington gave that warning, he had, as President of the United States, approved and signed an act of Congress enforcing the prohibition of slavery in the Northwestern Territory, which act embodied the policy of government upon that subject, up to and at the very moment he penned that warning; and about one year after he penned it he wrote La Fayette that he considered that prohibition a wise measure, expressing in the same connection his hope that we should sometime have a confederacy of free States.

Bearing this in mind, and seeing that sectionalism has since arisen upon this same subject, is that warning a weapon in your hands against us, or in our hands against you? Could Washington himself speak, would he cast the blame of that sectionalism upon us, who sustain his policy, or upon you, who repudiate it? We respect that warning of Washington, and we commend it to you, together with his example pointing to the right application of it.

But you say you are conservative—eminently conservative—while we are revolutionary, destructive, or something of the sort. What is conservatism? Is it not adherence to the old and tried, against the new and untried? We stick to, contend for, the identical old policy on the point in controversy which was adopted by our fathers who framed the Government under which we live; while you with one accord reject and scout and spit upon that old policy, and insist upon substituting something new. True, you disagree among yourselves as to what that substitute shall be. You have considerable variety of new propositions and plans, but you are unanimous in rejecting and denouncing the old policy of the fathers. Some of you are for reviving the foreign slave-trade; some for a congressional slave code for the Territories; some for

Congress forbidding the Territories to prohibit slavery within their limits; some for maintaining slavery in the Territories through the judiciary; some for the "gur-reat pur-rinciple" that if one man would enslave another, no third man should object—fantastically called "popular sovereignty." But never a man among you in favor of prohibition of slavery in Federal Territories, according to the practice of our fathers who framed the Government under which we live. Not one of all your various plans can show a precedent or an advocate in the century within which our Government originated. And yet you draw yourselves up and say, "We are eminently conservative."

It is exceedingly desirable that all parts of this great confederacy shall be at peace, and in harmony one with another. Let us Republicans do our part to have it so. Even though much provoked, let us do nothing through passion and ill-temper. Even though the Southern people will not so much as listen to us, let us calmly consider their demands, and yield to them if, in our deliberate view of our duty, we possibly can. Judging by all they say and do, and by the subject and nature of their controversy with us, let us determine, if we can, what will satisfy them.

Will they be satisfied if the Territories be unconditionally surrendered to them? We know they will not. In all their present complaints against us, the Territories are scarcely mentioned. Invasions and insurrections are the rage now. Will it satisfy them, in the future, if we have nothing to do with invasions and insurrections? We know it will not. We so know because we know we never had anything to do with invasions and insurrections; and yet this total abstaining does not exempt us from the charge and the denunciation.

The question recurs, what will satisfy them? Simply this: we must not only let them alone, but we must, somehow, convince them that we do let them alone. This, we know by experience, is no easy task. We have been so trying to convince them, from the very beginning of our organization, but with no success. In all our platforms and speeches, we have constantly protested our purpose to let them alone; but this had no tendency to convince them. Alike unavailing to convince them is the fact that they have never detected a man of us in any attempt to disturb them.

These natural and apparently adequate means all failing, what will convince them? This, and this only: cease to call slavery wrong, and join them in calling it right. And this must be done thoroughly—done in acts as well as in words. Silence will not be tolerated—we must place ourselves avowedly with them. Douglas's new sedition law must be enacted and enforced, suppressing all declarations that slavery is wrong, whether made in politics, in presses, in pulpits, or in private. We must arrest and return their fugitive slaves with greedy pleasure. We must pull down our free State constitutions. The whole atmosphere must be disinfected of all taint of opposition to slavery, before they will cease to believe that all their troubles proceed from us. So long as we call slavery wrong, whenever a slave runs away they will overlook the obvious fact that he ran away because he was oppressed, and declare he was stolen off. Whenever a master cuts his slaves with a lash, and they cry out under it, he will overlook the obvious fact that the negroes cry out because they are hurt, and insist that they were put up to it by some rascally abolitionist.

I am quite aware that they do not state their case precisely in this way. Most of them would probably say to us, "Let us alone, do nothing to us, and say what you please about slavery." But we do let them alone—have never disturbed them—so that, after all, it is what we say which dissatisfies them. They will continue to accuse us of doing, until we cease saying.

I am also aware that they have not as yet in terms demanded the overthrow of our free-State constitutions. Yet those constitutions declare the wrong of slavery with more solemn emphasis than do all other sayings against it; and when all these other sayings shall have been silenced, the overthrow of these constitutions will be demanded. It is nothing to the contrary that they do not demand the whole of this just now. Demanding what they do, and for the reason they do, they can voluntarily stop nowhere short of this consummation. Holding as they do that slavery is morally right, and socially elevating, they cannot cease to demand a full national recognition of it, as a legal right, and a social blessing.

Nor can we justifiably withhold this on any ground save our conviction that slavery is wrong. If slavery is right, all words, acts, laws, and constitutions against it are themselves wrong and should be silenced and swept away. If it is right, we cannot justly object to its nationality—its universality: if it is wrong, they cannot justly insist upon its extension—its enlargement. All they ask, we could readily grant, if we thought slavery right; all we ask, they could as readily grant, if they thought it wrong. Their thinking it right and our thinking it wrong is the precise fact on which depends the whole controversy. Thinking it right as they do, they are not to blame for desiring its full recognition, as being right; but, thinking it wrong, as we do, can we yield to them? Can we cast our votes with their view, and against our own? In view of our moral, social, and political responsibilities, can we do this?

Wrong as we think slavery is, we can yet afford to let it alone where it is because that much is due to the necessity arising from its actual presence in the nation; but can we, while our votes will prevent it, allow it to spread into the national Territories, and to overrun us here in these free States?

If our sense of duty forbids this, then let us stand by our duty, fearlessly and effectively. Let us be diverted by none of those sophistical contrivances wherewith we are so industriously plied and belabored—contrivances such as groping for some middle ground between the right and the wrong, vain as the search for a man who would be neither a living man nor a dead man—such as a policy of "don't care" on a question about which all free men do care—such as Union appeals beseeching true Union men to yield to Disunionists, reversing the divine rule, and caning, not the sinners, but the righteous to repentance—such as invocations of Washington, imploring men to unsay what Washington did.

Neither let us be slandered from our duty by false accusations against us, nor frightened from it by menaces of destruction to the Government, nor of dungeons to ourselves. Let us have faith that right makes might; and in that faith, let us, to the end, dare to do our duty as we understand it.

[As Mr. Lincoln concluded his address, there was witnessed the wildest scene of enthusiasm and excitement that has been in New Haven for years. The *Palladium* editorially says: "We give up most of our space to-day to a very full report of the eloquent speech of the Hon. Abraham Lincoln, of Illinois, delivered last night at Union Hall."]

FAREWELL ADDRESS AT SPRINGFIELD, ILLINOIS, FEBRUARY 11, 1861.

MY FRIENDS:—One who has never been placed in a like position cannot understand my feelings at this hour, nor the oppressive sadness I feel at this parting. For more than twenty-five years I have lived among you, and during all that time I have received nothing but kindness at your hands. Here the most cherished ties of earth were assumed. Here my children were born, and here one of them lies buried. To you, my friends, I owe all that I have, all that I am. All the strange checkered past seems to crowd upon my mind. To-day I leave you. I go to assume a task more difficult than that which devolved upon General Washington. Unless the great God who assisted him shall be with and aid me I cannot prevail; but if the same almighty arm that directed and protected him shall guide and support me I shall not fail; I shall succeed. Let us pray that the God of our fathers may not forsake us now. To Him I commend you all. Permit me to ask that with equal sincerity and faith you will all invoke His wisdom and goodness for me.

With these words I must leave you; for how long I know not. Friends, one and all, I must now wish you an affectionate farewell.

ADDRESS TO THE NEW JERSEY STATE SENATE, TRENTON,
NEW JERSEY, FEBRUARY 21, 1861.

MR. PRESIDENT AND GENTLEMEN OF THE SENATE OF THE STATE OF
NEW JERSEY:—I am very grateful to you for the honorable reception of
which I have been the object. I cannot but remember the place that New
Jersey holds in our early history. In the Revolutionary struggle few of
the States among the Old Thirteen had more of the battle-fields of the
country within their limits than New Jersey. May I be pardoned if, upon
this occasion, I mention that away back in my childhood, the earliest
days of my being able to read, I got hold of a small book, such a one as
few of the younger members have ever seen Weems's Life of
Washington. I remember all the accounts there given of the battle-fields
and struggles for the liberties of the country; and none fixed themselves
upon my imagination so deeply as the struggle here at Trenton, New
Jersey. The crossing of the river, the contest with the Hessians, the
great hardships endured at that time, all fixed themselves on my
memory more than any single Revolutionary event; and you all know,
for you have all been boys, how these early impressions last longer than
any others. I recollect thinking then, boy even though I was, that there
must have been something more than common that these men struggled
for. I am exceedingly anxious that that thing that something even more
than national independence, that something that held out a great
promise to all the people of the world to all time to come—I am
exceedingly anxious that this Union, the Constitution, and the liberties
of the people shall be perpetuated in accordance with the original idea
for which that struggle was made; and I shall be most happy indeed if I
shall be a humble instrument in the hands of the Almighty, and of this
his almost chosen people, for perpetuating the object of that great
struggle. You give me this reception, as I understand, without
distinction of party. I learn that this body is composed of a majority of
gentlemen who, in the exercise of their best judgment in the choice of a
chief magistrate, did not think I was the man. I understand,
nevertheless, that they come forward here to greet me as the
constitutionally elected President of the United States—as citizens of
the United States to meet the man who, for the time being, is the
representative of the majesty of the nation—united by the single
purpose to perpetuate the Constitution, the union, and the liberties of
the people. As such, I accept this reception more gratefully than I could
do did I believe it were tendered to me as an individual.

SPEECH AT INDEPENDENCE HALL, PHILADELPHIA,
PENNSYLVANIA, FEBRUARY 22, 1861.

MR. CUYLER:—I am filled with deep emotion at finding myself standing here, in this place, where were collected together the wisdom, the devotion to principle, from which sprang the institutions under which we live. You have kindly suggested to me that in my hands is the task of restoring peace to the present distracted condition of the country. I can say in return, sir, that all the political sentiments I entertain have been drawn, so far as I have been able to draw them, from the sentiments which originated and were given to the world from this hall. I have never had a feeling politically that did not spring from the sentiments embodied in the Declaration of Independence. I have often pondered over the dangers which were incurred by the men who assembled here and framed and adopted that Declaration of Independence. I have pondered over the toils that were endured by the officers and soldiers of the army who achieved that independence. I have often inquired of myself what great principle or idea it was that kept the confederacy so long together. It was not the mere matter of separation of the colonies from the motherland, but that sentiment in the Declaration of Independence which gave liberty, not alone to the people of this country, but, I hope, to the world for all future time. It was that which gave promise that in due time the weight would be lifted from the shoulders of all men. This is the sentiment embodied in the Declaration of Independence. Now, my friends, can the country be saved upon that basis? If it can, I will consider myself one of the happiest men in the world if I can help to save it. If it cannot be saved upon that principle, it will be truly awful. But if this country cannot be saved without giving up that principle, I was about to say I would rather be assassinated on this spot than surrender it. Now, in my view of the present aspect of affairs, there need be no bloodshed or war. There is no necessity for it. I am not in favor of such a course, and I may say, in advance, that there will be no bloodshed unless it is forced upon the Government, and then it will be compelled to act in self-defense.

My friends; this is wholly an unexpected speech, and I did not expect to be called upon to say a word when I came here. I supposed it was merely to do something toward raising the flag. I may, therefore, have said something indiscreet. I have said nothing but what I am willing to live by and, if it be the pleasure of Almighty God, die by.

FIRST INAUGURAL ADDRESS, WASHINGTON, DC, MARCH 4, 1861.

FELLOW-CITIZENS OF THE UNITED STATES:—In compliance with a custom as old as the Government itself, I appear before you to address you briefly, and to take in your presence the oath prescribed by the Constitution of the United States to be taken by the President "before he enters on the execution of his office."

I do not consider it necessary at present for me to discuss those matters of administration about which there is no special anxiety or excitement.

Apprehension seems to exist among the people of the Southern States that by the accession of a Republican administration their property and their peace and personal security are to be endangered. There has never been any reasonable cause for such apprehension. Indeed, the most ample evidence to the contrary has all the while existed and been open to their inspection. It is found in nearly all the published speeches of him who now addresses you. I do but quote from one of those speeches when I declare that "I have no purpose, directly or indirectly, to interfere with the institution of slavery in the States where it exists. I believe I have no lawful right to do so, and I have no inclination to do so." Those who nominated and elected me did so with full knowledge that I had made this and many similar declarations, and had never recanted them. And, more than this, they placed in the platform for my acceptance, and as a law to themselves and to me, the clear and emphatic resolution which I now read:

"Resolved, That the maintenance inviolate of the rights of the States, and especially the right of each State to order and control its own domestic institutions according to its own judgment exclusively, is essential to that balance of power on which the perfection and endurance of our political fabric depend, and we denounce the lawless invasion by armed force of the soil of any State or Territory, no matter under what pretext, as amongst the gravest of crimes."

I now reiterate these sentiments; and, in doing so, I only press upon the public attention the most conclusive evidence of which the case is susceptible, that the property, peace, and security of no section are to be in any wise endangered by the now incoming administration. I add, too, that all the protection which, consistently with the Constitution and the laws, can be given, will be cheerfully given to all the States when lawfully demanded, for whatever cause—as cheerfully to one section as to another.

There is much controversy about the delivering up of fugitives from service or labor. The clause I now read is as plainly written in the

Constitution as any other of its provisions:

"No person held to service or labor in one State, under the laws thereof, escaping into another, shall in consequence of any law or regulation therein be discharged from such service or labor, but shall be delivered up on claim of the party to whom such service or labor may be due."

It is scarcely questioned that this provision was intended by those who made it for the reclaiming of what we call fugitive slaves; and the intention of the lawgiver is the law. All members of Congress swear their support to the whole Constitution—to this provision as much as to any other. To the proposition, then, that slaves whose cases come within the terms of this clause "shall be delivered up," their oaths are unanimous. Now, if they would make the effort in good temper, could they not with nearly equal unanimity frame and pass a law by means of which to keep good that unanimous oath?

There is some difference of opinion whether this clause should be enforced by national or by State authority; but surely that difference is not a very material one. If the slave is to be surrendered, it can be of but little consequence to him or to others by which authority it is done. And should any one in any case be content that his oath shall go unkept on a merely unsubstantial controversy as to how it shall be kept?

Again, in any law upon this subject, ought not all the safeguards of liberty known in civilized and humane jurisprudence to be introduced, so that a free man be not, in any case, surrendered as a slave? And might it not be well at the same time to provide by law for the enforcement of that clause in the Constitution which guarantees that "the citizens of each State shall be entitled to all privileges and immunities of citizens in the several States"?

I take the official oath to-day with no mental reservations, and with no purpose to construe the Constitution or laws by any hypercritical rules. And, while I do not choose now to specify particular acts of Congress as proper to be enforced, I do suggest that it will be much safer for all, both in official and private stations, to conform to and abide by all those acts which stand unrepealed, than to violate any of them, trusting to find impunity in having them held to be unconstitutional.

It is seventy-two years since the first inauguration of a President under our national Constitution. During that period fifteen different and greatly distinguished citizens have, in succession, administered the executive branch of the Government. They have conducted it through many perils, and generally with great success. Yet, with all this scope of precedent, I now enter upon the same task for the brief constitutional term of four years under great and peculiar difficulty. A disruption of the Federal Union, heretofore only menaced, is now formidably attempted.

I hold that, in contemplation of universal law and of the Constitution, the Union of these States is perpetual. Perpetuity is implied, if not expressed, in the fundamental law of all national governments. It is safe to assert that no government proper ever had a provision in its organic law for its own termination. Continue to execute all the express provisions of our national Constitution, and the Union will endure forever—it being impossible to destroy it except by some action not provided for in the instrument itself.

Again, if the United States be not a government proper, but an association of States in the nature of contract merely, can it as a contract be peaceably unmade by less than all the parties who made it? One party to a contract may violate it—break it, so to speak; but does it not require all to lawfully rescind it?

Descending from these general principles, we find the proposition that in legal contemplation the Union is perpetual confirmed by the history of the Union itself. The Union is much older than the Constitution. It was formed, in fact, by the Articles of Association in 1774. It was matured and continued by the Declaration of Independence in 1776. It was further matured, and the faith of all the then thirteen States expressly plighted and engaged that it should be perpetual, by the Articles of Confederation in 1778. And, finally, in 1787 one of the declared objects for ordaining and establishing the Constitution was "to form a more perfect Union."

But if the destruction of the Union by one or by a part only of the States be lawfully possible, the Union is less perfect than before the Constitution, having lost the vital element of perpetuity.

It follows from these views that no State upon its own mere motion can lawfully get out of the Union; that resolves and ordinances to that effect are legally void; and that acts of violence, within any State or States, against the authority of the United States, are insurrectionary or revolutionary, according to circumstances.

I therefore consider that, in view of the Constitution and the laws, the Union is unbroken; and to the extent of my ability I shall take care, as the Constitution itself expressly enjoins upon me, that the laws of the Union be faithfully executed in all the States. Doing this I deem to be only a simple duty on my part; and I shall perform it so far as practicable, unless my rightful masters, the American people, shall withhold the requisite means, or in some authoritative manner direct the contrary. I trust this will not be regarded as a menace, but only as the declared purpose of the Union that it will constitutionally defend and maintain itself.

In doing this there needs to be no bloodshed or violence; and there shall be none, unless it be forced upon the national authority. The power confided to me will be used to hold, occupy, and possess the property and places belonging to the Government, and to collect the duties and imposts; but beyond what may be necessary for these objects, there will be no invasion, no using of force against or among the people anywhere. Where hostility to the United States, in any interior locality, shall be so great and universal as to prevent competent resident citizens from holding the Federal offices, there will be no attempt to force obnoxious strangers among the people for that object. While the strict legal right may exist in the government to enforce the exercise of these offices, the attempt to do so would be so irritating, and so nearly impracticable withal, that I deem it better to forego for the time the uses of such offices.

The mails, unless repelled, will continue to be furnished in all parts of the Union. So far as possible, the people everywhere shall have that sense of perfect security which is most favorable to calm thought and reflection. The course here indicated will be followed unless current events and experience shall show a modification or change to be proper, and in every case and exigency my best discretion will be exercised according to circumstances actually existing, and with a view and a hope of a peaceful solution of the national troubles and the restoration of fraternal sympathies and affections.

That there are persons in one section or another who seek to destroy the Union at all events, and are glad of any pretext to do it, I will neither affirm nor deny; but if there be such, I need address no word to them. To those, however, who really love the Union may I not speak?

Before entering upon so grave a matter as the destruction of our national fabric, with all its benefits, its memories, and its hopes, would it not be wise to ascertain precisely why we do it? Will you hazard so desperate a step while there is any possibility that any portion of the ills you fly from have no real existence? Will you, while the certain ills you fly to are greater than all the real ones you fly from—will you risk the commission of so fearful a mistake?

All profess to be content in the Union if all constitutional rights can be maintained. Is it true, then, that any right, plainly written in the Constitution, has been denied? I think not. Happily the human mind is so constituted that no party can reach to the audacity of doing this. Think, if you can, of a single instance in which a plainly written provision of the Constitution has ever been denied. If by the mere force of numbers a majority should deprive a minority of any clearly written constitutional right, it might, in a moral point of view, justify revolution—certainly would if such a right were a vital one. But such is not our case. All the vital rights of minorities and of individuals are so plainly assured to them by affirmations and negations, guaranties and prohibitions, in the Constitution, that controversies never arise concerning them. But no organic law can ever be framed with a provision specifically applicable to every question which may occur in practical administration. No foresight can anticipate, nor any document of reasonable length contain, express provisions for all possible questions. Shall fugitives from labor be surrendered by national or by State authority? The Constitution does not expressly say. May Congress prohibit slavery in the Territories? The Constitution does not expressly say. Must Congress protect slavery in the Territories? The Constitution does not expressly say.

From questions of this class spring all our constitutional controversies, and we divide upon them into majorities and minorities. If the minority will not acquiesce, the majority must, or the Government must cease. There is no other alternative; for continuing the Government is acquiescence on one side or the other.

If a minority in such case will secede rather than acquiesce, they make a precedent which in turn will divide and ruin them; for a minority of their own will secede from them whenever a majority refuses to be controlled by such minority. For instance, why may not any portion of a new confederacy a year or two hence arbitrarily secede again, precisely as portions of the present Union now claim to secede from it? All who cherish disunion sentiments are now being educated to the exact temper of doing this.

Is there such perfect identity of interests among the States to compose a new Union as to produce harmony only, and prevent renewed secession?

Plainly, the central idea of secession is the essence of anarchy. A majority held in restraint by constitutional checks and limitations, and always changing easily with deliberate changes of popular opinions and sentiments, is the only true sovereign of a free people. Whoever rejects it does, of necessity, fly to anarchy or to despotism. Unanimity is impossible; the rule of a minority, as a permanent arrangement, is wholly inadmissible; so that, rejecting the majority principle, anarchy or despotism in some form is all that is left.

I do not forget the position assumed by some, that constitutional questions are to be decided by the Supreme Court; nor do I deny that such decisions must be binding, in any case, upon the parties to a suit, as to the object of that suit, while they are also entitled to very high respect and consideration in all parallel cases by all other departments of the government. And, while it is obviously possible that such decision may be erroneous in any given case, still the evil effect following it, being limited to that particular case, with the chance that it may be overruled and never become a precedent for other cases, can better be borne than could the evils of a different practice. At the same time, the candid citizen must confess that if the policy of the government, upon vital questions affecting the whole people, is to be irrevocably fixed by decisions of the Supreme Court, the instant they are made, in ordinary litigation between parties in personal actions, the people will have ceased to be their own rulers, having to that extent practically resigned the government into the hands of that eminent tribunal. Nor is there in this view any assault upon the court or the judges. It is a duty from which they may not shrink to decide cases properly brought before them, and it is no fault of theirs if others seek to turn their decisions to political purposes.

One section of our country believes slavery is right, and ought to be extended, while the other believes it is wrong, and ought not to be extended. This is the only substantial dispute. The fugitive slave clause of the Constitution and the law for the suppression of the foreign slave trade are each as well enforced, perhaps, as any law can ever be in a community where the moral sense of the people imperfectly supports the law itself. The great body of the people abide by the dry legal obligation in both cases, and a few break over in each. This, I think, cannot be perfectly cured; and it would be worse in both cases after the separation of the sections than before. The foreign slave trade, now imperfectly suppressed, would be ultimately revived, without restriction, in one section, while fugitive slaves, now only partially surrendered, would not be surrendered at all by the other.

Physically speaking, we cannot separate. We cannot remove our respective sections from each other, nor build an impassable wall between them. A husband and wife may be divorced and go out of the presence and beyond the reach of each other; but the different parts of our country cannot do this. They cannot but remain face to face, and intercourse, either amicable or hostile, must continue between them. Is it possible, then, to make that intercourse more advantageous or more satisfactory after separation than before? Can aliens make treaties easier than friends can make laws? Can treaties be more faithfully enforced between aliens than laws can among friends? Suppose you go to war, you cannot fight always; and when, after much loss on both sides, and no gain on either, you cease fighting, the identical old questions as to terms of intercourse are again upon you.

This country, with its institutions, belongs to the people who inhabit it. Whenever they shall grow weary of the existing government, they can exercise their constitutional right of amending it, or their revolutionary right to dismember or overthrow it. I cannot be ignorant of the fact that many worthy and patriotic citizens are desirous of having the national Constitution amended. While I make no recommendation of amendments, I fully recognize the rightful authority of the people over the whole subject, to be exercised in either of the modes prescribed in the instrument itself, and I should, under existing circumstances, favor rather than oppose a fair opportunity being afforded the people to act upon it. I will venture to add that to me the convention mode seems preferable, in that it allows amendments to originate with the people themselves, instead of only permitting them to take or reject propositions originated by others not especially chosen for the purpose, and which might not be precisely such as they would wish to either accept or refuse. I understand a proposed amendment to the Constitution which amendment, however, I have not seen—has passed Congress, to the effect that the Federal Government shall never interfere with the domestic institutions of the States, including that of persons held to service. To avoid misconstruction of what I have said, I depart from my purpose not to speak of particular amendments so far as to say that, holding such a provision to now be implied constitutional law, I have no objection to its being made express and irrevocable.

The chief magistrate derives all his authority from the people, and they have conferred none upon him to fix terms for the separation of the States. The people themselves can do this also if they choose; but the executive, as such, has nothing to do with it. His duty is to administer the present government, as it came to his hands, and to transmit it, unimpaired by him, to his successors.

Why should there not be a patient confidence in the ultimate justice of the people? Is there any better or equal hope in the world? In our present differences is either party without faith of being in the right? If the Almighty Ruler of nations, with his eternal truth and justice, be on your side of the North, or on yours of the South, that truth and that justice will surely prevail by the judgment of this great tribunal of the American people.

By the frame of the government under which we live, this same people have wisely given their public servants but little power for mischief; and have, with equal wisdom, provided for the return of that little to their own hands at very short intervals. While the people retain their virtue and vigilance, no administration, by any extreme of wickedness or folly, can very seriously injure the government in the short space of four years.

My countrymen, one and all, think calmly and well upon this whole subject. Nothing valuable can be lost by taking time. If there be an object to hurry any of you in hot haste to a step which you would never take deliberately, that object will be frustrated by taking time; but no good object can be frustrated by it. Such of you as are now dissatisfied still have the old Constitution unimpaired, and, on the sensitive point, the laws of your own framing under it; while the new administration will have no immediate power, if it would, to change either. If it were admitted that you who are dissatisfied hold the right side in the dispute, there still is no single good reason for precipitate action. Intelligence, patriotism, Christianity, and a firm reliance on Him who has never yet forsaken this favored land, are still competent to adjust in the best way all our present difficulty.

In your hands, my dissatisfied fellow-countrymen, and not in mine, is the momentous issue of civil war. The government will not assail you. You can have no conflict without being yourselves the aggressors. You have no oath registered in heaven to destroy the government, while I shall have the most solemn one to "preserve, protect, and defend" it.

I am loath to close. We are not enemies, but friends. We must not be enemies. Though passion may have strained, it must not break, our bonds of affection. The mystic chords of memory, stretching from every battle-field and patriot grave to every living heart and hearthstone all over this broad land, will yet swell the chorus of the Union when again touched, as surely they will be, by the better angels of our nature.

MESSAGE TO THE SPECIAL SESSION OF THE 37TH CONGRESS, WASHINGTON, DC, JULY 4, 1861.

FELLOW-CITIZENS OF THE SENATE AND HOUSE OF REPRESENTATIVES:—Having been convened on an extraordinary occasion, as authorized by the Constitution, your attention is not called to any ordinary subject of legislation.

At the beginning of the present Presidential term, four months ago, the functions of the Federal Government were found to be generally suspended within the several States of South Carolina, Georgia, Alabama, Mississippi, Louisiana, and Florida, excepting only those of the Post-Office Department.

Within these States all the forts, arsenals, dockyards, custom-houses, and the like, including the movable and stationary property in and about them, had been seized, and were held in open hostility to this government, excepting only Forts Pickens, Taylor, and Jefferson, on and near the Florida coast, and Fort Sumter, in Charleston Harbor, South Carolina. The forts thus seized had been put in improved condition, new ones had been built, and armed forces had been organized and were organizing, all avowedly with the same hostile purpose.

The forts remaining in the possession of the Federal Government in and near these States were either besieged or menaced by warlike preparations, and especially Fort Sumter was nearly surrounded by well-protected hostile batteries, with guns equal in quality to the best of its own, and outnumbering the latter as perhaps ten to one. A disproportionate share of the Federal muskets and rifles had somehow found their way into these States, and had been seized to be used against the government. Accumulations of the public revenue lying within them had been seized for the same object. The navy was scattered in distant seas, leaving but a very small part of it within the immediate reach of the government. Officers of the Federal army and navy had resigned in great numbers; and of those resigning a large proportion had taken up arms against the government. Simultaneously, and in connection with all this, the purpose to sever the Federal Union was openly avowed. In accordance with this purpose, an ordinance had been adopted in each of these States, declaring the States respectively to be separated from the national Union. A formula for instituting a combined government of these States had been promulgated; and this illegal organization, in the character of confederate States, was already invoking recognition, aid, and intervention from foreign powers.

Finding this condition of things, and believing it to be an imperative duty upon the incoming executive to prevent, if possible, the consummation of such attempt to destroy the Federal Union, a choice of means to that end became indispensable. This choice was made and was declared in the inaugural address. The policy chosen looked to the exhaustion of all peaceful measures before a resort to any stronger ones. It sought only to hold the public places and property not already wrested from the government, and to collect the revenue, relying for the rest on time, discussion, and the ballot-box. It promised a continuance of the mails, at government expense, to the very people who were resisting the government; and it gave repeated pledges against any disturbance to any of the people, or any of their rights. Of all that which a President might constitutionally and justifiably do in such a case, everything was forborne without which it was believed possible to keep the government on foot.

On the 5th of March (the present incumbent's first full day in office), a letter of Major Anderson, commanding at Fort Sumter, written on the 28th of February and received at the War Department on the 4th of March, was by that department placed in his hands. This letter expressed the professional opinion of the writer that reinforcements could not be thrown into that fort within the time for his relief, rendered necessary by the limited supply of provisions, and with a view of holding possession of the same, with a force of less than twenty thousand good and well-disciplined men. This opinion was concurred in by all the officers of his command, and their memoranda on the subject were made enclosures of Major Anderson's letter. The whole was immediately laid before Lieutenant-General Scott, who at once concurred with Major Anderson in opinion. On reflection, however, he took full time, consulting with other officers, both of the army and the navy, and at the end of four days came reluctantly but decidedly to the same conclusion as before. He also stated at the same time that no such sufficient force was then at the control of the government, or could be raised and brought to the ground within the time when the provisions in the fort would be exhausted. In a purely military point of view, this reduced the duty of the administration in the case to the mere matter of getting the garrison safely out of the fort.

It was believed, however, that to so abandon that position, under the circumstances, would be utterly ruinous; that the necessity under which it was to be done would not be fully understood; that by many it would be construed as a part of a voluntary policy; that at home it would discourage the friends of the Union, embolden its adversaries, and go far to insure to the latter a recognition abroad; that in fact, it would be our national destruction consummated. This could not be allowed. Starvation was not yet upon the garrison, and ere it would be reached Fort Pickens might be reinforced. This last would be a clear indication of policy, and would better enable the country to accept the evacuation of Fort Sumter as a military necessity. An order was at once directed to be sent for the landing of the troops from the steamship Brooklyn into Fort Pickens. This order could not go by land, but must take the longer and slower route by sea. The first return news from the order was received just one week before the fall of Fort Sumter. The news itself was that the officer commanding the Sabine, to which vessel the troops had been transferred from the Brooklyn, acting upon some quasi armistice of the late administration (and of the existence of which the present administration, up to the time the order was despatched, had only too vague and uncertain rumors to fix attention), had refused to land the troops. To now reinforce Fort Pickens before a crisis would be reached at Fort Sumter was impossible—rendered so by the near exhaustion of provisions in the latter-named fort. In precaution against such a conjuncture, the government had, a few days before, commenced preparing an expedition as well adapted as might be to relieve Fort Sumter, which expedition was intended to be ultimately used, or not, according to circumstances. The strongest anticipated case for using it was now presented, and it was resolved to send it forward. As had been intended in this contingency, it was also resolved to notify the governor of South Carolina that he might expect an attempt would be made to provision the fort; and that, if the attempt should not be resisted, there would be no effort to throw in men, arms, or ammunition, without further notice, or in case of an attack upon the fort. This notice was accordingly given; whereupon the fort was attacked and bombarded to its fall, without even awaiting the arrival of the provisioning expedition.

It is thus seen that the assault upon and reduction of Fort Sumter was in no sense a matter of self-defense on the part of the assailants. They well knew that the garrison in the fort could by no possibility commit aggression upon them. They knew—they were expressly notified—that the giving of bread to the few brave and hungry men of the garrison was all which would on that occasion be attempted, unless themselves, by resisting so much, should provoke more. They knew that this government desired to keep the garrison in the fort, not to assail them, but merely to maintain visible possession, and thus to preserve the Union from actual and immediate dissolution—trusting, as hereinbefore stated, to time, discussion, and the ballot-box for final adjustment; and they assailed and reduced the fort for precisely the reverse object—to drive out the visible authority of the Federal Union, and thus force it to immediate dissolution. That this was their object the executive well understood; and having said to them in the inaugural address, "You can have no conflict without being yourselves the aggressors," he took pains not only to keep this declaration good, but also to keep the case so free from the power of ingenious sophistry that the world should not be able to misunderstand it. By the affair at Fort Sumter, with its surrounding circumstances, that point was reached. Then and thereby the assailants of the government began the conflict of arms, without a gun in sight or in expectancy to return their fire, save only the few in the fort sent to that harbor years before for their own protection, and still ready to give that protection in whatever was lawful. In this act, discarding all else, they have forced upon the country the distinct issue, "immediate dissolution or blood."

And this issue embraces more than the fate of these United States. It presents to the whole family of man the question whether a constitutional republic or democracy—a government of the people by the same people—can or cannot maintain its territorial integrity against its own domestic foes. It presents the question whether discontented individuals, too few in numbers to control administration according to organic law in any case, can always, upon the pretenses made in this case, or on any other pretenses, or arbitrarily without any pretense, break up their government, and thus practically put an end to free government upon the earth. It forces us to ask: Is there in all republics this inherent and fatal weakness? Must a government, of necessity, be too strong for the liberties of its own people, or too weak to maintain its own existence?

So viewing the issue, no choice was left but to call out the war power of the government, and so to resist force employed for its destruction by force for its preservation.

The call was made, and the response of the country was most gratifying, surpassing in unanimity and spirit the most sanguine expectation. Yet none of the States commonly called slave States, except Delaware, gave a regiment through regular State organization. A few regiments have been organized within some others of those States by individual enterprise, and received into the government service. Of course the seceded States, so called (and to which Texas had been joined about the time of the inauguration), gave no troops to the cause of the Union. The border States, so called, were not uniform in their action, some of them being almost for the Union, while in others—as Virginia, North Carolina, Tennessee, and Arkansas—the Union sentiment was nearly repressed and silenced. The course taken in

Virginia was the most remarkable—perhaps the most important. A convention elected by the people of that State to consider this very question of disrupting the Federal Union was in session at the capital of Virginia when Fort Sumter fell. To this body the people had chosen a large majority of professed Union men. Almost immediately after the fall of Sumter, many members of that majority went over to the original disunion minority, and with them adopted an ordinance for withdrawing the State from the Union. Whether this change was wrought by their great approval of the assault upon Sumter, or their great resentment at the government's resistance to that assault, is not definitely known. Although they submitted the ordinance for ratification to a vote of the people, to be taken on a day then somewhat more than a month distant, the convention and the Legislature (which was also in session at the same time and place), with leading men of the State not members of either, immediately commenced acting as if the State were already out of the Union. They pushed military preparations vigorously forward all over the State. They seized the United States armory at Harper's Ferry, and the navy-yard at Gosport, near Norfolk. They received perhaps invited—into their State large bodies of troops, with their warlike appointments, from the so-called seceded States. They formally entered into a treaty of temporary alliance and co-operation with the so-called "Confederate States," and sent members to their congress at Montgomery. And finally, they permitted the insurrectionary government to be transferred to their capital at Richmond.

The people of Virginia have thus allowed this giant insurrection to make its nest within her borders; and this government has no choice left but to deal with it where it finds it. And it has the less regret as the loyal citizens have, in due form, claimed its protection. Those loyal citizens this government is bound to recognize and protect, as being Virginia.

In the border States, so called,—in fact, the middle States,—there are those who favor a policy which they call "armed neutrality"; that is, an arming of those States to prevent the Union forces passing one way, or the disunion the other, over their soil. This would be disunion completed. Figuratively speaking, it would be the building of an impassable wall along the line of separation—and yet not quite an impassable one, for under the guise of neutrality it would tie the hands of Union men and freely pass supplies from among them to the insurrectionists, which it could not do as an open enemy. At a stroke it would take all the trouble off the hands of secession, except only what proceeds from the external blockade. It would do for the disunionists that which, of all things, they most desire—feed them well and give them disunion without a struggle of their own. It recognizes no fidelity to the Constitution, no obligation to maintain the Union; and while very many who have favored it are doubtless loyal citizens, it is, nevertheless, very injurious in effect.

Recurring to the action of the government, it may be stated that at first a call was made for 75,000 militia; and, rapidly following this, a proclamation was issued for closing the ports of the insurrectionary districts by proceedings in the nature of blockade. So far all was believed to be strictly legal. At this point the insurrectionists announced their purpose to enter upon the practice of privateering.

Other calls were made for volunteers to serve for three years, unless sooner discharged, and also for large additions to the regular army and navy. These measures, whether strictly legal or not, were ventured upon, under what appeared to be a popular demand and a public necessity; trusting then, as now, that Congress would readily ratify them. It is believed that nothing has been done beyond the constitutional competency of Congress.

Soon after the first call for militia, it was considered a duty to authorize the commanding general in proper cases, according to his discretion, to suspend the privilege of the writ of habeas corpus, or, in other words, to arrest and detain, without resort to the ordinary processes and forms of law, such individuals as he might deem dangerous to the public safety. This authority has purposely been exercised but very sparingly. Nevertheless, the legality and propriety of what has been done under it are questioned, and the attention of the country has been called to the proposition that one who has sworn to "take care that the laws be faithfully executed" should not himself violate them. Of course some consideration was given to the questions of power and propriety before this matter was acted upon. The whole of the laws which were required to be faithfully executed were being resisted and failing of execution in nearly one third of the States. Must they be allowed to finally fail of execution, even had it been perfectly clear that by the use of the means necessary to their execution some single law, made in such extreme tenderness of the citizen's liberty that, practically, it relieves more of the guilty than of the innocent, should to a very limited extent be violated? To state the question more directly, are all the laws but one to go unexecuted, and the government itself go to pieces lest that one be violated? Even in such a case, would not the official oath be broken if the government should be overthrown when it was believed that disregarding the single law would tend to preserve it? But it was not believed that this question was presented. It was not believed that any law was violated. The provision of the Constitution that "the privilege of the writ of habeas corpus shall not be suspended, unless when, in cases of rebellion or invasion, the public safety may require it," is equivalent to a provision—is a provision— that such privilege may be suspended when, in case of rebellion or invasion, the public safety does require it. It was decided that we have a case of rebellion, and that the public safety does require the qualified suspension of the privilege of the writ which was authorized to be made. Now it is insisted that Congress, and not the executive, is vested with this power. But the Constitution itself is silent as to which or who is to exercise the power; and as the provision was plainly made for a dangerous emergency, it cannot be believed the framers of the instrument intended that in every case the danger should run its course until Congress could be called together, the very assembling of which might be prevented, as was intended in this case, by the rebellion.

No more extended argument is now offered, as an opinion at some length will probably be presented by the attorney-general. Whether there shall be any legislation upon the subject, and if any, what, is submitted entirely to the better judgment of Congress.

The forbearance of this government had been so extraordinary and so long continued as to lead some foreign nations to shape their action as if they supposed the early destruction of our national Union was probable. While this, on discovery, gave the executive some concern, he is now happy to say that the sovereignty and rights of the United States are now everywhere practically respected by foreign powers; and a general sympathy with the country is manifested throughout the world.

The reports of the Secretaries of the Treasury, War, and the Navy will give the information in detail deemed necessary and convenient for your deliberation and action; while the executive and all the departments will stand ready to supply omissions, or to communicate new facts considered important for you to know.

It is now recommended that you give the legal means for making this contest a short and decisive one: that you place at the control of the government for the work at least four hundred thousand men and $400,000,000. That number of men is about one-tenth of those of proper ages within the regions where, apparently, all are willing to engage; and the sum is less than a twenty-third part of the money value owned by the men who seem ready to devote the whole. A debt of $600,000,000 now is a less sum per head than was the debt of our Revolution when we came out of that struggle; and the money value in the country now bears even a greater proportion to what it was then than does the population. Surely each man has as strong a motive now to preserve our liberties as each had then to establish them.

A right result at this time will be worth more to the world than ten times the men and ten times the money. The evidence reaching us from the country leaves no doubt that the material for the work is abundant, and that it needs only the hand of legislation to give it legal sanction, and the hand of the executive to give it practical shape and efficiency. One of the greatest perplexities of the government is to avoid receiving troops faster than it can provide for them. In a word, the people will save their government if the government itself will do its part only indifferently well.

It might seem, at first thought, to be of little difference whether the present movement at the South be called "secession" or "rebellion." The movers, however, well understand the difference. At the beginning they knew they could never raise their treason to any respectable magnitude by any name which implies violation of law. They knew their people possessed as much of moral sense, as much of devotion to law and order, and as much pride in and reverence for the history and government of their common country as any other civilized and patriotic people. They knew they could make no advancement directly in the teeth of these strong and noble sentiments. Accordingly, they commenced by an insidious debauching of the public mind. They invented an ingenious sophism which, if conceded, was followed by perfectly logical steps, through all the incidents, to the complete destruction of the Union. The sophism itself is that any State of the Union may consistently with the national Constitution, and therefore lawfully and peacefully, withdraw from the Union without the consent of the Union or of any other State. The little disguise that the supposed right is to be exercised only for just cause, themselves to be the sole judges of its justice, is too thin to merit any notice.

With rebellion thus sugar-coated they have been drugging the public mind of their section for more than thirty years, and until at length they have brought many good men to a willingness to take up arms against the government the day after some assemblage of men have enacted the farcical pretense of taking their State out of the Union, who could have been brought to no such thing the day before.

This sophism derives much, perhaps the whole, of its currency from the assumption that there is some omnipotent and sacred supremacy pertaining to a State—to each State of our Federal Union. Our States have neither more nor less power than that reserved to them in the Union by the Constitution—no one of them ever having been a State out of the Union. The original ones passed into the Union even before they cast off their British colonial dependence; and the new ones each came into the Union directly from a condition of dependence, excepting Texas. And even Texas in its temporary independence was never designated a State. The new ones only took the designation of States on coming into the Union, while that name was first adopted for the old ones in and by the Declaration of Independence. Therein the "United Colonies" were declared to be "free and independent States"; but even then the object plainly was not to declare their independence of one another or of the Union, but directly the contrary, as their mutual pledge and their mutual action before, at the time, and afterward, abundantly show. The express plighting of faith by each and all of the original thirteen in the Articles of Confederation, two years later, that the Union shall be perpetual, is most conclusive. Having never been States either in substance or in name outside of the Union, whence this magical omnipotence of "State rights," asserting a claim of power to lawfully destroy the Union itself? Much is said about the "sovereignty" of the States; but the word even is not in the national Constitution, nor, as is believed, in any of the State constitutions. What is "sovereignty" in the political sense of the term? Would it be far wrong to define it as "a political community without a political superior"? Tested by this, no one of our States except Texas ever was a sovereignty. And even Texas gave up the character on coming into the Union; by which act she acknowledged the Constitution of the United States, and the laws and treaties of the United States made in pursuance of the Constitution, to be for her the supreme law of the land. The States have their status in the Union, and they have no other legal status. If they break from this, they can only do so against law and by revolution. The Union, and not themselves separately, procured their independence and their liberty. By conquest or purchase the Union gave each of them whatever of independence or liberty it has. The Union is older than any of the States, and, in fact, it created them as States. Originally some dependent colonies made the Union, and, in turn, the Union threw off their old dependence for them, and made them States, such as they are. Not one of them ever had a State constitution independent of the Union. Of course, it is not forgotten that all the new States framed their constitutions before they entered the Union nevertheless, dependent upon and preparatory to coming into the Union.

Unquestionably the States have the powers and rights reserved to them in and by the national Constitution; but among these surely are not included all conceivable powers, however mischievous or destructive, but, at most, such only as were known in the world at the time as governmental powers; and certainly a power to destroy the government itself had never been known as a governmental, as a merely administrative power. This relative matter of national power and State rights, as a principle, is no other than the principle of generality and locality. Whatever concerns the whole should be confided to the whole—to the General Government; while whatever concerns only the State should be left exclusively to the State. This is all there is of original principle about it. Whether the national Constitution in defining boundaries between the two has applied the principle with exact accuracy, is not to be questioned. We are all bound by that defining, without question.

What is now combated is the position that secession is consistent with the Constitution—is lawful and peaceful. It is not contended that there is any express law for it; and nothing should ever be implied as law which leads to unjust or absurd consequences. The nation purchased with money the countries out of which several of these

States were formed. Is it just that they shall go off without leave and without refunding? The nation paid very large sums (in the aggregate, I believe, nearly a hundred millions) to relieve Florida of the aboriginal tribes. Is it just that she shall now be off without consent or without making any return? The nation is now in debt for money applied to the benefit of these so-called seceding States in common with the rest. Is it just either that creditors shall go unpaid or the remaining States pay the whole? A part of the present national debt was contracted to pay the old debts of Texas. Is it just that she shall leave and pay no part of this herself?

Again, if one State may secede, so may another; and when all shall have seceded, none is left to pay the debts. Is this quite just for creditors? Did we notify them of this sage view of ours when we borrowed their money? If we now recognize this doctrine by allowing the seceders to go in peace, it is difficult to see what we can do if others choose to go or to extort terms upon which they will promise to remain.

The seceders insist that our Constitution admits of secession. They have assumed to make a national constitution of their own, in which of necessity they have either discarded or retained the right of secession as they insist it exists in ours. If they have discarded it, they thereby admit that on principle it ought not to be in ours. If they have retained it, by their own construction of ours, they show that to be consistent they must secede from one another whenever they shall find it the easiest way of settling their debts, or effecting any other selfish or unjust object. The principle itself is one of disintegration and upon which no government can possibly endure.

If all the States save one should assert the power to drive that one out of the Union, it is presumed the whole class of seceder politicians would at once deny the power and denounce the act as the greatest outrage upon State rights. But suppose that precisely the same act, instead of being called "driving the one out," should be called "the seceding of the others from that one," it would be exactly what the seceders claim to do, unless, indeed, they make the point that the one, because it is a minority, may rightfully do what the others, because they are a majority, may not rightfully do. These politicians are subtle and profound on the rights of minorities. They are not partial to that power which made the Constitution and speaks from the preamble calling itself "We, the People."

It may well be questioned whether there is to-day a majority of the legally qualified voters of any State except perhaps South Carolina in favor of disunion. There is much reason to believe that the Union men are the majority in many, if not in every other one, of the so-called seceded States. The contrary has not been demonstrated in any one of them. It is ventured to affirm this even of Virginia and Tennessee; for the result of an election held in military camps, where the bayonets are all on one side of the question voted upon, can scarcely be considered as demonstrating popular sentiment. At such an election, all that large class who are at once for the Union and against coercion would be coerced to vote against the Union.

It may be affirmed without extravagance that the free institutions we enjoy have developed the powers and improved the condition of our whole people beyond any example in the world. Of this we now have a striking and an impressive illustration. So large an army as the government has now on foot was never before known without a soldier in it but who has taken his place there of his own free choice. But more than this, there are many single regiments whose members, one and another, possess full practical knowledge of all the arts, sciences, professions, and whatever else, whether useful or elegant, is known in the world; and there is scarcely one from which there could not be selected a President, a Cabinet, a Congress, and perhaps a court, abundantly competent to administer the government itself. Nor do I say this is not true also in the army of our late friends, now adversaries in this contest; but if it is, so much better the reason why the government which has conferred such benefits on both them and us should not be broken up. Whoever in any section proposes to abandon such a government would do well to consider in deference to what principle it is that he does it; what better he is likely to get in its stead; whether the substitute will give, or be intended to give, so much of good to the people. There are some foreshadowings on this subject. Our adversaries have adopted some declarations of independence in which, unlike the good old one, penned by Jefferson, they omit the words "all men are created equal." Why? They have adopted a temporary national constitution, in the preamble of which, unlike our good old one, signed by Washington, they omit "We, the People," and substitute, "We, the deputies of the sovereign and independent States." Why? Why this deliberate pressing out of view the rights of men and the authority of the people?

This is essentially a people's contest. On the side of the Union it is a struggle for maintaining in the world that form and substance of government whose leading object is to elevate the condition of men to lift artificial weights from all shoulders; to clear the paths of laudable pursuit for all; to afford all an unfettered start, and a fair chance in the race of life. Yielding to partial and temporary departures, from necessity; this is the leading object of the government for whose existence we contend.

I am most happy to believe that the plain people understand and appreciate this. It is worthy of note that, while in this the government's hour of trial large numbers of those in the army and navy who have been favored with the offices have resigned and proved false to the hand which had pampered them, not one common soldier or common sailor is known to have deserted his flag.

Great honor is due to those officers who remained true, despite the example of their treacherous associates; but the greatest honor, and most important fact of all, is the unanimous firmness of the common soldiers and common sailors. To the last man, so far as known, they have successfully resisted the traitorous efforts of those whose commands, but an hour before, they obeyed as absolute law. This is the patriotic instinct of the plain people. They understand, without an argument, that the destroying of the government which was made by Washington means no good to them.

Our popular government has often been called an experiment. Two points in it our people have already settled—the successful establishing and the successful administering of it. One still remains—its successful maintenance against a formidable internal attempt to overthrow it. It is now for them to demonstrate to the world that those who can fairly carry an election can also suppress a rebellion; that ballots are the rightful and peaceful successors of bullets; and that when ballots have fairly and constitutionally decided, there can be no successful appeal back to bullets; that there can be no successful appeal, except to ballots themselves, at succeeding elections. Such will be a great lesson of peace: teaching men that what they cannot take by an election, neither can they take it by a war; teaching all the folly of being the beginners of a war.

Lest there be some uneasiness in the minds of candid men as to what is to be the course of the government toward the Southern States after the rebellion shall have been suppressed, the executive deems it proper to say it will be his purpose then, as ever, to be guided by the Constitution and the laws; and that he probably will have no different understanding of the powers and duties of the Federal Government relatively to the rights of the States and the people, under the Constitution, than that expressed in the inaugural address.

He desires to preserve the government, that it may be administered for all as it was administered by the men who made it. Loyal citizens everywhere have the right to claim this of their government, and the government has no right to withhold or neglect it. It is not perceived that in giving it there is any coercion, any conquest, or any subjugation, in any just sense of those terms.

The Constitution provides, and all the States have accepted the provision, that "the United States shall guarantee to every State in this Union a republican form of government." But if a State may lawfully go out of the Union, having done so it may also discard the republican form of government, so that to prevent its going out is an indispensable means to the end of maintaining the guarantee mentioned; and when an end is lawful and obligatory, the indispensable means to it are also lawful and obligatory.

It was with the deepest regret that the executive found the duty of employing the war power in defense of the government forced upon him. He could but perform this duty or surrender the existence of the government. No compromise by public servants could, in this case, be a cure; not that compromises are not often proper, but that no popular government can long survive a marked precedent that those who carry an election can only save the government from immediate destruction by giving up the main point upon which the people gave the election. The people themselves, and not their servants, can safely reverse their own deliberate decisions.

As a private citizen the executive could not have consented that these institutions shall perish; much less could he in betrayal of so vast and so sacred a trust as these free people had confided to him. He felt that he had no moral right to shrink, nor even to count the chances of his own life, in what might follow. In full view of his great responsibility he has, so far, done what he has deemed his duty. You will now, according to your own judgment, perform yours. He sincerely hopes that your views and your action may so accord with his as to assure all faithful citizens who have been disturbed in their rights of a certain and speedy restoration to them, under the Constitution and the laws.

And having thus chosen our course, without guile and with pure purpose, let us renew our trust in God, and go forward without fear and with manly hearts.

PROCLAMATION OF A NATIONAL FAST-DAY, AUGUST 12, 1861.

A Proclamation.

Whereas a joint committee of both houses of Congress has waited on the President of the United States and requested him to "recommend a day of public humiliation, prayer, and fasting to be observed by the people of the United States with religious solemnities and the offering of fervent supplications to Almighty God for the safety and welfare of these States, His blessings on their arms, and a speedy restoration of peace"; and

Whereas it is fit and becoming in all people at all times to acknowledge and revere the supreme government of God, to bow in humble submission to His chastisements, to confess and deplore their sins and transgressions in the full conviction that the fear of the Lord is the beginning of wisdom, and to pray with all fervency and contrition for the pardon of their past offences and for a blessing upon their present and prospective action; and

Whereas when our own beloved country, once, by the blessing of God, united, prosperous, and happy, is now afflicted with faction and civil war, it is peculiarly fit for us to recognize the hand of God in this terrible visitation, and in sorrowful remembrance of our own faults and crimes as a nation and as individuals to humble ourselves before Him and to pray for His mercy-to pray that we may be spared further punishment, though most justly deserved, that our arms may be blessed and made effectual for the re-establishment of order, law, and peace throughout the wide extent of our country, and that the inestimable boon of civil and religious liberty, earned under His guidance and blessing by the labors and sufferings of our fathers, may be restored in all its original excellence.

Therefore I, Abraham Lincoln, President of the United States, do appoint the last Thursday in September next as a day of humiliation, prayer, and fasting for all the people of the nation. And I do earnestly recommend to all the people, and especially to all ministers and teachers of religion of all denominations and to all heads of families, to observe and keep that day according to their several creeds and modes of worship in all humility and with all religious solemnity, to the end that the united prayer of the nation may ascend to the Throne of Grace and bring down plentiful blessings upon our country.

In testimony whereof I have hereunto set my hand and caused the seal of the United States to be affixed, this twelfth day of August, A. D. 1861, and of the independence of the United States of America the eighty-sixth.

ABRAHAM LINCOLN.

By the President:
WILLIAM H. SEWARD, *Secretary of State.*

FIRST ANNUAL MESSAGE TO CONGRESS, WASHINGTON, DC, DECEMBER 3, 1861.

FELLOW-CITIZENS OF THE SENATE AND HOUSE OF REPRESENTATIVES:—In the midst of unprecedented political troubles we have cause of great gratitude to God for unusual good health and most abundant harvests.

You will not be surprised to learn that in the peculiar exigencies of the times our intercourse with foreign nations has been attended with profound solicitude, chiefly turning upon our own domestic affairs.

A disloyal portion of the American people have during the whole year been engaged in an attempt to divide and destroy the Union. A nation which endures factious domestic division is exposed to disrespect abroad, and one party, if not both, is sure sooner or later to invoke foreign intervention.

Nations thus tempted to interfere are not always able to resist the counsels of seeming expediency and ungenerous ambition, although measures adopted under such influences seldom fail to be unfortunate and injurious to those adopting them.

The disloyal citizens of the United States who have offered the ruin of our country in return for the aid and comfort which they have invoked abroad have received less patronage and encouragement than they probably expected. If it were just to suppose, as the insurgents have seemed to assume, that foreign nations in this case, discarding all moral, social, and treaty obligations, would act solely and selfishly for the most speedy restoration of commerce, including especially the acquisition of cotton, those nations appear as yet not to have seen their way to their object more directly or clearly through the destruction than through the preservation of the Union. If we could dare to believe that foreign nations are actuated by no higher principle than this, I am quite sure a sound argument could be made to show them that they can reach their aim more readily and easily by aiding to crush this rebellion than by giving encouragement to it.

The principal lever relied on by the insurgents for exciting foreign nations to hostility against us, as already intimated, is the embarrassment of commerce. Those nations, however, not improbably saw from the first that it was the Union which made as well our foreign as our domestic commerce. They can scarcely have failed to perceive that the effort for disunion produces the existing difficulty, and that one strong nation promises more durable peace and a more extensive, valuable, and reliable commerce than can the same nation broken into hostile fragments.

It is not my purpose to review our discussions with foreign states, because, whatever might be their wishes or dispositions, the integrity of our country and the stability of our government mainly depend not upon them, but on the loyalty, virtue, patriotism, and intelligence of the American people. The correspondence itself, with the usual reservations, is herewith submitted.

I venture to hope it will appear that we have practiced prudence and liberality toward foreign powers, averting causes of irritation and with firmness maintaining our own rights and honor.

Since, however, it is apparent that here, as in every other state, foreign dangers necessarily attend domestic difficulties, I recommend that adequate and ample measures be adopted for maintaining the public defenses on every side. While under this general recommendation provision for defending our seacoast line readily occurs to the mind, I also in the same connection ask the attention of Congress to our great lakes and rivers. It is believed that some fortifications and depots of arms and munitions, with harbor and navigation improvements, all at well-selected points upon these, would be of great importance to the national defense and preservation I ask attention to the views of the Secretary of War, expressed in his report, upon the same general subject.

I deem it of importance that the loyal regions of east Tennessee and western North Carolina should be connected with Kentucky and other faithful parts of the Union by rail-road. I therefore recommend, as a military measure, that Congress provide for the construction of such rail-road as speedily as possible. Kentucky will no doubt co-operate, and through her Legislature make the most judicious selection of a line. The northern terminus must connect with some existing railroad, and whether the route shall be from Lexington or Nicholasville to the Cumberland Gap, or from Lebanon to the Tennessee line, in the direction of Knoxville, or on some still different line, can easily be determined. Kentucky and the General Government co-operating, the work can be completed in a very short time, and when done it will be not only of vast present usefulness but also a valuable permanent improvement, worth its cost in all the future.

Some treaties, designed chiefly for the interests of commerce, and having no grave political importance, have been negotiated, and will be submitted to the Senate for their consideration.

Although we have failed to induce some of the commercial powers to adopt a desirable melioration of the rigor of maritime war, we have removed all obstructions from the way of this humane reform except such as are merely of temporary and accidental occurrence.

I invite your attention to the correspondence between her Britannic Majesty's minister accredited to this government and the Secretary of State relative to the detention of the British ship Perthshire in June last by the United States steamer Massachusetts for a supposed breach of the blockade. As this detention was occasioned by an obvious misapprehension of the facts, and as justice requires that we should commit no belligerent act not founded in strict right as sanctioned by public law, I recommend that an appropriation be made to satisfy the reasonable demand of the owners of the vessel for her detention.

I repeat the recommendation of my predecessor in his annual message to Congress in December last in regard to the disposition of the surplus which will probably remain after satisfying the claims of American citizens against China, pursuant to the awards of the commissioners under the act of the 3d of March, 1859. If, however, it should not be deemed advisable to carry that recommendation into effect, I would suggest that authority be given for investing the principal, or the proceeds of the surplus referred to, in good securities, with a view to the satisfaction of such other just claims of our citizens against China as are not unlikely to arise hereafter in the course of our extensive trade with that empire.

By the act of the 5th of August last Congress authorized the President to instruct the commanders of suitable vessels to defend themselves against and to capture pirates. His authority has been exercised in a single instance only. For the more effectual protection of our extensive and valuable commerce in the Eastern seas especially, it seems to me that it would also be advisable to authorize the commanders of sailing vessels to recapture any prizes which pirates may make of United States vessels and their cargoes, and the consular courts now established by law in Eastern countries to adjudicate the cases in the event that this should not be objected to by the local authorities.

If any good reason exists why we should persevere longer in withholding our recognition of the independence and sovereignty of Haiti and Liberia, I am unable to discern it. Unwilling, however, to inaugurate a novel policy in regard to them without the approbation of Congress, I submit for your consideration the expediency of an appropriation for maintaining a charge d'affaires near each of those new States. It does not admit of doubt that important commercial advantages might be secured by favorable treaties with them.

The operations of the treasury during the period which has elapsed since your adjournment have been conducted with signal success. The patriotism of the people has placed at the disposal of the government the large means demanded by the public exigencies. Much of the national loan has been taken by citizens of the industrial classes, whose confidence in their country's faith and zeal for their country's deliverance from present peril have induced them to contribute to the support of the government the whole of their limited acquisitions. This fact imposes peculiar obligations to economy in disbursement and energy in action.

The revenue from all sources, including loans, for the financial year ending on the 30th of June, 1861, was $86,835,900.27, and the expenditures for the same period, including payments on account of the public debt, were $84,578,834.47, leaving a balance in the treasury on the 1st of July of $2,257,065.80. For the first quarter of the financial year ending on the 30th of September, 1861, the receipts from all sources, including the balance of the 1st of July, were $102,532,509.27, and the expenses $98,239733.09, leaving a balance on the 1st of October, 1861, of $4,292,776.18.

Estimates for the remaining three quarters of the year and for the financial year 1863, together with his views of ways and means for meeting the demands contemplated by them, will be submitted to Congress by the Secretary of the Treasury. It is gratifying to know that the expenditures made necessary by the rebellion are not beyond the resources of the loyal people, and to believe that the same patriotism which has thus far sustained the government will continue to sustain it till peace and union shall again bless the land.

I respectfully refer to the report of the Secretary of War for information respecting the numerical strength of the army and for recommendations having in view an increase of its efficiency and the well-being of the various branches of the service entrusted to his care. It is gratifying to know that the patriotism of the people has proved equal to the occasion, and that the number of troops tendered greatly exceeds the force which Congress authorized me to call into the field.

I refer with pleasure to those portions of his report which make allusion to the creditable degree of discipline already attained by our troops and to the excellent sanitary condition of the entire army.

The recommendation of the Secretary for an organization of the militia upon a uniform basis is a subject of vital importance to the future safety of the country, and is commended to the serious attention of Congress.

The large addition to the regular army, in connection with the defection that has so considerably diminished the number of its officers, gives peculiar importance to his recommendation for increasing the corps of cadets to the greatest capacity of the Military Academy.

By mere omission, I presume, Congress has failed to provide chaplains for hospitals occupied by volunteers. This subject was brought to my notice, and I was induced to draw up the form of a letter, one copy of which, properly addressed, has been delivered to each of the persons, and at the dates respectively named and stated in a schedule, containing also the form of the letter, marked A, and herewith transmitted.

These gentlemen, I understand, entered upon the duties designated at the times respectively stated in the schedule, and have labored faithfully therein ever since. I therefore recommend that they be compensated at the same rate as chaplains in the army. I further suggest that general provision be made for chaplains to serve at hospitals, as well as with regiments.

The report of the Secretary of the Navy presents in detail the operations of that branch of the service, the activity and energy which have characterized its administration, and the results of measures to increase its efficiency and power such have been the additions, by construction and purchase, that it may almost be said a navy has been created and brought into service since our difficulties commenced.

Besides blockading our extensive coast, squadrons larger than ever before assembled under our flag have been put afloat and performed deeds which have increased our naval renown.

I would invite special attention to the recommendation of the Secretary for a more perfect organization of the navy by introducing additional grades in the service.

The present organization is defective and unsatisfactory, and the suggestions submitted by the department will, it is believed, if adopted, obviate the difficulties alluded to, promote harmony, and increase the efficiency of the navy.

There are three vacancies on the bench of the Supreme Court—two by the decease of Justices Daniel and McLean and one by the resignation of Justice Campbell. I have so far forborne making nominations to fill these vacancies for reasons which I will now state. Two of the outgoing judges resided within the States now overrun by revolt, so that if successors were appointed in the same localities they could not now serve upon their circuits; and many of the most competent men there probably would not take the personal hazard of accepting to serve, even here, upon the Supreme bench. I have been unwilling to throw all the appointments north-ward, thus disabling myself from doing justice to the South on the return of peace; although I may remark that to transfer to the North one which has heretofore been in the South would not, with reference to territory and population, be unjust.

During the long and brilliant judicial career of Judge McLean his circuit grew into an empire-altogether too large for any one judge to give the courts therein more than a nominal attendance—rising in population from 1,470,018 in 1830 to 6,151,405 in 1860.

Besides this, the country generally has outgrown our present judicial system. If uniformity was at all intended, the system requires that all the States shall be accommodated with circuit courts, attended by Supreme judges, while, in fact, Wisconsin, Minnesota, Iowa, Kansas, Florida, Texas, California, and Oregon have never had any such courts. Nor can this well be remedied without a change in the system, because the adding of judges to the Supreme Court, enough for the accommodation of all parts of the country with circuit courts, would create a court altogether too numerous for a judicial body of any sort. And the evil, if it be one, will increase as new States come into the Union. Circuit courts are useful or they are not useful. If useful, no State should be denied them; if not useful, no State should have them. Let them be provided for all or abolished as to all.

Three modifications occur to me, either of which, I think, would be an improvement upon our present system. Let the Supreme Court be of convenient number in every event; then, first, let the whole country be divided into circuits of convenient size, the Supreme judges to serve in a number of them corresponding to their own number, and independent circuit judges be provided for all the rest; or, secondly, let the Supreme judges be relieved from circuit duties and circuit judges provided for all the circuits; or, thirdly, dispense with circuit courts altogether, leaving the judicial functions wholly to the district courts and an independent Supreme Court.

I respectfully recommend to the consideration of Congress the present condition of the statute laws, with the hope that Congress will be able to find an easy remedy for many of the inconveniences and evils which constantly embarrass those engaged in the practical administration of them. Since the Organization of the government, Congress has enacted some 5000 acts and joint resolutions, which fill more than 6000 closely printed pages and are scattered through many volumes. Many of these acts have been drawn in haste and without sufficient caution, so that their provisions are often obscure in themselves or in conflict with each other, or at least so doubtful as to render it very difficult for even the best-informed persons to ascertain precisely what the statute law really is.

It seems to me very important that the statute laws should be made as plain and intelligible as possible, and be reduced to as small a compass as may consist with the fullness and precision of the will of the Legislature and the perspicuity of its language. This well done would, I think, greatly facilitate the labors of those whose duty it is to assist in the administration of the laws, and would be a lasting benefit to the people, by placing before them in a more accessible and intelligible form the laws which so deeply concern their interests and their duties.

I am informed by some whose opinions I respect that all the acts of Congress now in force and of a permanent and general nature might be revised and rewritten so as to be embraced in one volume (or at most two volumes) of ordinary and convenient size; and I respectfully recommend to Congress to consider of the subject, and if my suggestion be approved to devise such plan as to their wisdom shall seem most proper for the attainment of the end proposed.

One of the unavoidable consequences of the present insurrection is the entire suppression in many places of all the ordinary means of administering civil justice by the officers and in the forms of existing law. This is the case, in whole or in part, in all the insurgent States; and as our armies advance upon and take possession of parts of those States the practical evil becomes more apparent. There are no courts or officers to whom the citizens of other States may apply for the enforcement of their lawful claims against citizens of the insurgent States, and there is a vast amount of debt constituting such claims. Some have estimated it as high as $200,000,000, due in large part from insurgents in open rebellion to loyal citizens who are even now making great sacrifices in the discharge of their patriotic duty to support the government.

Under these circumstances I have been urgently solicited to establish, by military power, courts to administer summary justice in such cases. I have thus far declined to do it, not because I had any doubt that the end proposed—the collection of the debts—was just and right in itself, but because I have been unwilling to go beyond the pressure of necessity in the unusual exercise of power. But the powers of Congress, I suppose, are equal to the anomalous occasion, and therefore I refer the whole matter to Congress, with the hope that a plan maybe devised for the administration of justice in all such parts of the insurgent States and Territories as may be under the control of this government, whether by a voluntary return to allegiance and order or by the power of our arms; this, however, not to be a permanent institution, but a temporary substitute, and to cease as soon as the ordinary courts can be reestablished in peace.

It is important that some more convenient means should be provided, if possible, for the adjustment of claims against the government, especially in view of their increased number by reason of the war. It is as much the duty of government to render prompt justice against itself in favor of citizens as it is to administer the same between private individuals. The investigation and adjudication of claims in their nature belong to the judicial department. Besides, it is apparent that the attention of Congress will be more than usually engaged for some time to come with great national questions. It was intended by the organization of the Court of Claims mainly to remove this branch of business from the halls of Congress; but, while the court has proved to be an effective and valuable means of investigation, it in great degree fails to effect the object of its creation for want of power to make its judgments final.

Fully aware of the delicacy, not to say the danger of the subject, I commend to your careful consideration whether this power of making judgments final may not properly be given to the court, reserving the right of appeal on questions of law to the Supreme Court, with such other provisions as experience may have shown to be necessary.

I ask attention to the report of the Postmaster general, the following being a summary statement of the condition of the department:

The revenue from all sources during the fiscal year ending June 30, 1861, including the annual permanent appropriation of $700,000 for the transportation of "free mail matter," was $9,049,296.40, being about 2 percent less than the revenue for 1860.

The expenditures were $13,606,759.11, showing a decrease of more than 8 percent as compared with those of the previous year and leaving an excess of expenditure over the revenue for the last fiscal year of $4,557,462.71.

The gross revenue for the year ending June 30, 1863, is estimated at an increase of 4 percent on that of 1861, making $8,683,000, to which should be added the earnings of the department in carrying free matter, viz., $700,000, making $9,383,000.

The total expenditures for 1863 are estimated at $12,528,000, leaving an estimated deficiency of $3,145,000 to be supplied from the treasury in addition to the permanent appropriation.

The present insurrection shows, I think, that the extension of this District across the Potomac River at the time of establishing the capital here was eminently wise, and consequently that the relinquishment of that portion of it which lies within the State of Virginia was unwise and dangerous. I submit for your consideration the expediency of regaining that part of the District and the restoration of the original boundaries thereof through negotiations with the State of Virginia.

The report of the Secretary of the Interior, with the accompanying documents, exhibits the condition of the several branches of the public business pertaining to that department. The depressing influences of the insurrection have been specially felt in the operations of the Patent and General Land Offices. The cash receipts from the sales of public lands during the past year have exceeded the expenses of our land system only about $200,000. The sales have been entirely suspended in the Southern States, while the interruptions to the business of the country and the diversion of large numbers of men from labor to military service have obstructed settlements in the new States and Territories of the Northwest.

The receipts of the Patent Office have declined in nine months about $100,000.00 rendering a large reduction of the force employed necessary to make it self-sustaining.

The demands upon the Pension Office will be largely increased by the insurrection. Numerous applications for pensions, based upon the casualties of the existing war, have already been made. There is reason to believe that many who are now upon the pension rolls and in receipt of the bounty of the government are in the ranks of the insurgent army or giving them aid and comfort. The Secretary of the Interior has directed a suspension of the payment of the pensions of such persons upon proof of their disloyalty. I recommend that Congress authorize that officer to cause the names of such persons to be stricken from the pension rolls.

The relations of the government with the Indian tribes have been greatly disturbed by the insurrection, especially in the southern superintendency and in that of New Mexico. The Indian country south of Kansas is in the possession of insurgents from Texas and Arkansas. The agents of the United States appointed since the 4th of March for this superintendency have been unable to reach their posts, while the most of those who were in office before that time have espoused the insurrectionary cause, and assume to exercise the powers of agents by virtue of commissions from the insurrectionists. It has been stated in the public press that a portion of those Indians have been organized as a military force and are attached to the army of the insurgents. Although the government has no official information upon this subject, letters have been written to the Commissioner of Indian Affairs by several prominent chiefs giving assurance of their loyalty to the United States and expressing a wish for the presence of Federal troops to protect them. It is believed that upon the repossession of the country by the

Federal forces the Indians will readily cease all hostile demonstrations and resume their former relations to the government.

Agriculture, confessedly the largest interest of the nation, has not a department nor a bureau, but a clerkship only, assigned to it in the government. While it is fortunate that this great interest is so independent in its nature as not to have demanded and extorted more from the government, I respectfully ask Congress to consider whether something more cannot be given voluntarily with general advantage.

Annual reports exhibiting the condition of our agriculture, commerce, and manufactures would present a fund of information of great practical value to the country. While I make no suggestion as to details, I venture the opinion that an agricultural and statistical bureau might profitably be organized.

The execution of the laws for the suppression of the African slave trade has been confided to the Department of the Interior. It is a subject of gratulation that the efforts which have been made for the suppression of this inhuman traffic have been recently attended with unusual success. Five vessels being fitted out for the slave trade have been seized and condemned. Two mates of vessels engaged in the trade and one person in equipping a vessel as a slaver have been convicted and subjected to the penalty of fine and imprisonment, and one captain, taken with a cargo of Africans on board his vessel, has been convicted of the highest grade of offense under our laws, the punishment of which is death.

The Territories of Colorado, Dakota, and Nevada, created by the last Congress, have been organized, and civil administration has been inaugurated therein under auspices especially gratifying when it is considered that the leaven of treason was found existing in some of these new countries when the Federal officers arrived there.

The abundant natural resources of these Territories, with the security and protection afforded by organized government, will doubtless invite to them a large immigration when peace shall restore the business of the country to its accustomed channels. I submit the resolutions of the Legislature of Colorado, which evidence the patriotic spirit of the people of the Territory. So far the authority of the United States has been upheld in all the Territories, as it is hoped it will be in the future. I commend their interests and defense to the enlightened and generous care of Congress.

I recommend to the favorable consideration of Congress the interests of the District of Columbia. The insurrection has been the cause of much suffering and sacrifice to its inhabitants, and as they have no representative in Congress that body should not overlook their just claims upon the government.

At your late session a joint resolution was adopted authorizing the President to take measures for facilitating a proper representation of the industrial interests of the United States at the exhibition of the industry of all nations to be holden at London in the year 1862. I regret to say I have been unable to give personal attention to this subject—a subject at once so interesting in itself and so extensively and intimately connected with the material prosperity of the world. Through the Secretaries of State and of the Interior a plan or system has been devised and partly matured, and which will be laid before you.

Under and by virtue of the act of Congress entitled "An act to confiscate property used for insurrectionary purposes," approved August 6, 1861, the legal claims of certain persons to the labor and service of certain other persons have become forfeited, and numbers of the latter thus liberated are already dependent on the United States, and must be provided for in some way. Besides this, it is not impossible that some of the States will pass similar enactments for their own benefit respectively, and by operation of which persons of the same class will be thrown upon them for disposal. In such case I recommend that Congress provide for accepting such persons from such States, according to some mode of valuation, in lieu, *pro tanto*, of direct taxes, or upon some other plan to be agreed on with such States respectively; that such persons, on such acceptance by the General Government, be at once deemed free, and that in any event steps be taken for colonizing both classes (or the one first mentioned if the other shall not be brought into existence) at some place or places in a climate congenial to them. It might be well to consider, too, whether the free colored people already in the United States could not, so far as individuals may desire, be included in such colonization.

To carry out the plan of colonization may involve the acquiring of territory, and also the appropriation of money beyond that to be expended in the territorial acquisition. Having practiced the acquisition of territory for nearly sixty years, the question of constitutional power to do so is no longer an open one with us. The power was questioned at first by Mr. Jefferson, who, however, in the purchase of Louisiana, yielded his scruples on the plea of great expediency. If it be said that the only legitimate object of acquiring territory is to furnish homes for white men, this measure effects that object, for emigration of colored men leaves additional room for white men remaining or coming here. Mr. Jefferson, however, placed the importance of procuring Louisiana more on political and commercial grounds than on providing room for population.

On this whole proposition, including the appropriation of money with the acquisition of territory, does not the expediency amount to absolute necessity—that without which the government itself cannot be perpetuated?

The war continues. In considering the policy to be adopted for suppressing the insurrection I have been anxious and careful that the inevitable conflict for this purpose shall not degenerate into a violent and remorseless revolutionary struggle. I have therefore in every case thought it proper to keep the integrity of the Union prominent as the primary object of the contest on our part, leaving all questions which are not of vital military importance to the more deliberate action of the Legislature.

In the exercise of my best discretion I have adhered to the blockade of the ports held by the insurgents, instead of putting in force by proclamation the law of Congress enacted at the late session for closing those ports.

So also, obeying the dictates of prudence, as well as the obligations of law, instead of transcending I have adhered to the act of Congress to confiscate property used for insurrectionary purposes. If a new law upon the same subject shall be proposed, its propriety will be duly considered. The Union must be preserved, and hence all indispensable means must be employed. We should not be in haste to determine that radical and extreme measures, which may reach the loyal as well as the disloyal, are indispensable.

The inaugural address at the beginning of the Administration and the message to Congress at the late special session were both mainly devoted to topics domestic controversy out of which the insurrection and consequent war have sprung. Nothing now occurs to add or subtract to or from the principles or general purposes stated and expressed in those documents.

The last ray of hope for preserving the Union peaceably expired at the assault upon Fort Sumter, and a general review of what has occurred since may not be unprofitable. What was painfully uncertain then is much better defined and more distinct now, and the progress of events is plainly in the right direction. The insurgents confidently claimed a strong support from north of Mason and Dixon's line, and the friends of the Union were not free from apprehension on the point. This, however, was soon settled definitely, and on the right side. South of the line noble little Delaware led off right from the first. Maryland was made to seem against the Union. Our soldiers were assaulted, bridges were burned, and railroads torn up within her limits, and we were many days at one time without the ability to bring a single regiment over her soil to the capital. Now her bridges and railroads are repaired and open to the government; she already gives seven regiments to the cause of the Union, and none to the enemy; and her people, at a regular election, have sustained the Union by a larger majority and a larger aggregate vote than they ever before gave to any candidate or any question. Kentucky, too, for some time in doubt, is now decidedly and, I think, unchangeably ranged on the side of the Union. Missouri is comparatively quiet, and, I believe, can, not again be overrun by the insurrectionists. These three States of Maryland,

Kentucky, and Missouri, neither of which would promise a single soldier at first, have now an aggregate of not less than forty thousand in the field for the Union, while of their citizens certainly not more than a third of that number, and they of doubtful whereabouts and doubtful existence, are in arms against us. After a somewhat bloody struggle of months, winter closes on the Union people of western Virginia, leaving them masters of their own country.

An insurgent force of about fifteen hundred, for months dominating the narrow peninsular region constituting the counties of Accomac and Northampton, and known as Eastern Shore of Virginia, together with some contiguous parts of Maryland, have laid down their arms, and the people there have renewed their allegiance to and accepted the protection of the old flag. This leaves no armed insurrectionist north of the Potomac or east of the Chesapeake.

Also we have obtained a footing at each of the isolated points on the southern coast of Hatteras, Port Royal, Tybee Island (near Savannah), and Ship Island; and we likewise have some general accounts of popular movements in behalf of the Union in North Carolina and Tennessee.

These things demonstrate that the cause of the Union is advancing steadily and certainly southward.

Since your last adjournment Lieutenant-General Scott has retired from the head of the army. During his long life the nation has not been unmindful of his merit; yet on calling to mind how faithfully, ably, and brilliantly he has served the country, from a time far back in our history, when few of the now living had been born, and thenceforward continually, I cannot but think we are still his debtors. I submit, therefore, for your consideration what further mark of recognition is due to him, and to ourselves as a grateful people.

With the retirement of General Scott came the Executive duty of appointing in his stead a general-in-chief of the army. It is a fortunate circumstance that neither in council nor country was there, so far as I know, any difference of opinion as to the proper person to be selected. The retiring chief repeatedly expressed his judgment in favor of General McClellan for the position, and in this the nation seemed to give a unanimous concurrence. The designation of General McClellan is therefore in considerable degree the selection of the country as well as of the Executive, and hence there is better reason to hope there will be given him the confidence and cordial support thus by fair implication promised, and without which he cannot with so full efficiency serve the country.

It has been said that one bad general is better than two good ones, and the saying is true if taken to mean no more than that an army is better directed by a single mind, though inferior, than by two superior ones at variance and cross-purposes with each other.

And the same is true in all joint operations wherein those engaged can have none but a common end in view and can differ only as to the choice of means. In a storm at sea no one on hoard can wish the ship to sink, and yet not unfrequently all go down together because too many will direct and no single mind can be allowed to control.

It continues to develop that the insurrection is largely, if not exclusively, a war upon the first principle of popular government—the rights of the people. Conclusive evidence of this is found in the most grave and maturely considered public documents, as well as in the general tone of the insurgents. In those documents we find the abridgment of the existing right of suffrage and the denial to the people of all right to participate in the selection of public officers except the legislative boldly advocated, with labored arguments to prove that large control of the people in government is the source of all political evil. Monarchy itself is sometimes hinted at as a possible refuge from the power of the people.

In my present position I could scarcely be justified were I to omit raising a warning voice against this approach of returning despotism.

It is not needed nor fitting here that a general argument should be made in favor of popular institutions, but there is one point, with its connections, not so hackneyed as most others, to which I ask a brief attention. It is the effort to place capital on an equal footing with, if not above, labor in the structure of government. It is assumed that labor is available only in connection with capital; that nobody labors unless somebody else, owning capital, somehow by the use of it induces him to labor. This assumed, it is next considered whether it is best that capital shall hire laborers, and thus induce them to work by their own consent, or buy them and drive them to it without their consent. Having proceeded so far, it is naturally concluded that all laborers are either hired laborers or what we call slaves. And further, it is assumed that whoever is once a hired laborer is fixed in that condition for life.

Now there is no such relation between capital and labor as assumed, nor is there any such thing as a free man being fixed for life in the condition of a hired laborer. Both these assumptions are false, and all inferences from them are groundless.

Labor is prior to and independent of capital. Capital is only the fruit of labor, and could never have existed if labor had not first existed. Labor is the superior of capital, and deserves much the higher consideration. Capital has its rights, which are as worthy of protection as any other rights. Nor is it denied that there is, and probably always will be, a relation between labor and capital producing mutual benefits. The error is in assuming that the whole labor of community exists within that relation. A few men own capital, and that few avoid labor themselves, and with their capital hire or buy another few to labor for them. A large majority belong to neither class—neither work for others nor have others working for them. In most of the Southern States a majority of the whole people of all colors are neither slaves nor masters, while in the Northern a large majority are neither hirers nor hired. Men, with their families—wives, sons, and daughters,—work for themselves on their farms, in their houses, and in their shops, taking the whole product to themselves, and asking no favors of capital on the one hand nor of hired laborers or slaves on the other. It is not forgotten that a considerable number of persons mingle their own labor with capital; that is, they labor with their own hands and also buy or hire others to labor for them; but this is only a mixed and not a distinct class. No principle stated is disturbed by the existence of this mixed class.

Again, as has already been said, there is not of necessity any such thing as the free hired laborer being fixed to that condition for life. Many independent men everywhere in these States a few years back in their lives were hired laborers. The prudent, penniless beginner in the world labors for wages awhile, saves a surplus with which to buy tools or land for himself, then labors on his own account another while, and at length hires another new beginner to help him. This is the just and generous and prosperous system which opens the way to all, gives hope to all, and consequent energy and progress and improvement of condition to all. No men living are more worthy to be trusted than those who toil up from poverty; none less inclined to take or touch aught which they have not honestly earned. Let them beware of surrendering a political power which they already possess, and which if surrendered will surely be used to close the door of advancement against such as they and to fix new disabilities and burdens upon them till all of liberty shall be lost.

From the first taking of our national census to the last are seventy years, and we find our population at the end of the period eight times as great as it was at the beginning. The increase of those other things which men deem desirable has been even greater. We thus have at one view what the popular principle, applied to government through the machinery of the States and the Union, has produced in a given time, and also what if firmly maintained it promises for the future. There are already among us those who if the Union be preserved will live to see it contain 200,000,000. The struggle of to-day is not altogether for to-day; it is for a vast future also. With a reliance on Providence all the more firm and earnest, let us proceed in the great task which events have devolved upon us.

MEMORANDUM OF INTERVIEW WITH JOHN W. CRISFELD,
WASHINGTON, DC, MARCH 10, 1862.

"DEAR SIR:—I called, at the request of the President, to ask you to come to the White House tomorrow morning, at nine o'clock, and bring such of your colleagues as are in town."

WASHINGTON, March 10, 1862.

Yesterday, on my return from church, I found Mr. Postmaster-General Blair in my room, writing the above note, which he immediately suspended, and verbally communicated the President's invitation, and stated that the President's purpose was to have some conversation with the delegations of Kentucky, Missouri, Maryland, Virginia, and Delaware, in explanation of his message of the 6th instant.

This morning these delegations, or such of them as were in town, assembled at the White House at the appointed time, and after some little delay were admitted to an audience. Mr. Leary and myself were the only members from Maryland present, and, I think, were the only members of the delegation at that time in the city. I know that Mr. Pearce, of the Senate, and Messrs. Webster and Calvert, of the House, were absent.

After the usual salutations, and we were seated, the President said, in substance, that he had invited us to meet him to have some conversation with us in explanation of his message of the 6th; that since he had sent it in several of the gentlemen then present had visited him, but had avoided any allusion to the message, and he therefore inferred that the import of the message had been misunderstood, and was regarded as inimical to the interests we represented; and he had resolved he would talk with us, and disabuse our minds of that erroneous opinion.

The President then disclaimed any intent to injure the interests or wound the sensibilities of the slave States. On the contrary, his purpose was to protect the one and respect the other; that we were engaged in a terrible, wasting, and tedious war; immense armies were in the field, and must continue in the field as long as the war lasts; that these armies must, of necessity, be brought into contact with slaves in the States we represented and in other States as they advanced; that slaves would come to the camps, and continual irritation was kept up; that he was constantly annoyed by conflicting and antagonistic complaints: on the one side a certain class complained if the slave was not protected by the army; persons were frequently found who, participating in these views, acted in a way unfriendly to the slaveholder; on the other hand, slaveholders complained that their rights were interfered with, their slaves induced to abscond and protected within the lines; these complaints were numerous, loud and deep; were a serious annoyance to him and embarrassing to the progress of the war; that it kept alive a spirit hostile to the government in the States we represented; strengthened the hopes of the Confederates that at some day the border States would unite with them, and thus tend to prolong the war; and he was of opinion, if this resolution should be adopted by Congress and accepted by our States, these causes of irritation and these hopes would be removed, and more would be accomplished toward shortening the war than could be hoped from the greatest victory achieved by Union armies; that he made this proposition in good faith, and desired it to be accepted, if at all, voluntarily, and in the same patriotic spirit in which it was made; that emancipation was a subject exclusively under the control of the States, and must be adopted or rejected by each for itself; that he did not claim nor had this government any right to coerce them for that purpose; that such was no part of his purpose in making this proposition, and he wished it to be clearly understood; that he did not expect us there to be prepared to give him an answer, but he hoped we would take the subject into serious consideration, confer with one another, and then take such course as we felt our duty and the interests of our constituents required of us.

Mr. Noell, of Missouri, said that in his State slavery was not considered a permanent institution; that natural causes were there in operation which would at no distant day extinguish it, and he did not think that this proposition was necessary for that; and, besides that, he and his friends felt solicitous as to the message on account of the different constructions which the resolution and message had received. The New York Tribune was for it, and understood it to mean that we must accept gradual emancipation according to the plan suggested, or get something worse.

The President replied that he must not be expected to quarrel with the New York Tribune before the right time; he hoped never to have to do it; he would not anticipate events. In respect to emancipation in Missouri, he said that what had been observed by Mr. Noell was probably true, but the operation of these natural causes had not prevented the irritating conduct to which he had referred, or destroyed the hopes of the Confederates that Missouri would at some time merge herself alongside of them, which, in his judgment, the passage of this resolution by Congress and its acceptance by Missouri would accomplish.

Mr. Crisfield, of Maryland, asked what would be the effect of the refusal of the State to accept this proposal, and he desired to know if the President looked to any policy beyond the acceptance or rejection of this scheme.

The President replied that he had no designs beyond the actions of the States on this particular subject. He should lament their refusal to accept it, but he had no designs beyond their refusal of it.

Mr. Menzies, of Kentucky, inquired if the President thought there was any power except in the States themselves to carry out his scheme of emancipation.

The President replied that he thought there could not be. He then went off into a course of remarks not qualifying the foregoing declaration nor material to be repeated to a just understanding of his meaning.

Mr. Crisfield said he did not think the people of Maryland looked upon slavery as a permanent institution; and he did not know that they would be very reluctant to give it up if provision was made to meet the loss and they could be rid of the race; but they did not like to be coerced into emancipation, either by the direct action of the government or by indirection, as through the emancipation of slaves in this District, or the confiscation of Southern property as now threatened; and he thought before they would consent to consider this proposition they would require to be informed on these points.

The President replied that, unless he was expelled by the act of God or the Confederate armies he should occupy that house for three years; and as long as he remained there Maryland had nothing to fear either for her institutions or her interests on the points referred to.

Mr. Crisfield immediately added: "Mr. President, if what you now say could be heard by the people of Maryland, they would consider your proposition with a much better feeling than I fear without it they will be inclined to do."

The President: "That [meaning a publication of what he said] will not do; it would force me into a quarrel before the proper time "; and, again intimating, as he had before done, that a quarrel with the "Greeley faction" was impending, he said he did not wish to encounter it before the proper time, nor at all if it could be avoided.

Governor Wickliffe, of Kentucky, then asked him respecting the constitutionality of his scheme.

The President replied: "As you may suppose, I have considered that; and the proposition now submitted does not encounter any constitutional difficulty. It proposes simply to co-operate with any State by giving such State pecuniary aid"; and he thought that the resolution, as proposed by him, would be considered rather as the expression of a sentiment than as involving any constitutional question.

Mr. Hall, of Missouri, thought that if this proposition was adopted at all it should be by the votes of the free States, and come as a proposition from them to the slave States, affording them an inducement to put aside this subject of discord; that it ought not to be expected that members representing slaveholding constituencies should declare at once, and in advance of any proposition to them, for the emancipation of slavery.

The President said he saw and felt the force of the objection; it was a fearful responsibility, and every gentleman must do as he thought best; that he did not know how this scheme was received by the members from the free States; some of them had spoken to him and received it kindly; but for the most part they were as reserved and chary as we had been, and he could not tell how they would vote. And in reply to some expression of Mr. Hall as to his own opinion regarding slavery, he said he did not pretend to disguise his anti-slavery feeling; that he thought it was wrong, and should continue to think so; but that was not the question we had to deal with now. Slavery existed, and that, too, as well by the act of the North as of the South; and in any scheme to get rid of it the North as well as the South was morally bound to do its full and equal share. He thought the institution wrong and ought never to have existed; but yet he recognized the rights of property which had grown out of it, and would respect those rights as fully as similar rights in any other property; that property can exist and does legally exist. He thought such a law wrong, but the rights of property resulting must be respected; he would get rid of the odious law, not by violating the rights, but by encouraging the proposition and offering inducements to give it up.

Here the interview, so far as this subject is concerned, terminated by Mr. Crittenden's assuring the President that, whatever might be our final action, we all thought him solely moved by a high patriotism and sincere devotion to the happiness and glory of his country; and with that conviction we should consider respectfully the important suggestions he had made.

After some conversation on the current war news, we retired, and I immediately proceeded to my room and wrote out this paper.

J. W. CRISFIELD.

We were present at the interview described in the foregoing paper of Mr. Crisfield, and we certify that the substance of what passed on the occasion is in this paper faithfully and fully given.

J. W. MENZIES,
J. J. CRITTENDEN,
R. MALLORY.

March 10, 1862.

APPEAL TO BORDER STATE REPRESENTATIVES TO FAVOR
COMPENSATED EMANCIPATION, WASHINGTON, DC, JULY 12, 1862.

GENTLEMEN:—After the adjournment of Congress now very near, I shall have no opportunity of seeing you for several months. Believing that you of the border States hold more power for good than any other equal number of members, I feel it a duty which I cannot justifiably waive to make this appeal to you. I intend no reproach or complaint when I assure you that, in my opinion, if you all had voted for the resolution in the gradual-emancipation message of last March, the war would now be substantially ended. And the plan therein proposed is yet one of the most potent and swift means of ending it. Let the States which are in rebellion see definitely and certainly that in no event will the States you represent ever join their proposed confederacy, and they cannot much longer maintain the contest. But you cannot divest them of their hope to ultimately have you with them so long as you show a determination to perpetuate the institution within your own States. Beat them at elections, as you have overwhelmingly done, and, nothing daunted, they still claim you as their own. You and I know what the lever of their power is. Break that lever before their faces, and they can shake you no more forever. Most of you have treated me with kindness and consideration and I trust you will not now think I improperly touch what is exclusively your own, when, for the sake of the whole country, I ask, Can you, for your States, do better than to take the course I urge? Discarding punctilio and maxims adapted to more manageable times, and looking only to the unprecedentedly stern facts of our case, can you do better in any possible event? You prefer that the constitutional relation of the States to the nation shall be practically restored without disturbance of the institution; and if this were done, my whole duty in this respect, under the Constitution and my oath of office, would be performed. But it is not done, and we are trying to accomplish it by war. The incidents of the war cannot be avoided. If the war continues long, as it must if the object be not sooner attained, the institution in your States will be extinguished by mere friction and abrasion—by the mere incidents of the war. It will be gone, and you will have nothing valuable in lieu of it. Much of its value is gone already. How much better for you and for your people to take the step which at once shortens the war and secures substantial compensation for that which is sure to be wholly lost in any other event! How much better to thus save the money which else we sink forever in war! How much better to do it while we can, lest the war ere long render us pecuniarily unable to do it! How much better for you as seller, and the nation as buyer, to sell out and buy out that without which the war could never have been, than to sink both the thing to be sold and the price of it in cutting one another's throats! I do not speak of emancipation at once, but of a decision at once to emancipate gradually. Room in South America for colonization can be obtained cheaply and in abundance, and when numbers shall be large enough to be company and encouragement for one another, the freed people will not be so reluctant to go.

I am pressed with a difficulty not yet mentioned—one which threatens division among those who, united, are none too strong. An instance of it is known to you. General Hunter is an honest man. He was, and I hope still is, my friend. I valued him none the less for his agreeing with me in the general wish that all men everywhere could be free. He proclaimed all men free within certain States, and I repudiated the proclamation. He expected more good and less harm from the measure than I could believe would follow. Yet, in repudiating it, I gave dissatisfaction, if not offence, to many whose support the country cannot afford to lose. And this is not the end of it. The pressure in this direction is still upon me, and is increasing. By conceding what I now ask you can relieve me, and, much more, can relieve the country in this important point. Upon these considerations, I have again begged your attention to the message of March last. Before leaving the Capital, consider and discuss it among yourselves. You are patriots and statesmen, and as such I pray you consider this proposition; and, at the least, commend it to the consideration of your States and people. As you would perpetuate popular government for the best people in the world, I beseech you that you do in nowise omit this. Our common country is in great peril, demanding the loftiest views and boldest action to bring a speedy relief. Once relieved, its form of government is saved to the world; its beloved history and cherished memories are vindicated, and its happy future fully assured and rendered inconceivably grand. To you, more than to any others, the privilege is given to assure that happiness and swell that grandeur, and to link your own names therewith forever.

ADDRESS ON COLONIZATION TO AN AFRICAN AMERICAN
DELEGATION, WASHINGTON, DC, AUGUST 14, 1862.

This afternoon the President of the United States gave an audience to a committee of colored men at the White House. They were introduced by Rev. J. Mitchell, Commissioner of Emigration, E. M. Thomas, the chairman, remarked that they were there by invitation to hear what the Executive had to say to them.

Having all been seated, the President, after a few preliminary observations, informed them that a sum of money had been appropriated by Congress, and placed at his disposition, for the purpose of aiding the colonization, in some country, of the people, or a portion of them, of African descent, thereby making it his duty, as it had for a long time been his inclination, to favor that cause. And why, he asked, should the people of your race be colonized, and where? Why should they leave this country? This is, perhaps, the first question for proper consideration. You and we are different races. We have between us a broader difference than exists between almost any other two races. Whether it is right or wrong I need not discuss; but this physical difference is a great disadvantage to us both, as I think. Your race suffer very greatly, many of them, by living among us, while ours suffer from your presence. In a word, we suffer on each side. If this is admitted, it affords a reason, at least, why we should be separated. You here are free men, I suppose.

[A voice—"Yes, sir!"]

Perhaps you have long been free, or all your lives. Your race are suffering, in my judgment, the greatest wrong inflicted on any people. But even when you cease to be slaves, you are yet far removed from being placed on an equality with the white race. You are cut off from many of the advantages which the other race enjoys. The aspiration of men is to enjoy equality with the best when free, but on this broad continent not a single man of your race is made the equal of a single man of ours. Go where you are treated the best, and the ban is still upon you. I do not propose to discuss this, but to present it as a fact, with which we have to deal. I cannot alter it if I would. It is a fact about which we all think and feel alike, I and you. We look to our condition. Owing to the existence of the two races on this continent, I need not recount to you the effects upon white men, growing out of the institution of slavery.

I believe in its general evil effects on the white race. See our present condition—the country engaged in war—white men cutting one another's throats—none knowing how far it will extend—and then consider what we know to be the truth: But for your race among us there could not be war, although many men engaged on either side do not care for you one way or the other. Nevertheless I repeat, without the institution of slavery and the colored race as a basis, the war could not have an existence. It is better for us both, therefore, to be separated. I know that there are free men among you, who, even if they could better their condition, are not as much inclined to go out of the country as those who, being slaves, could obtain their freedom on this condition. I suppose one of the principal difficulties in the way of colonization is that the free colored man cannot see that his comfort would be advanced by it. You may believe that you can live in Washington, or elsewhere in the United States, the remainder of your life, as easily, perhaps more so, than you can in any foreign Country; and hence you may come to the conclusion that you have nothing to do with the idea of going to a foreign country.

This is (I speak in no unkind sense) an extremely selfish view of the case. You ought to do something to help those who are not so fortunate as yourselves. There is an unwillingness on the part of our people, harsh as it may be, for you free colored people to remain with us. Now, if you could give a start to the white people, you would open a wide door for many to be made free. If we deal with those who are not free at the beginning, and whose intellects are clouded by slavery, we have very poor material to start with. If intelligent colored men, such as are before me, would move in this matter, much might be accomplished. It is exceedingly important that we have men at the beginning capable of thinking as white men, and not those who have been systematically oppressed. There is much to encourage you. For the sake of your race you should sacrifice something of your present comfort for the purpose of being as grand in that respect as the white people. It is a cheering thought throughout life that something can be done to ameliorate the condition of those who have been subject to the hard usages of the world. It is difficult to make a man miserable while he feels he is worthy of himself and claims kindred to the great God who made him. In the American Revolutionary war sacrifices were made by men engaged in it, but they were cheered by the future. General Washington himself endured greater physical hardships than if he had remained a British subject, yet he was a happy man because he had engaged in benefiting his race, in doing something for the children of his neighbors, having none of his own.

The colony of Liberia has been in existence a long time. In a certain sense it is a success. The old President of Liberia, Roberts, has just been with me—the first time I ever saw him. He says they have within the bounds of that colony between three and four hundred thousand people, or more than in some of our old States, such as Rhode Island or Delaware, or in some of our newer States, and less than in some of our larger ones. They are not all American colonists or their descendants. Something less than 12,000 have been sent thither from this country. Many of the original settlers have died; yet, like people else-where, their offspring outnumber those deceased. The question is, if the colored people are persuaded to go anywhere, why not there?

One reason for unwillingness to do so is that some of you would rather remain within reach of the country of your nativity. I do not know how much attachment you may have toward our race. It does not strike me that you have the greatest reason to love them. But still you are attached to them, at all events.

The place I am thinking about for a colony is in Central America. It is nearer to us than Liberia not much more than one fourth as far as Liberia, and within seven days' run by steamers. Unlike Liberia, it is a great line of travel—it is a highway. The country is a very excellent one for any people, and with great natural resources and advantages, and especially because of the similarity of climate with your native soil, thus being suited to your physical condition. The particular place I have in view is to be a great highway from the Atlantic or Caribbean Sea to the Pacific Ocean, and this particular place has all the advantages for a colony. On both sides there are harbors—among the finest in the world. Again, there is evidence of very rich coal-mines. A certain amount of coal is valuable in any country. Why I attach so much importance to coal is, it will afford an opportunity to the inhabitants for immediate employment till they get ready to settle permanently in their homes. If you take colonists where there is no good landing, there is a bad show; and so where there is nothing to cultivate and of which to make a farm. But if something is started so that you can get your daily bread as soon as reach you there, it is a great advantage. Coal land is the best thing I know of with which to commence an enterprise.

To return—you have been talked to upon this subject, and told that a speculation is intended by gentlemen who have an interest in the country, including the coal-mines. We have been mistaken all our lives if we do not know whites, as well as blacks, look to their self-interest. Unless among those deficient of intellect, everybody you trade with makes something. You meet with these things here and everywhere. If such persons have what will be an advantage to them, the question is whether it cannot be made of advantage to you. You are intelligent, and know that success does not so much depend on external help as on self-reliance. Much, therefore, depends upon yourselves. As to the coal-mines, I think I see the means available for your self-reliance. I shall, if I get a sufficient number of you engaged, have provision made that you shall not be wronged. If you will engage in the enterprise, I will spend some of the money entrusted to me. I am not sure you will succeed. The government may lose the money; but we cannot succeed unless we try, and we think with care we can succeed. The political affairs in Central America are not in quite as satisfactory a condition as I wish. There are contending factions in that quarter, but it is true all the factions are agreed alike on the subject of colonization, and want it, and are more generous than we are here.

To your colored race they have no objection I would endeavor to have you made the equals, and have the best assurance that you should be the equals, of the best.

The practical thing I want to ascertain is whether I can get a number of able-bodied men, with their wives and children, who are willing to go when I present evidence of encouragement and protection. Could I get a hundred tolerably intelligent men, with their wives and children, and able to "cut their own fodder," so to speak? Can I have fifty? If I could find twenty-five able-bodied men, with a mixture of women and children—good things in the family relation, I think,—I could make a successful commencement. I want you to let me know whether this can be done or not. This is the practical part of my wish to see you. These are subjects of very great importance, worthy of a month's study, instead of a speech delivered in an hour. I ask you, then, to consider seriously, not pertaining to yourselves merely, nor for your race and ours for the present time, but as one of the things, if successfully managed, the good of mankind—not confined to the present generation, but as

> "From age to age descends the lay
> To millions yet to be,
> Till far its echoes roll away
> Into eternity."

The above is merely given as the substance of the President's remarks.

The chairman of the delegation briefly replied that they would hold a consultation, and in a short time give an answer.

The President said: Take your full time-no hurry at all.

The delegation then withdrew.

REPLY TO EMANCIPATION MEMORIAL PRESENTED BY CHICAGO CHRISTIANS OF ALL DENOMINATIONS, WASHINGTON, DC, SEPTEMBER 13, 1862.

The subject presented in the memorial is one upon which I have thought much for weeks past, and I may even say for months. I am approached with the most opposite opinions and advice, and that by religious men, who are equally certain that they represent the Divine will. I am sure that either the one or the other class is mistaken in that belief, and perhaps in some respects both. I hope it will not be irreverent for me to say that if it is probable that God would reveal his will to others, on a point so connected with my duty, it might be supposed he would reveal it directly to me; for, unless I am more deceived in myself than I often am, it is my earnest desire to know the will of Providence in this matter. And if I can learn what it is I will do it! These are not, however, the days of miracles, and I suppose it will be granted that I am not to expect a direct revelation. I must study the plain physical facts of the case, ascertain what is possible, and learn what appears to be wise and right.

The subject is difficult, and good men do not agree. For instance, the other day, four gentlemen of standing and intelligence from New York called as a delegation on business connected with the war; but before leaving two of them earnestly besought me to proclaim general emancipation, upon which the other two at once attacked them. You know also that the last session of Congress had a decided majority of antislavery men, yet they could not unite on this policy. And the same is true of the religious people. Why, the rebel soldiers are praying with a great deal more earnestness, I fear, than our own troops, and expecting God to favor their side: for one of our soldiers who had been taken prisoner told Senator Wilson a few days since that he met nothing so discouraging as the evident sincerity of those he was among in their prayers. But we will talk over the merits of the case.

What good would a proclamation of emancipation from me do, especially as we are now situated? I do not want to issue a document that the whole world will see must necessarily be inoperative, like the Pope's bull against the comet! Would my word free the slaves, when I cannot even enforce the Constitution in the rebel States? Is there a single court, or magistrate or individual that would be influenced by it there? And what reason is there to think it would have any greater effect upon the slaves than the late law of Congress, which I approved, and which offers protection and freedom to the slaves of rebel masters who come within our lines? Yet I cannot learn that that law has caused a single slave to come over to us. And suppose they could be induced by a proclamation of freedom from me to throw themselves upon us, what should we do with them? How can we feed and care for such a multitude? General Butler wrote me a few days since that he was issuing more rations to the slaves who have rushed to him than to all the white troops under his command. They eat, and that is all; though it is true General Butler is feeding the whites also by the thousand; for it nearly amounts to a famine there. If, now, the pressure of the war should call off our forces from New Orleans to defend some other point, what is to prevent the masters from reducing the blacks to slavery again? for I am told that whenever the rebels take any black prisoners, free or slave, they immediately auction them off. They did so with those they took from a boat that was aground in the Tennessee River a few days ago. And then I am very ungenerously attacked for it! For instance, when, after the late battles at and near Bull Run, an expedition went out from Washington under a flag of truce to bury the dead and bring in the wounded, and the rebels seized the blacks who went along to help, and sent them into slavery, Horace Greeley said in his paper that the government would probably do nothing about it. What could I do?

Now, then, tell me, if you please, what possible result of good would follow the issuing of such a proclamation as you desire? Understand, I raise no objections against it on legal or constitutional grounds; for, as commander-in-chief of the army and navy, in time of war I suppose I have a right to take any measure which may best subdue the enemy; nor do I urge objections of a moral nature, in view of possible consequences of insurrection and massacre at the South. I view this matter as a practical war measure, to be decided on according to the advantages or disadvantages it may offer to the suppression of the rebellion.

I admit that slavery is the root of the rebellion, or at least its *sine qua non*. The ambition of politicians may have instigated them to act, but they would have been impotent without slavery as their instrument. I will also concede that emancipation would help us in Europe, and convince them that we are incited by something more than ambition. I grant, further, that it would help somewhat at the North, though not so much, I fear, as you and those you represent imagine. Still, some additional strength would be added in that way to the war, and then, unquestionably, it would weaken the rebels by drawing off their laborers, which is of great importance; but I am not so sure we could do much with the blacks. If we were to arm them, I fear that in a few weeks the arms would be in the hands of the rebels; and, indeed, thus far we have not had arms enough to equip our white troops. I will mention another thing, though it meet only your scorn and contempt. There are fifty thousand bayonets in the Union armies from the border slave States. It would be a serious matter if, in consequence of a proclamation such as you desire, they should go over to the rebels. I do not think they all would—not so many, indeed, as a year ago, or as six months ago—not so many to-day as yesterday. Every day increases their Union feeling. They are also getting their pride enlisted, and want to beat the rebels. Let me say one thing more: I think you should admit that we already have an important principle to rally and unite the people, in the fact that constitutional government is at stake. This is a fundamental idea going down about as deep as anything.

Do not misunderstand me because I have mentioned these objections. They indicate the difficulties that have thus far prevented my action in some such way as you desire. I have not decided against a proclamation of liberty to the slaves, but hold the matter under advisement; and I can assure you that the subject is on my mind, by day and night, more than any other. Whatever shall appear to be God's will, I will do. I trust that in the freedom with which I have canvassed your views I have not in any respect injured your feelings.

SECOND ANNUAL MESSAGE TO CONGRESS,
WASHINGTON, DC, DECEMBER 1, 1862.

FELLOW-CITIZENS OF THE SENATE AND HOUSE OF REPRESENTATIVES:—Since your last annual assembling another year of health and bountiful harvests has passed; and while it has not pleased the Almighty to bless us with a return of peace, we can but press on, guided by the best light he gives us, trusting that in his own good time and wise way all will yet be well.

The correspondence touching foreign affairs which has taken place during the last year is herewith submitted, in virtual compliance with a request to that effect, made by the House of Representatives near the close of the last session of Congress.

If the condition of our relations with other nations is less gratifying than it has usually been at former periods, it is certainly more satisfactory than a nation so unhappily distracted as we are might reasonably have apprehended. In the month of June last there were some grounds to expect that the maritime powers which, at the beginning of our domestic difficulties, so unwisely and unnecessarily, as we think, recognized the insurgents as a belligerent, would soon recede from that position, which has proved only less injurious to themselves than to our own country. But the temporary reverses which afterward befell the national arms, and which were exaggerated by our own disloyal citizens abroad, have hitherto delayed that act of simple justice.

The civil war, which has so radically changed, for the moment, the occupations and habits of the American people, has necessarily disturbed the social condition, and affected very deeply the prosperity, of the nations with which we have carried on a commerce that has been steadily increasing throughout a period of half a century. It has, at the same time, excited political ambitions and apprehensions which have produced a profound agitation throughout the civilized world. In this unusual agitation we have forborne from taking part in any controversy between foreign states, and between parties or factions in such states. We have attempted no propagandism and acknowledged no revolution, but we have left to every nation the exclusive conduct and management of its own affairs. Our struggle has been, of course, contemplated by foreign nations with reference less to its own merits than to its supposed and often exaggerated effects and consequences resulting to those nations themselves, nevertheless, complaint on the part of this government, even if it were just, would certainly be unwise.

The treaty with Great Britain for the suppression of the slave trade has been put into operation with a good prospect of complete success. It is an occasion of special pleasure to acknowledge that the execution of it on the part of her Majesty's government has been marked with a jealous respect for the authority of the United States and the rights of their moral and loyal citizens.

The convention with Hanover for the abolition of the state dues has been carried into full effect under the act of Congress for that purpose.

A blockade of 3000 miles of seacoast could not be established and vigorously enforced in a season of great commercial activity like the present without committing occasional mistakes and inflicting unintentional injuries upon foreign nations and their subjects.

A civil war occurring in a country where foreigners reside and carry on trade under treaty stipulations is necessarily fruitful of complaints of the violation of neutral rights. All such collisions tend to excite misapprehensions, and possibly to produce mutual reclamations between nations which have a common interest in preserving peace and friendship. In clear cases of these kinds I have so far as possible heard and redressed complaints which have been presented by friendly powers. There is still, however, a large and an augmenting number of doubtful cases upon which the government is unable to agree with the governments whose protection is demanded by the claimants. There are, moreover, many cases in which the United States or their citizens suffer wrongs from the naval or military authorities of foreign nations which the governments of those states are not at once prepared to redress. I have proposed to some of the foreign states thus interested mutual conventions to examine and adjust such complaints. This proposition has been made especially to Great Britain, to France, to Spain, and to Prussia. In each case it has been kindly received, but has not yet been formally adopted.

I deem it my duty to recommend an appropriation in behalf of the owners of the Norwegian bark Admiral P. Tordenskiold, which vessel was in May, 1861, prevented by the commander of the blockading force off Charleston from leaving that port with cargo, notwithstanding a similar privilege had shortly before been granted to an English vessel. I have directed the Secretary of State to cause the papers in the case to be communicated to the proper committees.

Applications have been made to me by many free Americans of African descent to favor their emigration, with a view to such colonization as was contemplated in recent acts of Congress, Other parties, at home and abroad—some from interested motives, others upon patriotic considerations, and still others influenced by philanthropic sentiments—have suggested similar measures, while, on the other hand, several of the Spanish American republics have protested against the sending of such colonies to their respective territories. Under these circumstances I have declined to move any such colony to any state without first obtaining the consent of its government, with an agreement on its part to receive and protect such emigrants in all the rights of freemen; and I have at the same time offered to the several states situated within the Tropics, or having colonies there, to negotiate with them, subject to the advice and consent of the Senate, to favor the voluntary emigration of persons of that class to their respective territories, upon conditions which shall be equal, just, and humane. Liberia and Haiti are as yet the only countries to which colonists of African descent from here could go with certainty of being received and adopted as citizens; and I regret to say such persons contemplating colonization do not seem so willing to migrate to those countries as to some others, nor so willing as I think their interest demands. I believe, however, opinion among them in this respect is improving, and that ere long there will be an augmented and considerable migration to both these countries from the United States.

The new commercial treaty between the United States and the Sultan of Turkey has been carried into execution.

A commercial and consular treaty has been negotiated, subject to the Senate's consent, with Liberia, and a similar negotiation is now pending with the Republic of Haiti. A considerable improvement of the national commerce is expected to result from these measures.

Our relations with Great Britain, France, Spain, Portugal, Russia, Prussia, Denmark, Sweden, Austria, the Netherlands, Italy, Rome, and the other European states remain undisturbed. Very favorable relations also continue to be maintained with Turkey, Morocco, China, and Japan.

During the last year there has not only been no change of our previous relations with the independent states of our own continent, but more friendly sentiments than have heretofore existed are believed to be entertained by these neighbors, whose safety and progress are so intimately connected with our own. This statement especially applies to Mexico, Nicaragua, Costa Rica, Honduras, Peru, and Chile.

The commission under the convention with the Republic of New Granada closed its session without having audited and passed upon all the claims which were submitted to it. A proposition is pending to revive the convention, that it may be able to do more complete justice. The joint commission between the United States and the Republic of Costa Rica has completed its labors and submitted its report.

I have favored the project for connecting the United States with Europe by an Atlantic telegraph, and a similar project to extend the telegraph from San Francisco to connect by a Pacific telegraph with the line which is being extended across the Russian Empire.

The Territories of the United States, with unimportant exceptions, have remained undisturbed by the civil war; and they are exhibiting such evidence of prosperity as justifies an expectation that some of them will soon be in a condition to be organized as States and be constitutionally admitted into the Federal Union.

The immense mineral resources of some of those Territories ought to be developed as rapidly as possible. Every step in that direction would have a tendency to improve the revenues of the government and diminish the burdens of the people. It is worthy of your serious consideration whether some extraordinary measures to promote that end cannot be adopted. The means which suggests itself as most likely to be effective is a scientific exploration of the mineral regions in those Territories with a view to the publication of its results at home and in foreign countries—results which cannot fail to be auspicious.

The condition of the finances win claim your most diligent consideration. The vast expenditures incident to the military and naval operations required for the suppression of the rebellion have hitherto been met with a promptitude and certainty unusual in similar circumstances, and the public credit has been fully maintained. The continuance of the war, however, and the increased disbursements made necessary by the augmented forces now in the field demand your best reflections as to the best modes of providing the necessary revenue without injury to business and with the least possible burdens upon labor.

The suspension of specie payments by the banks soon after the commencement of your last session made large issues of United States notes unavoidable. In no other way could the payment of troops and the satisfaction of other just demands be so economically or so well provided for. The judicious legislation of Congress, securing the receivability of these notes for loans and internal duties and making them a legal tender for other debts, has made them an universal currency, and has satisfied, partially at least, and for the time, the long-felt want of an uniform circulating medium, saving thereby to the people immense sums in discounts and exchanges.

A return to specie payments, however, at the earliest period compatible with due regard to all interests concerned should ever be kept in view. Fluctuations in the value of currency are always injurious, and to reduce these fluctuations to the lowest possible point will always be a leading purpose in wise legislation. Convertibility, prompt and certain convertibility, into coin is generally acknowledged to be the best and surest safeguard against them; and it is extremely doubtful whether a circulation of United States notes payable in coin and sufficiently large for the wants of the people can be permanently, usefully, and safely maintained.

Is there, then, any other mode in which the necessary provision for the public wants can be made and the great advantages of a safe and uniform currency secured?

I know of none which promises so certain results and is at the same time so unobjectionable as the organization of banking associations, under a general act of Congress, well guarded in its provisions. To such associations the government might furnish circulating notes, on the security of United States bonds deposited in the treasury. These notes, prepared under the supervision of proper officers, being uniform in appearance and security and convertible always into coin, would at once protect labor against the evils of a vicious currency and facilitate commerce by cheap and safe exchanges.

A moderate reservation from the interest on the bonds would compensate the United States for the preparation and distribution of the notes and a general supervision of the system, and would lighten the burden of that part of the public debt employed as securities. The public credit, moreover, would be greatly improved and the negotiation of new loans greatly facilitated by the steady market demand for government bonds which the adoption of the proposed system would create.

It is an additional recommendation of the measure, of considerable weight, in my judgment, that it would reconcile as far as possible all existing interests by the opportunity offered to existing institutions to reorganize under the act, substituting only the secured uniform national circulation for the local and various circulation, secured and unsecured, now issued by them.

The receipts into the treasury from all sources, including loans and balance from the preceding year, for the fiscal year ending on the 30th June, 1862, were $583,885,247.06, of which sum $49,056,397.62 were derived from customs; $1,795,331.73 from the direct tax; from public lands, $152,203.77; from miscellaneous sources, $931,787.64; from loans in all forms, $529,692,460.50. The remainder, $2,257,065.80, was the balance from last year.

The disbursements during the same period were: For congressional, executive, and judicial purposes, $5,939,009.29; for foreign intercourse, $1,339,710.35; for miscellaneous expenses, including the mints, loans, post-office deficiencies, collection of revenue, and other like charges, $14,129,771.50; for expenses under the Interior Department, $3,102,985.52; under the War Department, $394,368,407.36; under the Navy Department, $42,674,569.69; for interest on public debt, $13,190,324.45; and for payment of public debt, including reimbursement of temporary loan and redemptions, $96,096,922.09; making an aggregate of $570,841,700.25, and leaving a balance in the treasury on the 1st day of July, 1862, of $13,043,546.81.

It should be observed that the sum of $96,096,922.09, expended for reimbursements and redemption of public debt, being included also in the loans made, may be properly deducted both from receipts and expenditures, leaving the actual receipts for the year $487,788,324.97, and the expenditures $474,744,778.16.

Other information on the subject of the finances will be found in the report of the Secretary of the Treasury, to whose statements and views I invite your most candid and considerate attention.

The reports of the Secretaries of War and of the Navy are herewith transmitted. These reports, though lengthy, are scarcely more than brief abstracts of the very numerous and extensive transactions and operations conducted through those departments. Nor could I give a summary of them here upon any principle which would admit of its being much shorter than the reports themselves. I therefore content myself with laying the reports before you and asking your attention to them.

It gives me pleasure to report a decided improvement in the financial condition of the Post-Office Department as compared with several preceding years. The receipts for the fiscal year 1861 amounted to $8,349,296.40, which embraced the revenue from all the States of the Union for three quarters of that year. Notwithstanding the cessation of revenue from the so-called seceded States during the last fiscal year, the increase of the correspondence of the loyal States has been sufficient to produce a revenue during the same year of $8,299,820.90, being only $50,000 less than was derived from all the States of the Union during the previous year. The expenditures show a still more favorable result. The amount expended in 1861 was $13,606,759.11. For the last year the amount has been reduced to $11,125,364.13, showing a decrease of about $2,481,000 in the expenditures as compared with the preceding year, and about $3,750,000 as compared with the fiscal year 1860. The deficiency in the department for the previous year was $4,551,966.98. For the last fiscal year it was reduced to $2,112,814.57. These favorable results are in part owing to the cessation of mail service in the insurrectionary States and in part to a careful review of all expenditures in that department in the interest of economy. The efficiency of the postal service, it is believed, has also been much improved. The Postmaster-General has also opened a correspondence through the Department of State with foreign governments proposing a convention of postal representatives for the purpose of simplifying the rates of foreign postage and to expedite the foreign mails. This proposition, equally important to our adopted citizens and to the commercial interests of this country, has been favorably entertained and agreed to by all the governments from whom replies have been received.

I ask the attention of Congress to the suggestions of the Postmaster-General in his report respecting the further legislation required, in his opinion, for the benefit of the postal service.

The Secretary of the Interior reports as follows in regard to the public lands:

"The public lands have ceased to be a source of revenue. From the 1st July, 1861, to the 30th September, 1862, the entire cash receipts from the sale of lands were $137,476.2—a sum much less than the expenses of our land system during the same period. The homestead law, which will take effect on the 1st of January next, offers such inducements to settlers that sales for cash cannot be expected to an extent sufficient to meet the expenses of the General Land Office and the cost of surveying and bringing the land into market."

The discrepancy between the sum here stated as arising from the sales of the public lands and the sum derived from the same source as reported from the Treasury Department arises, as I understand, from the fact that the periods of time, though apparently were not really coincident at the beginning point, the Treasury report including a considerable sum now which had previously been reported from the Interior, sufficiently large to greatly overreach the sum derived from the three months now reported upon by the Interior and not by the Treasury.

The Indian tribes upon our frontiers have during the past year manifested a spirit of insubordination, and at several points have engaged in open hostilities against the white settlements in their vicinity. The tribes occupying the Indian country south of Kansas renounced their allegiance to the United States and entered into treaties with the insurgents. Those who remained loyal to the United States were driven from the country. The chief of the Cherokees has visited this city for the purpose of restoring the former relations of the tribe with the United States. He alleges that they were constrained by superior force to enter into treaties with the insurgents, and that the United States neglected to furnish the protection which their treaty stipulations required.

In the month of August last the Sioux Indians in Minnesota attacked the settlements in their vicinity with extreme ferocity, killing indiscriminately men, women, and children. This attack was wholly unexpected, and therefore no means of defense had been provided. It is estimated that not less than 800 persons were killed by the Indians, and a large amount of property was destroyed. How this outbreak was induced is not definitely known, and suspicions, which may be unjust, need not be stated. Information was received by the Indian Bureau from different sources about the time hostilities were commenced that a simultaneous attack was to be made upon white settlements by all the tribes between the Mississippi River and the Rocky Mountains. The State of Minnesota has suffered great injury from this Indian war. A large portion of her territory has been depopulated, and a severe loss has been sustained by the destruction of property. The people of that State manifest much anxiety for the removal of the tribes beyond the limits of the State as a guaranty against future hostilities. The Commissioner of Indian Affairs will furnish full details. I submit for your especial consideration whether our Indian system shall not be remodeled. Many wise and good men have impressed me with the belief that this can be profitably done.

I submit a statement of the proceedings of commissioners, which shows the progress that has been made in the enterprise of constructing the Pacific Railroad. And this suggests the earliest completion of this road, and also the favorable action of Congress upon the projects now pending before them for enlarging the capacities of the great canals in New York and Illinois, as being of vital and rapidly increasing importance to the whole nation, and especially to the vast interior region hereinafter to be noticed at some greater length. I purpose having prepared and laid before you at an early day some interesting and valuable statistical information upon this subject. The military and commercial importance of enlarging the Illinois and Michigan Canal and improving the Illinois River is presented in the report of Colonel Webster to the Secretary of War, and now transmitted to Congress. I respectfully ask attention to it.

To carry out the provisions of the act of Congress of the 15th of May last, I have caused the Department of Agriculture of the United States to be organized.

The Commissioner informs me that within the period of a few months this department has established an extensive system of correspondence and exchanges, both at home and abroad, which promises to effect highly beneficial results in the development of a correct knowledge of recent improvements in agriculture, in the introduction of new products, and in the collection of the agricultural statistics of the different States.

Also, that it will soon be prepared to distribute largely seeds, cereals, plants, and cuttings, and has already published and liberally diffused much valuable information in anticipation of a more elaborate report, which will in due time be furnished, embracing some valuable tests in chemical science now in progress in the laboratory.

The creation of this department was for the more immediate benefit of a large class of our most valuable citizens, and I trust that the liberal basis upon which it has been organized will not only meet your approbation, but that it will realize at no distant day all the fondest anticipations of its most sanguine friends and become the fruitful source of advantage to all our people.

On the 22d day of September last a proclamation was issued by the Executive, a copy of which is herewith submitted.

In accordance with the purpose expressed in the second paragraph of that paper, I now respectfully recall your attention to what may be called "compensated emancipation."

A nation may be said to consist of its territory, its people, and its laws. The territory is the only part which is of certain durability. "One generation passeth away and another generation cometh, but the earth abideth forever." It is of the first importance to duly consider and estimate this ever enduring part. That portion of the earth's surface which is owned and inhabited by the people of the United States is well adapted to be the home of one national family, and it is not well adapted for two or more. Its vast extent and its variety of climate and productions are of advantage in this age for one people, whatever they might have been in former ages. Steam, telegraphs, and intelligence have brought these to be an advantageous combination for one united people.

In the inaugural address I briefly pointed out the total inadequacy of disunion as a remedy for the differences between the people of the two sections. I did so in language which I cannot improve, and which, therefore, I beg to repeat:

"One section of our country believes slavery is right and ought to be extended, while the other believes it is wrong and ought not to be extended. This is the only substantial dispute. The fugitive-slave clause of the Constitution and the laws for the suppression of the foreign slave trade are each as well enforced, perhaps, as any law can ever be in a community where the moral Sense of the people imperfectly supports the law itself. The great body of the people abide by the dry legal obligation in both cases, and a few break over in each. This, I think, cannot be perfectly cured, and it would be worse in both cases after the separation of the sections than before. The foreign slave trade, now imperfectly suppressed, would be ultimately revived without restriction in one section, while fugitive slaves, now only partially surrendered, would not be surrendered at all by the other.

"Physically speaking, we can not separate. We can not remove our respective sections from each other nor build an impassable wall between them. A husband and wife may be divorced and go out of the presence and beyond the reach of each other, but the different parts of our country cannot do this. They cannot but remain face to face, and intercourse, either amicable or hostile, must continue between them. Is it possible, then, to make that intercourse more advantageous or more satisfactory after separation than before? Can aliens make treaties easier than friends can make laws? Can treaties be more faithfully enforced between aliens than laws can among friends? Suppose you go to war, you cannot fight always; and when, after much loss on both sides and no gain on either, you cease fighting, the identical old questions, as to terms of intercourse, are again upon you."

There is no line, straight or crooked, suitable for a national boundary upon which to divide. Trace through, from east to west, upon the line between the free and slave country, and we shall find a little more than one third of its length are rivers, easy to be crossed, and populated, or soon to be populated, thickly upon both sides; while nearly all its remaining length are merely surveyors' lines, over which people may walk back and forth without any consciousness of their presence. No part of this line can be made any more difficult to pass by writing it down on paper or parchment as a national boundary. The fact of separation, if it comes, gives up on the part of the seceding section the fugitive-slave clause along with all other constitutional obligations upon the section seceded from, while I should expect no treaty stipulation would ever be made to take its place.

But there is another difficulty. The great interior region bounded east by the Alleghenies, north by the British dominions, west by the Rocky Mountains, and south by the line along which the culture of corn and cotton meets, and which includes part of Virginia, part of Tennessee, all of Kentucky, Ohio, Indiana, Michigan, Wisconsin, Illinois, Missouri, Kansas, Iowa, Minnesota, and the Territories of Dakota, Nebraska, and part of Colorado, already has above 10,000,000 people, and will have 50,000,000 within fifty years if not prevented by any political folly or mistake. It contains more than one third of the country owned by the United States—certainly more than 1,000,000 square miles. Once half as populous as Massachusetts already is, it would have more than 75,000,000 people. A glance at the map shows that, territorially speaking, it is the great body of the Republic. The other parts are but marginal borders to it, the magnificent region sloping west from the Rocky Mountains to the Pacific being the deepest and also the richest in undeveloped resources. In the production of provisions, grains, grasses, and all which proceed from them this great interior region is naturally one of the most important in the world. Ascertain from statistics the small proportion of the region which has yet been brought into cultivation, and also the large and rapidly increasing amount of products, and we shall be overwhelmed with the magnitude of the prospect presented. And yet this region has no seacoast—touches no ocean anywhere. As part of one nation, its people now find, and may forever find, their way to Europe by New York, to South America and Africa by New Orleans, and to Asia by San Francisco; but separate our common country into two nations, as designed by the present rebellion, and every man of this great interior region is thereby cut off from some one or more of these outlets, not perhaps by a physical barrier, but by embarrassing and onerous trade regulations.

And this is true, wherever a dividing or boundary line may be fixed. Place it between the now free and slave country, or place it south of Kentucky or north of Ohio, and still the truth remains that none south of it can trade to any port or place north of it, and none north of it can trade to any port or place south of it, except upon terms dictated by a government foreign to them. These outlets, east, west, and south, are indispensable to the well-being of the people inhabiting and to inhabit this vast interior region. Which of the three may be the best is no proper question. All are better than either, and all of right belong to that people and to their successors forever. True to themselves, they will not ask where a line of separation shall be, but will vow rather that there shall be no such line. Nor are the marginal regions less interested in these communications to and through them to the great outside world. They, too, and each of them, must have access to this Egypt of the West without paying toll at the crossing of any national boundary.

Our national strife springs not from our permanent part; not from the land we inhabit; not from our national homestead. There is no possible severing of this but would multiply and not mitigate evils among us. In all its adaptations and aptitudes it demands union and abhors separation. In fact, it would ere long force reunion, however much of blood and treasure the separation might have cost.

Our strife pertains to ourselves—to the passing generations of men—and it can without convulsion be hushed forever with the passing of one generation.

In this view I recommend the adoption of the following resolution and articles amendatory to the Constitution of the United States:

Resolved by the Senate and House of Representatives of the United States of America, in Congress assembled, (two thirds of both Houses concurring), That the following articles be proposed to the Legislatures (or conventions) of the several States as amendments to the Constitution of the United States, all or any of which articles, when ratified by three fourths of the said Legislatures (or conventions), to be valid as part or parts of the said Constitution, viz.

ART.—Every State wherein slavery now exists which shall abolish the same therein at any time or times before the 1st day of January, A.D. 1900, shall receive compensation from the United States as follows, to wit:

The President of the United States shall deliver to every such State bonds of the United States bearing interest at the rate of — percent per annum to an amount equal to the aggregate sum of ——— for each slave shown to have been therein by the Eighth Census of the United States, said bonds to be delivered to such State by installments or in one parcel at the completion of the abolishment, accordingly as the same shall have been gradual or at one time within such State; and interest shall begin to run upon any such bond only from the proper time of its delivery as aforesaid. Any State having received bonds as aforesaid and afterwards reintroducing or tolerating slavery therein shall refund to the United States the bonds so received, or the value thereof, and all interest paid thereon.

ART.—All slaves who shall have enjoyed actual freedom by the chances of the war at any time before the end of the rebellion shall be forever free; but all owners of such who shall not have been disloyal shall be compensated for them at the same rates as is provided for States adopting abolishment of slavery, but in such way that no slave shall be twice accounted for.

ART.—Congress may appropriate money and otherwise provide for colonizing free colored persons with their own consent at any place or places without the United States.

I beg indulgence to discuss these proposed articles at some length. Without slavery the rebellion could never have existed; without slavery it could not continue.

Among the friends of the Union there is great diversity of sentiment and of policy in regard to slavery and the African race amongst us. Some would perpetuate slavery; some would abolish it suddenly and without compensation; some would abolish it gradually and with compensation; some would remove the freed people from us, and some would retain them with us; and there are yet other minor diversities. Because of these diversities we waste much strength in struggles among ourselves. By mutual concession we should harmonize and act together. This would be compromise, but it would be compromise among the friends and not with the enemies of the Union. These articles are intended to embody a plan of such mutual concessions. If the plan shall be adopted, it is assumed that emancipation will follow, at least in several of the States.

As to the first article, the main points are, first, the emancipation; secondly, the length of time for consummating it (thirty-seven years); and, thirdly, the compensation.

The emancipation will be unsatisfactory to the advocates of perpetual slavery, but the length of time should greatly mitigate their dissatisfaction. The time spares both races from the evils of sudden derangement—in fact, from the necessity of any derangement—while most of those whose habitual course of thought will be disturbed by the measure will have passed away before its consummation. They will never see it. Another class will hail the prospect of emancipation, but will deprecate the length of time. They will feel that it gives too little to the now living slaves. But it really gives them much. It saves them from the vagrant destitution which must largely attend immediate emancipation in localities where their numbers are very great, and it gives the inspiring assurance that their posterity shall be free forever. The plan leaves to each State choosing to act under it to abolish slavery now or at the end of the century, or at any intermediate tune, or by degrees extending over the whole or any part of the period, and it obliges no two States to proceed alike. It also provides for compensation, and generally the mode of making it. This, it would seem, must further mitigate the dissatisfaction of those who favor perpetual slavery, and especially of those who are to receive the compensation. Doubtless some of those who are to pay and not to receive will object. Yet the measure is both just and economical. In a certain sense the liberation of slaves is the destruction of property— property acquired by descent or by purchase, the same as any other property. It is no less true for having been often said that the people of the South are not more responsible for the original introduction of this property than are the people of the North; and when it is remembered how unhesitatingly we all use cotton and sugar and share the profits of dealing in them, it may not be quite safe to say that the South has been more responsible than the North for its continuance. If, then, for a common object this property is to be sacrificed, is it not just that it be done at a common charge?

And if with less money, or money more easily paid, we can preserve the benefits of the Union by this means than we can by the war alone, is it not also economical to do it? Let us consider it, then. Let us ascertain the sum we have expended in the war Since compensated emancipation was proposed last March, and consider whether if that measure had been promptly accepted by even some of the slave States the same sum would not have done more to close the war than has been otherwise done. If so, the measure would save money, and in that view would be a prudent and economical measure. Certainly it is not so easy to pay something as it is to pay nothing, but it is easier to pay a large sum than it is to pay a larger one. And it is easier to pay any sum when we are able than it is to pay it before we are able. The war requires large sums, and requires them at once. The aggregate sum necessary for compensated emancipation of course would be large. But it would require no ready cash, nor the bonds even any faster than the emancipation progresses. This might not, and probably would not, close before the end of the thirty-seven years. At that time we shall probably have a hundred millions of people to share the burden, instead of thirty-one millions as now. And not only so, but the increase of our population may be expected to continue for a long time after that period as rapidly as before, because our territory will not have become full. I do not state this inconsiderately. At the same ratio of increase which we have maintained, on an average, from our first national census, in 1790, until that of 1860, we should in 1900 have a population of 103,208,415. And why may we not continue that ratio far beyond that period? Our abundant room, our broad national homestead, is our ample resource. Were our territory as limited as are the British Isles, very certainly our population could not expand as stated. Instead of receiving the foreign born as now, we should be compelled to send part of the native born away. But such is not our condition. We have 2,963,000 square miles. Europe has 3,800,000, with a population averaging 73 ⅓ persons to the square mile. Why may not our country at some time average as many? Is it less fertile? Has it more waste surface by mountains, rivers, lakes, deserts, or other causes? Is it inferior to Europe in any natural advantage? If, then, we are at some time to be as populous as Europe, how soon? As to when this may be, we can judge by the past and the present; as to when it will be, if ever, depends much on whether we maintain the Union. Several of our States are already above the average of Europe—seventy-three and a third to the square mile. Massachusetts 157; Rhode Island 133; Connecticut 99; New York and New Jersey, each 80. Also two other great States, Pennsylvania and Ohio, are not far below, the former having 63 and the latter 59. The States already above the European average, except New York, have increased in as rapid a ratio, since passing that point, as ever before; while no one of them is equal to some other parts of our country in natural capacity for sustaining a dense population.

Taking the nation in the aggregate, and we find its population and ratio of increase, for the several decennial periods, to be as follows:

1799....	3,929,827				
1800....	5,305,937	35.02 per cent. ratio of increase.			
1810....	7,239,814	36.45	"	"	"
1820....	9,638,131	33.13	"	"	"
1830....	12,866,020	33.49	"	"	"
1840....	17,069,453	32.67	"	"	"
1850....	23,191,876	35.87	"	"	"
1860....	31,443,790	35.58	"	"	"

This shows an average decennial increase of 34.60 percent in population through the seventy years, from our first to our last census yet taken. It is seen that the ratio of increase, at no one of these two periods, is either two percent below or two percent above the average; thus showing how inflexible, and consequently how reliable, the law of increase in our case is. Assuming that it will continue, it gives the following results:

1870	42,323,341
1880	56,967,216
1890	76,677,872
1900	103,208,415
1910	138,918,526
1920	186,984,335
1930	251,680,914

These figures show that our country may be as populous as Europe now is at some point between 1920 and 1930, say about 1925—our territory, at 73 ⅓ persons to the square mile, being of capacity to contain 217,186,000.

And we will reach this, too, if we do not ourselves relinquish the chance by the folly and evils of disunion or by long and exhausting war springing from the only great element of national discord among us. While it cannot be foreseen exactly how much one huge example of secession, breeding lesser ones indefinitely, would retard population, civilization, and prosperity, no one can doubt that the extent of it would be very great and injurious.

The proposed emancipation would shorten the war, perpetuate peace, insure this increase of population, and proportionately the wealth of the country. With these we should pay all the emancipation would cost, together with our other debt, easier than we should pay our other debt without it. If we had allowed our old national debt to run at six percent per annum, simple interest, from the end of our revolutionary struggle until to-day, without paying anything on either principal or interest, each man of us would owe less upon that debt now than each man owed upon it then; and this because our increase of men through the whole period has been greater than six percent—has run faster than the interest upon the debt. Thus time alone relieves a debtor nation, so long as its population increases faster than unpaid interest accumulates on its debt.

This fact would be no excuse for delaying payment of what is justly due, but it shows the great importance of time in this connection—the great advantage of a policy by which we shall not have to pay until we number 100,000,000 what by a different policy we would have to pay now, when we number but 31,000,000. In a word, it shows that a dollar will be much harder to pay for the war than will be a dollar for emancipation on the proposed plan. And then the latter will cost no blood, no precious life. It will be a saving of both.

As to the second article, I think it would be impracticable to return to bondage the class of persons therein contemplated. Some of them, doubtless, in the property sense belong to loyal owners, and hence Provision is made in this article for compensating such.

The third article relates to the future of the freed people. It does not oblige, but merely authorizes Congress to aid in colonizing such as may consent. This ought nut to be regarded as objectionable on the one hand or on the other, insomuch as it comes to nothing unless by the mutual consent of the people to be deported and the American voters through their representatives in Congress.

I cannot make it better known than it already is that I strongly favor colonization; and yet I wish to say there is an objection urged against free colored persons remaining in the country which is largely imaginary, if not sometimes malicious.

It is insisted that their presence would injure and displace white labor and white laborers. If there ever could be a proper time for mere catch arguments that time surely is not now. In times like the present men should utter nothing for which they would not willingly be responsible through time and in eternity. Is it true, then, that colored people can displace any more white labor by being free than by remaining slaves? If they stay in their old places, they jostle no white laborers; if they leave their old places, they leave them open to white laborers. Logically, there is neither more nor less of it. Emancipation, even without deportation, would probably enhance the wages of white labor, and very surely would not reduce them. Thus the customary amount of labor would still have to be performed. The freed people would surely not do more than their old proportion of it, and very probably for a time would do less, leaving an increased part to white laborers, bringing their labor into greater demand, and consequently enhancing the wages of it. With deportation, even to a limited extent, enhanced wages to white labor is mathematically certain. Labor is like any other commodity in the market-increase the demand for it and you increase the price of it. Reduce the supply of black labor by colonizing the black laborer out of the country, and by precisely so much you increase the demand for and wages of white labor.

But it is dreaded that the freed people will swarm forth and cover the whole land. Are they not already in the land? Will liberation make them any more numerous? Equally distributed among the whites of the whole country, and there would be but one colored to seven whites. Could the one in any way greatly disturb the seven? There are many communities now having more than one free colored person to seven whites, and this without any apparent consciousness of evil from it. The District of Columbia and the States of Maryland and Delaware are all in this condition. The District has more than one free colored to six whites, and yet in its frequent petitions to Congress I believe it has never presented the presence of free colored persons as one of its grievances. But why should emancipation South send the free people North? People of any color seldom run unless there be something to run from. Heretofore colored people to some extent have fled North from bondage, and now, perhaps, from both bondage and destitution. But if gradual emancipation and deportation be adopted, they will have neither to flee from. Their old masters will give them wages at least until new laborers can be procured, and the freedmen in turn will gladly give their labor for the wages till new homes can be found for them in congenial climes and with people of their own blood and race. This proposition can be trusted on the mutual interests involved. And in any event, cannot the North decide for itself whether to receive them?

Again, as practice proves more than theory in any case, has there been any irruption of colored people northward because of the abolishment of slavery in this District last spring?

What I have said of the proportion of free colored persons to the whites in the District is from the census of 1860, having no reference to persons called contrabands nor to those made free by the act of Congress abolishing slavery here.

The plan consisting of these articles is recommended, not but that a restoration of the national authority would be accepted without its adoption.

Nor will the war nor proceedings under the proclamation of September 22, 1862, be stayed because of the recommendation of this plan. Its timely adoption, I doubt not, would bring restoration, and thereby stay both.

And notwithstanding this plan, the recommendation that Congress provide by law for compensating any State which may adopt emancipation before this plan shall have been acted upon is hereby earnestly renewed. Such would be only an advance part of the plan, and the same arguments apply to both.

This plan is recommended as a means, not in exclusion of, but additional to, all others for restoring and preserving the national authority throughout the Union. The subject is presented exclusively in its economical aspect. The plan would, I am confident, secure peace more speedily and maintain it more permanently than can be done by force alone, while all it would cost, considering amounts and manner of payment and times of payment, would be easier paid than will be the additional cost of the war if we rely solely upon force. It is much, very much, that it would cost no blood at all.

The plan is proposed as permanent constitutional law. It cannot become such without the concurrence of, first, two thirds of Congress, and afterwards three fourths of the States. The requisite three fourths of the States will necessarily include seven of the slave States. Their concurrence, if obtained, will give assurance of their severally adopting emancipation at no very distant day upon the new constitutional terms. This assurance would end the struggle now and save the Union forever.

I do not forget the gravity which should characterize a paper addressed to the Congress of the nation by the chief magistrate of the nation, nor do I forget that some of you are my seniors, nor that many of you have more experience than I in the conduct of public affairs. Yet I trust that in view of the great responsibility resting upon me you will perceive no want of respect to yourselves in any undue earnestness I may seem to display.

Is it doubted, then, that the plan I propose, if adopted, would shorten the war, and thus lessen its expenditure of money and of blood? Is it doubted that it would restore the national authority and national prosperity and perpetuate both indefinitely? Is it doubted that we here—Congress and executive—can secure its adoption? Will not the good people respond to a united and earnest appeal from us? Can we, can they, by any other means so certainly or so speedily assure these vital objects? We can succeed only by concert. It is not "Can any of us imagine better?" but "Can we all do better?" Object whatsoever is possible, still the question recurs, "Can we do better?" The dogmas of the quiet past are inadequate to the stormy present. The occasion is piled high with difficulty, and we must rise with the occasion. As our case is new, so we must think anew and act anew. We must disenthrall ourselves, and then we shall save our country.

Fellow-citizens, we can not escape history. We of this Congress and this administration will be remembered in spite of ourselves. No personal significance or insignificance can spare one or another of us. The fiery trial through which we pass will light us down in honor or dishonor to the latest generation. We say we are for the Union. The world will not forget that we say this. We know how to save the Union. The world knows we do know how to save it. We, even we here, hold the power and bear the responsibility. In giving freedom to the slave we assure freedom to the free—honorable alike in what we give and what we preserve. We shall nobly save or meanly lose the last, best hope of earth. Other means may succeed; this could not fail. The way is plain, peaceful, generous, just—a way which if followed the world will forever applaud and God must forever bless.

FINAL EMANCIPATION PROCLAMATION, JANUARY 1, 1863.

A Proclamation.

Whereas on the 22d day of September, A.D. 1862, a proclamation was issued by the President of the United States, containing, among other things, the following, to wit:

"That on the 1st day of January, A.D., 1863, all persons held as slaves within any State or designated part of a State the people whereof shall then be in rebellion against the United States shall be then, thenceforward, and forever free; and the executive government of the United States, including the military and naval authority thereof, will recognize and maintain the freedom of such persons and will do no act or acts to repress such persons, or any of them, in any efforts they may make for their actual freedom.

"That the executive will on the 1st day of January aforesaid, by proclamation, designate the States and parts of States, if any, in which the people thereof, respectively, shall then be in rebellion against the United States; and the fact that any State or the people thereof shall on that day be in good faith represented in the Congress of the United States by members chosen thereto at elections wherein a majority of the qualified voters of such States shall have participated shall, in the absence of strong countervailing testimony, be deemed conclusive evidence that such State and the people thereof are not then in rebellion against the United States."

Now, therefore, I, Abraham Lincoln, President of the United States, by virtue of the power in me vested as Commander-in-Chief of the Army and Navy of the United States in time of actual armed rebellion against the authority and government of the United States, and as a fit and necessary war measure for suppressing said rebellion, do, on this 1st day of January, A. D. 1863, and in accordance with my purpose so to do, publicly proclaimed for the full period of one hundred days from the first day above mentioned, order and designate as the States and parts of States wherein the people thereof, respectively, are this day in rebellion against the United States the following, to wit:

Arkansas, Texas, Louisiana (except the parishes of St. Bernard, Plaquemines, Jefferson, St. John, St. Charles, St. James, Ascension, Assumption, Terre Bonne, Lafourche, St. Mary, St. Martin, and

Orleans, including the city of New Orleans), Mississippi, Alabama, Florida, Georgia, South Carolina, North Carolina, and Virginia (except the forty-eight counties designated as West Virginia, and also the counties of Berkeley, Accomac, Northampton, Elizabeth City, York, Princess Anne, and Norfolk, including the cities of Norfolk and Portsmouth), and which excepted parts are for the present left precisely as if this proclamation were not issued.

And by virtue of the power and for the purpose aforesaid, I do order and declare that all persons held as slaves within said designated States and parts of States are, and henceforward shall be, free; and that the Executive Government of the United States, including the military and naval authorities thereof, will recognize and maintain the freedom of said persons.

And I hereby enjoin upon the people so declared to be free to abstain from all violence, unless in necessary self-defense; and I recommend to them that, in all cases when allowed, they labor faithfully for reasonable wages.

And I further declare and make known that such persons of suitable condition will be received into the armed service of the United States to garrison forts, positions, stations, and other places, and to man vessels of all sorts in said service.

And upon this act, sincerely believed to be an act of justice, warranted by the Constitution upon military necessity, I invoke the considerate judgment of mankind and the gracious favor of Almighty God.

In witness whereof I have hereunto set my hand and caused the seal of the United States to be affixed.

Done at the city of Washington, this first day of January, A.D. 1863, and of the independence of the United States of America the eighty-seventh.

ABRAHAM LINCOLN.

By the President:
WILLIAM H. SEWARD, *Secretary of State.*

LETTER TO JAMES C. CONKLING, WASHINGTON, DC, AUGUST 26, 1863.

EXECUTIVE MANSION,
WASHINGTON, August 26, 1863.

HON. JAMES C. CONKLING.

MY DEAR SIR:—Your letter inviting me to attend a mass meeting of unconditional Union men, to be held at the capital of Illinois, on the 3d day of September, has been received.

It would be very agreeable for me thus to meet my old friends at my own home, but I cannot just now be absent from here so long as a visit there would require.

The meeting is to be of all those who maintain unconditional devotion to the Union, and I am sure that my old political friends will thank me for tendering, as I do, the nation's gratitude to those other noble men whom no partisan malice or partisan hope can make false to the nation's life.

There are those who are dissatisfied with me. To such I would say: You desire peace, and you blame me that we do not have it. But how can we obtain it? There are but three conceivable ways.

First—to suppress the rebellion by force of arms. This I am trying to do. Are you for it? If you are, so far we are agreed. If you are not for it, a second way is to give up the Union. I am against this. Are you for it? If you are you should say so plainly. If you are not for force nor yet for dissolution, there only remains some imaginable compromise. I do not believe that any compromise embracing the maintenance of the Union is now possible. All that I learn leads to a directly opposite belief. The strength of the rebellion is its military, its army. That army dominates all the country and all the people within its range. Any offer of terms made by any man or men within that range, in opposition to that army, is simply nothing for the present; because such man or men have no power whatever to enforce their side of a compromise, if one were made with them. To illustrate: Suppose refugees from the South and peace men of the North get together in convention, and frame and proclaim a compromise embracing a restoration of the Union. In what way can that compromise be used to keep Lee's army out of Pennsylvania? Meade's army can keep Lee's army out of Pennsylvania, and, I think, can ultimately drive it out of existence.

But no paper compromise to which the controllers of Lee's army are not agreed can at all affect that army. In an effort at such compromise we would waste time, which the enemy would improve to our disadvantage; and that would be all. A compromise, to be effective, must be made either with those who control the rebel army, or with the people, first liberated from the domination of that army by the success of our own army. Now allow me to assure you that no word or intimation from that rebel army, or from any of the men controlling it, in relation to any peace compromise, has ever come to my knowledge or belief.

All charges and insinuations to the contrary are deceptive and groundless. And I promise you that if any such proposition shall hereafter come, it shall not be rejected and kept a secret from you. I freely acknowledge myself to be the servant of the people, according to the bond of service, the United States Constitution, and that, as such, I am responsible to them.

But, to be plain: You are dissatisfied with me about the negro. Quite likely there is a difference of opinion between you and myself upon that subject.

I certainly wish that all men could be free, while you, I suppose, do not. Yet, I have neither adopted nor proposed any measure which is not consistent with even your view, provided you are for the Union. I suggested compensated emancipation; to which you replied you wished not to be taxed to buy negroes. But I had not asked you to be taxed to buy negroes, except in such way as to save you from greater taxation to save the Union exclusively by other means.

You dislike the Emancipation Proclamation, and perhaps would have it retracted. You say it is unconstitutional. I think differently. I think the Constitution invests its commander-in-chief with the law of war in time of war. The most that can be said, if so much, is, that slaves are property. Is there, has there ever been, any question that by the law of war, property, both of enemies and friends, may be taken when needed?

And is it not needed whenever it helps us and hurts the enemy? Armies, the world over, destroy enemies' property when they cannot use it, and even destroy their own to keep it from the enemy. Civilized belligerents do all in their power to help themselves or hurt the enemy, except a few things regarded as barbarous or cruel.

Among the exceptions are the massacre of vanquished foes and non-combatants, male and female.

But the proclamation, as law, either is valid or is not valid.

If it is not valid it needs no retraction. If it is valid it cannot be retracted, any more than the dead can be brought to life. Some of you profess to think its retraction would operate favorably for the Union.

Why better after the retraction than before the issue? There was more than a year and a half of trial to suppress the rebellion before the proclamation was issued, the last one hundred days of which passed under an explicit notice that it was coming, unless averted by those in revolt returning to their allegiance.

The war has certainly progressed as favorably for us since the issue of the proclamation as before.

I know, as fully as one can know the opinions of others, that some of the commanders of our armies in the field, who have given us our most important victories, believe the emancipation policy and the use of colored troops constitute the heaviest blows yet dealt to the rebellion, and that at least one of those important successes could not have been achieved when it was but for the aid of black soldiers. Among the commanders who hold these views are some who have never had any affinity with what is called "Abolitionism," or with "Republican Party politics," but who hold them purely as military opinions. I submit their opinions are entitled to some weight against the objections often urged that emancipation and arming the blacks are unwise as military measures, and were not adopted as such in good faith.

You say that you will not fight to free negroes. Some of them seem willing to fight for you; but no matter.

Fight you, then, exclusively, to save the Union. I issued the proclamation on purpose to aid you in saving the Union. Whenever you shall have conquered all resistance to the Union, if I shall urge you to continue fighting, it will be an apt time then for you to declare you will not fight to free negroes.

I thought that in your struggle for the Union, to whatever extent the negroes should cease helping the enemy, to that extent it weakened the enemy in his resistance to you. Do you think differently? I thought that whatever negroes can be got to do as soldiers, leaves just so much less for white soldiers to do in saving the Union. Does it appear otherwise to you?

But negroes, like other people, act upon motives. Why should they do anything for us if we will do nothing for them? If they stake their lives for us they must be prompted by the strongest motive, even the promise of freedom. And the promise, being made, must be kept.

The signs look better. The Father of Waters again goes unvexed to the sea. Thanks to the great Northwest for it; nor yet wholly to them. Three hundred miles up they met New England, Empire, Keystone, and Jersey, hewing their way right and left. The sunny South, too, in more colors than one, also lent a helping hand.

On the spot, their part of the history was jotted down in black and white. The job was a great national one, and let none be slighted who bore an honorable part in it And while those who have cleared the great river may well be proud, even that is not all. It is hard to say that anything has been more bravely and well done than at Antietam, Murfreesboro, Gettysburg, and on many fields of less note. Nor must Uncle Sam's web-feet be forgotten. At all the watery margins they have been present; not only on the deep sea, the broad bay, and the rapid river, but also up the narrow, muddy bayou, and wherever the ground was a little damp, they have been and made their tracks. Thanks to all. For the great Republic—for the principle it lives by and keeps alive— for man's vast future—thanks to all.

Peace does not appear so distant as it did. I hope it will come soon, and come to stay, and so come as to be worth the keeping in all future time. It will then have been proved that among freemen there can be no successful appeal from the ballot to the bullet, and that they who take such appeal are sure to lose their case and pay the cost. And there will be some black men who can remember that with silent tongue, and clinched teeth, and steady eye, and well-poised bayonet, they have helped mankind on to this great consummation; while I fear there will be some white ones unable to forget that with malignant heart and deceitful speech they have striven to hinder it.

Still, let us not be over-sanguine of a speedy, final triumph. Let us be quite sober. Let us diligently apply the means, never doubting that a just God, in His own good time, will give us the rightful result.

Yours very truly,

A. LINCOLN.

PROCLAMATION FOR THANKSGIVING, OCTOBER 3, 1863.

A Proclamation.

The year that is drawing towards its close has been filled with the blessings of fruitful fields and healthful skies. To these bounties, which are so constantly enjoyed that we are prone to forget the source from which they come, others have been added which are of so extraordinary a nature that they cannot fail to penetrate and soften even the heart which is habitually insensible to the ever-watchful providence of Almighty God. In the midst of a civil war of unequalled magnitude and severity which has sometimes seemed to invite and provoke the aggressions of foreign states; peace has been preserved with all nations, order has been maintained, the laws have been respected and obeyed, and harmony has prevailed everywhere except in the theatre of military conflict; while that theatre has been greatly contracted by the advancing armies and navies of the Union. The needful diversion of wealth and strength from the fields of peaceful industry, to the national defense has not arrested the plough, the shuttle, or the ship: The axe has enlarged the borders of our settlements, and the mines, as well of, iron and coal as of the precious metals, have yielded even more abundantly than heretofore. Population has steadily increased, notwithstanding the waste that has been made in the camp, the siege, and the battle-field; and the country, rejoicing in the consciousness of augmented strength and vigor, is permitted to expect a continuance of years, with large increase of freedom. No human counsel hath devised, nor hath any mortal hand worked out these great things. They are the gracious gifts of the Most High God, who, while dealing with us in anger for our sins, hath nevertheless remembered mercy.

It has seemed to me fit and proper that they should be reverently, solemnly, and gratefully acknowledged, as with one heart and voice, by the whole American people. I do, therefore, invite my fellow-citizens in every part of the United States, and also those who are at sea, and those who are sojourning in foreign lands, to set apart and observe the last Thursday of November next as a day of thanksgiving and prayer to our beneficent Father who dwelleth in the heavens. And I recommend to them that, while offering up the ascriptions justly due to Him for such singular deliverances and blessings, they do also, with humble penitence for our national perverseness and disobedience, commend to His tender care all those who have become widows, orphans, mourners, or sufferers in the lamentable civil strife in which we are unavoidably engaged, and fervently implore the interposition of the Almighty hand to heal the wounds of the nation, and to restore it, as soon as may be consistent with divine purposes, to the full enjoyment of peace, harmony, tranquility, and union.

In testimony whereof, I have hereunto set my hand, and caused the seal of the United States to be affixed.

Done at the city of Washington, this third day of October, in the year of our Lord one thousand eight hundred and sixty-three, and of the independence of the United States the eighty-eighth.

ABRAHAM LINCOLN.

By the President:

WILLIAM H. SEWARD, *Secretary of State.*

ADDRESS DELIVERED AT THE DEDICATION OF THE CEMETERY AT GETTYSBURG, NOVEMBER 19, 1863.

Four score and seven years ago our fathers brought forth on this continent, a new nation, conceived in Liberty, and dedicated to the proposition that all men are created equal.

Now we are engaged in a great civil war, testing whether that nation or any nation so conceived and so dedicated, can long endure. We are met on a great battle-field of that war. We have come to dedicate a portion of that field, as a final resting place for those who here gave their lives that that nation might live. It is altogether fitting and proper that we should do this.

But, in a larger sense, we can not dedicate—we can not consecrate—we can not hallow—this ground. The brave men, living and dead, who struggled here, have consecrated it, far above our poor power to add or detract. The world will little note, nor long remember what we say here, but it can never forget what they did here. It is for us the living, rather, to be dedicated here to the unfinished work which they who fought here have thus far so nobly advanced. It is rather for us to be here dedicated to the great task remaining before us—that from these honored dead we take increased devotion to that cause for which they gave the last full measure of devotion that we here highly resolve that these dead shall not have died in vain—that this nation, under God, shall have a new birth of freedom—and that government of the people, by the people, for the people, shall not perish from the earth.

To Albert G. Hodges, Washington, DC, April 4, 1864.

Executive Mansion, Washington, April 4, 1864.

A. G. Hodges, Esq., Frankfort, Kentucky:

My Dear Sir:—You ask me to put in writing the substance of what I verbally said the other day, in your presence, to Governor Bramlette and Senator Dixon. It was about as follows:

"I am naturally anti-slavery. If slavery is not wrong, nothing is wrong. I cannot remember when I did not so think and feel, and yet I have never understood that the Presidency conferred upon me an unrestricted right to act officially upon this judgment and feeling. It was in the oath I took that I would to the best of my ability preserve, protect, and defend the Constitution of the United States. I could not take the office without taking the oath. Nor was it my view that I might take an oath to get power, and break the oath in using the power. I understood, too, that in ordinary civil administration this oath even forbade me to practically indulge my primary abstract judgment on the moral question of slavery. I had publicly declared this many times, and in many ways. And I aver that, to this day, I have done no official act in mere deference to my abstract judgment and feeling on slavery. I did understand, however, that my oath to preserve the Constitution to the best of my ability, imposed upon me the duty of preserving, by every indispensable means, that government, that nation, of which that Constitution was the organic law. Was it possible to lose the nation and yet preserve the Constitution? By General law, life and limb must be protected; yet often a limb must be amputated to save a life; but a life is never wisely given to save a limb. I felt that measures, otherwise unconstitutional, might become lawful, by becoming indispensable to the preservation of the Constitution, through the preservation of the nation. Right or wrong, I assumed this ground, and now avow it. I could not feel that to the best of my ability I had even tried to preserve the Constitution, if, to save slavery, or any minor matter, I should permit the wreck of government, country, and Constitution, altogether. When, early in the war, General Fremont attempted military emancipation, I forbade it, because I did not then think it an indispensable necessity. When, a little later, General Cameron, then Secretary of War, suggested the arming of the blacks, I objected, because I did not yet think it an indispensable necessity. When, still later, General Hunter attempted military emancipation, I again forbade it, because I did not yet think the indispensable necessity had come. When, in March, and May, and July, 1862, I made earnest and successive appeals to the Border States to favor compensated emancipation, I believed the indispensable necessity for military emancipation and arming the blacks would come, unless averted by that measure. They declined the proposition, and I was, in my best judgment, driven to the alternative of either surrendering the Union, and with it the Constitution, or of laying strong hand upon the colored element. I chose the latter. In choosing it, I hoped for greater gain than loss, but of this I was not entirely confident. More than a year of trial now shows no loss by it in our foreign relations, none in our home popular sentiment, none in our white military force, no loss by it any how, or anywhere. On the contrary, it shows a gain of quite one hundred and thirty thousand soldiers, seamen, and laborers. These are palpable facts, about which, as facts, there can be no caviling. We have the men; and we could not have had them without the measure.

"And now let any Union man who complains of the measure test himself by writing down in one line that he is for subduing the rebellion by force of arms; and in the next, that he is for taking these hundred and thirty thousand men from the Union side, and placing them where they would be but for the measure he condemns. If he cannot face his case so stated, it is only because he cannot face the truth."

I add a word which was not in the verbal conversation. In telling this tale I attempt no compliment to my own sagacity. I claim not to have controlled events, but confess plainly that events have controlled me. Now, at the end of three years' struggle, the nation's condition is not what either party, or any man, devised or expected. God alone can claim it. Whither it is tending seems plain. If God now wills the removal of a great wrong, and wills also that we of the North, as well as you of the South, shall pay fairly for our complicity in that wrong, impartial history will find therein new cause to attest and revere the justice and goodness of God.

Yours truly,
A. LINCOLN.

SPEECH TO THE ONE HUNDRED SIXTY-SIXTH OHIO REGIMENT,
WASHINGTON, DC, AUGUST 22, 1864.

SOLDIERS:—I suppose you are going home to see your families and friends. For the services you have done in this great struggle in which we are engaged, I present you sincere thanks for myself and the country.

I almost always feel inclined, when I say anything to soldiers, to impress upon them, in a few brief remarks, the importance of success in this contest. It is not merely for the day, but for all time to come, that we should perpetuate for our children's children that great and free government which we have enjoyed all our lives. I beg you to remember this, not merely for my sake, but for yours. I happen, temporarily, to occupy this big White House. I am a living witness that any one of your children may look to come here as my father's child has. It is in order that each one of you may have, through this free government which we have enjoyed, an open field, and a fair chance for your industry, enterprise, and intelligence; that you may all have equal privileges in the race of life with all its desirable human aspirations—it is for this that the struggle should be maintained, that we may not lose our birthrights—not only for one, but for two or three years, if necessary. The nation is worth fighting for, to secure such an inestimable jewel.

RESPONSE TO A SERENADE, WASHINGTON, DC, NOVEMBER 10, 1864.

FRIENDS AND FELLOW CITIZENS: It has long been a grave question whether any government, not too strong for the liberties of its people, can be strong enough to maintain its existence in great emergencies. On this point the present rebellion brought our government to a severe test, and a presidential election occurring in regular course during the rebellion, added not a little to the strain.

If the loyal people united were put to the utmost of their strength by the rebellion, must they not fail when divided and partially paralyzed by a political war among themselves?

But the election was a necessity. We cannot have free government without elections; and if the election could force us to forego or postpone a national election, it might fairly claim to have already conquered and ruined us. The strife of the election is but human nature practically applied to the facts of the case. What has occurred in this case must ever recur in similar cases. Human nature will not change. In any future great national trial, compared with the men of this, we will have as weak and as strong, as silly and as wise, as bad and as good.

Let us, therefore, study the incidents of this as philosophy to learn wisdom from, and none of them as wrongs to be revenged.

But the election, along with its incidental and undesirable strife, has done good, too. It has demonstrated that a people's government can sustain a national election in the midst of a great civil war. Until now, it has not been known to the world that this was a possibility. It shows, also, how sound and strong we still are. It shows that even among the candidates of the same party, he who is most devoted to the Union and most opposed to treason can receive most of the people's votes. It shows, also, to the extent yet known, that we have more men now than we had when the war began. Gold is good in its place; but living, brave, and patriotic men are better than gold.

But the rebellion continues, and, now that the election is over, may not all have a common interest to reunite in a common effort to save our common country? For my own part, I have striven and shall strive to avoid placing any obstacle in the way. So long as I have been here, I have not willingly planted a thorn in any man's bosom.

While I am duly sensible to the high compliment of a re-election, and duly grateful, as I trust, to Almighty God, for having directed my countrymen to a right conclusion, as I think, for their good, it adds nothing to my satisfaction that any other man may be disappointed by the result.

May I ask those who have not differed with me to join with me in this same spirit towards those who have? And now, let me close by asking three hearty cheers for our brave soldiers and seamen, and their gallant and skillful commanders.

LETTER TO MRS. BIXBY, NOVEMBER 21, 1864.

EXECUTIVE MANSION, WASHINGTON, November 21, 1864.

MRS. BIXBY, Boston, Massachusetts.

DEAR MADAM:—I have been shown in the files of the War Department a statement of the Adjutant-General of Massachusetts that you are the mother of five sons who have died gloriously on the field of battle. I feel how weak and fruitless must be any words of mine which should attempt to beguile you from the grief of a loss so overwhelming. But I cannot refrain from tendering to you the consolation that may be found in the thanks of the Republic they died to save. I pray that our Heavenly Father may assuage the anguish of your bereavement, and leave you only the cherished memory of the loved and lost, and the solemn pride that must be yours to have laid so costly a sacrifice upon the altar of freedom.

Yours very sincerely and respectfully,

A. LINCOLN.

RESPONSE TO A SERENADE, WASHINGTON, DC, FEBRUARY 1, 1865.

He supposed the passage through Congress of the Constitutional amendment for the abolishing of slavery throughout the United States was the occasion to which he was indebted for the honor of this call.

The occasion was one of congratulation to the country, and to the whole world. But there is a task yet before us—to go forward and consummate by the votes of the States that which Congress so nobly began yesterday. He had the honor to inform those present that Illinois had already done the work. Maryland was about half through, but he felt proud that Illinois was a little ahead.

He thought this measure was a very fitting if not an indispensable adjunct to the winding up of the great difficulty. He wished the reunion of all the States perfected, and so effected as to remove all causes of disturbance in the future; and, to attain this end, it was necessary that the original disturbing cause should, if possible, be rooted out. He thought all would bear him witness that he had never shirked from doing all that he could to eradicate slavery, by issuing an Emancipation Proclamation. But that proclamation falls short of what the amendment will be when fully consummated. A question might be raised whether the proclamation was legally valid. It might be added, that it only aided those who came into our lines, and that it was inoperative as to those who did not give themselves up; or that it would have no effect upon the children of the slaves born hereafter; in fact, it would be urged that it did not meet the evil. But this amendment is a king's cure for all evils. It winds the whole thing up. He would repeat, that it was the fitting if not the indispensable adjunct to the consummation of the great game we are playing. He could not but congratulate all present— himself, the country, and the whole world upon this great moral victory.

SECOND INAUGURAL ADDRESS, WASHINGTON, DC, MARCH 4, 1865.

FELLOW-COUNTRYMEN:—At this second appearing to take the oath of the presidential office there is less occasion for an extended address than there was at the first. Then a statement somewhat in detail of a course to be pursued seemed fitting and proper. Now, at the expiration of four years, during which public declarations have been constantly called forth on every point and phase of the great contest which still absorbs the attention and engrosses the energies of the nation, little that is new could be presented. The progress of our arms, upon which all else chiefly depends, is as well known to the public as to myself, and it is, I trust, reasonably satisfactory and encouraging to all. With high hope for the future, no prediction in regard to it is ventured.

On the occasion corresponding to this four years ago all thoughts were anxiously directed to an impending civil war. All dreaded it, all sought to avert it. While the inaugural address was being delivered from this place, devoted altogether to saving the Union without war, insurgent agents were in the city seeking to destroy it without war seeking to dissolve the Union and divide effects by negotiation. Both parties deprecated war, but one of them would make war rather than let the nation survive, and the other would accept war rather than let it perish, and the war came.

One eighth of the whole population was colored slaves, not distributed generally over the Union, but localized in the southern part of it. These slaves constituted a peculiar and powerful interest. All knew that this interest was somehow the cause of the war. To strengthen, perpetuate, and extend this interest was the object for which the insurgents would rend the Union even by war, while the Government claimed no right to do more than to restrict the territorial enlargement of it. Neither party expected for the war the magnitude or the duration which it has already attained. Neither anticipated that the cause of the conflict might cease with or even before the conflict itself should cease. Each looked for an easier triumph, and a result less fundamental and astounding. Both read the same Bible and pray to the same God, and each invokes His aid against the other. It may seem strange that any men should dare to ask a just God's assistance in wringing their bread from the sweat of other men's faces, but let us judge not, that we be not judged. The prayers of both could not be answered. That of neither has been answered fully. The Almighty has His own purposes. "Woe unto the world because of offenses; for it must needs be that offenses come, but woe to that man by whom the offense cometh." If we shall suppose that American slavery is one of those offenses which, in the providence of God, must needs come, but which, having continued through His appointed time, He now wills to remove, and that He gives to both North and South this terrible war as the woe due to those by whom the offense came, shall we discern therein any departure from those divine attributes which the believers in a living God always ascribe to Him? Fondly do we hope, fervently do we pray, that this mighty scourge of war may speedily pass away. Yet, if God wills that it continue until all the wealth piled by the bondsman's two hundred and fifty years of unrequited toil shall be sunk, and until every drop of blood drawn with the lash shall be paid by another drawn with the sword, as was said three thousand years ago, so still it must be said, "The judgments of the Lord are true and righteous altogether."

With malice toward none, with charity for all, with firmness in the right as God gives us to see the right, let us strive on to finish the work we are in, to bind up the nation's wounds, to care for him who shall have borne the battle and for his widow and his orphan, to do all which may achieve and cherish a just and lasting peace among ourselves and with all nations.

ADDRESS ON RECONSTRUCTION, WASHINGTON, DC, APRIL 11, 1865.

FELLOW-CITIZENS:—We meet this evening not in sorrow, but in gladness of heart. The evacuation of Petersburg and Richmond, and the surrender of the principal insurgent army, give hope of a righteous and speedy peace, whose joyous expression cannot be restrained. In the midst of this, however, He from whom blessings flow must not be forgotten. A call for a national thanksgiving is being prepared, and will be duly promulgated. Nor must those whose harder part gives us the cause of rejoicing be overlooked. Their honors must not be parceled out with others. I myself was near the front, and had the pleasure of transmitting much of the good news to you. But no part of the honor for plan or execution is mine. To General Grant, his skillful officers, and brave men, all belongs. The gallant navy stood ready, but was not in reach to take active part.

By these recent successes, the reinauguration of the national authority—reconstruction which has had a large share of thought from the first, is pressed much more closely upon our attention. It is fraught with great difficulty. Unlike a case of war between independent nations, there is no authorized organ for us to treat with—no one man has authority to give up the rebellion for any other man. We simply must begin with and mould from disorganized and discordant elements. Nor is it a small additional embarrassment that we, the loyal people, differ among ourselves as to the mode, manner, and measure of reconstruction. As a general rule, I abstain from reading the reports of attacks upon myself, wishing not to be provoked by that to which I cannot properly offer an answer. In spite of this precaution, however, it comes to my knowledge that I am much censured for some supposed agency in setting up and seeking to sustain the new State government of Louisiana.

In this I have done just so much and no more than the public knows. In the Annual Message of December, 1863, and the accompanying proclamation, I presented a plan of reconstruction, as the phrase goes, which I promised, if adopted by any State, would be acceptable to and sustained by the Executive Government of the nation. I distinctly stated that this was not the only plan that might possibly be acceptable, and I also distinctly protested that the Executive claimed no right to say when or whether members should be admitted to seats in Congress from such States. This plan was in advance submitted to the then Cabinet, and approved by every member of it. One of them suggested that I should then and in that connection apply the Emancipation Proclamation to the theretofore excepted parts of Virginia and Louisiana; that I should drop the suggestion about apprenticeship for freed people, and that I should omit the protest against my own power in regard to the admission of members of Congress. But even he approved every part and parcel of the plan which has since been employed or touched by the action of Louisiana.

The new constitution of Louisiana, declaring emancipation for the whole State, practically applies the proclamation to the part previously excepted. It does not adopt apprenticeship for freed people, and is silent, as it could not well be otherwise, about the admission of members to Congress. So that, as it applied to Louisiana, every member of the Cabinet fully approved the plan. The message went to Congress, and I received many commendations of the plan, written and verbal, and not a single objection to it from any professed emancipationist came to my knowledge until after the news reached Washington that the people of Louisiana had begun to move in accordance with it. From about July, 1862, I had corresponded with different persons supposed to be interested in seeking a reconstruction of a State government for Louisiana. When the message of 1863, with the plan before mentioned, reached New Orleans, General Banks wrote me that he was confident that the people, with his military co-operation, would reconstruct substantially on that plan. I wrote to him and some of them to try it. They tried it, and the result is known. Such has been my only agency in getting up the Louisiana government.

As to sustaining it my promise is out, as before stated. But, as bad promises are better broken than kept, I shall treat this as a bad promise and break it, whenever I shall be convinced that keeping it is adverse to the public interest; but I have not yet been so convinced. I have been shown a letter on this subject, supposed to be an able one, in which the writer expresses regret that my mind has not seemed to be definitely fixed upon the question whether the seceded States, so called, are in the Union or out of it. It would perhaps add astonishment to his regret were he to learn that since I have found professed Union men endeavoring to answer that question, I have purposely forborne any public expression upon it. As appears to me, that question has not been nor yet is a practically material one, and that any discussion of it, while it thus remains practically immaterial, could have no effect other than the mischievous one of dividing our friends. As yet, whatever it may become, that question is bad as the basis of a controversy, and good for nothing at all—a merely pernicious abstraction.

We all agree that the seceded States, so called, are out of their proper practical relation with the Union, and that the sole object of the Government, civil and military, in regard to those States, is to again get them into their proper practical relation. I believe that it is not only possible, but in fact easier, to do this without deciding or even considering whether those States have ever been out of the Union, than with it. Finding themselves safely at home, it would be utterly immaterial whether they had been abroad. Let us all join in doing the acts necessary to restore the proper practical relations between these States and the Union, and each forever after innocently indulge his own opinion whether, in doing the acts he brought the States from without into the Union, or only gave them proper assistance, they never having been out of it. The amount of constituency, so to speak, on which the Louisiana government rests, would be more satisfactory to all if it contained fifty thousand, or thirty thousand, or even twenty thousand, instead of twelve thousand, as it does. It is also unsatisfactory to some that the elective franchise is not given to the colored man. I would myself prefer that it were now conferred on the very intelligent, and on those who serve our cause as soldiers.

Still, the question is not whether the Louisiana government, as it stands, is quite all that is desirable. The question is, will it be wiser to take it as it is and help to improve it, or to reject and disperse? Can Louisiana be brought into proper practical relation with the Union sooner by sustaining or by discarding her new State government? Some twelve thousand voters in the heretofore Slave State of Louisiana have sworn allegiance to the Union, assumed to be the rightful political power of the State, held elections, organized a State government, adopted a Free State constitution, giving the benefit of public schools equally to black and white, and empowering the Legislature to confer the elective franchise upon the colored man. This Legislature has already voted to ratify the Constitutional Amendment recently passed by Congress, abolishing slavery throughout the nation. These twelve thousand persons are thus fully committed to the Union and to perpetuate freedom in the State—committed to the very things, and nearly all things, the nation wants—and they ask the nation's recognition and its assistance to make good this committal.

Now, if we reject and spurn them, we do our utmost to disorganize and disperse them. We, in fact, say to the white man: You are worthless or worse; we will neither help you nor be helped by you. To the blacks we say: This cup of liberty which these, your old masters, held to your lips, we will dash from you, and leave you to the chances of gathering the spilled and scattered contents in some vague and undefined when, where, and how. If this course, discouraging and paralyzing both white and black, has any tendency to bring Louisiana into proper practical relations with the Union, I have so far been unable to perceive it. If, on the contrary, we recognize and sustain the new government of Louisiana, the converse of all this is made true. We encourage the hearts and nerve the arms of twelve thousand to adhere to their work, and argue for it, and proselyte for it, and fight for it, and feed it, and grow it, and ripen it to a complete success. The colored man, too, in seeing all united for him, is inspired with vigilance, and energy, and daring to the same end. Grant that he desires the elective franchise, will he not attain it sooner by saving the already advanced steps towards it, than by running backward over them? Concede that the new government of Louisiana is only to what it should be as the egg is to the fowl, we shall sooner have the fowl by hatching the egg than by smashing it.

Again, if we reject Louisiana, we also reject one vote in favor of the proposed amendment to the National Constitution. To meet this proposition, it has been argued that no more than three fourths of those States which have not attempted secession are necessary to validly ratify the amendment. I do not commit myself against this, further than to say that such a ratification would be questionable, and sure to be persistently questioned, while a ratification by three fourths of all the States would be unquestioned and unquestionable. I repeat the question, Can Louisiana be brought into proper practical relation with the Union sooner by sustaining or by discarding her new State government? What has been said of Louisiana will apply to other States. And yet so great peculiarities pertain to each State, and such important and sudden changes occur in the same State, and withal so new and unprecedented is the whole case, that no exclusive and inflexible plan can safely be prescribed as to details and collaterals. Such exclusive and inflexible plan would surely become a new entanglement. Important principles may and must be inflexible. In the present situation as the phrase goes, it may be my duty to make some new announcement to the people of the South. I am considering, and shall not fail to act, when satisfied that action will be proper.

THE END